THE PLAYS AND
POEMS OF
Philip Massinger

The posthumous engraving of Philip Massinger (by Thomas Cross) published in *Three New Playes*, 1655

THE PLAYS AND POEMS OF
Philip Massinger

EDITED BY
PHILIP EDWARDS
AND
COLIN GIBSON

VOLUME I

OXFORD
AT THE CLARENDON PRESS
1976

Oxford University Press, Ely House, London W.1

GLASGOW NEW YORK TORONTO MELBOURNE WELLINGTON
CAPE TOWN IBADAN NAIROBI DAR ES SALAAM LUSAKA ADDIS ABABA
DELHI BOMBAY CALCUTTA MADRAS KARACHI DACCA
KUALA LUMPUR SINGAPORE HONG KONG TOKYO

ISBN 0 19 811894 5

© *Oxford University Press 1976*

All rights reserved. No part of this publication may be reproduced, stored in a retrieval system, or transmitted, in any form or by any means, electronic, mechanical, photocopying, recording, or otherwise, without the prior permission of Oxford University Press

PR
2701.5
.M3
1976
v.1

*Printed in Great Britain
at the University Press, Oxford
by Vivian Ridler
Printer to the University*

PREFACE

THIS edition of Philip Massinger's work contains seventeen plays and all his known poems. Fifteen of the plays are of his sole authorship, ten of them published under his name in his lifetime, three published under his name some years after his death, and two (*The Parliament of Love* and *Believe As You List*) first published from manuscript in the nineteenth century. The other two plays are collaborations: *The Fatal Dowry* with Field, and *A Very Woman* with Fletcher, published with title-page attribution to him. The edition does not include the very many plays written in collaboration with Fletcher which were published (without any acknowledgement of Massinger's authorship) in the Beaumont and Fletcher folio of 1647. Nor does it include *The Virgin Martyr*, written in collaboration with Dekker, which has been edited by Fredson Bowers for the Cambridge edition of Dekker's plays, nor *The Old Law*, which, though it has a title-page attribution (of 1656) to Massinger as joint-author with Middleton and Rowley, can scarcely if at all have been touched by him. This edition therefore continues the development of a canon begun in Coxeter's edition of 1759, as may be seen from the list of collected editions on p. lxviii.

The purpose of this edition is to present reliable and readable texts backed up by full introductory and explanatory material. The plays are printed in the presumed order of composition. The spelling of the original editions or manuscripts has been preserved, but the form of the stage-directions and speakers' names has been standardized for the ease of the reader. A general introduction gives a biography of Massinger, together with a history of the reception of his plays by critics and of their fortunes in the theatre. Each work is prefaced by an introduction which presents as succinctly as possible the available evidence on authorship, date, sources, stage-history, and the foundation of the text. Full details of editorial method are given in Section IV of the General Introduction.

Footnotes to the text record all substantive departures from the contemporary copy-texts, and an Appendix to the edition lists all minor corrections. In the final volume, there will be found the explanatory notes; these notes do not usually gloss individual words, which are defined in a general glossary, also in the final volume. This glossary is combined with an index of all the topics discussed in the commentary and of the more important proper names in the plays; it is hoped that this combined glossary and index will be of value not only to Massinger's readers but to all students of the period looking for information on the meanings of words and phrases, on customs and events, on proverbs and mythology, not to speak of food, drink, and aphrodisiacs.

The editorial work has been divided as follows:

Philip Edwards	Colin Gibson
The Fatal Dowry	*The Duke of Milan*
The Maid of Honour	*The Renegado*
The Bondman	*The Unnatural Combat*
The Parliament of Love	*The Roman Actor*
A New Way to Pay Old Debts	*The Picture*
The Great Duke of Florence	*Believe As You List*
The Emperor of the East	*The City Madam*
The Guardian	*The Bashful Lover*
A Very Woman	The poems

The history of this edition goes back into the 1920s, when A. K. McIlwraith, a Canadian scholar, was working at Oxford under Percy Simpson on a study of Massinger's collaboration with Fletcher and an edition of the plays (the present seventeen plus *The Virgin Martyr*) for the degree of D.Phil. The degree was awarded in 1931, the examiners being F. P. Wilson and E. K. Chambers. In December 1930 McIlwraith wrote to the Clarendon Press suggesting an edition of all of Massinger's plays including the collaborative plays in the Beaumont and Fletcher canon—35 in all. Full proposals were submitted in October 1931. The Press eventually agreed to undertake the edition, provided it was fully annotated and limited to the 'non-Fletcher' plays. McIlwraith's labours in preparing his D.Phil. edition had been extraordinary, but his progress in the years that followed was very slow. He made revisions and improvements, and carried out investigations on a number of important bibliographical problems, but what he left behind him when he died in October 1955 was basically the edition which he had prepared in 1931, together with a handwritten account of Massinger's life, and an elaborate and invaluable index of words and phrases. On material for the introductions, explanatory notes, and glossary, he appears to have made little headway.

The Clarendon Press wished to have the edition completed and in January 1957 Philip Edwards agreed to re-edit the plays, using McIlwraith's work where possible. In 1962, Colin Gibson, who was completing an edition of *The Roman Actor* for his doctorate at the University of Otago, was invited to become joint-editor. McIlwraith's materials have been indispensable in the preparation of this edition, particularly on bibliographical matters such as the collation of copies of the original quartos in the search for press-corrections, on biographical matters, and on Massinger's collaboration with Fletcher. The editors have tried to acknowledge at every point their use of McIlwraith's findings, but here they wish to record their profound indebtedness to their predecessor's work in general. At times perhaps, both editors have thought as they puzzled their way through manuscripts and photostats 30 to 40 years old that it would be quicker to edit Massinger *ab initio*, but they readily and gratefully acknowledge that their work rests on foundations laid by A. K. McIlwraith.

The other major editor of Massinger on whose work we have been glad to build is William Gifford, who established the definitive text of the nineteenth century. Indispensable also have been the scholarly editions of individual plays prepared in the United States in this century, some of them as dissertations which have not been published; they are named in the appropriate introductions, and here we express our gratitude to those editors who made available the results of their researches.

Our general indebtedness to the work of scholars in the Jacobean and Caroline field will be everywhere apparent in this edition; we particularly mention the great work of G. E. Bentley and W. W. Greg, without which this edition could hardly have been undertaken.

It is unfortunate that in our ignorance we cannot now acknowledge those who helped McIlwraith in his work, except Professor G. B. A. Fletcher, whose letter telling McIlwraith of the source of *The Bondman* was among the material handed over to us by the Clarendon Press. For our own part, we have many people to thank for help of many kinds:

The Clarendon Press, for extraordinary patience, for generosity in supplying books and materials, and for financial assistance, particularly in joining with the University of Essex in providing a research assistant in 1969–70;

Colleagues and the library staffs of universities we have taught in, particularly the University of Birmingham, Trinity College, Dublin, the University of Essex, and the University of Otago. The librarians and library staff of the many English, European, American, and Australasian libraries who have supplied information and material, particularly the Bodleian Library, the British Museum, the Folger Shakespeare Library, the Huntington Library, and the Victoria and Albert Museum;

G. E. Bentley, K. N. Chaudhuri, M. A. R. Colledge, Elsie Duncan-Jones, Roma Gill, June Harley (Mrs. Rowe), Bernard Harris, Bertha Hensman, Richard Hosley, Rex Ingram, D. S. Lawless, J. C. Maxwell, Patricia Smith, John Steele, O. J. Villarejo, the late F. P. Wilson, for communication of notable information, discoveries, and advice;

Allardyce Nicoll and his colleagues at the Shakespeare Institute, Stratford-upon-Avon (University of Birmingham) for organising a graduate seminar on the canon and dating of Massinger's plays in 1957;

Arthur Colby Sprague, James G. McManaway, Bryn Mawr College, and Ball State University for gifts of books;

All Souls College, Oxford, for a visiting fellowship, 1971, and the Huntington Library, California, for a research grant, 1965 (P. E.); the Grants Committee of the University of New Zealand for research grants (1962, 1966, and 1968), and the University of Otago for generous leave provision in 1962 and 1970 (C. G.);

Charmian Arbuckle, Sylvia Bressey, Margaret Harris, Roger Haydon, Dorothy Jones, and Carol Kagay for valuable research assistance. Leonie Henderson, Margaret Hine, Marian Littlechild, Marjorie McGlashan, Caroline Miller and Elsie Moodie for help in preparing material;

Finally, our deepest thanks go to our families for their patience and their help during the many years when Philip Massinger has been a conspicuous presence in our homes.

PHILIP EDWARDS
COLIN GIBSON

Brightlingsea and Dunedin
1973

CONTENTS

VOLUME I

LIST OF PLATES	xiii
GENERAL INTRODUCTION	
I. Massinger's life and theatrical career	xv
II. Massinger's reputation	xlv
III. The collected editions of Massinger's plays	lxviii
IV. Editorial practice	lxx
V. Abbreviations and short-titles	lxxviii

THE FATAL DOWRY
Introduction	1
Text	13
Appendix A (Verse)	96
Appendix B (Music)	98

THE MAID OF HONOUR
Introduction	105
Text	117

THE DUKE OF MILAN
Introduction	199
Text	213

THE BONDMAN
Introduction	301
Text	311

VOLUME II

THE RENEGADO
Introduction	1
Text	11

THE PARLIAMENT OF LOVE
Introduction	97
Text	107
Appendix (Malone Society Reprint)	177

x *Contents*

THE UNNATURAL COMBAT
Introduction 181
Text 195

A NEW WAY TO PAY OLD DEBTS
Introduction 273
Text 293
Appendix (Wright's excerpts, 1640) 378

VOLUME III

THE ROMAN ACTOR
Introduction 1
Text 13

THE GREAT DUKE OF FLORENCE
Introduction 95
Text 101

THE PICTURE
Introduction 181
Text 193
Appendix (Music) 288

BELIEVE AS YOU LIST
Introduction 293
Text 303

THE EMPEROR OF THE EAST
Introduction 391
Text 401

VOLUME IV

THE CITY MADAM
Introduction 1
Text 17

THREE NEW PLAYS
Introduction 101

THE GUARDIAN
Introduction — 107
Text — 113
Appendix (Verse) — 198

A VERY WOMAN
Introduction — 201
Text — 207

THE BASHFUL LOVER
Introduction — 291
Text — 299
Appendix (Verse) — 381

POEMS

THE COPY OF A LETTER
Introduction — 386
Text — 389

A NEW YEAR'S GIFT
Introduction — 392
Text — 393

TO SIR FRANCIS FOLJAMBE
Introduction — 395
Text — 396

LONDON'S LAMENTABLE ESTATE
Introduction — 397
Text — 399

THE VIRGIN'S CHARACTER
Introduction — 406
Text — 409

TO JAMES SHIRLEY
Introduction — 414
Text — 416

SERO, SED SERIO
Introduction — 417
Text — 418

POEMS (cont.)

  TO HIS SON
    Introduction   421
    Text   423

VOLUME V

APPENDICES
  I. Running Corrections to the Text   1
  II. Massinger's Spellings   73

COMMENTARY   96
  The Fatal Dowry   96
  The Maid of Honour   110
  The Duke of Milan   117
  The Bondman   128
  The Renegado   138
  The Parliament of Love   150
  The Unnatural Combat   158
  A New Way to Pay Old Debts   168
  The Roman Actor   179
  The Great Duke of Florence   192
  The Picture   197
  Believe As You List   208
  The Emperor of the East   216
  The City Madam   226
  The Guardian   242
  A Very Woman   249
  The Bashful Lover   256
  Poems   262

GLOSSARY AND INDEX TO THE COMMENTARY   269

INDEX OF NAMES APPEARING IN THE INTRODUCTIONS   355

CORRIGENDA

page

VOLUME I

lxxvii	penultimate line: for *nominorum* read *nominum*
51	line 117: *insert* F3^r *in left-hand margin*
77	line 69: *for* strumpet. *read* strumpet,
121	scene heading: for *Secne* read *Scene*
159	line 21: *insert* G1^r *in left-hand margin*
182	line 61: for *Fulgento* read *Fulgentio*
217	line 9: for *serve* read *serue*

VOLUME II

283	entry for ?1883: *for* Dick's *read* Dicks'

VOLUME III

297	note 3, line 2: *for* Wedgewood *read* Wedgwood
390	29^v, lines 2 and 3: *move to left, as line 6*

VOLUME IV

3	note 1: *for* Mathews *read* Mathew
195	headline: *for* vi *read* iv

VOLUME V

8	Verse, line 12: for (second) *thee* read *thee.*
16	II.iv.85: *for* (second) diues *read* diue^s
77	*for* (second) comãnd *read* comãnde

LIST OF PLATES

Portrait of Massinger. The posthumous engraving by Thomas Cross, published in *Three New Playes*, 1655.

Frontispiece

The manuscript of *Believe As You List*, in Massinger's hand. Part of folio 8 verso, and part of folio 20 recto.

Volume III, between pp. 302 and 303

GENERAL INTRODUCTION

I

MASSINGER'S LIFE AND THEATRICAL CAREER[1]

PHILIP MASSINGER, the second child and only son of Arthur and Anne Massinger, was baptized in the church of St. Thomas, Salisbury, on 24 November 1583. The original register is not preserved, but a seventeenth-century transcript reads:

> *Nouember*
> Phillip: Messenger: sone
> of Arthur: g[ent]: bapt: the 24

'Mr Messengers wiffe' was churched on 16 December.[2] Arthur Massinger, gentleman, had been a fellow of Merton College, Oxford, from 1573 to 1579. He was probably the Arthur Massinger who sailed with Humphrey Gilbert in 1578.[3] On 14 December 1579, a meeting of Senior Fellows of Merton College, which included Arthur Massinger, noted that he had for three months been a married man,[4] and he therefore relinquished, or was forced to relinquish, his fellowship. He had married Anne, daughter of William Crompton, a mercer, of Stafford and London.[5] William Crompton's will, dated 8 March 1582, reads:

> For Anne my daughter beinge married to an honest gentleman and a lovinge manne Arthure Massinger, to her I gyve over that alreadye she hathe hadd the somme of fourtye poundes to her and her daughter little Elizabethe eche twentye poundes and the Lorde God blesse theme bothe.[6]

[1] The main sources for the biographical material in this section are (*a*) a manuscript by A. K. McIlwraith probably prepared about 1947 as a draft of the biography for his edition; (*b*) Donald S. Lawless's *Philip Massinger and His Associates* (1967), and the Birmingham Ph.D. thesis (1965) of which it is an abridgement. Both these contain documentary and manuscript records which supplement the full and up-to-date biography in T. A. Dunn's *Philip Massinger* (1957).
[2] From transcripts in McIlwraith MS.
[3] Mark Eccles, *Times Literary Supplement*, 16 July 1931.
[4] From transcript of Merton College *Registrum*, pp. 69–70, in McIlwraith MS.
[5] Lawless, Thesis, pp. 2 and 269, and Monograph, p. 1.
[6] Lawless, Thesis, p. 269.

Massinger's mother was not as we see an heiress, but the Cromptons were people of substance. Massinger's uncle, Thomas Crompton, for example, was a D.C.L., Chancellor of the Diocese of London, and judge in the court of Admiralty.

After Oxford and his marriage, Arthur Massinger made his career in the service of Henry Herbert, second Earl of Pembroke, of Wilton. The first mention of this service is in 1587. Working more from London than from Wilton, Arthur Massinger was engaged in negotiating the public and private business of the earl: the Bishop of Salisbury once referred to him as 'the Earl's solicitor'.[1] He was Examiner to the Council of the Welsh Marches and was three times returned as a member of Parliament. When Henry Herbert died in 1601, Arthur Massinger continued to serve the family under the new earl, William, until his own death in June 1603.[2] His father's intimacy with one of the greatest families in the land was quite clearly a matter of great pride to Philip Massinger throughout his life.

In May 1602, Philip Massinger was entered as an undergraduate at St. Alban Hall, Oxford (his father's first college); he may have been in residence from the previous autumn. Langbaine and Wood give quite different accounts of his university career. According to Langbaine,[3] he was sent to the university by his father, and he 'closely pursued his Studies . . . for Three or Four years space.' According to Wood,[4] 'tho incouraged in his studies by the Earl of *Pembroke*, yet, he applied his mind more to Poetry and Romances for about four years or more, than to Logick and Philosophy, which he ought to have done, and for that end was patronized.' Wood's account is almost certainly fanciful, particularly as regards Pembroke's patronage. Massinger never took a degree, and if indeed he was at Oxford for four years he must certainly have wasted his time; but there is no evidence to support Langbaine's 'Three or Four years' or Wood's 'about four years or more'. It is quite possible that Massinger was forced to leave the university for financial reasons on his father's death in the summer of 1603 after only two years' study.

The next time we hear of Massinger he is in prison for debt, one

[1] Dunn, p. 5.
[2] McIlwraith MS., citing registers of the parish of St. Dunstan in the West; Register 1, fol. 196^r and Register 2, fol. 242^v.
[3] *Account of the English Dramatick Poets*, 1691, pp. 352–3.
[4] *Athenae Oxonienses*, 1691, i. 536.

of three dramatists appealing to Henslowe their employer to buy them out. The other two are Nathan Field and Robert Daborne. The date of this famous letter is not known, but Greg's conjectural date of 1613 has not been disputed.

Mr Hinchlow

You understand o^r vnfortunate extremitie, and I doe not thincke you so void of christianitie, but that you would throw so much money into the Thames as wee request now of you; rather then endanger so many innocent liues; you know there is x^l more at least to be receaued of you for the play, wee desire you to lend vs v^l. of that, wch shall be allowed to you w^{t}hout wch wee cannot be bayled, nor I play any more till this be dispatch'd, it will loose you xx^l. ere the end of the next weeke, beside the hinderance of the next new play, pray Sr Consider our Cases wth humanitie, and now giue vs cause to acknowledge you our true freind in time of neede; wee haue entreated Mr Dauison to deliuer this note, as well to wittnesse yor loue as o^r promises, and allwayes acknowledgment to be euer
  yor most thanckfull; and louing freinds,
        Nat: Field

The mony shall be abated out of the mony remayns for the play of m^r Fletcher & owrs
        Rob: Daborne

I have ever founde yow a true louinge freind to mee & in soe small a suite it beeinge honest I hope yow will not faile vs.
        Philip Massinger

To our most loving friend, Mr Philip Hinchlow, esquire, These.[1]

Daborne later wrote to Henslowe (it could have been with reference to yet another joint request for money): 'S^r I did think I deservd as much mony as m^r messenger', and, 'I beseech y^u way my great occation this once and make vp my mony even with m^r messengers which is to let me have x^s more.'[2] Two years later Massinger was still drawing money from Henslowe; on 4 July 1615, he and Daborne signed a bond in £6 for the repayment of a loan of £3.[3]

In the dedication to his first printed play, *The Duke of Milan* (1623), Massinger spoke of 'my misfortunes hauing cast me on this course'; and at the end of his life listed himself among those 'whose

---

[1] W. W. Greg, *Henslowe Papers*, 1907, pp. 65-6, and photograph in A. H. Cruickshank, *Philip Massinger*, 1920.
[2] *Henslowe Papers*, pp. 70-1.   [3] Ibid., p. 85.

necessitous fortunes' made poetry their profession.[1] The most important evidence of his condition, his ambitions, and his regard for the kind of work he was doing for Henslowe and the King's men in these early years of his career is the verse-letter 'written upon occasion' to the Earl of Pembroke (*The Copy of a Letter*, vol. IV, pp. 389–91), which probably belongs to the period 1615–20. The poem is the first of several appeals to the Herberts which put forward his father's relationship with the family as a ground for patronage. Massinger makes much of his financial distress, asking Pembroke to 'cast an eye / Of fauour, on my trodd downe pouertie'. He lays a modest claim to the name of poet, though he says he is 'Scarce yet allowed one of the Company'. To establish oneself as a poet, he argues, one needs a patron:

> could I obteyne
> A noble Fauorer, I might write and doe
> Like others of more name.

Unfortunately (the argument goes on) acquiring a patron demands a boldness and an insincerity which he cannot muster:

> I would not for a pension or A place
> Part soe wth myne owne Candor; lett me rather
> Liue poorely on those toyes I would not father,
> Not knowne beyond A Player or A Man
> That does pursue the course that I haue ran,
> Ere soe grow famous.

This passage is not crystal-clear (it has been used to argue that Massinger was an actor), but it is a fair interpretation that Massinger was at this time getting a very meagre living from writing which he took no pride in, and thought himself unknown as a writer except to the actors and those who were in the same trade as himself. He may have been over-modest about his reputation. In 1620, John Taylor's *The Praise of Hemp-Seed* mentioned him along with Drayton, Jonson, Chapman, Marston, Middleton, Heywood and others as one of the writers

> liuing at this day
> Which doe in *paper* their true worth display.

---

[1] Dedication to *The Unnatural Combat*, 1639. Similar statements by Jonson and Daniel, deploring the poverty which has driven them to write for the stage, are recorded by G. E. Bentley, *The Profession of Dramatist in Shakespeare's Time*, 1971, p. 39.

But he seems to have cared little about recognition for the work he was doing. Though it is always possible that some of Massinger's lost plays belong to this early period and were his unaided compositions, all the evidence we have argues that up to about 1620, when he was 37, Massinger spent all his time working on plays in collaboration with other dramatists. We have the evidence of the 'tripartite' letter that in or around 1613 he, Field, and Daborne were working on a play with Fletcher. He collaborated with Field again in *The Fatal Dowry* (?1617-19); this play was not published until 1632, and then, issued as the work of 'P. M. and N. F.', it carried none of the usual signs that Massinger had himself initiated and supervised the publication. He collaborated with Dekker in *The Virgin Martyr*, a most uncharacteristic work written for the Red Bull perhaps in 1620. Unlike *The Fatal Dowry*, this was published early (1622) and was attributed to him: 'Written by *Phillip Messenger* and *Thomas Decker*.'[1]

Massinger's main work from 1616 to 1622, however, was his collaboration with John Fletcher. His share in the long series of plays was never acknowledged in his own lifetime nor for a long time afterwards. In 1658, Massinger's friend Aston Cokayne published *A Chain of Golden Poems* and in it made several references to the injustice done to both Fletcher and Massinger in ascribing the 1647 folio to Beaumont and Fletcher; he addresses the publishers:

> In the large book of Playes you late did print
> (In *Beaumonts* and in *Fletchers* name) why in't
> Did you not justice? give to each his due?
> For *Beaumont* (of those many) writ in few:
> And *Massinger* in other few; the Main
> Being sole Issues of sweet *Fletchers* brain.
> But how came I (you ask) so much to know?
> *Fletchers* chief bosome-friend inform'd me so.[2]

---

[1] Another play of this period, *The Old Law* (? 1618), was published in 1656 and attributed on the title-page to Massinger, Middleton, and Rowley. It was printed in Massinger's works from Coxeter to Gifford and Cunningham, but on evidence of style and manner it is now generally agreed that Massinger can have had little or nothing to do with the writing of the play. It has been argued that Massinger revised it, but the evidence is not strong. There are discussions by E. C. Morris, *PMLA*, xvii (1902), 1-70; B. Maxwell, *Studies in Beaumont, Fletcher and Massinger*, 1939, pp. 138-46; G. R. Price, *Huntington Library Quarterly*, xvi (1953), 117-139.

[2] '*To Mr.* Humphrey Mosley, *and Mr.* Humphrey Robinson.'; *A Chain of Golden Poems*, sig. P5^r (p. 117 incorrectly for 217); the friend is Charles Cotton.

In another place Cokayne writes:

> And my good friend Old *Philip Massinger*
> With *Fletcher* writ in some that we see there.[1]

In his epitaph on Fletcher and Massinger, Cokayne refers to their collaboration again:

> In the same Grave *Fletcher* was buried here
> Lies the Stage-Poet *Philip Massinger*:
> Playes they did write together, were great friends,
> And now one Grave includes them at their ends.[2]

The extent of Massinger's collaboration with Fletcher has been analysed by a large number of investigators, relying almost entirely on the internal evidence of style.[3] The whole matter was exhaustively and judiciously surveyed by A. K. McIlwraith in his unpublished Oxford dissertation (1931). Very similar results were arrived at in another thorough survey thirty years later published by Cyrus Hoy in the Virginia *Studies in Bibliography*.[4] Massinger's style and prosody are very easily recognizable but there are many problems in dividing the Fletcher plays among their contributors. One such problem is the matter of revision. *A Very Woman*, for example, seems to be a revision by Massinger of an earlier play which was itself a collaboration between him and Fletcher. *Cleander*, licensed in the same year as *A Very Woman* (1634), is unknown under that name but it is probably *The Lovers' Progress*, included in the Beaumont and Fletcher folio, a revision by Massinger of an earlier play by Fletcher. A conservative list of the plays which Massinger wrote with Fletcher follows.[5]

1616–17	*The Queen of Corinth* (with Field)
	The Jeweller of Amsterdam (with Field): lost
1616–18	*The Knight of Malta* (with Field)
1619–20	*The Custom of the Country*

---

[1] *A Chain of Golden Poems*, p. 92 (G7^r).
[2] Ibid., p. 186 (N5^v).
[3] See Lawless, Monograph, pp. 22–3.
[4] Hoy, 'The Shares of Fletcher and his Collaborators in the Beaumont and Fletcher Canon', *Studies in Bibliography* (Bibliographical Society of the University of Virginia), viii (1956), 129–46; xi (1957), 143–62; xi (1958), 85–106; xii (1959), 91–116; xiii (1960), 77–108; xiv (1961), 45–63; xv (1962), 71–90.
[5] We exclude the impossible problem of *Rollo, or the Bloody Brother* and refer the reader to Bentley, iii. 401–7, and Hoy, loc. cit., xiv. 56–63. McIlwraith did not accept *The Honest Man's Fortune* as being in part by Massinger.

1619	*Sir John van Olden Barnavelt*
1620	*The False One*
1619–23	*The Little French Lawyer*
1621	*The Double Marriage*
1607–21	*Thierry and Theodoret*
1615–22	*Beggars Bush*
1622	*The Prophetess*
1622	*The Sea Voyage*
1622	*The Spanish Curate*
1625	*The Elder Brother*
1625	*Love's Cure*
pre-1625	original of *A Very Woman*

In the early 1620s Massinger began to assert himself as a dramatist in his own right and to create his own plays. This must not be seen as a kind of graduation from the apprenticeship of the master's workshop. He was 38 in 1621, and he may well have become reconciled, or more reconciled, to making a career out of writing for the public stage. *The Maid of Honour* (?1621–2) is probably the first of a series of plays which Massinger wrote for the companies controlled by Christopher Beeston at the Phoenix (or Cockpit) in Drury Lane (converted into a 'private' theatre in 1617). All the plays written in collaboration with Fletcher were for the King's company, playing at the Globe and the indoor Blackfriars theatre. So was *The Fatal Dowry*, and so were two early non-collaborative plays, *The Duke of Milan* (?1622) and *The Unnatural Combat* (?1624–5). These last three plays were tragedies: all the plays written for the Cockpit were tragicomedies or comedies. Following *The Maid of Honour*, there were *The Bondman* (1623), *The Renegado* and *The Parliament of Love* (1624), and *A New Way to Pay Old Debts* (1625). Massinger wrote one other play for a Beeston company, *The Great Duke of Florence* (1627). *The Virgin Martyr* (?1620) had been written for the Revels Company at the Red Bull. *The Bondman* was probably the most popular of the early plays: it was the first of Massinger's plays to be given at Court (27 December 1623); it was published quickly (sometimes a sign of failure on the stage but here a sign of success) and went into a second edition in 1638; it was his most popular play in the Restoration.

In 1624, Massinger was associated with one William Bagnall in a Chancery suit. McIlwraith surmised that Bagnall was the 'W. B.' who wrote commendatory verses for *The Duke of Milan* and for *The*

Bondman (published in 1623 and 1624).[1] The Chancery proceedings[2] may have been dropped. There exists only a Bill presented in the Court of Chancery by Massinger and Bagnall against Thomas Smith and Tristram Horner, with interlineation indicating the bringing of additional charges. There is no answer to the Bill, no judgement, and no depositions. The matter is a debt of £10. 15s. 11d. plus 40s. damages and costs. Smith had successfully sued Horner for the above debt, and Massinger and Bagnall had stood bail. Smith and Horner had then joined forces and rounded on Massinger and Bagnall for the money. Hence the suit, asking the Chancellor to subpoena Smith and Horner. The interlineation in the document suggests that Horner's debt to Smith never existed; the implication is that the whole thing was an elaborate trick to get money out of Massinger and Bagnall. The Bill is signed by John Selden, as surety that the complainants would proceed with the case.[3]

On 27 March 1625 King James died. In the months that followed, London endured one of the worst outbreaks of plague in her history; in August, deaths were standing at over 4,000 a week.[4] What with Lent, the period of mourning, and the plague, the theatres were closed for many months. Plays started to be given again in early December.[5] Massinger probably wrote *A New Way to Pay Old Debts* during the summer of plague, and when the theatres reopened it was performed at the Phoenix by the company which Beeston formed for sponsorship by the new Queen, Henrietta Maria. It is almost certainly the 1625 visitation that Massinger commemorates in his long moral poem on the plague, 'London's Lamentable Estate'.

One of the plague's victims was John Fletcher, who in Aubrey's account was escaping to the country and 'stayd but to make himselfe a suite of Cloathes, and while it was makeing, fell sick of the Plague and dyed'.[6]

Massinger inherited Fletcher's position as chief dramatist for the King's company; except for *The Great Duke of Florence*, all Massinger's plays from this point were written for the King's men, beginning with *The Roman Actor* in 1626 and ending with *The*

[1] *RES*, iv (1928), 326–7; *The Library*, 4th Series, xi (1930), 81–2.
[2] Series I (C. 2), Charles I, Bundle M 60, no. 10.
[3] Summarized from McIlwraith MS.
[4] F. P. Wilson, *The Plague in Shakespeare's London*, 1927; reprinted 1963, p. 136.
[5] Bentley, ii. 654–7.
[6] *Brief Lives*, ed. Clark, i. 254.

Fair Anchoress of Pausilippo (lost) in 1640, a total of at least eighteen plays in fourteen years. There is no record of any contract between Massinger and the King's company, such as is known to have existed later between Richard Brome and the Salisbury Court Theatre,[1] but it is hardly conceivable that there was not an agreement of some kind. Massinger was the Blackfriars dramatist as Shirley was the Phoenix dramatist.[2]

Something like half the plays which Massinger wrote from 1625 until his death are lost. The extant plays, in the probable order of composition, are: *The Roman Actor* (1626), *The Great Duke of Florence* (Phoenix, 1627), *The Picture* (1629), *Believe As You List* (1631), *The Emperor of the East* (1631), *The City Madam* (1632), *The Guardian* (1633), *A Very Woman* (1634), *The Bashful Lover* (1636). Establishing the list of lost plays is a difficult task. We start on fairly firm ground with nine records of licenses by the Master of the Revels, Sir Henry Herbert, for plays which he noted were written by Massinger but which are not now known.[3]

The Judge	6 June 1627	(*Herbert*, p. 31)[4]
The Honour of Women	6 May 1628[5]	(,, p. 31)
Minerva's Sacrifice	3 November 1629	(,, p. 33)[4]
The Unfortunate Piety	13 June 1631	(,, p. 33)
Cleander	7 May 1634	(,, p. 35)[6]
The Orator	10 January 1635	(,, p. 36)
The King and the Subject	5 June 1638	(,, pp. 22–3)
Alexius or The Chaste Lover	25 September 1639	(,, p. 38)[4]
The Fair Anchoress	26 January 1640	(,, p. 38)

On 9 September 1653, thirteen years after Massinger's death, Humphrey Moseley entered a very large number of plays in the Stationers' Register in order to establish his copyright. There are

---

[1] See Bentley, iii. 52–4, and the same author's *The Profession of Dramatist in Shakespeare's Time*, 1971, pp. 112–17.

[2] For further discussion see the introduction to *The Great Duke of Florence*.

[3] These records are in Herbert's Office-book. This Office-book was begun by Sir John Astley when he became Master of the Revels in May, 1622, and was continued by Herbert, who bought the office from Astley in the summer of 1623. The Office-book has long since disappeared, but many extracts were made by Malone and Chalmers and most of these were collected by J. Q. Adams and published in 1917 as *The Dramatic Records of Sir Henry Herbert*.

[4] Also listed in the plays protected from publication for the King's Men in August 1641; see Bentley, i. 65–6.

[5] Malone's note in his copy of *The Maid of Honour* (Bodl. Mal. 236) says 26 May.

[6] It is generally agreed that this is *The Lovers' Progress*, the revision of a Fletcher play published in the 1647 Beaumont and Fletcher folio.

ten entries of plays 'by Phill: Massinger' as follows (from the transcript by Plomer which Greg printed in *The Library* in 1911):[1]

> The Noble Choice, or the Orato^r
> The Wandring Louers, or ye Painter
> The Italian Night peece, or The Vnfortunate, Piety
> Alexius the Chast Gallant or. The Bashfull Louer.
> A Very Woman, or ye Womans Plot.
> The Iudge, or Beleiue, as yo^u list
> The Prisoner, or ye Faire Anchoress
> The Citie honest man, or ye Guardian.
> The Spanish ViceRoy, or ye Hono^r: of Women.
> Minerva's Sacrifice, or ye Forc'd Lady

It seems that the respectable Moseley was here engaged in a delicate piece of fraud, securing his copyright for two plays for the price of one by entering the title of one play as the alternative or sub-title of another.[2] *Alexius* and *The Bashful Lover* are the subject of quite separate licences by Herbert, and for those plays still extant in the above list the alternative titles given are irrelevant or inappropriate. Moreover, when Moseley re-entered a number of his plays on 29 June 1660 (unnecessarily including some he had already published) he gave single titles only. It seems therefore that the above list contains the titles of twenty Massinger plays, not ten. For the first time, *The Spanish Viceroy*, a play known to have been acted by the King's men in 1624, is attributed to Massinger.[3]

Moseley's 1660 entry in the Register gives some titles from the 1653 entry but adds yet more (the new ones are asterisked):

> The Womans Plott. a Comedy.
> The Prisoners. a TragiComedy.
> The Honour of Women. a Comedy.
> Believe as you list. a Tragedy.
> The forced Lady. a Tragedy.

---

[1] Reprinted in Greg, *Collected Papers*, p. 60.

[2] J. C. Reed, in *Proceedings of the Oxford Bibliographical Society*, II. ii (1928, pub. 1929), 67–8, argued that Moseley was too wealthy and respectable to engage in such a deceit, and that 'the lists were probably made up inaccurately, and were not verified either by Moseley or by the Stationers' Company.' A strange carelessness, to insert 'or' so often! Though it is just conceivable that someone mistook a list of titles in two columns for a list of double titles in a single column, one fears that fraud is the more likely hypothesis.

[3] On 20 December 1624, the King's men had to apologize to Herbert for acting the play without having it licensed; the author is not mentioned in their letter. See Bentley, v. 1412.

*The Tyrant. a Tragedy.
The Bashfull Lovers.
The Gardian
*Philenzo & Hypollita. a TragiComedy
*Antonio & Vallia. a Comedy.
*Fast & Welcome. a Comedy

All of the above are 'by Phillip Massinger'. Moseley also entered *The Parliament of Love*, but he attributed it to Rowley.[1] (There are many such misattributions in Moseley's lists. We cannot accept any of the entries as proof positive that he had in his hands an unpublished play by Massinger.) We may now list the titles which can be extracted from his entries, noting when there is confirmation of his entry from another source.

Alexius the Chaste Gallant (or *Lover*)	Herbert
Antonio and Vallia	
The Bashful Lover	extant
Believe As You List	extant
The City Honest Man	
The Fair Anchoress	Herbert
Fast and Welcome	
The Forced Lady	
The Guardian	extant
The Honour of Women	Herbert
The Italian Nightpiece	
The Judge	Herbert
Minerva's Sacrifice	Herbert
The Noble Choice	
The Orator	Herbert
The Painter	
The Parliament of Love	extant
Philenzo and Hippolyta	
The Prisoner(s)	
The Spanish Viceroy	acted
The Tyrant	
The Unfortunate Piety	Herbert
A Very Woman	extant
The Wandering Lovers	
The Woman's Plot	

All of Herbert's nine licensed lost plays are here except *Cleander* which is assumed to be the same as the extant *Lovers' Progress*,

[1] Greg, *Collected Papers*, pp. 61–2.

xxvi *General Introduction*

and *The King and the Subject* which Herbert specifically says was only allowed to be played under another title; it is quite possible that (as Fleay once suggested) Moseley's *The Tyrant* was the new name for the play. If that is correct we are left with a possible total of twenty-two plays still unpublished by 1660, only two of which, *Believe As You List* and *The Parliament of Love*, have been found.

At this point it is necessary to bring in John Warburton (1682–1759), Somerset Herald, and the famous story of his cook. Warburton had at some time written out a list of manuscript plays[1] in which occur the following:

>Minervas Sacrifise Phill. Masenger
>The forc'd Lady A T. Phill. Massinger
>Antonio & Vallia by Phill. Massinger
>The Parliam^t of Love by W^m. Rowley
>The Womans Plott Phill. Massinger
>The Tyrant A Tragedy by Phill. Massenger
>Philenzo & Hipolito A C. by Phill. Massenger
>The Judge A C. by Phill. Massenger.
>Fast and Welcome C. by Phill. Massinger
>Belive as yo^u. list C. by Phill. Massinger
>The Hon^r. of Women A. C. by P. Massinger
>Alexias or ye chast Glallant T. P Massinger
>The Noble choise T. C. P. Massinger

At the foot of the first side of the sheet, Warburton at some later time wrote:

>After I had been many years Collecting these MSS Playes, through my own carlesness and the Ignorace of my Ser[vant] in whose hands I had lodgd them they was unluckely burnd or put under Pye bottoms, excepting ye three which followes.   J. W.

In his full and careful study of Warburton's and Moseley's lists, Greg produced clear evidence that Warburton had copied from Moseley's lists in making his own. He inferred that Warburton's list was *not* basically a list of manuscript plays which he had owned and then had carelessly allowed to disappear into the oven. He concluded that Warburton had copied from Moseley's list the titles of manuscript plays which he wanted to add to his collection; he obtained some of these, and acquired other manuscripts not listed

---

[1] B.M. Lansdowne MS. 807, printed by Greg in 'The Bakings of Betsy', *The Library*, ii (1921), 225–59, reprinted in *Collected Papers*, pp. 48–74.

by Moseley. (Warburton catalogues fifty-six plays, thirty-eight of which are in Moseley's list.) His cook may well have used some of the plays for her baking, and when Warburton discovered his loss of all but three of his plays, 'no longer in the least remembering either the extent of his collection or the nature of his list, [he] added in a fit of natural vexation the famous memorandum.'[1]

It is certainly true that several plays which Warburton claimed he possessed and claimed were destroyed were not in fact destroyed. Among the Massinger items, *Believe As You List* and *The Parliament of Love* were not baked and still exist, *The Tyrant* got as far as Warburton's sale in November 1759,[2] and J. P. Collier said in 1845 that the manuscript of 'Philenzo and Hippolyto' had been found among the Conway papers.[3] It is also certain that some common readings in Warburton and Moseley can only be explained on the grounds that Warburton copied from Moseley. Greg's theory that there was no major collection by Warburton and no major holocaust has been generally accepted for 60 years, but the subject has recently been reopened by J. Freehafer in his article 'John Warburton's Lost Plays'.[4] He argues that the credibility of Warburton's list is established by the presence of information which the Stationers' Register entries do not have.[5] The list was known earlier than Greg realized—Malone knew it before 1778—and it was accepted; Warburton was not deceived by the false double-titles in Moseley's list, as he must have been had he known of the plays only from Moseley's list. Freehafer argues that Warburton bought Moseley's stock of play manuscripts and made his catalogue from a list which had been used in making the Stationers' Register entries for Moseley. He concludes (having noted that there was in fact an extraordinary consumption of waste paper, including books, by bakers and grocers) that Warburton's cook has indeed caused a very severe loss to our knowledge of seventeenth-century drama.

[1] *Collected Papers*, p. 74.
[2] Ibid., p. 50.
[3] Bentley, iv. 808, thinks Collier must have been mistaken, for nothing further has been heard of the manuscript; but it is a curious mistake to make.
[4] *Studies in Bibliography* (Virginia), xxiii (1970), 154–64.
[5] A minor point not discussed by Greg or Freehafer is Warburton's restoration of the 'or' in 'Alexias or ye chast Glallant'. Herbert had licensed (according to Malone) 'Alexius or The Chaste Lover'; Moseley's entry, however, is 'Alexius the Chast Gallant or. The Bashfull Louer.' He erased the 'or' to provide the 'or' for his spurious subtitle; Warburton therefore had another source for his title. Herbert's 'Lover' for 'Gallant' is probably a mistake: a chaste gallant provides a better paradox-title.

Freehafer's arguments are persuasive, but unfortunately we cannot be *certain* that inclusion in Warburton's list is independent testimony of the existence of a manuscript play by Massinger, and as Moseley is far from being absolutely reliable, there must remain a shadowy area in the list of Massinger's lost plays. There are seven plays mentioned by Herbert and confirmed by Moseley: there can be no doubt that these existed, and we can add *The Spanish Viceroy*, though Herbert does not mention the author. With regard to the other twelve in Moseley's list, it is possible to think that inclusion in Warburton's list is an additional argument that the play existed and was Massinger's. Again there are seven such plays. There remain five plays which are not known except for their appearance in Moseley's list, and the authenticity of these is the least certain: *The City Honest Man*, *The Italian Nightpiece*,[1] *The Painter*, *The Prisoner(s)*, and *The Wandering Lovers*.[2]

Massinger's playwriting career is presented as a table on pp. xxx–xxxi. It will be seen that Massinger was associated in the writing of some 55 plays. Of these, 22 are lost, or at least are not known under the given title. Of the 33 extant plays, 18 were written in collaboration with others, and 15 Massinger wrote on his own. This is over a period of about 27 years; we can be fairly certain that Massinger was also associated with a number of plays of which we have no record in the years before 1615.

Publication of plays

It will be helpful to discuss publication and patronage as subjects on their own, and to take them in that order since the published play was important for Massinger in his dealings with patrons.

As the century proceeded, plays came more and more to have a literary life outside the theatre; as well as actions to be witnessed they had an independent life as books to be bought and read. The publication of his plays became more and more an essential part of the dramatist's literary life. The printed play smoothly took the

[1] It was suggested by Logan Pearsall Smith that *The Italian Night Masque*, mentioned by Sir Henry Wotton in an undated letter as acted by the King's players, is the same as *The Italian Nightpiece* (see Bentley, iv. 792). A further identification with Suckling's *Aglaura* is suggested by J. Freehafer in *JEGP*, lxvii (1968), 249–65.

[2] Bentley (iv. 818) suggested that the entry '*Massingers Secretary*' in a list of works made use of by Joshua Poole in his *The English Parnassus* (1657) was 'some sort of writers' guide'; it is in fact John Massinger: *The Secretary in Fashion*, 1640 [*STC* 20491], a translation of a work by Jean Puget de la Serre.

place of the specially prepared manuscript as an offering to a prospective patron, and it had the advantage that it could be a public means of recognizing the bounty of an existing patron.[1] Massinger did not, as Shirley did, tend to deal with a single publisher: there are six publishers for the ten plays he published in his lifetime (this is excluding *The Virgin Martyr* and *The Fatal Dowry*).[2] There was some tension between theatre and dramatist over publication, and it was normal for a year or two to pass before a theatre or company was willing to allow a new play to become common property in print. Three of Massinger's plays were published very soon after their first performance: *The Bondman* (registered for publication three months after being licensed for the stage), *The Picture* (published in the year following licensing), and *The Emperor of the East* (registered eight months after licensing). In the case of *The Emperor of the East*, early publication seems to follow a lack of success on the stage; Massinger is anxious perhaps to justify himself before a more discerning audience and the theatre has no interest in protecting the play.

Massinger did not publish any of the plays which he wrote after *The Emperor of the East* (written 1631 and published 1632) but he continued to bring out older plays, *The Maid of Honour*, *A New Way to Pay Old Debts*, and *The Great Duke of Florence*, all of which had been in Beeston's possession, and finally in 1639 *The Unnatural Combat*, at least 15 years old and presented as a kind of curiosity from the past. But *The City Madam*, *The Guardian*, *A Very Woman*, and *The Bashful Lover* (and plays now lost) remained unpublished. There was a five-year gap after the publication of Massinger's first two plays, *The Duke of Milan* and *The Bondman* in 1623 and 1624, and then in the following five years (1629–33) he published no fewer than six of his plays. The silence must be connected with his new position with the King's company; the breaking of the silence with the publication of *The Roman Actor* in 1629 is very much a sign of his confidence and success, for it is an ambitious publication, dedicated in gratitude to three patrons who are also his friends, with no less than six sets of commendatory verses whose authors include his fellow gentleman-dramatists, John Ford, Thomas May,

---

[1] But by 1639 Massinger noted that the formal dedication of a play to a patron was considered 'obsolete and out of fashion'; see the dedication to *The Unnatural Combat*.

[2] John Waterson published three plays, Robert Allott and Edward Blackmore two each. The printers are different for all except two plays.

xxx *General Introduction*

THE PLAYS OF PHILIP MASSINGER

	Date	Title (* = included in this edition)	Authorship	Company or Theatre	Publication	Evidence for lost play
1	?1613	unknown	Massinger, Fletcher, Daborne, Field	(Henslowe)	unknown	Tripartite letters to Henslowe
2	1616–17	The Queen of Corinth	Massinger, Fletcher, Field	King's	1647 Folio	
3	?1616–17	The Jeweller of Amsterdam	Massinger, Fletcher, Field	?King's	lost	S.R. entry to Moseley, 1654
4	1616–18	The Knight of Malta	Massinger, Fletcher, Field	King's	1647 Folio	
5	?1611–19	*The Fatal Dowry	Massinger, Field	King's	1632	
6	?1619–20	The Custom of the Country	Massinger, Fletcher	King's	1647 Folio	
7	1619	Sir John Van Olden Barnavelt	Massinger, Fletcher	King's	1883	
8	?1620	The Virgin Martyr	Massinger, Dekker	Red Bull	1622	
9	?1620	The False One	Massinger, Fletcher	King's	1647 Folio	
10	?1619–23	The Little French Lawyer	Massinger, Fletcher	King's	1647 Folio	
11	?1621	The Double Marriage	Massinger, Fletcher	King's	1647 Folio	
12	1607–21	Thierry and Theodoret	Massinger, Fletcher (?Beaumont)	King's	1621	
13	1615–22	Beggars' Bush	Massinger, Fletcher (?Beaumont)	King's	1647 Folio	
14	?1621–2	*The Maid of Honour	Massinger	Phoenix	1632	
15	?1621–2	The Duke of Milan	Massinger	King's	1623	
16	1622	The Spanish Curate	Massinger, Fletcher	King's	1647 Folio	
17	1622	The Prophetess	Massinger, Fletcher	King's	1647 Folio	
18	1622	The Sea Voyage	Massinger, Fletcher	King's	1647 Folio	
19	1623	*The Bondman	Massinger	Phoenix	1624	
20	1624	*The Renegado	Massinger	Phoenix	1630	
21	1624	*The Parliament of Love	Massinger	Phoenix	1805	
22	1624	The Spanish Viceroy	Massinger	King's	lost	Memorandum by Herbert
23	?1624–5	*The Unnatural Combat	Massinger	King's	1639	
24	?1625	The Elder Brother	Massinger, Fletcher	King's	1647 Folio	
25	?1625	Love's Cure	Massinger, Fletcher	?King's	1647 Folio	
26	>1625	[original of *A Very Woman*]	Massinger		—	Revised as *A Very Woman* (q.v.)
27	1625	*A New Way to Pay Old Debts	Massinger	Phoenix	1633	

28	1626	*The Roman Actor	Massinger	King's	1629	Herbert, Moseley, Warburton
29	1627	The Judge	Massinger	King's	lost	Herbert, Moseley, Warburton
30	1627	*The Great Duke of Florence	Massinger	Phoenix	1636	Herbert, Moseley, Warburton
31	1628	The Honour of Women	Massinger	?	lost	
32	1629	*The Picture	Massinger	King's	1630	Herbert, Moseley, Warburton
33	1629	Minerva's Sacrifice	Massinger	King's	lost	
34	1631	*Believe As You List	Massinger	King's	1849	Herbert, Moseley, Warburton
35	1631	*The Emperor of the East	Massinger	King's	1632	
36	1631	The Unfortunate Piety	Massinger	King's	lost	Herbert, Moseley
37	1632	*The City Madam	Massinger	King's	1658	
38	1633	*The Guardian	Massinger	King's	1655	
39	1634	Cleander	Massinger, Fletcher	King's	1647 Folio	Herbert (= The Lovers' Progress)
40	1634	*A Very Woman	Massinger, Fletcher	King's	1655	Herbert, Moseley
41	1635	The Orator	Massinger	King's	lost	
42	1636	*The Bashful Lover	Massinger	King's	1655	Herbert (Moseley, Warburton)
43	1638	The King and The Subject (? = The Tyrant)	Massinger	King's	lost	Herbert, Moseley, Warburton
44	1639	Alexius or the Chaste Gallant/Lover	Massinger	King's	lost	
45	1640	The Fair Anchoress of Pausilippo	Massinger	King's	lost	Herbert, Moseley
46	?	Antonio and Vallia	?Massinger	?	lost	Moseley, Warburton
47	?	The City Honest Man	?Massinger	?	lost	Moseley
48	?	Fast and Welcome	?Massinger	?	lost	Moseley, Warburton
49	?	The Forced Lady	?Massinger	King's	lost	(Ld. Chamberlain) Moseley, Warburton
50	?	The Italian Night-piece	?Massinger	?	lost	(Wotton) Moseley
51	?	The Noble Choice	?Massinger	?	lost	Moseley, Warburton
52	?	The Painter	?Massinger	?	lost	Moseley
53	?	Philenzo and Hippolyta	?Massinger	?	lost	Moseley, Warburton
54	?	The Prisoner(s)	?Massinger	?	lost	Moseley
55	?	The Wandering Lovers	?Massinger	?	lost	Moseley
56	?	The Woman's Plot	?Massinger	?	lost	(Ld. Chamberlain) Moseley, Warburton

and Thomas Goffe, as well as Joseph Taylor who is presumably to be identified as the leading actor in the King's men, who had taken the part of Paris in the play. *The Bondman* in 1624 had had a single commendatory poem from W. B.

It can be shown that Massinger was accustomed to visit the printing-house to check the printing of his plays.[1] Perhaps the clearest evidence of his interest in his own publications, however, is the Harbord volume, now in the Folger Library in Washington. This was a collection of eight of Massinger's plays, bound in one volume, containing extensive corrections in Massinger's own hand. The plays, listed in the order in which a seventeenth-century hand has inscribed them on what was the fly-leaf of the bound volume, are *The Bondman* (1624), *The Renegado* (1630), *The Emperor of the East* (1632), *The Roman Actor* (1629), *The Picture* (1630), *The Fatal Dowry* (1632), *The Maid of Honour* (1632), and *The Duke of Milan* (1623). This makes the entire set of Massinger's publications up to 1633, except for *The Virgin Martyr*, and presumably the collection was brought together about that time. The volume, which may possibly be one referred to by William Oldys in 1737, or that owned by George Lillo (see below, p. xlix), was sold from the Harbord Library at Gunton in Norfolk in 1853. John Addington Symonds bought it from an Oxford bookseller and later in life (1877) gave it to Edmund Gosse. Gosse (to use his own words) 'unfortunately broke up the volume, and had the eight plays separately bound.'[2] Swinburne examined the ink corrections and some of them were published by Cruickshank in his book *Philip Massinger* (1920). Greg published in *The Library* in 1924 a long and informative account, putting forward the theory that Massinger had been working through the plays individually, making his corrections. When he had reached the second act of *The Picture* he stopped and sent the quartos to be bound. When the bound volume came back, he found that *The Duke of Milan* had been cropped, and he wrote in two lines which had been damaged; but he did not return to the task of correcting, and the remainder of *The Picture*, *The Fatal Dowry*, and *The Maid of Honour* are without any corrections. The corrections, although they are at their best fitful, are naturally of great importance and interest textually, and they are also unique

---

[1] See, for example, the introductions (text section) to *Renegado* and *Emperor of the East*.
[2] A. H. Cruickshank, *Philip Massinger*, 1920, pp. 222–3.

as an illustration of a dramatist of this period checking through his own printed work. What purpose Massinger had in preparing this volume can only be guessed at. What he has done is to get together a first volume of his 'works'; probably he wanted to present it to a patron.

Patronage

We have already looked at the earliest evidence of Massinger's search for patronage, the poem to Pembroke, which probably belongs to 1615–20. The second document is his first published play, *The Duke of Milan* (1623). This is dedicated to Lady Katherine Stanhope (later Countess of Chesterfield). She was the sister of Fletcher's patron, the Earl of Huntingdon, and this relationship is surely the reason for Massinger's approaching her. At another time, he presented a poem to her as a 'Newyeares Guift' (see vol. iv, p. 393). It is not easy to say whether poem or dedication came first. The poem contains the phrase 'since I / Haue heretofore been silent' which certainly seems to establish its priority, but the silence may refer only to commendatory poems, like the one he is writing, which a poet was expected to write for his patron. Both poem and dedication seem to indicate that Lady Stanhope has already helped the poet. The poem talks of a time 'Before I ow'd to you the name / Of Seruant', and in the dedication Massinger speaks of his wish to publish to the world 'that I am euer your Ladyships creature'; in neither case are the words those of a stranger making his first approach.

Lady Stanhope is the centre of a small web, which shows how important kinship was in the strategy of a client-poet. We saw that she was the sister of the patron of Massinger's colleague, Fletcher. Her grandson was Aston Cokayne, who tended to collect poets,[1] and whom Massinger called 'my worthy friend' in the dedication of *The Emperor of The East* (1632) to Lord John Mohun, who was Cokayne's uncle and Lady Stanhope's son-in-law:

your Nephew, to my extraordinarie content, deliuer'd to mee, that your Lordship at your vacant hours sometimes vouchsaf'd to peruse such trifles of mine, as haue passed the Presse, & not alone warranted them in your gentle suffrage, but disdain'd not to bestow a remembrance of your loue, and intended fauour to mee.

The Renegado, 1630, is dedicated to George Harding, Lord Berkeley,

[1] '*Donne, Suckling, Randolph, Drayton, Massinger, / Habbington, Sandy's, May*, my Acquaintance were.' *Poems*, 1662, sig. Q5ᵛ.

and Massinger states that he is not known to him. But it is not alone that Lord Berkeley is, as Massinger too fulsomely points out, well known for 'the Patronage, and Protection of the Dramatique Poem' that makes Massinger approach him; he was related by marriage to Lady Stanhope.[1]

To return to *The Duke of Milan*, on its publication in 1623 Massinger sent one copy of the play to Sir Francis Foljambe and wrote in it a presentation poem for him (see vol. iv, p. 396). Foljambe was a hospitable and extravagant man, younger than Massinger; he was made a baronet in 1622. He had extensive property chiefly in Derbyshire and the West Riding; some of his income came from lead- and coal-mines.[2] The poem asks Foljambe to 'looke / vpon the sender . . . wth your / accustomde favor'. Foljambe's generosity to Massinger, already begun, was long-lasting. Nine years later, Massinger dedicated *The Maid of Honour* (1632) to him and Sir Thomas Bland, his 'most honour'd friends'. 'I had not to this time subsisted, but that I was supported by your frequent courtesies, and favours.' This confession appears in a dedication, and it does not mean (or does not need to mean) that Massinger was near starvation and was rescued by Foljambe and Bland, but it is of importance in underlining the plain fact that a dramatist could not live by his writing, even if he wrote as regularly and professionally as Massinger did, and had the seeming security of writing for the most prosperous of the theatre-companies. An alternative source of income was essential.[3]

It seems very likely that Massinger was successful in getting the regular help of a small pension from Philip Herbert, Earl of Montgomery, who succeeded his brother William and became fourth Earl of Pembroke in 1630. There is no evidence that Massinger's suit to the third earl (see above, p. xviii) was successful. In 1624 he dedicated *The Bondman* to Philip Herbert in the following terms:

> How euer I could neuer arriue at the happinesse to be made knowne to your Lordship, yet a desire borne with me, to make tender of all duties, and seruice, to the Noble Family of the *Herberts*, descended to me as an inheritance from my dead Father, *Arthur Massinger*. Many yeares hee

---

[1] Lawless, Monograph, pp. 44, 50–1.
[2] Lawless, Thesis, pp. 242–7.
[3] The case has been made that dramatists made more money than they would had they followed other professions open to them, and that Massinger's complaints of his poverty are not evidence of low income; G. E. Bentley, *The Profession of Dramatist in Shakespeare's Time* (1971), pp. 108–10.

happily spent in the seruice of your Honourable House, and dyed a seruant to it: leauing his, to be euer most glad, and ready, to be at the command of al such, as deriue themselues from his most honour'd Master, your Lordships most noble Father.

When the play was first acted, Massinger goes on, 'your Lordships liberall suffrage taught others to allow it for currant, it hauing receaued the vndoubted stampe of your Lordships allowance.' Massinger must have been sure of his ground to speak thus: he is presumably referring to the reception of the court performance at Christmas 1623. Whatever sign of approval Philip Herbert gave, Massinger lost no time in following it up with his dedication; the publication of the play is unusually early. The evidence that Massinger got a pension from him is in John Aubrey's *The Natural History of Wiltshire*.[1] Aubrey spoke of three persons he knew of who received pensions from Philip Herbert, Massinger, the last, being the odd man out.

> Philip Earle of Pembroke . . . did not delight in books or poetry but exceedingly loved painting and building, in which he had singular judgement . . . Mr Philip Massinger, author of severall good playes, was a servant to his lordship, and had a pension of twenty or thirty pounds per annum, which was payed to his wife after his decease. She lived at Cardiffe, in Glamorganshire. There were others also had pensions, that I have forgot.

Massinger's rather embarrassing poem of 1636, *Sero, sed Serio*, addressed to his 'most singular good Lord and Patron Philip Earle of Pembrooke' on the death of his son, bears all the signs of a duty-offering from a pensioner and there is no reason to doubt Aubrey's account.

The third time Massinger used his father's connection with the Herberts in a bid for patronage was the dedication of *A New Way to Pay Old Debts* in 1633 to Robert Dormer, Earl of Carnarvon, who married Philip Herbert's daughter in 1625: 'I was borne a deuoted seruant, to the thrice noble Family of your incomparable Lady.' He makes it clear that he does not know Carnarvon, but hopes that he may be admitted to his acquaintance and acknowledge him as his 'noble Patron'.

So much for Massinger's relations as client with the aristocracy. The rest of his patrons were of the gentry and lesser nobility like

---

[1] Ed. J. Britton, 1847, p. 91.

Sir Francis Foljambe, patrons whom in general he seems to have been able to call his friends. *The Roman Actor* was dedicated in 1629 to his 'much Honoured, and most *true Friends*', Sir Philip Knyvett, Sir Thomas Jay, and Thomas Bellingham. He acknowledges himself bound for 'so many, & extraordinary fauors' and says that they were his 'only Supporters' during the composition of the play and that they have now encouraged him to print the play. Sir Philip Knyvett of Buckenham in Norfolk (1583–1654) was created a baronet at the institution of the order in 1611 and was a man of substance in his county:[1] it is assumed that Massinger addressed his poem *The Virgins Character* to his daughter Dorothy (see vol. iv, p. 406). Sir Thomas Jay or Jeay was one of Massinger's close associates; he was of Netheravon in Wiltshire, was knighted in 1625, sat in Parliament, was a Middlesex magistrate, and went with Buckingham to the Ile de Rhé in 1627. As keeper of the King's armoury at Greenwich and the Tower, he was in trouble about the sale of unwanted arms and armour in 1628, and in 1641 he was put out of the Commission of the Peace after being accused of extortion as a Justice of the Peace.[2] He had pretensions to verse, and contributed commendatory poems to *The Roman Actor*, *The Picture*, and *A New Way to Pay Old Debts*;[3] poems of his in manuscript are in the library of Trinity College, Dublin. Thomas Bellingham was the son of a Sussex knight and his mother was a Foljambe; he has some fame for being convicted in the Star Chamber before James in 1617 for duelling; the penalty of a £1,000 fine and imprisonment in the Tower was revoked but the case gave James the opportunity for his speech against duelling.[4]

Sir Thomas Bland, who shares the dedication of *The Maid of Honour* with Sir Francis Foljambe, was a Yorkshireman who was at the Inner Temple and was knighted in 1616, having succeeded to the large family estates in 1614. Sir Robert Wiseman of Essex was the dedicatee of *The Great Duke of Florence* in 1636; Massinger speaks of 'the many benefits you have heretofore conferr'd upon me', and, in words similar to those of the *Maid of Honour* dedication, says, 'for many yeares I had but faintly subsisted, if I had not often tasted of your Bounty.' Finally in 1639, the year before his

[1] G. E. C., *Complete Baronetage*, i. 24; F. Blomefield, *History of Norfolk*, 1805, i. 380.
[2] Lawless, Thesis, pp. 253–7.
[3] He may be the 'T. I.' who contributes a commendatory poem to Shirley's *Royal Master* (McIlwraith MS).
[4] Lawless, Thesis, pp. 157–8.

Massinger's Life and Theatrical Career

death, Massinger dedicated *The Unnatural Combat* to his 'much Honoured Friend' Anthony St. Leger ('Sentliger') of Ulcombe and Leeds Castle. Massinger acknowledges the support that his father, Sir Warham St. Leger (who had died in 1631),[1] had given him and that the son had continued. The whole dedication is interesting as a document on dedications written by one who feels himself to belong to a past generation. He says he knows that the patronage of drama no longer requires these dedications and that they are 'obsolete, and out of fashion'. But he feels the need to make a 'free and glad profession' of his patron's bounty and his own indebtedness. And perhaps patrons may take pride in the public announcement of their support for the arts:

> Many of eminence, and the best of such, who disdained not to take notice of mee, have not thought themselves disparaged, I dare not say honoured, to be celebrated the Patrons of my humble studies.

'Ambitious of *Fame* / As *Poets* are', Massinger says of himself in *Sero, sed Serio*. It is in this dedication to *The Unnatural Combat* that Massinger calls himself one of those whose 'necessitous fortunes' have forced them to try to make a profession of poetry. Massinger generally speaks of his plays as trifles, and it is interesting to watch the conflict between pride in his art and contempt for his trade. Massinger's hopes in his verse-letter to Pembroke that he would be lifted out of the servitude of writing for the theatre were never realized. At the same time, it is clear that (not without continuous effort and suit) he was able to rely on a support from patrons which with his earnings from the theatre made the financial circumstances of his later life much easier than they seem to have been in the uncertain days before 1620.[2] If at times his irritation at depending on the acclaim of a public audience is extreme he can also, in *The Roman Actor*, eulogize the public drama and call the play not a toy he will not father but 'the most perfit birth of my *Minerua*'.

We may add here a few notes on Massinger's associates other than his patrons. Of his fellow-dramatists, there are his collaborators, Daborne, Dekker, Field, and Fletcher, and others who write epistles for his plays, John Ford, Thomas May, Thomas Goffe, James Shirley, and John Clavell (a very minor dramatist who was at

---

[1] The elder St. Leger had sailed with Ralegh on his last expedition and gave testimony against him on their return.

[2] Although he was sued for £60 by Nathaniel Field the printer in 1629; see Malone Society Collections, ii. 3 (1931), p. 402. Possibly the debt was for books.

one time sentenced to death for highway robbery). Others who contribute commendatory poems to the plays are Joseph Taylor the actor (*The Roman Actor*); Daniel Lakyn (*The Renegado*), who is identified by Alice Senob and D. S. Lawless as a man who became a remarkable and much-travelled physician; Robert Harvey (*The Roman Actor*), who was at Gray's Inn in 1626 and also wrote verses for Shirley's *The Wedding*; Henry Moody (*A New Way to Pay Old Debts*), who succeeded to a baronetcy in 1629; he was at Oxford and Gray's Inn, wrote verses for the Beaumont and Fletcher Folio of 1647 and was one of the scientific virtuosi of the time; after the Civil War he went to America where he died in 1661.[1] Of William Singleton, the 'true friend and kinsman' of *The Emperor of the East*, little is known: he is probably the William Singleton who was at Oxford from 1621-4, wrote verses for Ford's *Lover's Melancholy*, and was M.P. for Gloucester in 1640. George Donne is identified as John Donne's second son; he was about 31 when he wrote verses for *The Great Duke of Florence* and had spent some years as a prisoner of war of the Spaniards; he went to Virginia as 'Muster-Master General and Marshal'; he died in 1638 on his way back to Virginia after getting into serious financial trouble in England.[2] Henry Parker, the political theorist, wrote a poem of condolence for Massinger on the failure of one of his plays (see below); James Smith, a very minor poet, Massinger called his 'son' in a poem he wrote for him (see vol. iv, p. 423). John Selden the jurist who signed the Chancery bond in 1624 need not have been more than an acquaintance, but he was of course a friend of poets.

A point of interest which emerges about Massinger's younger associates is that six of them, Singleton, Harvey, Moody, Smith, Parker, and Clavell, were together at Oxford in the early 1620s—possibly George Donne too—and they may well have been a group of friends with an enthusiasm for the theatre and an admiration for the dramatist who was twenty years their senior.

Massinger was several times involved in brushes with the censorship of the drama. In 1619, *Sir John van Olden Barnavelt*, which he wrote with Fletcher, a play on political and religious conflict in the Netherlands of immediate topical reference, was licensed by the Master of the Revels, but performance was prohibited by the Bishop of London. (In time, the players managed to get round the

---

[1] Lawless, Thesis, pp. 296-301.   [2] Ibid., pp. 221-6.

Massinger's Life and Theatrical Career

prohibition.) In 1631, Herbert banned *Believe As You List* because it was considered that Massinger's subject, the deposing and persecution of Sebastian of Portugal by Philip II of Spain, was 'dangerous' matter when there was a peace sworn between England and Spain. Massinger had to rewrite the play and he set the story back in the world of ancient Rome (see the Introduction to the play). The next banning, in 1638, involved Massinger in less work. The ban is a particularly interesting case for it shows not only the King's personal interest in the stage but also the sensitivity of the monarchy as the divisions in the country deepened. In an entry in his Officebook for 5 June 1638, Henry Herbert quoted six and a half lines of a speech by Massinger (it is all we possess of the lost play):

> 'Monys? Wee'le rayse supplies what ways we please,
> 'And force you to subscribe to blanks, in which
> 'We'le mulct you as wee shall thinke fitt. The Caesars
> 'In Rome were wise, acknowledginge no lawes
> 'But what their swords did ratifye, the wives
> 'And daughters of the senators bowinge to
> 'Their wills, as deities,' &c.

This is a peece taken out of Phillip Messingers play, called *The King and the Subject*, and entered here for ever to bee remembered by my son and those that cast their eyes on it, in honour of Kinge Charles, my master, who readinge over the play at Newmarket, set his marke upon the place with his owne hande, and in thes words:

> 'This is too insolent, and to bee changed.'

Note, that the poett makes it the speech of a king, Don Pedro, king of Spayne, and spoken to his subjects.[1]

But the king did not wish to ban the play as a whole. Herbert writes, 'At Greenwich the 4 of June, Mr. W. Murray, gave mee power from the king to allowe of the play, and tould me that hee would warrant it.' On the understanding that the title of the play was altered and that the required reformations were 'most strictly observed', Herbert allowed the play to be acted. It was noted above that the new title may have been *The Tyrant*; but the play is not extant. It is a point to notice that although all three censored plays were allowed to be acted after reformation, not one of them was printed. *Sir John van Olden Barnavelt* was first printed in 1883, *Believe As You List* in 1849, and *The King and the Subject* has not survived. It is

[1] Adams, *Herbert*, pp. 22–3.

a question whether this is a coincidence, or a sign of the wariness of publishers in handling plays which had already caused trouble for their political content.

Evidence of the contemporary reception of Massinger's plays is rather thin. He maintained the privileged and important position of chief dramatist for the leading theatrical company for the whole of his life from 1625, and with all exaggeration allowed for, the tributes of title-pages and commendatory poems continue to indicate the success of his plays. It is clear, however, that around 1631-2 he was having trouble with a section of his audience. In the 'Prologue at the Blackfriers' written for *The Emperor of the East* (licensed for the stage in March 1631; registered for publication in November 1631 and published 1632) Massinger says he would much rather *not* write a prologue since 'many are apt to wound / His credit in this kind'. Whatever tone he adopts will be criticized by those who 'delight / To misapplie what euer hee shall write'. This complaint is strictly about prologues, but it is evident that his critics were not satisfied with the plays. Massinger wrote a prologue for a Court performance which may never have taken place,[1] complaining that:

> this poore worke suffer'd by the rage,
> And enuie of some Catos of the stage:

he appealed to the King as to a higher court of judgement. In the commendatory poems, John Clavell talks about those who had no appetite for the play and left without giving thanks; William Singleton more sharply speaks of the play having been 'cri'd downe' by those whose 'malice' would simply not allow them to be fair to a work by Massinger. Singleton's words suggest, like the Prologue, a feeling of a general ill-will towards Massinger in some section of the Blackfriars audience rather than the simple failure of a new play. But Henry Parker seems to be speaking of a single and most unusual failure in his poem, 'To his hono[d]: frend M[r]. Phillip Massinger, having not had that iust applause for one of his playes w[ch] was due to him'.[2] *The Emperor of the East* is the play he is most likely to be talking of. The poem speaks of a 'hissing croude', and 'the gallants' not liking the play. Parker's argument is that Massinger

---

[1] A Massinger play *was* given at Court that season, however: *The Fatal Dowry*, on 3 Feb. 1631 (Bentley, i. 28).

[2] Printed by G. Thorn-Drury, *A Little Ark*, 1921, p. 2, and reprinted by T. A. Dunn, *Philip Massinger*, 1957, p. 33.

Massinger's Life and Theatrical Career

has 'soe ponderous a masse of Fame' that the detraction of a few cannot hurt him: he ought not to be as upset as he is. But if in fact the play is not up to standard:

> it doth not cast
> Dislike upon that play wch pleased last.
> If in a fragrant vineyard wee espie
> one whithered grape wch wants maturitie,
> Wee do not blame the soyle, or els impute
> that small defect unto the Noble roote.

According to the Prologue to *The Guardian* in 1633, two plays had failed:

> After twice putting forth to Sea, his Fame
> Shipwrack'd in either, and his once known Name
> In two years silence buried, perhaps lost
> I' the general opinion . . .
> Our Author weighs up anchors, and once more
> Forsaking the security of the shore,
> Resolves to prove his fortune . . .

This prologue presents insoluble problems. What was the other play that failed, besides *The Emperor of the East*? How are we to explain 'two years silence'? *The Emperor of the East* was licensed on 11 March 1631, *The Guardian* on 31 October 1633. In between these two plays come the revised *Believe As You List* (licensed 6 May 1631), which *may* have been a failure, *The Unfortunate Piety* (13 June 1631) and *The City Madam* (25 May 1632). For all we know, *The Unfortunate Piety* may have been a failure, but it is hard to think of *The City Madam* in this dismal role, and in any case it is only 15 months away from *The Guardian*, which seems to make nonsense of the 'two years silence'. If one took the rather desperate solution that the prologue to *The Guardian* really belonged to some other play and became attached to *The Guardian* by mistake, we should be hard put to it to find a 'two years silence' anywhere else: perhaps between *The Orator* and *The Bashful Lover* in 1636 and *The King and the Subject* in 1638. The hypothesis is hardly worth pursuing; if the Prologue is not *The Guardian's* it need not be Massinger's, and no problem exists. The best that can be said is that the 'two years silence' is a vague rhetorical phrase, and that the other failure besides *The Emperor of the East* must have been one of the three plays, *Believe As You List*, *The Unfortunate Piety*, or

The City Madam. Fortunately, *The Guardian* was a success: it was acted at Court on 12 January 1634 and according to Herbert was 'well likte'.[1]

Other evidence of the reception of Massinger's plays is scattered and miscellaneous. William Hemminge in his 'Elegy on Randolph's Finger' (? 1630-2) puts him in the best of company:

> The fluente Flettcher, Beaumonte riche In sence
> for Complement and Courtshypes quintesence,
> Ingenious Shakespeare, Messenger that knowes
> the strength to wright or plott In verse or prose,
> Whose easye pegasus Can Ambell ore
> some threscore Myles of fancye In an hower . . .[2]

William Cartwright paid Massinger the compliment of imitating *The Bondman* in a number of the scenes of *The Royal Slave*, 1636.[3] A little epigram in *Wits Recreations*, 1640 (signature B8^r) takes up the pun created by Cokayne in his prefatory poem to *The Emperor of the East*:

> *Apollo's Messenger*, who doth impart
> To us the edicts of his learned art
> We cannot but respect thee, for we know,
> Princes are honour'd in their Legats so.

The praise is so curious that one wonders if it is ironical.

There can be no doubt that in his lifetime Massinger's plays were bought and read. His first two published plays, *The Duke of Milan* and *The Bondman* went into second editions in 1638, and there is a note of their being supplied to a customer by Humphrey Moseley in 1640 along with *The Duke of Florence* and *The Unnatural Combat*.[4] No fewer than twelve of Massinger's plays were in the collection of John Horne, who was a fellow of Oriel College, Oxford, from 1617 until 1648 (some of the copies came into the Bodleian via Malone).[5] Not all readers were pleased with what they found. About the year of Massinger's death, Abraham Wright, clergyman, fellow of St. John's College, Oxford, and a keen student of the theatre (information about which he passed on to his son James Wright who included

---

[1] Adams, *Herbert*, p. 54.
[2] Ed. G. C. Moore Smith, 1923, lines 55-8.
[3] Cartwright, *Plays and Poems*, ed. G. B. Evans, pp. 186, 605, and W. G. Rice *MLN*, xlv (1930), 515-18.
[4] Greg, *Bibliography*, iii. 1317-18.
[5] A. C. Baugh, 'A Seventeenth-century Play-list', *MLR*, xiii (1918), 401-11.

it in his indispensable *Historia Histrionica,* 1699), was compiling a commonplace book of excerpts from chronicles and plays which he chose for their rhetorical power and vividness of language. He added brief comments on the plays which he excerpted.[1] He got half-way through *A New Way to Pay Old Debts* transcribing his selected passages and then wrote, 'The rest not worth ye reading.' In going on to call it 'A silly play' he put it in the company of *Hamlet,* which he thought 'but an indifferent play'. In his disappointment at Massinger's flow of unmetaphorical language, Wright strangely anticipates the burden of the complaint against Massinger's language running from Lamb to Eliot which we shall be looking at shortly: 'no expressions, but onely plaine downright relating ye matter; without any new dress either of language or fancy.'[2]

An interesting comment on the popularity of Massinger among women as an erotic writer is given by John Johnson in his *Academy of Love* in 1641. A dreamer makes a visit to the University of Love, and in Love's Library sees the tomes which 'our Courtly Dames study':

[I] saw chained up in golden linkes two Spanish Poets, *Dante* and *Cost,* and an English one called *Messenger,* which Messenger they entertaine, hoping still to see the good and gratefull newes of a well-filled purse ...[3]

Massinger died in March 1640, and was buried on 18 March in St. Saviour's Church, Southwark (the church on the southern bank of the Thames, across London Bridge, which was then generally referred to as St. Mary Overy's and which is now Southwark Cathedral). Aubrey said that he 'went to bed well, and dyed suddenly—but not of the plague';[4] he was 56 years old. The Register of the church entered him as 'Philip Massenger stranger'. This must mean that his home was not in the parish. D. S. Lawless discovered that the reason for the high fee for the burial, two pounds, is simply that it was a regulation at Southwark to double the fee for a

[1] The document, now in the British Museum (Add. MS. 22608), is headed *Excerpta quaedam per A. W. Adolescentem.* It was described in 1967 by J. G. McManaway, *Studies,* pp. 279-91, and more extensively by A. C. Kirsch, *Modern Philology,* lxvi (1969), 256-61.

[2] As the excerpts have never been printed, they are given in full as an Appendix to *A New Way to Pay Old Debts.* James Wright thought better of Massinger than his father did; see *Country Conversations,* 1694, pp. 15-16.

[3] Quoted by L. B. Wright, 'The Reading of Renaissance English Women', *SP,* xxviii (1931), 151-2.

[4] *Brief Lives,* ed. Clark, 1898, ii. 55.

'stranger';[1] previous comment had even gone so far as to suggest that the high fee was for Roman rites. Aubrey collected his information 'at the place where he dyed, which was by the Bankes side neer the then playhouse'. If he was a 'stranger', he must only have been lodging there; we have no idea where his home was. There has been some dispute about the place of his burial. Aubrey, who was followed by Wood, said 'he was buryed about the middle of the Bullhead-churchyard', but the account books of the church (which record the fee) say categorically 'in the Church'. Cokayne's emphatic statement that Massinger was buried in Fletcher's grave is in both the title and text of his poem '*An Epitaph on M^r. John Fletcher, and M^r. Philip Massinger, who lie buried both in one Grave*'.[2] An engraved slab now lies in the chancel of the church. A commemorative window was unveiled by Sir Walter Besant in July 1896.[3]

The only evidence that Massinger was married is in Aubrey's mention of his pension from Pembroke being paid to his widow (see above, p. xxxv) and he says a second time 'his wife dyed at Cardiffe in Wales'.[4] T. A. Dunn searched London parish registers for records of children; he found references to a 'Katheren Messinger' married in the church of Allhallows-in-the-wall in 1633, and a Thomas Messenger, gentleman, who, as a 29-year-old widower, remarried in St. Peter's, Paul's Wharf, on 24 January 1637. Dunn notes that the name is not at all uncommon and that it is no more than a possibility that these are Massinger's children. One cannot put much faith in the report that a Miss Henrietta Massinger who died in 1762 was 'a descendant of Massinger, the dramatic poet'.[5]

As for personal possessions and tokens, we are very fortunate to have the manuscript of *Believe As You List* and the copy of *The Duke of Milan* which Massinger sent to Foljambe, as well as the quartos which he corrected and had bound. A copy of Phineas Fletcher's academic play, *Sicelides* (1631), in the Dyce collection at the Victoria and Albert Museum bears the faintly inked inscription, 'Philip Massinger his booke'. It was accepted as genuine by Dyce and Greg, but it so closely resembles the signature at the foot of the 'tripartite' letter to Henslowe, which Malone had reproduced in his *Enquiry* (1796), that there must be some suspicion that it is a forgery. Whether Massinger owned or borrowed the very many books which

---

[1] Lawless, Monograph, pp. 10, 15.
[2] See above, p. xx.
[3] *NQ*, 18 July 1896, p. 44.
[4] *Brief Lives*, ii. 54.
[5] *The London Magazine*, 4 Aug. 1762.

the study of his plays shows him to be familiar with is impossible to say. Our ignorance about his books, like our ignorance about his marriage or his home, and our ignorance about what sort of a man he was, is part of the general obscurity which surrounds the personal lives of most Tudor and Stuart dramatists.[1] There has been much discussion since Gifford's day of the possibility that Massinger was a Roman Catholic; the evidence is not very convincing. The debate has been usefully surveyed by T. A. Dunn.[2]

II

MASSINGER'S REPUTATION

There is only a short period between Massinger's death and the closing of the theatres in 1642. From the list of plays which the Lord Chamberlain protected for Beeston in 1639 it is evident that all the plays which Massinger wrote for the Cockpit companies, with the interesting exception of *The Parliament of Love*, were still in the repertory. Seven of his unpublished plays were protected from unauthorized publication for the Lord Chamberlain on behalf of the King's company in 1641; neither *Believe As You List* nor *A Very Woman* is included. During the long period in which the theatres remained closed, there was little to do with plays except print them. To judge from the very large number of manuscripts of Massinger's plays which Humphrey Moseley acquired, it seems possible that he was thinking of a collected edition, but he contented himself with *Three New Playes* in 1655 (*The Bashful Lover*, *The Guardian*, and *A Very Woman*), to accompany the *Six New Playes* of Shirley, and the *Five New Playes* of Brome, both published in 1653. In 1658, Andrew Pennycuick brought out *The City Madam*, and that was the last of Massinger's plays to be published until the manuscripts of *The Parliament of Love* and *Believe As You List* were printed in the nineteenth century.

In 1655, John Cotgrave published his anthology, *The English Treasury of Wit and Language, collected out of the most, and best of our English Drammatick Poems*.[3] The passages from plays which he prints are irritatingly without their origins, but in a copy in the

[1] For the posthumous 'portrait' of Massinger, see vol. iv, p. 104.
[2] Dunn, pp. 49–51, 184–91.
[3] See a description by G. E. Bentley, *SP*, xl (1943), 180–203.

British Museum (1451.c.49) a late seventeenth-century or early eighteenth-century hand has painstakingly inked in most of the attributions. There are 49 excerpts from Massinger's plays, *The Emperor of the East* being the favourite play with no fewer than fifteen extracts, followed by *The Fatal Dowry*. Since the extracts are, as in later anthologies, moral passages 'digested into commonplaces for general use', it must be that *The Emperor of the East* is more than usually sententious. Hence perhaps its failure on the stage.

Allusions to Massinger in the second half of the seventeenth century tend to take the form of including him in those rather tiresome shopping lists of poets that are exceedingly uninformative.[1] Some have a little more character. Samuel Sheppard, in *The Times Displayed* of 1646 (C4r), spoke of Davenant, Shirley, Goffe, Beaumont and Fletcher, and him 'that the sweet Renegaddo pend', adding in the margin, 'Mr *Philip Massenger*'. Richard Washington in 1650 wrote a little poem in his copy of *The Picture*, 'To the Memory of that great Architect of Poetry Mr. Phillip Massinger' which contains the lines:

> Apelles in his arte did all surpas
> But Massinger to thee he nothing was
> sterne Johnson and our smoth tongued Shakespeares Layes
> May crye them up but thou shalt weare the Bayse

Philip Kynder writing in 1656 suggests that the figures of *A New Way to Pay Old Debts* are becoming folk-lore; he talks of the danger of thinking that literature is history:

as if one in future age should make all *England* in ages past to be a *Bartholomew*-Faire, because Ben. Johnson hath writ it ... Or from *Massingers* Mr. *Greedy*, a hungry Justice of Peace in *Nottingham*-shire: or *Will-doe* the Parson of *Gotham* the Condition of all the Country.[2]

---

[1] e.g. George Wither, *The Great Assises holden in Parnassus* (1645), A2r, B4r, E3r; Samuel Holland, *Don Zara del Fogo*, 1656, Bk. 2, Ch. 4, p. 102; Sir Richard Baker, *Chronicles of the Kings of England*, 1660, pp. 502-3 (Massinger is included in the 1664 edition but dropped in 1670 and 1679—almost certainly because of a typographical error which led to Shakespeare's disappearance in 1670 also); Anon., 'An Elegy upon the death of Sir William Davenant', ?1668, reprinted in G. Thorn-Drury, *A Little Ark*, 1921, p. 35; Edward Phillips, *Compendiosa Enumeratio Poetarum*, 1669 (see R. G. Howarth, *MLR*, liv (1959), 328); Anon., 'An Essay on Dramatic Poesy', 1681 (see *HLQ*, xxviii (1964-5), 89-91); Charles Gildon, *Lives of the English Dramatick Poets* (1699), p. 98.

[2] *The Surfeit to A B C*, pp. 57-8.

Massinger's Reputation

When playing was resumed in 1660, the old plays were all that could be offered to the public. J. G. McManaway claimed that if we include nineteen plays written with Fletcher (Chelli's figure), twelve of which were revived between 1660 and 1720, no fewer than twenty-three out of thirty-six plays of Massinger 'were revived in one form or another' in the Restoration period, and that of the seventeen printed plays of Massinger available eleven 'were adapted wholly or in part' before the death of Betterton, and five others 'were acted in a form about which we have no specific record'.[1] This is perhaps too generous a picture; if we exclude adaptations which were in fact little more than the pilfering of an idea or a scene, we find we have records of only five plays which we know were staged: *The Bondman*, *The Renegado*, *The Virgin Martyr*, *A Very Woman*, and *A New Way to Pay Old Debts*—all of them in the years immediately following the reopening of the theatres. *The Bondman* drew the most attention, as Pepys's frequent references show. There must have been other plays staged, for in 1668–9, when the question of the rights of the directors of the two theatres, Davenant and Killigrew, over the old plays was settled by an official carving-up, Killigrew's list contained *The Duke of Milan*, *The Unnatural Combat*, *The Bashful Lover*, *The Emperor of the East*, *The Fatal Dowry*, *The Roman Actor*, and *The Guardian* (this last possibly not Massinger's but Cowley's). McManaway thought that ownership of the plays 'was not just an academic question' and considered it possible that all the plays mentioned had in fact been acted.[2]

At the end of the seventeenth century the antiquarian interest which is such a feature of the eighteenth century began to show itself. In his *Theatrum Poetarum Anglicanorum*, 1675, Edward Phillips calls Massinger 'a sufficiently famous and very copious writer, both comic and tragic, to the English Stage', and lists ten of his plays. William Winstanley borrows the phrase 'sufficiently famous' for his paragraph on Massinger in *The Lives of the most Famous English Poets*, 1687; he gives the titles of sixteen plays in print (with *A Very Woman* as *the merry Woman*). Anthony à Wood again found Massinger 'sufficiently fam'd' in his account in *Athenae Oxonienses*, 1691, which used the researches of John Aubrey which have been referred to. The other main 'biographer' at the end of the

---

[1] J. G. McManaway, 'Massinger and the Restoration Drama' (1931), reprinted in *Studies*, p. 8.
[2] Ibid., p. 17.

century was Gerard Langbaine (see above, p. xvi). In his *Momus Triumphans*, 1688, he made an interesting reference to the ease of getting away with plunder from authors 'not so generally known' as Shakespeare and Fletcher, like Marston, Middleton, and Massinger. He gave Massinger fair space in his *Account of the English Dramatick Poets*, 1691, though the confidence of his remarks may conceal the fact that his information has little independent authority. He singled out *A New Way to Pay Old Debts* and *The City Madam* as particularly good plays.

In the early days of the eighteenth century,[1] Nicholas Rowe was thinking of an edition of Massinger's collected plays. The preface to the 1719 alteration of *The Bondman* says of Massinger: '*He has publish'd 14 Plays, entirely of his own Writing, (which, I have been inform'd, were revis'd by Mr Rowe before his Death* [1718], *and design'd by him for the Press.*' Gifford said, without authority (1805, I. lviii), that Rowe was 'seduced from his purpose' by finding how good *The Fatal Dowry* was and deciding to rewrite it as *The Fair Penitent*. As it turns out, *The Fair Penitent* (1703) has to serve as Rowe's tribute to Massinger, though Rowe did not acknowledge his pillage. *The Fair Penitent* became famous; Johnson, who never mentions Massinger, praised Rowe's play very highly. There was a good deal of indignation later in the century both at Rowe's unscrupulousness, and the unfairness of public judgement in praising Rowe and ignoring Massinger. In 1786 Richard Cumberland devoted three numbers of *The Observer* (88-90) to an extended comparison of the two plays (it was the first real critical analysis of a Massinger play) and came down overwhelmingly on the side of the original play.

Though no new edition appeared, collectors were busy seeking out the original editions, and manuscripts, of Massinger's plays in the general revival of interest in the literature of the early seventeenth century. It must have been in the early part of the century that John Warburton (1682-1759) made his famous collection or non-collection of the manuscripts of the now-lost plays (see p. xxvi). George Lillo the dramatist, who died in 1739, had a fine collection of seventeenth-century plays including a volume catalogued as

[1] This section on the eighteenth century has been helped at every point by the very thorough M.A. dissertation of Miss M. J. Harley, 'The Eighteenth-Century Interest in English Drama before 1640' (University of Birmingham, 1962; unpublished). Miss Harley very kindly allowed us to make free use of her work. References to it will be to 'Harley'.

'Massinger's Works. 1633'.[1] Garrick (died 1779) had original quartos in his collection, which passed to the British Museum. William Oldys, noting with anxiety the increasing difficulty of finding early plays, reported on 27 September 1737 that 'a volume of ten of Massinger's *Plays*' had been sold at an auction to the Countess of Pomfret's footman for £3. 10s. 0d.[2]

William Oldys (1696–1761) is of great importance in the story of the revival of interest in Massinger in the eighteenth century, because of his work for the very influential anthology of 1738, *The British Muse, or, A Collection of Thoughts Moral, Natural, and Sublime, of our English Poets: Who flourished in the Sixteenth and Seventeenth Centuries.* The work is attributed to Thomas Hayward, but it is generally agreed that Oldys was the guiding spirit.[3] The anthology was expressly designed to rescue the pre-Restoration poets and dramatists from obscurity. The compiler, says Oldys's preface (p. xx) 'has chosen . . . to devote himself to neglected and expiring merit; conceiving it more useful and meritorious to revive and preserve the excellencies, which time and oblivion were upon the point of cancelling for ever, than to repeat what others had extracted before.' Oldys worked chiefly from the collection of plays in the library of Edward Harley, second Earl of Oxford (to whom he had sold his own collection): the range and scope of the anthology are quite extraordinary. Extracts are as cheerfully given from Webster, Tourneur, and Marston as from Shakespeare, Jonson, and Beaumont and Fletcher, and there are extracts from completely forgotten plays, like Burnell's *Landgartha*. There are over eighty extracts from Massinger's plays, and the selection is a very good one, though, from the plan of the volume, most of the passages are aphoristic, gnomic, or sententious. All of Massinger's then-known plays are represented, the two most popular being *The Emperor of the East* and *The Duke of Milan*, followed by *The Fatal Dowry*, *The Maid of Honour*, and *The Bondman*. Oddly, *The Roman Actor* is given only one excerpt.

The British Muse achieved Oldys's object, and its importance in re-establishing the 'lesser' early seventeenth-century dramatists is perhaps still not fully recognized. The anthology was reissued in

---

[1] *HLQ*, xxix (1965–6), 275–86.
[2] *NQ*, 2nd Series, xi (16 Feb. 1861), 123; *The British Muse*, I. xxii; Harley, p. 233.
[3] See, e.g., O. Gilchrist, *Letter to William Gifford* (1811), and R. D. Williams *PMLA*, liii (1938), 434–44.

1740 as *The Quintessence of English Poetry* and it was used for the later anthologies like *The Beauties of English Drama* (1777). Octavius Gilchrist, in his *Letter to Gifford* of 1811 wrote, 'To this judicious compilation . . . selected chiefly from the dramatic writers anterior to the Restoration, I think, may be attributed the attention subsequently bestowed on their writings' (p. 9). He also thought that, without it, Dodsley would not have thought of publishing his *Old Plays* in 1744. A later critic is convinced that Lamb used *The British Muse* for his even more influential *Specimens of the English Dramatic Poets* of 1808.[1]

Robert Dodsley devoted one volume of his *Select Collection of Old Plays* (1744) to Massinger, choosing the two social comedies, *A New Way to Pay Old Debts* and *The City Madam*, two romantic comedies, *The Guardian* and *The Picture*, and a tragedy, *The Unnatural Combat*. This selection is the first modern edition of Massinger's plays and Dodsley shares with Oldys much of the credit for bringing Massinger to the attention of readers. It is possibly because of the existence of Dodsley that Garrick was led to put on *A New Way to Pay Old Debts* at Drury Lane in 1748—perhaps its first production for 85 years, and its first London production since Massinger's lifetime. Unfortunately Garrick did not take the part of Overreach himself. The revival lasted for only four performances.

In 1751 (29 October), the *London Gazeteer* printed proposals for publishing Massinger's complete works in 5 volumes for 12 shillings and 6 pence, sewn.[2] 400 subscriptions were needed, but 'the Subscription went on so slowly that the Project was dropt'.[3] Almost certainly this was Coxeter's edition. Thomas Coxeter was born in Gloucestershire in 1689 and had gone to Oxford in 1705. Instead of pursuing the law, he 'became acquainted with booksellers and authors', and began collecting books and materials for the biographies of the poets. In 1744, his proposals for an edition of Thomas May spoke of his 'intending to revive the best of our OLD PLAYS, faithfully collated with all the editions that could be found in a search of above thirty years.'[4] But he died in 1747 with nothing in print. In 1759 there appeared *The Dramatic Works of Mr Philip Massinger, Compleat. In Four Volumes. Revised, Corrected, and all the Various*

---

[1] R. D. Williams, op. cit.   [2] Gifford, 1813, I. xci.
[3] Thomas Davies, Massinger's *Works*, 1779, I. xlix–l.
[4] Oldys gave Coxeter help towards his edition—some of it unintentionally. See his manuscript notes in the British Museum copy of Langbaine's *English Dramatick Poets* (C. 28. g. 1), p. 353.

Editions Collated, By Mr Coxeter. With Notes Critical and Explanatory, By the Editor, And by Various Authors . . . Printed for Henry Dell. . . . An anonymous Very Humble Servant dedicates the work to Garrick, who is one of the 124 subscribers. The Preface remarks that:

> Several Attempts have been made to re-publish a Compleat Edition of the Works of PHILIP MASSINGER; which, by the death of the Editors, or other casual Accidents, have hitherto all proved abortive . . . The late ingenious Mr. COXETER had corrected and collated all the various Editions; and, if I may judge from his Copies, he had spared no diligence and care to make them as correct as possible. Several ingenious Observations and Notes he had likewise prepared for his intended Edition, which are all inserted in the present. Had he lived to have compleated his Design, I dare say he would have added many more . . .

There is a brief and derivative 'Account of the Life' of Massinger. The 'Editor' and author of the prefatory material is presumably Henry Dell, the publisher. He is also, presumably, the author of some of the vapid notes, pointing to the beauties of a scene or making comparisons with Shakespeare. One or two notes are signed 'The Rev. Mr. Dodd', 'The Rev. Mr. Spence', etc. Coxeter's notes (again one presumes) are those which discuss readings 'in the old Copies', note parallel passages in Massinger himself, and (occasionally) gloss obscure terms: one or two critical comments written in quite an energetic clipped style may be his also (e.g. ii. 412).

Coxeter's edition gives the seventeen plays which were published with Massinger's name on the title-page (including *The Old Law*), and it thus set the canon for all succeeding editions of Massinger, including the present, though the two manuscript plays, *Believe As You List* and *The Parliament of Love*, have since come to light; and *The Old Law* is no longer accepted as Massinger's. While the edition, as given by Dell, commits countless errors of omission and commission, Coxeter did a great deal to tidy up and improve the text of Massinger as found in the early editions. He certainly did not deserve the contempt and abuse which Gifford unceasingly poured on his head in the introduction and notes to his own edition (e.g., 'every page of his work bears the strongest impression of imbecility'; 1813 edn., I. xciii). Against Gifford's comment that 'his conjectures are void alike of ingenuity and probability', A. K. McIlwraith pencilled in his copy, 'But you accept about three quarters of them.'

A notable reviewer of the 1759 edition was Oliver Goldsmith:[1] 'What mighty reason our editor had to disturb his repose, we cannot see at present, especially as his best plays have been already published in Dodsley's collection.' Massinger 'seldom rises to any pitch of sublimity, and yet it must be owned is never so incorrigibly absurd, as we often find his predecessor [Shakespeare]. His performances are all crowded with incident, but want character, the genuine mark of genius in a dramatic poet.' Goldsmith was no friend of the early drama, and elsewhere wrote against the stage-revival of 'those hashes of absurdity'.[2] He reviewed Colman's *Critical Reflections* in 1761 and said that Massinger and his fellows had 'already proceeded too far in the road to oblivion, ever to be brought back, whatever may be the endeavours of their few remaining friends, for that purpose.'[3]

Thomas Davies, bookseller and actor, bought up the sheets of Dell's edition and reissued them without amendment (even including the original errata-list!) in 1761. But he prefaced the edition with *Critical Reflections on the Old English Dramatick Writers*, addressed to David Garrick. This piece, which was also published as a separate pamphlet, was by George Colman (the Elder), then only 29. It would be clear from internal evidence alone that the piece was written to eulogize Massinger and thus boost Davies's sales, and in later years Colman said that the *Reflections* were 'thrown together at the instance of Mr. Garrick, to serve his old subject Davies; who, converted from an Actor into a Bookseller, had purchased the remaining copies of Coxeter's Edition.'[4] *Critical Reflections* puts the case that Garrick has been too exclusively absorbed in reviving Shakespeare, and is wrongly ignoring Shakespeare's contemporaries, especially Massinger, who has been 'permitted to languish in Obscurity, and remained almost entirely unknown' (p. 4). Colman quotes extensively from *The Picture*, remarking that 'the Workings of the human Heart are accurately set down'; he particularly commends the verse as preferable to 'that empty Swell of Phraseology, so frequent in our late Tragedies' and suggests that Garrick substitute *The City Madam* for the 'annual affront' of *The London*

---

[1] *The Critical Review*, July 1759; *Essays and Criticisms by Dr. Goldsmith*, 1798, iii. 229–31; see Harley, p. 238.
[2] *Works*, ed. Cunningham, 1854, ii. 58; see R. D. Williams, *PMLA*, liii (1938), 439.
[3] *Monthly Review*, xxiv (March 1761), 200–1, cited by Harley, p. 242.
[4] Colman, *Prose on Several Occasions*, 1787, I. x; see E. R. Page, *George Colman the Elder*, 1935, p. 51.

Cuckolds on Lord-Mayor's Day. Colman was widely read, and was quoted approvingly as far away as Germany (by H. W. von Gerstenberg in his *Bibliothek der schoenen Wissenschaften und freien Kuenste*).[1]

The reissue of Coxeter was only the beginning of Davies's efforts to commend Massinger to the English public.[2] He praised him to his correspondents,[3] and wrote a study which was prefaced to the third collected edition of Massinger in 1779, *Some Account of the Life of Philip Massinger*. (This was later republished as a separate pamphlet, 1789.) Davies's work, which had the advantage of using Oldys's manuscript notes on Langbaine, is a cheerful, knowledgeable, and enthusiastic survey of Massinger's life and works, in general not profound but remarkable in one respect, its comments on Massinger as a political writer, anticipating S. R. Gardiner by a hundred years.[4]

> But, besides the occasional Censure which *Massinger* passed upon the growing Vices of the Times in which he lived he aimed at higher Game. He boldly attacked the Faults of Ministers and of Kings themselves. He pointed his Arrows against *Carr* and *Buckingham*, against *James* and *Charles* the First.

Davies then goes on to describe the controversy over assistance to Frederick, Elector Palatine, and what Davies calls James's 'pusilanimous Temper' in coming to the aid of his son-in-law:

> *Massinger* . . . was not a Favourer of Arbitrary Power, or inclined to put an implicit Faith in the Word of Kings; he was averse from embracing the Doctrines of Passive Obedience and Non-Resistance . . . *Massinger* was a good Subject, but not like other Poets, his Contemporaries, a slavish Flatterer of Power, and an Abettor of despotick Principles.

---

[1] See H. S. Arnold, 'The Reception of Ben Jonson, Beaumont and Fletcher, and Massinger in Eighteenth-Century Germany' (unpub. Ph.D. thesis, Maryland, 1962).

[2] E. R. Wasserman, in 'Henry Headley and the Elizabethan Revival', *SP*, xxxvi (1939), 491–502, calls Davies 'a popular champion of the Elizabethans in the early years of the Revival. . . . Apparently without decided tastes of his own, he served largely to reflect the ideas of his associates, Warton, Farmer, Percy, Reed, and Steevens.' Davies also republished William Browne and Sir John Davies.

[3] There is an autograph letter to James Granger in the Huntington Library, HM 7312 Harley (p. 244) notes a printed version in Granger's *Letters*, ed. Malcolm, 1805, pp. 26–7.

[4] Gardiner's views on the political content of the plays appeared in *The Contemporary Review*, xxviii (1876), 495–507, reprinted in New Shakespere Society *Transactions*, 1875–6, pp. 314–31. The article was extremely influential because of the authority of the writer as historian. It demonstrates that Massinger was a political dramatist sensitive to the tensions and crises of his day, but it is less happy in its view of the plays as political allegories for the Pembrokian opposition party.

Davies gives a two-page demonstration of his case that in Roberto and Fulgentio in *The Maid of Honour*, Massinger 'undoubtedly drew the Portraits of *James* and his Minion, *Carr* or *Buckingham*, or perhaps both'. In Bertoldo's speech (I. i. 215-39), 'The Poet spoke the genuine Sense of the Nation' against James's caution towards a military engagement. In Fulgentio's effeminacy, Massinger hit at James's sexual tastes. And in *The Emperor of the East*, '*Massinger* vindicates the Cause of the Nation against unjust and exorbitant Impositions, and the Excesses of regal and ministerial Authority.'

Davies deserves great credit for his pioneer work on Massinger as a social and political commentator, and one can only wish it outweighed his indiscretion in publishing Monck Mason's disastrous edition. John Monck Mason, 1726-1809, was an Irishman who flirted with opposition causes but became more conformist as a commissioner for revenue, 1772-93, and in the last Irish Parliament voted for the Union. He had a taste for literature and old plays, but he engagingly states in the 1779 Preface, 'I never heard of *Massinger* till about two Years ago, when a Friend of mine, who knew my Inclination, sent me a Copy of his Works, from whence I received that high Degree of Pleasure, which they cannot fail to give to every Reader of Taste and Feeling.' He explains that he found the Coxeter edition very faulty and that following his habit he rectified in the margin the mistakes he discovered.[1]

Two of his friends then persuaded him to have his corrections published. 'I flatter myself', he said in conclusion, 'that this Edition of *Massinger* will be found more correct, (and Correctness is the only Merit it pretends to) than the best of those which have as yet been published of any other ancient dramatic Writer.' It never seems to have crossed Monck Mason's mind (or Davies's) that he should have consulted the original editions, and while he certainly amended errors in Coxeter, he achieved absurdities of unnecessary speculation about true readings which laid him open to the merciless scorn of the reviewers and Gifford. The 1779 edition of Massinger's works is merely a reprint of Coxeter (with all its errors, original and invented) with cursory amendments by Monck Mason. It is more Davies's edition than Monck Mason's. Davies inserts Mason's readings, and

[1] Monck Mason's copy of Coxeter with his annotations came into P. A. Daniel's possession, whence Dobell sold it in 1934 to J. G. McManaway, who very kindly gave it to the present editors.

his notes (which he marks 'M. M.'), and he adds notes of his own (marked 'D'.) An Appendix in the last volume carries longer notes, chiefly by Davies. Textually, it has no authority, though Mason's lucky hits will be found from time to time in the footnotes of the present edition. The dry conclusion of the harsh but informed review in *The Critical Review* was: 'Work enough remains for any critic who may think the plays of Massinger worth a third edition.'[1] But if Davies has done less than he might for the text of Massinger, he succeeded as propagandist.

The period between the publication of the Monck Mason edition in 1779 and the publication of Harness's edition in 1830, 'Adapted for family reading, and the use of young persons, by the omission of objectionable passages', is Massinger's great half-century. It is the period when *A New Way to Pay Old Debts* established itself as the rival to *Richard III* and *Hamlet* as an histrionic spectacle, and each successive Overreach—Henderson, Pope, Cooke, Kemble, and Kean—strove to outdo his predecessor; the period when six other Massinger plays were performed by the London theatre; when a new edition of the *Biographia Dramatica* referred to 'this very great man'; when Huber commended him to Goethe's attention;[2] when Gifford produced his standard edition, and brought out a second revised version within eight years; when the younger poets all read him and wrote about him—Coleridge, Scott, Byron, Lamb, Southey, Keats; when Hazlitt wrote the brilliant reviews of Kean as Sir Giles Overreach.

D. J. Rulfs has shown that between 1776 and 1790 there was a noticeable increase in the non-Shakespearian Elizabethan drama produced in London, although the reasons for the revival lay more in academic interest than in popular demand.[3] *The Westminster Gazette*, reviewing the 1779 revival of *The Bondman*, grumbled at 'the business of rummaging old libraries, and reviving plays which have long been consigned to oblivion, or to Circulating Libraries.' Beaumont and Fletcher were highest in esteem, followed by Massinger. *A New Way to Pay Old Debts* was revived at Covent Garden in 1781, with Henderson as Sir Giles (the untiring Davies had sent him a copy of his *Life*).[4] Cumberland's version of *The Bondman*

[1] *The Critical Review*, xlvii (1779), 293–300, quoted by Harley, p. 251.
[2] In *Flora*, ii (1793), 232; see H. S. Arnold, op. cit., p. 176.
[3] 'Reception of the Elizabethan Playwrights on the London Stage 1776–1833', *SP*, xlvi (1949), 54–69.
[4] R. H. Ball, *The Amazing Career of Sir Giles Overreach*, 1939, pp. 40–1.

had not been very successful at Covent Garden in 1779. *The City Madam* appeared sporadically and in different versions from 1771 onwards. A version of *The Picture* appeared in 1783. *The Duke of Milan* was revived in 1779 and 1816, *The Maid of Honour* in 1785 and 1831, *The Fatal Dowry* in 1825. Only *A New Way to Pay Old Debts* really held the stage and its success is unmatched. Kean electrified London with his performance on 12 January 1816; the effect of his final entry as the crazed, outwitted villain is spoken of in terms, and in volume, which probably no other single piece of acting has ever brought forth.

In 1796, Charles Lamb wrote to Coleridge asking 'Are you acquainted with Massinger?'[1] He then quoted a passage about slighted affection from *The Very Woman* (IV. iii) which so entranced him that he wanted it as an epigraph for his projected *Poems*; he also included it in his *Specimens*. But it is not by Massinger: it is Fletcher's. Coleridge borrowed Mason's Massinger from the Bristol Library in 1797 or 1798[2] and presumably began that intent and affectionate study of Massinger's verse which he seems to have continued right up to his death. Southey, writing from Bristol in 1779, speaks rather slightingly of the plot of *The Picture* ('well for his days; but we have outgrown it'); but in later years he copied out a great many passages from the plays into his commonplace books.[3]

It was necessary for a reliable edition of Massinger to be issued before detailed comments on his work—especially his verse—could be of real value. *The Plays of Philip Massinger in Four Volumes* of 1805 was Gifford's first major editorial work (his Jonson was published in 1816) and although it is possible to point out many faults in the reading and notes, there is no doubt that it is a great editorial achievement. Gifford collected and borrowed the early copies, and he collated copies of the same edition—discovering that press correction could produce variant readings. He was helped by Malone's extracts from Herbert's Office-book in dating plays from the licensing dates,[4] and Malone helped him generously by allowing him to use his own collection of plays. Malone also lent him the decayed manuscript of *The Parliament of Love*, which was now printed for the first time. Gifford weakened his edition by reprinting

[1] *Letters*, ed. Lucas, 1912, i. 28–9.
[2] *Notebooks*, ed. K. Coburn, ii, 1962, 3187 *note*.
[3] *Letters*, 1856, i. 65, and the commonplace books, ed. J. W. Warter, 4 vols. 1849-51, especially iv. 331–3.
[4] Malone had published these in 1790.

a long essay by John Ferriar, a physician, which had first appeared in the transactions of the Manchester Literary and Philosophical Society in 1786, and critical comment on each play by Dr. Ireland. Ferriar's piece is thoughtful and knowledgeable, but, like Dr. Ireland's comments, lacks distinction.

The most formidable review of Gifford did not appear until 1808, and this took exception to the 'dull and pious dissertations' of Ireland. This was in *The Edinburgh Review*, a twenty-page discussion (xii (April 1808), 99–119). It is not really hostile, but it is strong in its censure of Gifford's abuse of his predecessors. 'His constant aim', it remarks, is 'to build his own reputation on the ruin of that of his predecessors'. It pointed out a number of mistakes which, it thought, proved that Gifford had no justification for his self-righteous denunciation of the errors of Coxeter and Mason. (Gifford replied at very great length to this review in the acrimonious 'Advertisement' prefixed to the 1813 edition. Honours are about even, except in courtesy). *The Edinburgh Review* thought Gifford overestimated Massinger. 'Massinger . . . is an eloquent writer; but an indifferent dramatist. His comedies have no wit; his tragedies no propriety . . . Massinger's talents appear to have been better fitted by nature for heroic than dramatic writing: he excels in dignified scenes . . . but his flowing, stately periods are perhaps too lofty for the stage, and contribute to render his plays heavy and wearisome to the reader. . .'. Gifford's revised edition of 1813 contains a great many additional notes and corrections, though the text remains basically the same.[1]

Charles Lamb's *Specimens of the English Dramatic Poets who lived about the time of Shakespeare* was published in 1808. There are extracts from *The City Madam*, *A New Way to Pay Old Debts*, *The Picture*, *Parliament of Love*, *A Very Woman*, and *The Unnatural Combat*; from *The Fatal Dowry*, Lamb chose a passage by Field, and from *The Virgin Martyr*, a passage by Dekker. The comments are mostly left-handed compliments and polite insults: the balancing of Webster–Tourneur–Ford against Massinger–Shirley, to last for over a century and a half, had begun. Ignoring Massinger's consistent attack on aristocratic corruption, Lamb remarks of *The City Madam* that 'this bitter satire against the city women . . . must have been particularly gratifying to the females of the Herbert family and the rest of Massinger's patrons and patronesses.' Lamb thought

[1] It cost £2. 12s. in boards, or in royal octavo £4. 4s. in boards.

Massinger incapable of 'deeper passion and more tragical interest. Massinger had not the higher requisites of his art in anything like the degree in which they were possessed by Ford, Webster, Tourneur, Heywood, and others. . . . He is read with composure and placid delight.' Passages which he quoted from *The Virgin Martyr* and *The Old Law* he thought 'above Massinger'. But he could praise 'the good sense, rational fondness, and chastised feeling' of a passage from *The Picture*, and yield that his English style is 'the purest and most free from violent metaphor and harsh constructions, of any of the dramatists who were his contemporaries'.[1]

It seems clear that Scott did not know the less-published Jacobean dramatists as well as Lamb did, and in his 'essay on the Drama' of 1819 'Shirley, Ford, Webster, Decker and others' are rather vaguely nodded to.[2] He had mentioned Massinger in his Life of Dryden in 1808 (*Works of Dryden*, i. 5) as one who 'approached to Shakespeare in dignity'. In 1819, he treats him more fully, as one who had studied both Shakespeare and Jonson 'with the intention of uniting their excellences'. He particularly praised him for the structure of his plots: 'in unravelling the intricacy of his intrigues, he often displays the management of a master'. His 'peculiar excellence' was 'a full conception of character, a strength in bringing out, and consistency in adhering to it'. When there seem to be violent changes, as in Pisander/Marullo in *The Bondman* or Luke in *The City Madam*, 'upon looking back, we are always surprised and delighted to trace from the very beginning, intimations of what the personage is to prove'.

Byron gave Massinger a high rank in *English Bards and Scotch Reviewers* (lines 590–3); attacking the modern stage he asked:

> Shall sapient managers new scenes produce
> From Cherry, Skeffington, and Mother Goose?
> While Shakespeare, Otway, Massinger, forgot,
> On stalls must moulder, or in closets rot?

Other passing references show he knew *A New Way to Pay Old Debts* well, and especially remembered the first night of Kean's Sir Giles;[3] he also valued Gifford's 'excellent edition of Massinger'.[4] Hazlitt's reviews of Kean (1816) are discussed in the introduction to *A New*

---

[1] *Specimens*, etc., edition of 1895, pp. 356–82.
[2] *Miscellaneous Works*, vi (1870), 342–3.
[3] Letters of 1 Aug., 12 Aug. 1819, and 8 Oct. 1820.
[4] *Letters and Journals*, ii. 183; *Don Juan*, ix. 63.

Way to Pay Old Debts; he also, like Cumberland before him, preferred the Massinger and Field *Fatal Dowry* to Rowe's *Fair Penitent*, though he liked neither *The Duke of Milan* nor Kean's performance in it.[1] His general, and unflattering, opinions on Massinger are given in the fourth of the *Lectures on the Age of Elizabeth*, delivered in 1819 and published in 1820. Massinger is 'harsh and crabbed', 'makes an impression by hardness and repulsiveness of manner', 'he seldom touches the heart or kindles the fancy'. In his plays, 'the interest arises principally from the conflict between the absurdity of the passion and the obstinacy with which it is persisted in'. In spite of his calling Massinger's villains 'a sort of *lusus naturae*', he appends to his published text the long and brilliant analysis of Sir Giles Overreach's character which he had written for the preface to *A New Way to Pay Old Debts* in Oxberry's 'New English Drama'.[2]

T. L. Beddoes was a good deal influenced by Massinger, but, like Lamb, preferred the more exotic effects of some of his contemporaries. Towards the end of *The Bride's Tragedy* (1822), where there is a poisoning through smelling flowers, Beddoes adds a footnote, 'The reader will recollect Massinger's Duke of Milan.'[3] In 1824 he was reading *The Fatal Dowry*: 'The first four acts . . . have improved my opinion of Massinger: he is a very effective "stage-poet" after all.'[4] In 1825 he was very annoyed with the 'cobbling' of the play for its stage-revival (see p. 12). In a letter of 1830, he wonders why Tieck has attributed *The Second Maiden's Tragedy* to Massinger: 'it is too imaginative for old Philip.'[5]

Thomas Campbell edited *Specimens of the British Poets* in 1819; he gave an intelligent critical estimate of Massinger (i. 201) and devoted a generous 26 pages to his work: several extracts from *The Bondman*, including the parting of Leosthenes and Cleora and, inevitably, the appeal by Pisander to the more humane relations of a happier age (IV. ii. 53–88), one from *The Great Duke of Florence*, one from *The Fatal Dowry*, and another favourite of the anthologists, the big scene of temptation and revelation in *The Duke of Milan* between Francisco and Marcelia (II. i). Keats was reading Massinger in 1819: he referred to *A Very Woman* in a letter of 22 September, and in a letter to Fanny Brawne of 1 July he wrote, 'Some lines I

---

[1] *Works*, ed. Howe, v. 289–91.   [2] Ibid., vi. 265–9.
[3] *Works*, ed. Donner, 1935, p. 234.
[4] Ibid., p. 593. The printed text reads 'the four first acts'.   [5] Ibid., p. 650.

read the other day are continually ringing a peal in my ears': he then quoted Sforza's passionate expression of his jealous fears to Francisco in *Duke of Milan*, I. iii. 203–8, with some amendments, including a characteristic 'press'd' for 'touch'd' in the fourth line:

> To see those eyes I prize above mine own
> Dart favors on another—
> And those sweet lips (yielding immortal nectar)
> Be gently press'd by any but myself—
> Think, think Francesca, what a cursed thing
> It were beyond expression!

At this period the most important comments on Massinger are those by Coleridge. They are conveniently brought together by R. F. Brinkley in her book *Coleridge on the Seventeenth Century*. Coleridge spoke on Massinger in Lecture VII of the 1818 series (17 Feb.)[1] but the comments which have been preserved are scattered in notes and marginalia which seem to spread over many years. The most valuable observations are on the verse, but we take first general judgements (all references are to the pages of Miss Brinkley's book).

'Massinger is always entertaining; his plays have the interest of novels' (678). Developing this, Coleridge has a curious image for the Massingerian structure: 'Two or three tales, each in itself independent of the others, and united only by making the persons that are the agents in the story the *relations* of those in the other, as when a bindweed or thread is twined round a bunch of flowers, each having its own root—and this novel narrative in *dialogue*—such is the *character* of Massinger's plays . . .' (676). Presumably Coleridge meant the distinct aims and ends which (say) Welborn, Lovell, and Alworth have as they join in the single action against Overreach, or the different personal interests involved in *The Renegado* or *The Guardian*.

Coleridge differs completely from Scott on Massinger's consistency of character: he doesn't have 'a guiding point' in his characters; 'you never know what they are about', instancing in Camiola in *The Maid of Honour* an 'utter want of preparation' (674). For another curious opinion, one would again very much like to know which play or plays Coleridge had in mind: 'He is not a poet of high imagination; he is like a Flemish painter, in whose delineations objects appear as they do in nature, have the same force and truth, and produce the same effect upon the spectator' (675).

[1] T. M. Raysor, *Coleridge's Miscellaneous Criticism*, 1936, p. 4.

Massinger's Reputation

In talking of Massinger's general ideas, Coleridge is clearly influenced by the opinions of Gifford and Davies. He follows Gifford in saying that Massinger 'had a half-in-half hankering for Popery' (515); Gifford had been 'convinced . . . that he was a Catholick' (1805, p. lx). Politically, Massinger was 'a Democrat' (655), 'a decided Whig' (656); he opposed 'the morals which it was fashionable to teach in the reigns of James I, and his Successor'. Coleridge introduces personal reasons into Massinger's politics: 'Hence too the continued Flings at Kings, Courtiers, and all the favourites of Fortune, like one who had enough of intellect to see the injustice of his own inferiority in the share of the good things of life, but not genius enough to rise above it & forget himself—envy demonstrated' (674).

Massinger's verse continuously fascinated Coleridge. He contrasted it at one time with Shakespeare's ('both excellent in their kind', 433) and at another with Milton's: 'The style is differenced, but differenced in the smallest degree possible, from animated conversation, by the vein of poetry' (606–7). 'The language is most pure, equally free from bookishness and from vulgarism' (676). 'It is the nearest approach to the language of real life at all compatible with a fixed metre' (673). It is this combination of regular prosody and natural speech which roused Coleridge's admiration. 'The rhythm and metre are incomparably good . . . flexible and seeming to rise out of the passions, so that whenever a line sounds immetrical, the reader may be certain he has recited it amiss . . . Read aright, the blank verse is not less smooth than varied, a rich harmony, puzzling the fingers, but satisfying the ear' (676).

Coleridge argued that there could be no 'authentic edition of our Elder *dramatic Poets*' without a study of 'the philosophy of metre', and he proposed a rhetorical approach, observing emphasis, 'retardation & acceleration of the Times of Syllables according to the meaning of the words, the passion that accompanies them, and even the character of the Person that uses them. By these means, Massinger 'might be reduced to a rich and yet regular metre'. The details are complicated; here is an example: 'He who does not find a line (not corrupted) of Massinger's flow to the *Time total* of an Iambic Pentameter Hyperacatalectic, i.e. four Iambics (∪ —) and an Amphibrach (∪ — ∪) has not read it aright' (653–4). To achieve this 'Time total' one has to allow for the acceleration and retardation of the voice 'all which the mood or passion would have produced in the real Agent, and therefore demand from the Actor' (676). Apparent irregularity then becomes regular. Coleridge also notes that when a speech ends in mid-line, and a new speaker joins in, there is often a hypermetrical syllable because the last syllable of one speech and the first of the next are to be spoken simultaneously.

Since quality of verse becomes the burning issue in deciding the merit of Massinger, it is worthwhile spending time on Coleridge's respect for its diction and rhythm, and it is well worth comparing his view with those of Middleton Murry in 1922, that Massinger's blank verse is 'really excellent prose—lucid, well shaped, and sinewy'. 'Massinger would have been much happier, had he been freed from the obligation of cutting his prose up into lines.'[1]

Massinger was widely read in the nineteenth century. Stendhal knew him, and in his *Racine et Shakespeare* (1825) said, 'J'aime mieux une vieille pièce de Massinger que le *Caton* d'Addisson'.[2] Harness's expurgated edition presumably brought the plays to a wider English audience in 1830. *The Mirror of Taste and Dramatic Censor*, published in New York and Philadelphia in 1810, had given the American public expurgated versions of *A New Way to Pay Old Debts*, *The Fatal Dowry*, *The Bondman*, and *The Maid of Honour*. Gifford's edition was reissued in a single volume in 1840 'with a design of meeting the spirit of the age for cheap literature.' In the same year, Hartley Coleridge brought out a one-volume edition of Massinger and Ford, using Gifford's text. In 1836, Count von Baudissin published German translations of four of Massinger's plays, *The Fatal Dowry*, *The Duke of Milan*, *A New Way to Pay Old Debts*, and *The City Madam*. (A French translation of four plays, by Ernest Lafond, appeared in 1864: *The Fatal Dowry*, *The Bondman*, *The Picture*, *The Virgin Martyr*.) In 1849, the manuscript of *Believe As You List* was edited for the Percy Society by T. Crofton Croker: the play was first included in Massinger's works in the compact one-volume edition of Massinger's plays edited by Lieutenant-Colonel Francis Cunningham, using Gifford's text, in 1868. This was widely read, and is still the only portable complete Massinger. Massinger was not published in the Mermaid Series until 1887–9, when Arthur Symons edited two volumes containing *The Duke of Milan*, *A New Way to Pay Old Debts*, *The Great Duke of Florence*, *The Maid of Honour*, *The City Madam*, *The Roman*

---

[1] *The Problem of Style*, pp. 56–7.
[2] *Racine et Shakespeare*, ed. P. Martino, 1925, ii. 233.

Actor, The Fatal Dowry, The Guardian, The Virgin Martyr, and *Believe As You List*. This is the most recent edition of a substantial collection of Massinger's plays,[1] and the lack of editions in the last 80 years or so is a sign of the change in taste which we shall now describe.

Henry Hallam's *Introduction to the Literature of Europe*, 1837-9, gave space and a high place to Massinger—'Massinger, as a tragic writer, appears to me second only to Shakespeare; in the higher comedy, I can hardly think him inferior to Jonson.' This is probably the last time this sort of claim, common enough in the eighteenth century, was ever made. A. W. Ward in his *History of English Dramatic Literature* of 1875 said firmly he was 'not ... to be ranked among the most gifted of Shakspere's successors'. He was a moralist, and his genius was 'essentially rhetorical'.[2]

In 1877 there appeared a brilliant and very influential essay in the *Cornhill Magazine* by Leslie Stephen, which he reprinted in 1879 in *Hours in a Library* (Third Series).[3] Stephen presents Massinger as a man whose artistic defects are made more glaring by the predominant sentiment of his cultural environment in the period before the Civil War. Massinger was a grave and serious man, 'a moraliser by temperament', who could not transmute his thoughts and emotions into high art. 'He is throughout a sentimentalist and a rhetorician. . . . He is a man . . . of much real feeling and extraordinary facility of utterance, who finds in his stories convenient occasions for indulging in elaborate didactic utterances upon moral topics. . . .' 'His plays are apt to be a continuous declamation, cut up into fragments, and assigned to different actors.' Of this morality, Stephen says that it represents 'the voice of a society still inspired with the traditional sentiments of honour and self-respect, but a little afraid of contact with the rough realities of life. Its chivalry is a survival from a past epoch, not a spontaneous outgrowth of the most vital elements of contemporary development'. Massinger's hero–villains have lost the vital energy which informed those of the great Elizabethans preceding him: Marlowe, Shakespeare, Chapman. The blood has gone cold, there is no 'provisional sympathy' with them, and they become mere monsters. This is

---

[1] Four plays were published in a volume devoted to Massinger in a 'Masterpieces of English Drama' series in New York in 1912. The editor was L. A. Sherman and the plays were *Roman Actor, Maid of Honour, New Way,* and *Believe As You List*.

[2] Edition of 1899, iii. 1–47.

[3] pp. 1–49.

morbid, argues Stephen; it lands us in an unnatural atmosphere. In the way characters are persuaded by eloquent speeches, there is a further sign of the lack of 'rich blood in their veins'. There is 'a marked absence of downright wholesome commonsense'.

Symons's introduction to the Mermaid edition (1887) is very much affected by Stephen's approach, but introduces an element which will reappear: that Massinger represents the decadence of his time *both* because he is a keen observer of its growing corruptions *and* because his art is enfeebled by the atrophy of the period. Massinger may be commended as a keen observer, but, writing in an enfeebled age he has not the power to transmute 'recorded observation into vital fact' (p. xix). At the same time he is 'an admirable story-teller' (p. xxxii), but he has no passage of verse that 'makes us pause and brood... with the true epicure's relish' (p. xv).

Stripped of its rhetoric, a great deal of what Swinburne said about Massinger[1] turns out to have been said before. Even the phrase, 'He was the Falkland as Fletcher was the Rupert of the stage' is an epigrammatization of Stephen's remark that Massinger represented the misgivings felt by the more thoughtful members of his party as Fletcher represented 'the careless vitality of the cavalier spirit'. Swinburne puts more forcefully than others the view that Massinger sacrificed his art both to morality and to the theatre: 'The preacher or scene-shifter supplants the poet or the playwright' (p. 7). Swinburne found a great deal to praise in Massinger, however, and although he felt that 'his highest and most distinctive claims to honour are rather moral and intellectual ... than imaginative and creative', he was confident that 'the fame of Philip Massinger is secure against all chance of oblivion or eclipse' (p. 23).

The most characteristic voice of the end of the nineteenth century is that of Edmund Gosse, writing a 'University Extension Manual' on *The Jacobean Poets* (1894). Saintsbury, some years previously, had felt it necessary to protest against the 'rather low estimate' given Massinger since the time of Lamb, though he confessed 'I have nothing like the enthusiasm for him that I have for Webster, or for Dekker, or for Middleton'.[2] Gosse is not divided in his loyalties. He says that everyone vaguely thought that all Jacobean drama was like Massinger, 'until Lamb began to show quite clearly

---

[1] *The Fortnightly Review*, lii (1 July 1889), 1-23, reprinted in *Contemporaries of Shakespeare*, ed. Gosse and Wise, 1919, pp. 169-209.

[2] *A History of Elizabethan Literature*, 1907 (first ed. 1887), pp. 400-1.

what the old English drama really was' (p. 216). Massinger has a 'negation of qualities', 'the absence of what is brilliant, eccentric and passionate'; 'there can be no question that the decline in the essential part of poetry from Webster or Tourneur, to go no further back, to Massinger is very abrupt' (pp. 202–3). Massinger is 'scarcely a poet' (p. 206). 'It is very natural, especially for a young reader, to fling Massinger to the other end of the room, and to refuse him all attention' (p. 207). The best that Gosse can say for Massinger is that he is an 'admirable artificer', 'the Scribe of the seventeenth century'.

As there is little of interest in the criticism of the first two decades of this century (Emil Koeppel contributed a jejune piece to the *Cambridge History of English Literature* in 1910 containing such comments as 'his use of alliteration is very discreet'), it is convenient to go straight from Gosse to T. S. Eliot's essay of 1920. This was written as a review of A. H. Cruickshank's book *Philip Massinger*, 1920 (the first book devoted to Massinger) and collected in *The Sacred Wood* (1920). Eliot lays a formidable charge against Massinger: nothing less than having been responsible for the seventeenth-century dissociation of sensibility, causing 'the destruction of the old drama', and altering the whole course of English literature. 'Had Massinger been a greater man, a man of more intellectual courage, the current of English literature immediately after him might have taken a different course' (pp. 142–3). The particulars of the charge are that Massinger's work is doubly ossified; in words and in ideas Massinger is facile: using stock counters instead of minting things from his experience and imagination. Eliot describes Massinger as 'a man . . . of so exceptionally superior a literary talent . . . and so paltry an imagination'; a man with 'the highest degree of verbal excellence compatible with the most rudimentary development of the senses' (pp. 134–5). His 'feeling for language had outstripped his feeling for things . . . his eye and his vocabulary were not in co-operation.' The great period of English literature, when, the intellect being 'at the tips of the senses', 'sensation became word and word was sensation' was now over. 'The next period is the period of Milton . . . and this period is initiated by Massinger' (pp. 128–9).

Similarly with Massinger's ideas: 'he inherits the traditions of conduct, female chastity, hymeneal sanctity, the fashion of honour, without either criticising or informing them from his own experience'. In an important sentence which, however, lacks clarity (pp. 133–4), Eliot argues that what is decadent in the morals of Massinger is not an alteration of morality, but a preservation of morality when the emotions bonded to that morality have disappeared. 'As soon as the emotions disappear the morality which ordered it [*sic*] appears hideous.' In the second section of his essay, Eliot was much more laudatory about Massinger as a writer of comedy, in which he 'was one of the few masters in the language', and he closed the essay with this remark (p. 143): 'He is not . . . the only man of letters who, at the moment when a new view of life is wanted, has looked at life through the eyes of his predecessors, and only at manners through his own.'

It will be seen that so far from being a totally new assessment of Massinger, Eliot's essay is the culmination of a feeling of discomfort with the poetry and morality of Massinger which had been growing for over 100 years, and is associated with the gradual rehabilitation of metaphysical poetry—and Webster—during the nineteenth century. But Eliot's authority had a profound effect on the study of Massinger; over twenty years afterwards, the centenary article in *The Times Literary Supplement*, observing that Massinger's reputation had steadily declined in the last fifty years, remarked that students at universities felt safe in omitting him from their reading because he scarcely figured in the examinations set. Professor Una Ellis-Fermor, in her very widely read *Jacobean Drama* of 1936, defended her exclusion of Massinger on chronological grounds—but she allowed Ford in, as belonging essentially to the Jacobean age (pp. ix–x). The same manœuvre, Ford in, Massinger out, may be seen in Robert Ornstein's *The Moral Vision of Jacobean Tragedy*, 1959. It must be said that Massinger has suffered a little from his advocates. A. H. Cruickshank's book, though knowledgeable, is an amateurish work, and his praise is something of an embarrassment. 'Antonio, the Prince of Tarent, reminds us of a clean-limbed, honest English public-school boy; he is slow to take offence, but brave when provoked (*etc.*)' William Archer is perhaps no more helpful. He lectured on Massinger in a series at London in 1920 and 1921, published as *The Old Drama and the New* in 1923. His analysis of the reasons for Massinger's fall from grace is acute:

Massinger has been pointedly omitted from the general apotheosis of the minor Elizabethans. While Webster, Ford, and Tourneur have been lauded to the skies, Massinger has been treated almost as a negligible quantity. And why? Simply because we seldom or never find in his work those patches of verbal poetry on which nineteenth-century criticism fastened its attention; and because he had not the gift of those unexpectednesses, if I may so call them—like the famous 'Cover her face: mine eyes dazzle: she died young'—which had come to be regarded as the final proof of dramatic genius.

But when he praises Massinger, it is in such terms as this, of *The Great Duke of Florence*: 'The whole play is one that might have been written by a gentleman.'

A useful and balanced, though brief, account of Massinger appeared in 1937, in L. C. Knights's *Drama and Society in the Age of Jonson*. It rejects Eliot's contention that Massinger's verse and values were petrified. The verse is 'capable of sudden vividness... and it is almost always a serviceable dramatic medium'. In his two admirable comedies 'there is fresh perception of a contemporary world': Knights praises Massinger's discernment in perceiving and evaluating the social and economic issues of his day. The superficial snobbery of *The City Madam* is not its real meaning: there lies behind it a Jonsonian sense of order and limitations, 'something founded on religion, common sense and decency'. Massinger was 'a creator inspired by his predecessors, not a mere imitator' and in comedy, 'the last of the Elizabethans'.[1]

[1] As this study of Massinger's reputation is intended as a miniature history of taste, and not as an account of work done, no attempt is made to record the scholarly investigation of the last hundred years on the canon, on sources, on the text and its meaning, since the contributions will be noted in their proper places in the introductions and commentaries to the plays, and elsewhere in this General Introduction. But a note must be made here of the first thorough and scholarly investigation of Massinger's life and work. This was carried through by a young French scholar, Maurice Chelli, just before the First World War. Chelli was wounded in 1914 and never really recovered, eventually dying of 'flu in 1918. His work was published posthumously, and it is most unfortunate that it was brought out in two parts, *Le Drame de Massinger* in 1923 and *Étude sur la collaboration de Massinger avec Fletcher et son groupe* in 1926. The second work contained a bibliography essential for the first.

III

THE COLLECTED EDITIONS OF MASSINGER'S PLAYS

Collections containing at least three of Massinger's plays are listed below. A name in bold type beneath the date gives the short-title by which the edition is identified in the textual apparatus. The distinction between **Gifford**[1] and **Gifford**[2] is rarely required in the text-notes, and **Gifford** is to be understood as referring to the standard revised edition of 1813. The key to the abbreviations used for titles will be found on p. lxxviii.

1655 **55**	Three New Playes; *viz*. The Bashful Lover, Guardian, Very Woman ... Written by Philip Massenger, Gent. ... London, Printed for Humphrey Moseley ... 1655. *BL*, *Guard.*, *VW*.
1744 **Dodsley**	A Select Collection of Old Plays ... London: Printed for R. Dodsley ... MDCCXLIV [Vol. viii]. *CM*, *Guard.*, *NWP*, *Pict.*, *UC*.
1759 **Coxeter**	The Dramatic Works of Mr. Philip Massinger, Compleat.... Revised, Corrected, and all the Various Editions Collated, By Mr. Coxeter. With Notes Critical and Explanatory, By the Editor, And by Various Authors ... London: Printed for Henry Dell ... MDCCLIX. *BL*, *Bond.*, *CM*, *DM*, *EE*, *FD*, *GDF*, *Guard.*, *MH*, *NWP*, *The Old Law*, *Pict.*, *Ren.*, *RA*, *SSS*, *THS*, *TJS*, *UC*, *VW*, *The Virgin Martyr*.
1761	The Dramatic Works of Philip Massinger, Compleat. ... Revised ... By Thomas Coxeter ... London: Printed for T. Davies ... MDCCLXI. (Contents as before.)
1779 **Mason**	The Dramatick Works of Philip Massinger ... with notes critical and explanatory, by John Monck Mason, Esq. ... London ... MDCCLXXIX. (Contents as before.)
1804	The British Drama ... London, published by William Miller ... 1804 [vols. i and ii]. *Bond.*, *FD*, *GDF*, *NWP*.
1805 **Gifford**[1]	The Plays of Philip Massinger, ... with notes critical and explanatory, By W. Gifford, Esq. ... London: ... 1805. (Contents as **Coxeter**, with the addition of *PL*.)

The Collected Editions of Massinger's Plays   lxix

1811   The Modern British Drama . . . London: Printed for William Miller . . . 1811 [vols. i and iii]. *Bond.*, *FD*, *NWP*.

1813 **Gifford**[2]   The Plays of Philip Massinger, . . . with notes . . . By W. Gifford, Esq. . . . The Second Edition . . . London . . . 1813.
(Contents as **Gifford**[1], with the addition of *LTF*.)

1830   The Plays of Philip Massinger. Adapted for family reading, and the use of young persons, by the omission of objectionable passages. [By William Harness.] . . . London: . . . MDCCCXXX. [Also New York, 1831.] *BL*, *Bond.*, *CM*, *DM*, *EE*, *FD*, *GDF*, *MH*, *NWP*, *Pict.*, *RA* (selections), *UC*, *VW*, *The Virgin Martyr*.

1836   Ben Jonson und seine Schule . . . übersetzt . . . durch Wolf Grafen von Baudissin . . . Leipzig . . . 1836 [vol. ii]. *CM*, *DM*, *FD*, *NWP* (German texts).

1840   The Plays of Philip Massinger, with notes . . . by William Gifford. . . . Third Edition. London . . . MDCCCXL.
(Contents as **Gifford**[2].)

1840   The Dramatic Works of Massinger and Ford. With an Introduction, by Hartley Coleridge. London . . . MDCCCXL.
(Contents as **Gifford.**[2])
[*Later editions not recorded.*]

1864   Contemporains de Shakespeare. Massinger, traduit par Ernest Lafond . . . Paris . . . 1864. *Bond.*, *FD*, *Pict.*, *The Virgin Martyr*.

1868 **Cunningham**   The Plays of Philip Massinger. From the Text of William Gifford. With the addition of the tragedy 'Believe As You List.' Edited by Lieut.-Colonel F. Cunningham. London . . . 1868.
(Contents as **Gifford**[2], with the addition of *BAYL*)
[*Later reprints not recorded.*]

1870   The Works of the British Dramatists . . . from the Best Editions . . . by John S. Keltie . . . Edinburgh: William P. Nimmo. 1870.
DM, *NWP*, *The Virgin Martyr*.

1887–9 **Symons**   The Best Plays of the Old Dramatists. Philip Massinger. Edited, with an introduction and notes, By Arthur

	Symons. . . . London . . . [vol. i] 1887; [vol. ii] 1889. *BAYL, CM, DM, GDF, FD, Guard., MH, NWP, RA, The Virgin Martyr.*
1912	Masterpieces of the English Drama. Philip Massinger. Edited by Lucius A. Sherman . . . New York, Cincinnati, Chicago . . . [1912]. *BAYL, MH, NWP, RA.*
[1931] **McIlwraith**	The Life and Works of Philip Massinger by A. K. McIlwraith. [Unpublished doctoral thesis, Oxford University, 1931.] *BL, BAYL, Bond., CM, CL, DM, EE, FD, GDF, Guard., LTF, LLE, MH, NWP, NYG, PL, Pict., Ren., RA, SSS, THS, TJS, UC, VW, The Virgin Martyr, VC.*

IV
EDITORIAL PRACTICE

1. INTRODUCTIONS

Each play is prefaced by an introduction which gives an account of (*a*) any problems of authorship, (*b*) the date of the play and all important circumstances relating to its composition and first appearance, (*c*) the sources, (*d*) the foundation of the text, (*e*) the later history of the text, and (*f*) the history of the play upon the stage (including adaptations and alterations).

When, as is usual (see the following section), a single printed edition of the seventeenth century is the copy-text, the section of the introduction dealing with the text runs as follows:

(i) the relevant entries in the Stationers' Register;
(ii) a short bibliographical description of the primary edition;
(iii) an account of the printing of the edition, which is normally limited to discussion of the number of skeleton-formes and their employment, the evidence for differentiating compositors, the general quality of the composition, and the number and quality of the press-corrections (based on McIlwraith's collations);
(iv) an investigation of the nature of the manuscript used by the printer;
(v) a list of the extant copies of the primary edition available in university and public libraries and institutions;

Editorial Practice

(vi) the later history of the text, including any manuscript corrections by the author.

Each of Massinger's poems is prefaced by a short introduction dealing with questions of date and the circumstances of composition, the nature of the text and its later history.

2. TEXT

In their treatment of the text and its apparatus the editors have in general followed the principles and practice of Fredson Bowers in his edition of Thomas Dekker's plays (Cambridge University Press, 1953–61).

Of the seventeen plays included in this edition, ten were published in Massinger's lifetime, almost certainly at his instigation and with his approval:

The Duke of Milan (1623)   *The Emperor of the East* (1632)
The Bondman (1624)   *The Maid of Honour* (1632)
The Roman Actor (1629)   *A New Way to Pay Old Debts* (1633)
The Picture (1630)   *The Great Duke of Florence* (1636)
The Renegado (1630)   *The Unnatural Combat* (1639)

Two of these plays went into second editions in Massinger's lifetime, *The Duke of Milan* and *The Bondman*, both in 1638. The second edition of *The Bondman* has no independent authority; it is possible that Massinger oversaw the final stages of the printing of the 1638 *Duke of Milan*, but only five new readings, all from sheet M, three of them concerned with punctuation, have been adopted from that edition.

Five other plays were printed in single editions only in the seventeenth century. The publication of *The Fatal Dowry* (a collaboration with Field) in 1632 was probably not instigated or supervised by Massinger. *The Bashful Lover*, *The Guardian*, and *A Very Woman* were published together as *Three New Playes* in 1655, fifteen years after Massinger's death, and *The City Madam* was published in 1658.

The two remaining plays, *The Parliament of Love* and *Believe As You List*, were first printed from manuscript in 1805 and 1849 respectively.

For each of the fifteen plays published in the seventeenth century an early edition is the sole authoritative copy-text. The texts of these plays in the present edition have been set up from corrected photocopies of one copy of this primary edition. To faciliate reference to or from the original editions, the commencement of each new page of the original is marked by its signature in the margin of the present edition.

There exist copies of the original editions of six of these plays with ink corrections by Massinger himself (see above, p. xxxii). These corrections are (normally) incorporated in the text; this is the first edition of Massinger's plays to carry these 'authorized' readings.

Treatment of printed copy-text

The original spelling has been preserved, but abbreviations and contractions like 'M^{rs}', 'commaũd', '&' have been expanded. Speakers' names have been printed out in full; so far as possible, the conventions of the original editions in regard to the names given in stage-directions and speech-headings to disguised characters, servants, and extras have been preserved.

Stage-directions have been made consistent in position and type-fount throughout the edition. Directions are in italic with the full names of the characters in small capitals.[1]

Entries are centred; exits are set at the right-hand side. All editorial additions or alterations to the wording of the directions appear within square brackets.[2] It was Massinger's habit to head a new scene with a list of the first group of characters, without 'Enter', and with full-stops between the names; when this convention has survived into the printed texts it has been preserved. Asides have been added sparingly by the editors (within square brackets) where they have felt them necessary to clarify the action; the change to or from direct speech in such cases is normally marked by a dash.

Most of the early editions mark both scene and act divisions and these titles are kept (a standard italic type being used); in addition, the present edition records in the margin the beginning of all new scenes (whether marked in the original or not) thus: [III. v]. For some plays, the editors have thought it occasionally useful to insert in the Commentary the scene-locations given by Gifford, but in general locations are not given.

Whatever the practice of the original, all new speeches begin on a new line, and when (as so often in Massinger) a new speaker

[1] For a minor exception, see text-introduction to *The Maid of Honour*.
[2] It has therefore been necessary to remove some original square brackets from directions in *The Guardian* and *The Bashful Lover*.

Editorial Practice

finishes a verse-line begun by the previous speaker the new speech is indented to show more clearly the movement of the verse.

Punctuation has not been modernized, but the editors have allowed themselves considerable freedom in adding, removing or altering punctuation in the interest of clarity. (All changes in punctuation are noted, as described below.) In exclamations, ? has been replaced by ! unless the editor has felt that a logical distinction had been observed in the use of these two forms (e.g., ? after 'How...' and 'What...'). At the end of an interrupted or uncompleted speech the punctuation of the original is preserved if it is a dash, or colon-dash, or comma, colon, or semi-colon; otherwise, a dash has been inserted.

After much hesitation, the editors decided to impose no uniformity in the practice of capitalizing nouns or italicizing names even within the confines of a single play, and we have allowed the vagaries of the original to stand except in some individual cases which seemed grossly anomalous. The consequent lack of conformity may seem untidy, but to impose regularity in the use of italics in a text like that of *The Great Duke of Florence* would be not so much restoring as faking.

In the matter of emendation, we leave it to the reader to decide whether we have been too free or too conservative. We have preserved the readings of the original whenever we believed a case could be made out for them, and we have emended as infrequently as possible; nevertheless, faith in the reliability of seventeenth-century compositors has in the past at times resembled fanaticism, and we have accepted that all copyists are likely to corrupt their texts. We have found it necessary to introduce comparatively few new readings ourselves, thanks to the work of our predecessors, especially Coxeter and Gifford.

Treatment of manuscript copy-text

The two plays for which the copy-text is a manuscript, *The Parliament of Love* and *Believe As You List*, have been treated differently in the present edition. *Believe As You List* is probably the most important dramatic manuscript of the great age of English drama; a play in the dramatist's own handwriting fully marked for use in the theatre. The editor (C. G.) has produced a text which follows the original manuscript as closely as possible and translates the physical characteristics of Massinger's work into print; the accretions and corrections of the book-keeper and others who have written on the manuscript are removed to the textual notes (their appearance on the page is preserved in the Malone Society Reprint of the play, edited by C. J. Sisson). *The Parliament of Love*, on the other hand, is not in Massinger's hand and the editor (P. E.) has not thought preservation of the accidentals and the scanty punctuation worth what it would cost in trouble to the reader. The practice of Fredson Bowers in editing the fellow-manuscript of *The Welsh Ambassador* (Dekker, *Dramatic Works*, vol. iv) has therefore been followed; that is to say, the text has been treated as a seventeenth-century printer might have printed it, initial capitals being inserted at the beginning of lines etc., to bring it into conformity with the appearance of plays in this edition set up from printed texts. The accidents of the original manuscript have been reproduced in the Malone Society Reprint of the play, edited by Miss K. M. Lea.

The details of the treatment of each manuscript and the conventions and symbols used are fully described in the introduction to each play. For both, independent transcripts of the manuscripts made by A. K. McIlwraith, checked against the originals by the editors, have been used as the basis of the texts printed here.

The Poems

For two of Massinger's poems, *To His Son* and *To James Shirley* there is a printed copy-text; for another, *The Copy of a Letter*, there is a manuscript copy-text supported by a printed text. For each of three more poems, the *Letter to Foljambe*, *A New Year's Gift*, and *Sero, sed Serio* there is a single manuscript copy-text; the first in Massinger's hand, and the last carrying his signature. There are three manuscript copies of *The Virgin's Character*, and two of *London's Lamentable Estate*. *To His Son* and *To James Shirley* have been treated in the same way as the other printed copy-texts; for the other poems, the punctuation has been dealt with as in the printed texts, but the remaining accidentals of the original have been preserved. Massinger's *Letter to Foljambe* is, of course, reproduced exactly.

3. TEXTUAL APPARATUS

All alterations of the copy-text have been noted, except the following, which have been made silently:

(i) Expansion of speakers' names in speech-headings.

(ii) Centring of directions for entries.
(iii) Expansion and normalizing of names, and change of type, in stage-directions.
(iv) Indenting of new speeches which continue the verse-line.
(v) Commencing new speeches on a new line of print.
(vi) Substitution of capital initial for lower-case, or vice versa, after a change in punctuation involving a full-stop.
(vii) Changes of factotum initials, swash capitals, wrong-fount letters and punctuation-marks, broken letters, and turned letters.
(viii) Correction of faulty punctuation at the end of a completed speech.
(ix) Correction of faulty or missing punctuation at the end of stage-directions or speakers' names in speech-headings.
(x) Changes of punctuation and type in the act-and-scene headings.

All substantial alterations of the copy-text, that is, those which are considered to affect the meaning, are recorded in the text-notes at the foot of the page. The order of the items is always the same: line number / the reading of this edition / square bracket / the authority for this reading / the rejected reading / the authority for the rejected reading. The symbol used for the copy-text is normally the last two digits of the year of publication. Examples are as follows:

162 praye] *Gifford*; prayd *32*

'162' is the line number; 'praye' is the reading of the present edition; Gifford first made the emendation; 'prayd' is the rejected reading of the original quarto, '32'. This note does not insist that Gifford's reading is given with literal exactness; in this case he reads 'pray'. If, however, the editor desires to call attention to the exact form of an earlier editor's reading in such circumstances he brackets it thus:

84 sind] *Gifford* (sinn'd); sine *36*

or he may use the notation '*after Gifford*' to indicate that the basis or concept of the emendation is Gifford's though the form differs. '*conj. Gifford*' indicates that the reading was conjectured by Gifford, but not admitted into his text.

The apparatus makes no attempt to give the history of the text; its concern is to record and attribute all departures from the copy-text. But when important emendations made by previous editors are rejected, it is usual to record them, thus:

>   310 participate] *32*; precipitate *Coxeter*
>   8 sleepy] *Coxeter*; sleep *55*; asleep *Dodsley*

Other sigla and forms are:

> *editor* = the editor of the play in the present edition;
> *not in 32* = the reading is not found or is omitted in the named edition;
> *Massinger MS* = Massinger's inked corrections in the Harbord–Gosse–Folger quartos or the Foljambe quarto;
> 32^1, 32^2, 32^3 = the readings of uncorrected formes, and of later corrected stages;

The wavy dash (∼) is used to save the repetition of a word given in the lemma when attention is being called to a change elsewhere; in the punctuation, for example:

>   146 it] *Coxeter*; ∼, *32*

The caret mark (∧) is used to call attention to an absence of punctuation, thus:

>   61 Ladiship,] *Coxeter*; ∼∧ *32*

(Here it is indicated that the 1632 quarto reads 'Ladiship' without any punctuation following.)

In some plays, the misdivision of the verse is so extensive that the corrections have been listed in an appendix to avoid crowding the text-notes. Normally, however, correction of the lining of the verse is made at the foot of the page in the following way:

>   262–4 *rearranged by Gifford*; *32 reads* O . . . end / He

Where the error consists of two half-lines run together, the note is as follows:

>   2–3 abroad, / Must] *Coxeter*; *undivided 32*

Minor corrections which can hardly be said to affect the meaning of the text have been recorded in tables of Running Corrections, which are assembled as an appendix to the edition (vol. v). These are given in simple form and without attribution:

>   90 boldnesse] bodlnesse
>   34 'Tis] 'tis
>   43 inioy,] ∼;

Non-substantive press corrections are recorded in these tables also, and these are attributed, e.g.:

>   16 haunt] 32^2; haund 32^1

4. THE COMMENTARY

The commentary on the plays consists of explanatory notes placed in the final volume (v). These notes elucidate obscure passages, discuss problems of corruption in the text, explain references and allusions to events, customs, legends, and so on which may cause difficulty, and give sources or analogues for passages where desirable. *They do not explain the meaning of individual words*, unless there is some unusual problem to discuss: all glossing is done in the main Glossary described below.

In quotations from and references to Shakespeare we have used Peter Alexander's edition (Collins, 1951).[1]

5. GLOSSARY AND INDEX

A combined glossary and index is placed at the end of the final volume. It contains a glossary of all words which are obsolete or whose meanings have changed, an index of the topics discussed in the explanatory notes, and an index of the more important proper names in the text.

The conventions for entering words in the Glossary are given in full at the head of the Index, vol. v, p. 269, but the following points may be noted here:

(i) when the meaning of a word is not fully covered in the *Oxford English Dictionary*, the entry is asterisked, and there is a supporting note in the Commentary.

(ii) when (as with asterisked words) the play–act–scene–line reference is followed by 'n', attention is drawn to a fuller discussion in the Commentary. Some very well-known classical names are simply indexed, without gloss or explanatory note.

(iii) topics in the Commentary are distinguished from words in the text by the use of initial capitals in the entry.

(iv) all Glossary entries are in standardized modern spelling, with cross-references from the original spellings where these show considerable difference.

A separate *index nominorum* to the General Introduction, and to the introductions to the individual works, is also supplied.

---

[1] Some approximation must therefore be accepted in line-references to prose-passages, since the line-numbering in Alexander's edition is keyed not to itself but to the old Cambridge edition; see, e.g., *As You Like It*, Act V, Scene iv.

6. APPENDICES

A list of Massinger's spellings taken from what he left in his own handwriting is given as an appendix to the edition; the list contains some 3,357 separate entries with as many as five spellings recorded for a single word. A further appendix, as described above, is the list of Running Corrections for all plays.

V

ABBREVIATIONS AND SHORT-TITLES

1. MASSINGER'S WORKS

The abbreviated titles used for Massinger's plays and poems are as follows, with the number of the volume in which the work will be found.

BAYL	*Believe As You List* (III)
BL	*The Bashful Lover* (IV)
Bond.	*The Bondman* (I)
CL	'The Copy of a Letter to the Earl of Pembroke' (IV)
CM	*The City Madam* (IV)
DM	*The Duke of Milan* (I)
EE	*The Emperor of the East* (III)
FD	*The Fatal Dowry* (I)
GDF	*The Great Duke of Florence* (III)
Guard.	*The Guardian* (IV)
LLE	'London's Lamentable Estate' (IV)
LTF	'A Letter to Sir Francis Foljambe' (IV)
MH	*The Maid of Honour* (I)
NWP	*A New Way to Pay Old Debts* (II)
NYG	'A New Year's Gift' (IV)
Pict.	*The Picture* (III)
PL	*The Parliament of Love* (II)
RA	*The Roman Actor* (III)
Ren.	*The Renegado* (II)
SSS	'Sero, sed Serio' (IV)
THS	'To His Son' (IV)
TJS	'To James Shirley' (IV)
UC	*The Unnatural Combat* (II)
VC	'The Virgin's Character' (IV)
VW	*A Very Woman* (IV)

II. EDITIONS OF INDIVIDUAL PLAYS

A list of the short-titles used for collected editions of Massinger will be found on pp. lxviii–lxx. Editions of single plays frequently cited are referred to as follows.

Baldwin	*The Duke of Milan*, ed. T. W. Baldwin, Lancaster, Pa., 1918
Bryne	*The Maid of Honour*, ed. E. A. W. Bryne, 1927
Byrne	*A New Way to Pay Old Debts*, ed. M. St. Clare Byrne, 1950
Craik	*The City Madam*, ed. T. W. Craik, 1964 *A New Way to Pay Old Debts*, ed. T. W. Craik, 1964
Cruickshank	*A New Way to Pay Old Debts*, ed. A. H. Cruickshank, Oxford, 1926
Dawson	*The Picture*, ed. G. E. Dawson, unpublished doctoral thesis, Cornell University, 1931
Dunn	*The Fatal Dowry*, ed. T. A. Dunn, Edinburgh, 1969
Hoy	*The City Madam*, ed. C. Hoy, 1964
Kirk	*The City Madam*, ed. R. Kirk (Princeton Studies in English, 10), Princeton, 1934
Lockert	*The Fatal Dowry*, ed. C. L. Lockert, Lancaster, Pa., 1918
Phialas	*The Emperor of the East*, ed. P. G. Phialas, unpublished doctoral thesis, Yale University, 1948
Sandidge	*The Roman Actor*, ed. W. L. Sandidge (Princeton Studies in English, 4), 1929
Senob	*The Renegado*, ed. A. Senob, unpublished doctoral thesis, University of Chicago, 1939
Spencer	*The Bondman*, ed. B. T. Spencer, Princeton, 1932
Stochholm	*The Great Duke of Florence*, ed. J. M. Stochholm, Baltimore, 1933
Telfer	*The Unnatural Combat*, ed. R. S. Telfer (Princeton Studies in English, 7), Princeton, 1932

III. OTHER ABBREVIATIONS AND SHORT-TITLES

Abbott, *Shakespearian Grammar*	E. A. Abbott, *A Shakespearian Grammar*, 1869; 3rd edition, 1870
Adams, *Herbert*	*The dramatic records of Sir Henry Herbert*, ed. J. Q. Adams, New Haven, 1917
American NQ	*American Notes and Queries*

Arber	E. Arber, *A transcript of the registers of the Company of Stationers of London, 1554–1640*, 5 volumes, 1875–94
astrol.	astrological term
Babb, *Elizabethan Malady*	L. Babb, *The Elizabethan Malady: a study of melancholia in English literature from 1580–1642*, East Lansing, Michigan, 1951
Ball, *Amazing Career*	R. H. Ball, *The Amazing Career of Sir Giles Overreach*, 1939
Bentley	G. E. Bentley, *The Jacobean and Caroline stage*, 7 volumes, Oxford, 1941–68
cast	list of dramatis personae
Chamberlain, *Letters*	*The Letters of John Chamberlain*, ed. N. E. McClure, 2 volumes, Philadelphia, 1939
Cruickshank	A. H. Cruickshank, *Philip Massinger*, Oxford, 1920
C.S.P. Dom.	*Calendar of State Papers, Domestic*
ded.	dedication
DNB	*Dictionary of National Biography*
Dunn	T. A. Dunn, *Philip Massinger: The man and the playwright*, 1957
epil.	epilogue
Eyre and Rivington	G. E. B. Eyre and C. R. Rivington, *A transcript of the registers of the worshipful Company of Stationers, from 1640–1708 A.D.*, 3 volumes, 1913–14
Farmer and Henley	J. S. Farmer and W. E. Henley, *Slang and its analogues past and present*, 7 volumes, 1890–1904
Favyn	A. Favyn, *The theater of honour and knighthood. Or, A compendious chronicle and historie of the whole Christian world*, 1623
fig.	figurative usage
Gardiner	S. R. Gardiner, *History of England from the accession of James I. to the outbreak of the civil war, 1603–1642*, 10 volumes, 1883–4
Genest	J. Genest, *Some account of the English stage from the Restoration in 1660 to 1830*, 10 volumes, Bath, 1832

Abbreviations and Short-titles

Greg, *Bibliography*	W. W. Greg, *A Bibliography of the English printed drama to the Restoration*, 4 volumes, 1939–59
Collected Papers	W. W. Greg, *Collected Papers*, ed. J. C. Maxwell, Oxford, 1966
Harley	M. J. Harley, 'The eighteenth-century interest in English drama before 1640 outside Shakespeare', unpublished M.A. dissertation, University of Birmingham, 1962
HLQ	*Huntington Library Quarterly*
intrans.	intransitive verb
Jonson, *Works*	*Ben Jonson*, ed. C. H. Herford, P. and E. Simpson, 11 volumes, Oxford, 1925–52
Koeppel, *Quellen-Studien*	E. Koeppel, *Quellen-Studien zu den Dramen George Chapman's, Philip Massinger's, und John Ford's*. Quellen und Forschungen zur Sprach- und Culturgeschichte der germanischen Völker, lxxxii, Strassburg, 1897
Lawless, *Monograph*	D. S. Lawless, *Philip Massinger and his associates*, Muncie, Indiana, 1967
Poems	D. S. Lawless, *The Poems of Philip Massinger, with critical notes*, Muncie, Indiana, 1968
Thesis	D. S. Lawless, 'Massinger and his associates', unpublished doctoral thesis, University of Birmingham, 1965
Lilly	W. Lilly, *Christian astrology modestly treated of in three books*, 1647
Linthicum	M. C. Linthicum, *Costume in the drama of Shakespeare and his contemporaries*, 1936
lit.	literally
McManaway, *Studies*	J. G. McManaway, *Studies in Shakespeare, bibliography and theater*, ed. R. Hosley, A. C. Kirsch, and J. W. Velz, New York, 1969
MLN	*Modern Language Notes*
MLR	*Modern Language Review*
MP	*Modern Philology*
MSR	*Malone Society Reprints*
naut.	nautical usage
Nicoll, *History of English Drama*	A. Nicoll, *A history of English drama 1660–1900*, 6 volumes, 1952–9

NQ	*Notes and Queries*
ODP	*Oxford Dictionary of Proverbs*
ODQ	*Oxford Dictionary of Quotations*
OED	*Oxford English Dictionary*
PMLA	*Publications of the Modern Language Association of America*
ppl.	participial
PQ	*Philological Quarterly*
SD	stage-direction
SH	speech-heading
SP	*Studies in Philology*
STC	A. W. Pollard and G. R. Redgrave, *A Short-Title Catalogue of books printed . . . 1475–1640*, 1926
Sugden	E. H. Sugden, *A topographical dictionary to the works of Shakespeare and his fellow dramatists*, Manchester, 1925
Tilley	M. P. Tilley, *A Dictionary of the proverbs in England in the sixteenth and seventeenth centuries*, Ann Arbor, 1950
TLS	*Times Literary Supplement*
trans.	transitive verb
Wing	D. Wing, *A short-title catalogue of books printed . . . 1641–1700*, 3 volumes, New York, 1945–51
verse	commendatory verse

THE FATAL DOWRY

INTRODUCTION

(a) *Authorship*

The title-page of the earliest edition of *The Fatal Dowry*, 1632, assigns it to 'P. M. and N. F.' The absence of Massinger's name in full on the title-page, and of the customary dedication and commendatory verses, indicate that it was not Massinger who undertook the publication, but he acknowledged the play as his by including it in the Harbord volume (see section (d) below), and all the evidence points to a collaboration between Massinger and Nathan Field.[1] There can be little doubt that Acts I and V and all but the first scene of Act IV are by Massinger, that Act II and Act IV, Scene i are by Field, and that Act III is begun by Massinger and ended by Field. Field's hand is most easily seen in the scenes concerning the fop Novall Junior, which give most play to his characteristic brisk satire on the manners of the gallant and to his talent for sexual innuendo and badinage. The exuberance shown in plays entirely his own (*A Woman is a Weathercock* and *Amends for Ladies*) is perhaps somewhat subdued in *The Fatal Dowry*; but the similarities with his unaided plays are unmistakable and on some occasions amount to manifest repetition (see notes to II. i. 82–3, II. ii. 69–71, 96, IV. i. 65–6). The less witty and satirical parts are not really difficult to assign to their authors; the windy pathos of the rhetoric for the funeral in Act II, and for the quarrel in Act III, is not only as distinct from Massinger's style as may be, but is representative of what Field is likely to do in serious writing as shown in the few serious speeches in *Amends for Ladies*; it is not good verse, often irresponsible about the sense and containing ludicrous images, but since it is Field's it cannot lack spirit of a kind.

There are some fairly sound mechanical tests to confirm the evidence of style. Differences in kind in stage-directions are discussed

---

[1] For Field's career, see R. F. Brinkley, *Nathan Field, the Actor-Playwright*, 1928, and W. Peery, *The Plays of Nathan Field*, 1950.

under *Text* below. Spellings of name are sometimes significant: in Act I, we have *Charaloyes* (2), *Charloyes* (4) and *Charalois* (1); in Act II there is a marked change to *Charolois* (7) and *Charalois* (1). *Aymer* becomes *Aymeire* and *Aymiere* (1 each) in Massinger, but *Aymour* (4) in Field; Field is erratic in his spelling of Dijon. Cyrus Hoy has pointed out (*Studies in Bibliography*, viii (1956), pp. 129–46) that Massinger's unaided plays are remarkably free from contractions such as *o' th'*, *i' th'*, *'s* for *his* (*in's*, *on's* etc.), *h'as* for *he has*, etc. And almost invariably Massinger uses *you*; Hoy finds *ye* only twice in Massinger's whole work. Field's contractions may be studied from his own plays. *i' th'* and *o' th'* are found several times, as well as *'s* for *his*; *you* is preferred to *ye*, but *ye* is found. In *The Fatal Dowry*, II. i, we have *ye* five times, and *'s* for *his*; in II. ii, *i' th'* is found six times, *ye* once; in III. i (344–end), *'s* occurs twice, *ye* once; in IV. i, *'s* twice, *i' th'* and *o' th'* four times. None of these contractions, or *ye*, is found in any scene allotted above to Massinger. (Cf. Hoy, *Studies in Bibliography*, xii (1959), 91–5).

The only question is where we are to divide Act III. Up to line 315 (the entry of Novall Junior and his parasites) we are clearly in Massinger's hands; by line 344 we are clearly in Field's. Though I am inclined to put the break at line 320 (after the departure of Beaumelle), I think certainty is impossible.

It may be convenient to present the presumed division of work in tabular form.

Massinger:	I. i, ii		III. i. 1–320?
Field:		II. i, ii	III. i. 320?–505
Massinger:		IV. ii, iii, iv V. i, ii.	
Field:	IV. i		

(b) *Date*

The latest possible date for *The Fatal Dowry* is early 1620. Letters of administration for Field's estate were granted to his sister on 2 August 1620 (Brinkley, pp. 43–4, 153); his death could hardly have been later than the spring of that year; it might have been in 1619. The earlier limit for the date is less easy to fix. The play mentioned in the letter from Massinger, Field, and Daborne to Henslowe about the year 1613 (see General Introduction, p. xvii) could not be *The Fatal Dowry*, which was written for the King's men, but the letter establishes a fairly early relationship between the

Introduction

two dramatists. Field's co-operation in a play written for the King's men would probably belong to the period when he was himself a member of the company. His two unaided plays (1609–11) had been written for the companies in which he was then a leading actor. But it is not known exactly when he joined the King's men. Brinkley suggests that Field broke with Henslowe in 1615, but did not join the King's men until 1617 (pp. 32–3; Peery concurs, pp. 20–1); T. W. Baldwin suggests that Field took the share in the company made vacant by Shakespeare's death in 1616 (*Organization and Personnel of the Shakespearean Company*, 1927, pp. 51, 204–7); but Field, who was certainly a housekeeper by 1619, need not have been a sharer in the company from the beginning. Field's name appears in the actors' lists for the King's men plays *The Mad Lover* (?1616) and *The Queen of Corinth* (1616–17) (see Bentley, i. 72 and iii. 375). It is not possible to be more definite than to say that 1615 is the earliest date for Field's joining the company. Field collaborated with Fletcher and Massinger in the lost play, *The Jeweller of Amsterdam* (probably 1617; see Bentley, iii. 351) and is conjectured to have worked on other plays with the two men, or with Fletcher alone (Brinkley, chap. 5). I see no reason why *The Fatal Dowry* should be regarded as his last play, as Brinkley suggests. The topical allusions in the play might suggest a date of 1617; the allusions to the stern measures against duelling and to the 'Infanta Queen of Europe' might have lost their freshness by 1620 (see notes to IV. i. 120, IV. i. 68); 1617 would also suit the dig at the benevolence shown to Papists (II. ii. 111–13). If at III. i. 321–3 there is a reference to Daborne's transfiguration, a date of 1617–18 would be suitable. Thomas May seems to recall a passage of *The Fatal Dowry* (see note to V. ii. 169–172) in *The Heir*, which may have been in performance before 1620. But not too much weight can be put on these allusions. While a date of 1617–19 might be a reasonable inference, it is impossible to be definite within the limits 1615–20.

(c) *Source*

An article published by Eugene M. Waith in 1953 proved beyond doubt that *The Fatal Dowry* is based on one of the *controversiae* of Seneca the Elder.[1] The *controversiae* were imaginary problems of

---

[1] *PMLA*, lxviii (1953), 286–303. Waith gives an account of the *controversiae* and their influence on the English drama in the article, and also in *The Pattern of Tragicomedy in Beaumont and Fletcher*, 1952 (Yale Studies in English, vol. 120).

law devised for the training of rhetoricians; Seneca brought together many such problems, with examples of suitable methods of pleading a case, in his *Oratorum et rhetorum sententiae, divisiones, colores*.[1] A typical *controversia* begins by stating the relevant—if necessary fictitious—statutes, and by outlining the circumstances and the charge. The first *controversia* of Seneca's ninth book is based on the death of Miltiades, in the more romantic and less accurate version favoured by Valerius Maximus.

Cimon ungrateful to Callias.

Whoever shall take in the act an adulterer and an adultress shall not be culpable if he kills them both.
Ingratitude is actionable.

Miltiades, convicted of embezzlement, died in prison. Cimon his son gave himself as a substitute for his father's body, so that it might receive burial. Callias, a rich man of humble origin, redeemed him from the state and paid the debt; he married his daughter to him, who taking her in adultery, killed her, against the entreaties of her father. He is charged with ingratitude.[2]

This *controversia* is almost the plot of the play. Massinger does not accept the statutes, but, if ingratitude is not a crime, the play debates whether it is a sin. The low birth of Callias is barely hinted at, and with reason: Seneca's rhetors tend to smear Callias for using generosity as a means of advancing himself; such twisted motives would mar the play's clear distinction between the claims of gratitude and of honour on Charalois. Massinger found little useful in the collection of *sententiae*, *divisiones* and *colores* which follows the statement of the case, except in the arguments attributed to Porcius Latro, which insist, as in the first Act, on the real innocence of the father, the defender of his country, and which make a distinction between captivity and freedom which (as Waith noted) Massinger copied at V. ii. 202–5. There is also a slight borrowing from the arguments of Arellius Fuscus at I. i. 37–8.

[1] There is a convenient edition, with introduction, notes and a French parallel text by H. Bornecque, *Sénèque le Rhéteur. Controverses et Suasoires*; 2nd edn., Paris, 1932.
[2] Cimon ingratus Calliae. / Adulterum cum adultera qui deprenderit, dum utrumque corpus interficiat, sine fraude sit. / Ingrati sit actio. / Miltiades, peculatus damnatus, in carcere alligatus decessit; Cimon, filius eius, ut eum sepeliret, vicarium se pro corpore patris dedit. Callias dives sordide natus redemit eum a re publica et pecuniam solvit, filiam ei suam collocavit, quam ille deprensam in adulterio deprecante patre occidit. Ingrati reus est.

Introduction 5

The Athenian story is presented in the setting of fifteenth-century France, in a fictitious aftermath of the unsuccessful struggles of Charles the Bold of Burgundy against Louis XI of France. Massinger could have found all he wanted in Commines' *Historie*; Danett's translation (originally published in 1596) had been reissued in 1614. The 'three memorable overthrows' of Granson, Morat, and Nancy (I. ii. 169–70) are described in Book V of Commines. The name Charolois, one of the earldoms of Charles the Bold, is given in the first chapter of the work. The names of the other characters seem to have been drawn at random: the Earl of Romont was a Burgundian nobleman; Du Croy was suggested by 'Monseur de Beures of the house of Croy' (Book V, chap. 5; Tudor Translations, i. 308); there is a William of Rochefort who has no connection with Dijon (Book I, chap. 2; Tudor Translations, i. 37); there are several Beaumonts.

The search for Spanish originals of the play, particularly in Cervantes, has not been rewarding. But Lockert seems to be right in seeing a relationship between the judgement of Beaumelle by Rochfort, and a similar judgement in Daborne's *Poor Man's Comfort* (see note to IV. iv. 89).

(d) *Text*

The Fatal Dowry was entered in the Stationers' Register on 30 March 1632, to Francis Constable:

m^r. ffran: Constable   Entred for his Copy vnder the hands of S^r. Henry Herbert & m^r Smethwicke warden a Tragedy called the ffatall Dowry.

vj^d.

(Register D 241; Greg, *Bibliography*, i. 41; Arber, iv. 275)

The sole early edition of the play was published by Constable in the same year, printed by John Norton; it is henceforward referred to as *32*; the title-page is reproduced on p. 13. It is in quarto, [A]^2, B–L^4 (42 leaves). See Greg, *Bibliography*, no. 464 (ii. 612). The contents are as follows: [A]1^r, *title*; [A]1^v, *list of the names of characters*; [A]2^r, 'First Song.' *and* 'Second Song.'; [A]2^v, 'Cittizens Song of the Courtier.' *and* 'Courtiers Song of the Citizen.'; B1^r, 'The Fatall Dowry: A Tragedy.', *text begins*; L4^v, *text ends*, '*FINIS*.'. The text is in roman, 20 lines = 80 mm.; there are 37 lines to the page. Press corrections have been found in ten of the 21 formes; three formes were twice corrected. The variants which result from these press-corrections are for the most part trivial, significant differences occurring in five readings only. The evidence of headlines shows presswork which was a little erratic. Two skeletons were used, one for each inner forme and one for each outer forme, to the completion of Sheet D. (The inner forme of D was imposed with the skeleton reversed: the running title for C3^v becoming that for D1^v, etc.) After sheet D, the skeleton for the outer forme becomes the skeleton for the inner forme, and vice versa. The chase of the inner forme skeleton seems to have been unlocked and the head-lines reset and slightly rearranged in the imposing of almost every inner forme from Sheet F to the end; this resetting is apparently not connected with the press-corrections, and may be due to bad workmanship. The outer forme skeleton continues regularly until sheet I; the head-lines have been reset for K and again for L.

32 is not at all a well-printed text: the type is worn and the printing uneven; it is sometimes impossible, even after consulting several copies, to be certain whether a punctuation mark is a comma, a colon, or a semi-colon. The pages are cramped and untidy. Corruptions abound, and an unusually large number of emendations have been accepted in the present edition. Because of their great number, corrections of misdivided verse are given as a separate Appendix, instead of in the textual footnotes. It seems that two compositors set the play, composing *seriatim* rather than by cast-off formes, one compositor, X, having a much bigger share than the other, Y.[1] X's share is only slightly more than Y's to the end of sheet G; thereafter Y sets only two pages. X is a more careful and neat workman than Y; Y is responsible not only for a proportionately greater number of turned and omitted letters, but also for much of the corruption of the text; he will print, for example, *bushes, cal'd my cheekes* for [?] *blushes, scald my cheekes* (II. ii. 293) or *yet these eares* for *let these teares* (II. ii. 329); Y is also much less responsible in his punctuation, though X is no paragon.

The copy for *32* would seem to be the foul papers of the two dramatists, or conceivably a transcript of them, which had received

[1] The compositors are distinguished by purely typographical habits. X's page is much neater and tighter than Y's. Y puts an extraordinary number of quads before and after a punctuation mark, and sometimes between words; he also tends to leave much more space between the speaker's name and the first word of the speech than does X. As examples, E3^r [Y] may be compared with E4^v [X]. Spelling variants prove of little value in differentiating compositors, but there are significant differences in the spelling of *do, go,* and *here*.

Introduction

some annotation by the book-keeper in preparation for making the prompt-copy. In Massinger's share of the work, his idiosyncratic spellings are not preserved (such forms as *lowd, sawcily, sowre, blouded* are too few to be significant). But the stage-directions contain more pointers to the author than to the book-keeper. Characters are several times omitted in entries; groups are not defined in number (e.g., I. i. 102; I. ii; IV. iv. 91; V. i); Massinger is (for him) unusually reticent about necessary stage-business; at various points, there are no indications for beating, kneeling, blindfolding, stabbing, dying. In Field's parts of the play, the directions are much fuller and more detailed, and are very similar to those found in his own plays. The stage direction at II. i. 47 is a very good example; it is much like the manner of directions in *A Woman is a Weathercock*, II. i. 115 and 221. It is elaborate in its detail of what the author wishes to see on the stage: e.g., '*Scutchions, and very good order*'. It is distinctly 'authorial' and not 'prompt' in tone. The number of mourners is not stated, and two speaking parts, Gaoler and Priest, are omitted. Field's directions are full of details of the appearance and actions of the characters and while it might be argued that Novall's entry, 'as newly dressed', or the Creditors', 'loaden with money', could be book-keeper's entries, the fact that this type of entry occurs alone in Field's share of the play seems decisive in labelling them 'authorial'. Also significant of an author are two references to Beaumelle as 'Daug[hter]'; Bellapert has to trim '*her Lady*'; Novall addresses an aside 'to his M^{rs}'.

It is clear that the manuscript had been through the book-keeper's hands. Two lines before the elaborate direction for the funeral at II. i. 47 there is a marginal entry, '*Recorders | Musique*', 'doubling' the '*solemne Musique*' of the main direction. Another doubling is the marginal '*Hoboyes*' before the direction at the end of the second act, '*Here a passage ouer the Stage, while the Act is playing for the Marriage of Charalois with Beaumelle, &c.*' Again a general direction for music has been made precise, but the stage reviser has not particularized the procession itself.[1]

At IV. ii. 50, there is the following direction:

> *Song aboue.*
> *Musique and a Song, Beaumelle within—ha, ha, ha.*

[1] A similar anticipatory entry, probably from the same cause, is found in *A Woman is a Weathercock*, II. i. 220; the general direction, '*Loud Musicke*', is preceded by a marginal '*Cornets*'.

This again seems to be a doubling, the first part being a clarification for acting purposes.

The act and scene headings also seem to indicate preparation of the authors' foul papers for prompt-copy, but there are some problems not easy to solve. In *Believe As You List*, the stage-reviser struck out Massinger's careful indications of new scenes (e.g., 'Actus tertij, scæna secunda') and noted only the beginning of each act. In *The Fatal Dowry*, each new act is headed with act and scene number (*'Actus quartus. Scæna prima.'*); in the first two acts, no later scene is marked (there are two scenes in each act). Act III is one scene only. In Act IV, the second, third and fourth scenes are marked, without repetition of the Act number (e.g., '*Scæna 2.*'). In Act V, the second scene is indicated in the same way, but a third scene, which does not exist, is also marked (see text note to V. ii. 121). It seems probable that the book-keeper has struck out the scene divisions in the first and second acts (though it is true we do not know that Field would have inserted them in the second act in the first place); 'Actus primus. Scæna prima.' is a stock printer's legend and is not material (cf. Chambers, *Elizabethan Stage*, iii. 199). The scene markings in the last two acts are not in Massinger's known style; apart from the evidence of *Believe As You List*, most of his printed plays preserve the full act and scene reference at each new scene. It may be that someone has restored what was imperfectly deleted by the stage-reviser, and has inserted a gratuitous '*Scæna 3.*' in Act V. It would be unusual for a printer to mark a new scene which was not marked in his copy, and it may be that the act and scene headings in *The Fatal Dowry* point towards a transcript of annotated foul papers rather than the foul papers themselves. Such a theory would be supported by the comparative absence of Massinger's spellings.

The words of the play's four songs are not given at the appropriate points in the text but are gathered together in the preliminaries of *32*, as described in the listing of contents at the head of this section. It is unlikely that the songs were written specially for this play;[1] one of them is an excerpt from a song known in a fuller version elsewhere (see note to IV. ii. 51–8); the first song (II. i. 133–8) is ludicrously inappropriate for a funeral; though the last two songs have adultery as their theme they are not particularly suited to the occasion. The fact that the second song (II. ii. 134–45) is a duet is

[1] Cf. W. R. Bowden, *The English Dramatic Lyric*, 1951, pp. 108–9.

Introduction

not indicated in the text, which simply asks Aymer to sing. Music for the final song was found in Bodleian MS. Don. c. 57, fols. 96ᵛ, 97ʳ, and printed by J. P. Cutts, *La Musique de scène de la troupe de Shakespeare*, Paris, 1959, pp. 78–80.[1] Cutts believes that the music may be by Robert Johnson.

There are copies of 32 in the following libraries and institutions: All Souls College, Oxford; Bibliotheque Nationale; Bodleian Library (3 copies); Boston Public Library; British Museum (4 copies); Cambridge University Library; Chapin Library, Williamstown; Clark Library, University of California; Library of Congress; Folger Shakespeare Library (3 copies); University of Glasgow, Hunterian collection; Guildhall Library, London; Harvard College Library; Huntington Library; University of Illinois; University of Leeds, Brotherton Library; University of Liverpool; University of London; Merton College, Oxford; Pierpont Morgan Library; Newberry Library; University of Pennsylvania; Pforzheimer Collection; Princeton University; Royal Library, Stockholm; University of Texas; Alexander Turnbull Library, Wellington, New Zealand; Victoria and Albert Museum (2 copies); Worcester College, Oxford; Yale University.

The text of the present edition has been prepared from the Bodleian Library copy, Malone 236 (9).

The Fatal Dowry was one of the collection of eight plays, carrying corrections in Massinger's own hand, which were bound up together about the year 1633 (see General Introduction, p. xxxii); unfortunately, Massinger did not carry his corrections through to this play.

Besides appearing in the standard collected editions, *The Fatal Dowry* was published in *The British Drama*, 1804 (i. 77–104), *The Modern British Drama*, 1811 (i. 230–57), Dolby's *British Theatre* vol. x, 1825 (see below under Adaptations). There are two undated nineteenth-century editions published by Cumberland and by Lacy. There is an expurgated text in *The Mirror of Taste and Dramatic Censor*, Philadelphia and New York, 1810, vol. ii. The version in Dicks' Standard Plays, no. 365, c. 1884, is an inaccurate reprint of Dolby. The play was included by Arthur Symons in the second volume of his Mermaid selection, 1889. There have been two single-volume annotated editions in the present century, by C. L. Lockert (Lancaster, Pennsylvania), 1918, and by T. A. Dunn in the Fountain-

[1] See also J. P. Cutts, 'A Bodleian Song-Book', *Music and Letters*, xxxiv (1953), 192–212.

well Drama Texts series, 1969 (referred to in the textual notes as *Dunn*). The reference to *Adams* in the text notes is to a review by J. Q. Adams of Lockert's edition in *JEGP*, xviii (1919) 641–7; the reference to *F. P. Wilson* is to a letter to the editor.

There was a German translation of *The Fatal Dowry* by Baudissin in 1836 (*Die unselige Mitgift*) and a French translation by Lafond in 1864 (*La Dot fatale*); see the list of Collected Editions (p. lxviii).

(e) *Stage history and Adaptations*

When it was published, at least twelve years after its composition, *The Fatal Dowry* was described as a play that 'hath beene often Acted at the Priuate House in Blackefryers, by his Maiesties Seruants.' That it had remained in the repertory is confirmed by its being in the list of 'playes for the Kinge' given at court during the 1630–1 season. It was played at the Cockpit-in-Court at Whitehall on 3 February, 1631 (Bentley, i. 27–8). At the Restoration, the play was one of those allotted exclusively to Killigrew and the King's Company in the division of plays between him and Davenant on 12 January 1669.[1] McManaway (*Studies*, pp. 17–18) believes that the listed plays had all been revived on the Restoration stage, but there is no record of a performance of *The Fatal Dowry*.

In 1703 Nicholas Rowe rewrote the play as *The Fair Penitent*, not divulging his source. It was acted in Lincoln's Inn Fields in the same year, and it was extremely popular throughout the eighteenth century. Rowe completely reshaped the play, reducing the early legal activity, focusing much more attention on the marriage, and changing the catastrophe out of recognition (as the title suggests). The debate on the comparative quality of the two plays, once it was realized that Rowe had used Massinger's work, was warm (see General Introduction, p. xlviii, and below). A second eighteenth-century adaptation was by Aaron Hill, which he called *The Insolvent, or Filial Piety*. A series of letters between Hill and Colley Cibber gives a full and curious account of the occasion of the rewriting (printed in Hill's *Works*, 1753, ii. 312–20, and summarized in the Advertisement to *The Insolvent*, 1758). It is claimed that 'an old manuscript play' called *The Guiltless Adultress, or, The Judge in his Own Cause* was given by Wilks to Cibber after the latter had moved to the Theatre Royal in Drury Lane. This manuscript was 'suppos'd to be' a Davenant play, but examination showed at once that it was

---

[1] Nicoll, *History of English Drama*, i. 353–4.

Introduction

'founded on' *The Fatal Dowry* ('this last piece has often been enquired after in vain'). Cibber gave the manuscript to Hill in 1746 for him to correct, and Hill decided to rewrite it. It was not acted, however, until 1758, at the Haymarket. The most startling change is that Beaumelle is virtuous and wrongly suspected; this change must have been made in the 'old manuscript play', judging from its title.

The Fatal Dowry was revived at Drury Lane on 5 January 1825, with W. C. Macready as Romont and J. W. Wallack as Charalois (Genest, ix. 287-8). But this was again an adaptation though it is much more faithful to Massinger than the versions of Rowe or Hill. The adaptor is variously given as R. L. Sheil and J. S. Knowles. The Prologue, by Mr. R. B. Bourne, spoken by Macready, regretted that Massinger did not live in 'our chaster days' and thus obviate the need to prune the text of its impurities, underneath which a jewel lay hidden.

> Then let not Rowe's Fair Penitent—a tale
> Drawn feebly from our great original,
> With laboured phrase and specious eloquence,
> Usurp the place of Nature, Truth and Sense;
> If but the copy can applause command,
> Approve the earlier and the master hand:
> True taste at once and Massinger restore,
> 'And give the Stage one classic drama more.'

After three nights, the play had to be taken off because of Macready's serious illness. It was well received by the press: *The London Magazine* (N.S. i (February 1825), 287-8) said it was 'got up with great care' and 'met with deserved success'. 'Massinger's tragedy is full of poetry, downright vigorous dramatic dialogue, and full of character and stern passion'; but it thought *The Fair Penitent* 'a better acting piece'. Macready tried the play again on his recovery in April but it was not successful.[1] He played it in New York, however, in 1827, at the Park Theatre, and probably also at the Chestnut-street Theatre, Philadelphia.[2]

Six weeks after the London revival, the play was to be seen in Bath, on 18 and 21 February 1825, at the Theatre Royal, with

---

[1] *Macready's Reminiscences*, ed. F. Pollock, 1875, i. 301, 303; J. C. Trewin, *Mr. Macready*, 1955; and *DNB*, under R. L. Sheil.
[2] A. S. Downer, *The Eminent Tragedian*, 1966, p. 110.

Hamblin as Romont and Warde as Charalois.[1] It was also performed in Manchester in 1829 (20 June) with Waldron as Romont and Haines as Charalois.[2]

The adaptation was printed in 1825, '*The Fatal Dowry*, by Philip Massinger; altered and adapted for representation, as performed at the Theatre Royal, Drury Lane, January 5, 1825'. The Advertisement attacked the 'plagiarism under the title of The Fair Penitent' for unjustly defrauding Massinger's play of its rightful place in the theatrical list. It argued that acting length was one reason for altering the play. The 'unhappy method of inducing the catastrophe' was too gross and had to be changed; in the adaptation Beaumelle is killed off stage, and Charalois takes his own life. Thomas Love Beddoes disliked this version very much. He wrote in a letter:

The fatal dowry has been cobbled, I see, by some purblind ultracrepidarian. McReady's friend, Walker, very likely—but nevertheless I maintain 'tis a good play—& might have been rendered very effective by docking it of the whole fifth Act, which is an excrescence—re-creating Novall —& making Beaumelle a good deal more ghost-gaping & moonlightish— The cur-tailor has taken out the most purple piece in the whole weft— the end of the 4th act . . .[3]

In 1845, Samuel Phelps revived the 1825 adaptation at Sadler's Wells, and took the part of Romont himself. This seems to have been the last performance in England. Richard Beer-Hofmann rewrote the play as *Der Graf von Charolais, ein Trauerspiel*, and it was performed at the Neue Theater, Berlin, on 24 December 1904. This adaptation is discussed at length by Lockert in his edition, and by F. H. Schwarz in his Berne dissertation of 1907, *Nicholas Rowe's 'Fair Penitent'*.

[1] Playbill in Bath Public Library.
[2] Playbill in the Shakespeare Birthplace Library, Stratford-upon-Avon.
[3] *Works*, ed. H. W. Donner, 1935, p. 595.

THE
FATALL
DOVVRY:
A TRAGEDY.

As it hath beene often Acted at the Private House in Blackefryers, by his Maiesties Seruants.

Written by P. M. *and* N. F.

LONDON,
Printed by IOHN NORTON, for FRANCIS
CONSTABLE, and are to be sold at his
shop at the Crane, in Pauls Church-
yard. 1632.

[THE PERSONS PRESENTED]

Charalois, [*a young gentleman, son of the late Marshal.*]
Romont, [*his friend.*]
Charmi, [*an advocate.*]
Nouall Senior, [*premier president of the court of Dijon.*]
Liladam, [*a parasite.*] 5
Du Croy, [*a president of the court.*]
Rochfort, [*retiring premier president.*]
Baumont, [*secretary to* Rochfort.]
Pontalier, [*a soldier.*]
Malotin, [*his friend.*] 10
Beaumelle, [*daughter of* Rochfort.]
Florimel, } [*servants to* Beaumelle.]
Bellapert,
Aymer, [*a singer and keeper of a music-house.*]
Nouall Iunior, [*son of* Old Novall, *in love with* Beaumelle.] 15
Aduocates.
Creditors 3.
Officers.
Priest.
Taylor. 20
Barber.
Perfumer.
[Page.]
[Gaoler.]

The Fatall Dowry

A Tragedy

Actus primus. Scæna prima.

Enter CHARALOIS *with a paper*, ROMONT, CHARMI.

Charmi. SIR, I may moue the Court to serue your will,
But therein shall both wrong you and my selfe.
　Romont. Why thinke you so sir?
　Charmi. 　　　　　　　'Cause I am familiar
With what will be their answere: they will say,
Tis against law, and argue me of Ignorance　　　　　5
For offering them the motion.
　Romont. 　　　　You know not, Sir,
How in this cause they may dispence with Law,
And therefore frame not you their answere for them,
But doe your parts.
　Charmi. 　　　I loue the cause so well,
As I could runne the hazard of a checke for't.　　　　10
　Romont. From whom?
　Charmi. 　　　　　Some of the bench, that watch to giue it,
More then to doe the office that they sit for:
But giue me (sir) my fee.
　Romont. 　　　　Now you are Noble.
　Charmi. I shall deserue this better yet, in giuing
My Lord some counsell, (if he please to heare it)　　　15
Then I shall doe with pleading.
　Romont. 　　　　　　What may it be, sir?
　Charmi. That it would please his Lordship, as the Presidents,
And Counsaylors of Court come by, to stand
Heere, and but shew him selfe, and to some one
Or two, make his request: there is a minute　　　　20

I. i. 19. him selfe] *Gifford*; your selfe *32, McIlwraith*

When a mans presence speakes in his owne cause,
More then the tongues of twenty aduocates.
  Romont. I haue vrg'd that.

  Enter ROCHFORT, DU CROY.

  Charmi. Their Lordships here are comming,
I must goe get me a place, you'l finde me in Court,
And at your seruice.   *Exit* CHARMI.
  Romont.   Now put on your Spirits.   25
  Du Croy. The ease that you prepare your selfe, my Lord,
In giuing vp the place you hold in Court,
Will proue (I feare) a trouble in the State,
And that no slight one.
  Rochfort.   Pray you sir, no more.
  Romont. Now sir, lose not this offerd meanes: their lookes   30
Fixt on you, with a pittying earnestnesse,
Inuite you to demand their furtherance
To your good purpose.—This such a dulnesse,
So foolish and vntimely as——
  Du Croy.   You know him.
  Rochfort. I doe, and much lament the sudden fall   35
Of his braue house. It is young *Charaloyes*,
Sonne to the Marshall, from whom he inherits
His fame and vertues onely.
  Romont.   Ha, they name you.
  Du Croy. His father died in prison two daies since.
  Rochfort. Yes, to the shame of this vngratefull State,   40
That such a Master in the art of warre,
So noble, and so highly meriting
From this forgetfull Country, should, for want
Of meanes to satisfie his creditors,
The summes he tooke vp for the generall good,   45
Meet with an end so infamous.
  Romont.   Dare you euer
Hope for like oportunity?
  Du Croy.   My good Lord!
  Rochfort. My wish bring comfort to you.
  Du Croy.   The time calls vs.
  Rochfort. Good morrow Colonell. *Exeunt* ROCHFORT, DU CROY.

33. This] *32*; This is *Symons*

   Romont.   This obstinate spleene,
You thinke becomes your sorrow, and sorts wel
With your blacke suits: but grant me wit, or iudgement,
And by the freedome of an honest man,
And a true friend to boote, I sweare 'tis shamefull.
And therefore flatter not your selfe with hope,
Your sable habit, with the hat and cloake,
No though the ribons helpe, haue power to worke 'em
To what you would: for those that had no eyes
To see the great acts of your father, will not,
From any fashion sorrow can put on,
Bee taught to know their duties.
   Charalois.   If they will not,
They are too old to learne, and I too young
To giue them counsell, since if they partake
The vnderstanding, and the hearts of men,
They will preuent my words and teares: if not,
What can perswasion, though made eloquent
With griefe, worke vpon such as haue chang'd natures
With the most sauage beast? Blest, blest be euer
The memory of that happy age, when iustice
Had no gards to keepe off wrongd innocence
From flying to her succours, and in that,
Assurance of redresse: where now (*Romont*)
The damnd, with more ease may ascend from Hell,
Then we ariue at her. One Cerberus there
Forbids the passage, in our Courts a thousand,
As lowd, and fertyle headed, and the Client
That wants the sops, to fill their rauenous throats,
Must hope for no accesse: why should I then
Attempt impossibilities: you friend, being
Too well acquainted with my dearth of meanes,
To make my entrance that way?
   Romont.   Would I were not.
But Sir, you haue a cause, a cause so iust,
Of such necessitie, not to be deferd,
As would compell a mayde, whose foot was neuer
Set ore her fathers threshold, nor within
The house where she was borne, euer spake word,
Which was not vshered with pure virgin blushes,

To drowne the tempest of a pleaders tongue,
And force corruption to giue backe the hire
It tooke against her: let examples moue you.
You see great men in birth, esteeme and fortune, 90
Rather then lose a scruple of their right,
Fawne basely vpon such, whose gownes put off,
They would disdaine for Seruants.
   Charalois.   And to these
Can I become a suytor?
   Romont.   Without losse,
Would you consider, that to gaine their fauors, 95
Our chastest dames put off their modesties,
Soldiers forget their honors, vsurers
Make sacrifice of Gold, poets of wit,
And men religious, part with fame, and goodnesse!
Be therfore wonne to vse the meanes, that may 100
Aduance your pious ends.
   Charalois.   You shall orecome.
   Romont. And you receiue the glory, pray you now practise.

Enter OLD NOVALL, [ADVOCATES,] LILADAM, *and* 3 CREDITORS.

'Tis well.
   Charalois. Not looke on me!
   Romont.   You must haue patience—
Offer't againe.
   Charalois.   And be againe contemn'd?
   Nouall Senior. I know whats to be done.
   1 *Creditor.*   And that your Lordship
Will please to do your knowledge, we offer, first 106
Our thankefull hearts heere, as a bounteous earnest
To what we will adde—
   Nouall Senior.   One word more of this,
I am your enemie. Am I a man
Your bribes can worke on? ha?
   Liladam.   Friends, you mistake 110
The way to winne my Lord, he must not heare this,
But I, as one in fauour, in his sight,
May harken to you for my profit. Sir,

---

102 SD. ADVOCATES] *Gifford; not in 32*   108. adde—] *Coxeter;* ~∧ *32;* ~.
Gifford

I pray heare em.
   Nouall Senior. Tis well.
   Liladam. Obserue him now.
   Nouall Senior. Your cause being good, and your proceedings so,
Without corruption, I am your friend;   116
Speake your desires.
   2 Creditor.   Oh, they are charitable,
The Marshall stood ingag'd vnto vs three,
Two hundred thousand crownes, which by his death
We are defeated of. For which great losse   120
We ayme at nothing but his rotten flesh,
Nor is that cruelty.
   1 Creditor.   I haue a sonne,
That talkes of nothing but of Gunnes and Armors,
And sweares hee'll be a soldier, tis an humor
I would diuert him from, and I am told   125
That if I minister to him in his drinke
Powder, made of this banquerout Marshalls bones,
Prouided that the carcase rot aboue ground,
'T will cure his foolish frensie.
   Nouall Senior.   You shew in it
A fathers care. I haue a sonne my selfe,   130
A fashionable Gentleman and a peacefull:
And but I am assur'd he's not so giuen,
He should take of it too. Sir, what are you?
   Charalois. A Gentleman.
   Nouall Senior.   So are many that rake dunghills.
If you haue any suit, moue it in Court.   135
I take no papers in corners.
   Romont.   Yes as
The matter may be carried, and hereby
To mannage the conuayance—Follow him.
   Liladam. You are rude. I say, he shall not passe.
           Exit NOVALL, CHARALOIS *and* ADVOCATES.
   Romont.   You say so.
On what assurance?   140
For the well cutting of his Lordships cornes,
Picking his toes, or any office else
Neerer to basenesse!
   Liladam.   Looke vpon mee better,

Are these the ensignes of so coorse a fellow? 144
Be well aduis'd.
 Romont. Out, rogue, do not I know, *Kicks him.*
These glorious weedes spring from the sordid dunghill
Of thy officious basenesse? wert thou worthy
Of any thing from me, but my contempt,
I would do more then this, more, you Court-spider.
 Liladam. But that this man is lawlesse, he should find 150
That I am valiant.
 1 *Creditor.* If your eares are fast,
Tis nothing. Whats a blow or two? as much—
 2 *Creditor.* These chastisements, as vsefull are as frequent
To such as would grow rich.
 Romont.   Are they so Rascals?
I wil be-friend you then.   [*Beats them.*]
 1 *Creditor.*   Beare witnesse, Sirs. 155
 Liladam. Trueth, I haue borne my part already, friends.
In the Court you shall haue more.   *Exit.*
 Romont.   I know you for
The worst of spirits, that striue to rob the tombes
Of what is their inheritance from the dead.
For vsurers, bred by a riotous peace: 160
That hold the Charter of your wealth and freedome,
By being Knaues and Cuckolds: that ne're praye,
But when you feare the rich heires will grow wise,
To keepe their Lands out of your parchment toyles;
And then, the Diuell your father's cald vpon, 165
To inuent some wayes of Luxury ne're thought on.
Be gone, and quickly, or Ile leaue no roome
Vpon your forhead for your hornes to sprowt on,
Without a murmure, or I will vndoe you;
For I will beate you honest.
 1 *Creditor.*   Thrift forbid. 170
We will beare this, rather then hazard that. *Exeunt* CREDITORS.

     Enter CHARALOIS.

 Romont. I am some-what eas'd in this yet.
 Charalois.   (Onely friend)

  155 SD. *Beats them.*] *Coxeter* (Kicks them); *not in 32*   162. Cuckolds:]
Gifford (;) ; ~ ∧ *32* praye] *Gifford*; prayd *32* 171 SD. CREDITORS]
Gifford; Creditor *32*

To what vaine purpose do I make my sorrow
Wayte on the triumph of their cruelty?
Or teach their pride from my humilitie, 175
To thinke it has orecome? They are determin'd
What they will do: and it may well become me,
To robbe them of the glory they expect
From my submisse intreaties.
  Romont.   Thinke not so, Sir,
The difficulties that you incounter with, 180
Will crowne the vndertaking——Heauen! you weepe:
And I could do so too, but that I know,
Theres more expected from the sonne and friend
Of him, whose fatall losse now shakes our natures,
Then sighs, or teares, (in which a village nurse 185
Or cunning strumpet, when her knaue is hangd,
May ouercome vs.) We are men (young Lord)
Let vs not do like women. To the Court,
And there speake like your birth: wake sleeping iustice.
Or dare the Axe. This is a way will sort 190
With what you are. I call you not to that
I will shrinke from my selfe, I will deserue
Your thankes, or suffer with you—O how brauely
That sudden fire of anger shewes in you!
Giue fuell to it, since you are on a shelfe 195
Of extreme danger suffer like your selfe.   *Exeunt.*

Enter ROCHFORT, NOVALL SENIOR, CHARMI, DU CROY, ADVO-
CATES, BAUMONT, *and Officers, and* 3. PRESIDENTS [, CREDITORS].

  Du Croy. Your Lordship's seated. May this meeting proue
Prosperous to vs, and to the generall good
Of *Burgundy.*
  Nouall Senior. Speake to the poynt.
  Du Croy.   Which is,
With honour to dispose the place and power
Of primier President, which this reuerent man 5
Graue *Rochfort*, (whom for honours sake I name)
Is purpos'd to resigne, a place, my Lords,
In which he hath with such integrity,

I. ii. SD. CREDITORS] *Gifford; not in 32*   1. Your Lordship's seated. May] *32*;
Your lordships seated, may *Gifford*

Perform'd the first and best parts of a Iudge,
That as his life transcends all faire examples
Of such as were before him in *Dijon*,
So it remaines to those that shall succeed him,
A President they may imitate, but not equall.
  Rochfort. I may not sit to heare this.
  Du Croy.   Let the loue
And thankfulnes we are bound to pay to goodnesse,
In this o'recome your modestie.
  Rochfort.   My thankes
For this great fauour shall preuent your trouble.
The honourable trust that was impos'd
Vpon my weakenesse, since you witnesse for me
It was not ill discharg'd, I will not mention,
Nor now, if age had not depriu'd me of
The little strength I had to gouerne well
The Prouince that I vndertooke, forsake it.
  Nouall Senior. That we could lend you of our yeeres.
  Du Croy.   Or strength.
  Nouall Senior. Or as you are, perswade you to continue
The noble exercise of your knowing iudgement.
  Rochfort. That may not be, nor can your Lordships goodnes,
Since your imployments haue confer'd vpon me
Sufficient wealth, deny the vse of it,
And though old age, when one foot's in the graue,
In many, when all humors else are spent,
Feeds no affection in them, but desire
To adde height to the mountaine of their riches:
In me it is not so, I rest content
With the honours, and estate I now possesse,
And that I may haue liberty to vse,
What Heauen still blessing my poore industry,
Hath made me Master of: I pray the Court
To ease me of my burthen, that I may
Employ the small remainder of my life,
In liuing well, and learning how to dye so.

                Enter ROMONT, *and* CHARALOIS.

  Romont. See sir, our Aduocate.
  Du Croy.   The Court intreats,

Your Lordship will be pleasd to name the man,
Which you would haue your successor, and in me,
All promise to confirme it.
   Rochfort.   I embrace it,   45
As an assurance of their fauour to me,
And name my Lord *Nouall.*
   Du Croy.   The Court allows it.
   Rochfort. But there are suters waite heere, and their causes
May be of more necessity to be heard,
I therefore wish that mine may be defer'd,   50
And theirs haue hearing.
   Du Croy.   If your Lordship please
To take the place, we will proceed.
   Charmi.   The cause
We come to offer to your Lordships censure,
Is in it selfe so noble, that it needs not
Or Rhetorique in me that plead, or fauour   55
From your graue Lordships, to determine of it:
Since to the prayse of your impartiall iustice
(Which guilty, nay condemn'd men, dare not scandall)
It will erect a trophy of your mercy
Which married to that Iustice—
   Nouall Senior.   Speake to the cause.   60
   Charmi. I will, my Lord: to say, the late dead Marshall
The father of this young Lord heere, my Clyent,
Hath done his Country great and faithfull seruice,
Might taske me of impertinence, to repeate
What your graue Lordships cannot but remember.   65
He in his life, became indebted to
These thriftie men, I will not wrong their credits,
By giuing them the attributes they now merit,
And fayling by the fortune of the warres,
Of meanes to free himselfe, from his ingagements,   70
He was arrested, and for want of bayle
Imprisond at their suite, and not long after
With losse of liberty ended his life.

---

50. I] *Gifford*; And *32*   56. it:] *Mason* (;) ; ~. *32*   60. Which] *Coxeter*;
With *32*   Iustice—] *Mason*; ~. *32*   64. impertinence, to repeate] *Coxeter*;
impertinence to repeate, *32*   65. remember.] *Gifford*; ~, *32*   66. became]
Mason; become *32*

And though it be a *Maxime* in our Lawes,
All suites dye with the person, these mens malice 75
In death find matter for their hate to worke on,
Denying him the decent Rytes of buriall,
Which the sworne enemies of the Christian faith
Grant freely to their slaues: may it therefore please
Your Lordships, so to fashion your decree, 80
That what their crueltie doth forbid, your pittie
May giue allowance to.
   Nouall Senior.   How long haue you Sir
Practis'd in Court?
   Charmi.   Some twenty yeeres, my Lord.
   Nouall Senior. By your grosse ignorance it should appeare,
Not twentie dayes.
   Charmi.   I hope I haue giuen no cause 85
In this, my Lord—
   Nouall Senior.   How dare you moue the Court,
To the dispensing with an Act confirmd
By Parlament, to the terror of all banquerouts?
Go home, and with more care peruse the Statutes:
Or the next motion sauoring of this boldnesse, 90
May force you to leape (against your will)
Ouer the place you plead at.
   Charmi.   I foresaw this.
   Romont. Why does your Lordship thinke, the mouing of
A cause more honest then this Court had euer
The honor to determine, can deserue 95
A checke like this?
   Nouall Senior.   Strange boldnes!
   Romont.   Tis fit freedome:
Or do you conclude, an aduocate cannot hold
His credit with the Iudge, vnlesse he study
His face more then the cause for which he pleades?
   Charmi. Forbeare.
   Romont.   Or cannot you, that haue the power 100
To qualifie the rigour of the Lawes
When you are pleased, take a little from
The strictnesse of your sowre decrees, enacted
In fauor of the greedy creditors
Against the orethrowne debter?

Nouall Senior.   Sirra, you that prate
Thus sawcily, what are you?
  Romont.   Why Ile tell you,
Thou purple-colour'd man, I am one to whom
Thou owest the meanes thou hast of sitting there,
A corrupt Elder.
  Charmi.   Forbeare.
  Romont. The nose thou wear'st, is my gift, and those eyes,
That meete no obiect so base as their Master,
Had bin, long since, torne from that guiltie head,
And thou thy selfe slaue to some needy Swisse,
Had I not worne a sword, and vs'd it better
Then in thy prayers thou ere didst thy tongue.
  Nouall Senior. Shall such an Insolence passe vnpunisht?
  Charmi.   Heare mee.
  Romont. Yet I, that in my seruice done my Country,
Disdaine to bee put in the scale with thee,
Confesse my self vnworthy to bee valued
With the least part, nay haire of the dead Marshall,
Of whose so many glorious vndertakings,
Make choice of any one, and that the meanest
Performd against the subtill Fox of France,
The politique *Lewis,* or the more desperate Swisse,
And 'twyll outwaygh all the good purposes,
Though put in act, that euer Gowneman practizd.
  Nouall Senior. Away with him to prison.
  Romont.   If that curses,
Vrg'd iustly, and breath'd forth so, euer fell
On those that did deserue them, let not mine
Be spent in vaine now, that thou from this instant
Mayest in thy feare that they will fall vpon thee,
Be sensible of the plagues they shall bring with them.
And for denying of a little earth,
To couer what remaynes of our great soldyer,
May all your wiues proue whores, your factors theeues,
And while you liue, your ryotous heires vndoe you.
And thou, the patron of their cruelty,
Of all thy Lordships liue not to be owner
Of so much dung as will conceale a Dog,

                125. purposes] *Gifford*; purpose *32*

Or what is worse, thy selfe in. And thy yeeres, 140
To th'end thou mayst be wretched, I wish many,
And as thou hast denied the dead a graue,
May misery in thy life make thee desire one,
Which men and all the Elements keepe from thee:
I haue begun well, imitate, exceed. 145
   Rochfort. Good counsayle were it a prayseworthy deed.
                            Exeunt Officers with ROMONT.
   Du Croy. Remember what we are.
   Charalois.   Thus low my duty
Answeres your Lordships counsaile. I will vse
In the few words (with which I am to trouble
Your Lordships eares) the temper that you wish mee, 150
Not that I feare to speake my thoughts as lowd,
And with a liberty beyond *Romont*:
But that I know, for me that am made vp
Of all that's wretched, so to haste my end,
Would seeme to most, rather a willingnesse 155
To quit the burthen of a hopelesse life,
Then scorne of death, or duty to the dead.
I therefore bring the tribute of my prayse
To your seueritie, and commend the Iustice,
That will not for the many seruices 160
That any man hath done the Common wealth,
Winke at his least of ills: what though my father
Writ man before he was so, and confirmd it,
By numbring that day, no part of his life,
In which he did not seruice to his Country; 165
Was he to be free therefore from the Lawes,
And ceremonious forme in your decrees?
Or else because he did as much as man
In those three memorable ouerthrowes
At *Granson*, *Morat*, *Nancy*, where his Master, 170
The warlike *Charaloyes* (with whose misfortunes
I beare his name) lost treasure, men and life,
To be excus'd, from payment of those summes
Which (his owne patrimony spent) his zeale,
To serue his Countrey, forc'd him to take vp? 175
   Nouall Senior. The president were ill.

        146. it] *Coxeter*; ~, 32

Charalois. And yet, my Lord, this much
I know youll grant; after those great defeatures,

Enter Officers.

Which in their dreadfull ruines buried quick,
Courage and hope, in all men but himselfe,
He forst the proud foe, in his height of conquest, 180
To yeeld vnto an honourable peace.
And in it saued an hundred thousand liues,
To end his owne, that was sure proofe against
The scalding Summers heate, and Winters frost,
Ill ayres, the Cannon, and the enemies sword, 185
In a most loathsome prison.
   Du Croy. Twas his fault
To be so prodigall.
   Nouall Senior. He had from the state
Sufficient entertainment for the Army.
   Charalois. Sufficient? My Lord, you sit at home,
And though your fees are boundlesse at the barre, 190
Are thriftie in the charges of the warre:
But your wills be obeyd. To these I turne,
To these soft-hearted men, that wisely know
They are onely good men, that pay what they owe.
   2 Creditor. And so they are.
   1 Creditor. 'Tis the City Doctrine, 195
We stand bound to maintaine it.
   Charalois. Be constant in it,
And since you are as mercilesse in your natures,
As base, and mercenary in your meanes
By which you get your wealth, I will not vrge
The Court to take away one scruple from 200
The rigor of their lawes, or one good thought
In you to mend your disposition with.
I know there is no musique to your eares
So pleasing as the groanes of men in prison,
And that the teares of widows, and the cries 205
Of famish'd Orphants, are the feasts that take you.
That to be in your danger, with more care

---

201. rigor] *McIlwraith*; right *32*; weight *conj. Lockert*   or one] *32*; or [wish] one *Gifford*

Should be auoyded, then infectious ayre,
The loath'd embraces of diseased women,
A flatterers poyson, or the losse of honour.
Yet rather then my fathers reuerent dust
Shall want a place in that faire monument,
In which our noble Ancestors lye intomb'd,
Before the Court I offer vp my selfe
A prisoner for it: loade me with those yrons
That haue worne out his life, in my best strength
Ile run to th' incounter of cold hunger,
And choose my dwelling where no Sun dares enter,
So he may be releas'd.
 1 *Creditor.*   What meane you sir?
 2 *Aduocate.* Onely your fee againe: ther's so much sayd
Already in this cause, and sayd so well,
That should I onely offer to speake in it,
I should not bee heard, or laught at for it.
 1 *Creditor.* 'Tis the first mony aduocate ere gaue backe,
Though hee sayd nothing.
 Rochfort.   Be aduis'd, young Lord,
And well considerate, you throw away
Your liberty, and ioyes of life together:
Your bounty is imployd vpon a subiect
That is not sensible of it, with which, wise man
Neuer abus'd his goodnesse; the great vertues
Of your dead father vindicate themselues
From these mens malice, and breake ope the prison,
Though it containe his body.
 Nouall Senior.   Let him alone,
If he loue bonds, a Gods name let him weare 'em,
Prouided these consent.
 Charalois.   I hope they are not
So ignorant in any way of profit,
As to neglect a possibility
To get their owne, by seeking it from that
Which can returne them nothing, but ill fame,
And curses for their barbarous cruelties.

---

223. not bee heard, or laught at] *32*; be or not heard ∼ *Gifford*; or not be heard ∼ *Symons*; not bee heard, or be laught at *McIlwraith*   234. bonds] *McIlwraith, Dunn*; Lords *32*; Cords *Coxeter*

3 Creditor. What thinke you of the offer?
2 Creditor.   Very well.
1 Creditor. Accept it by all meanes: let's shut him vp,
He is well-shaped and has a villanous tongue,
And should he study that way of reuenge,
As I dare almost sweare he loues a wench,   245
We haue no wiues, nor neuer shall get daughters
That will hold out against him.
    Du Croy.   What's your answer?
    2 Creditor. Speake you for all.
    1 Creditor.   Why, let our executions
That lye vpon the father, bee return'd
Vpon the sonne, and we release the body.   250
    Nouall Senior. The Court must grant you that.
    Charalois.   I thanke your Lordships,
They haue in it confirm'd on me such glory,
As no time can take from me: I am ready,
Come lead me where you please: captiuity
That comes with honour, is true liberty.   255
        Exeunt [CHARALOIS,] CHARMI, CREDITORS *and Officers.*
    Nouall Senior. Strange rashnesse.
    Rochfort.   A braue resolution rather,
Worthy a better fortune, but howeuer
It is not now to be disputed, therefore
To my owne cause. Already I haue found
Your Lordships bountifull in your fauours to me,   260
And that should teach my modesty to end heere
And presse your loues no further.
    Du Croy.   There is nothing
The Court can grant, but with assurance you
May aske it, and obtaine it.
    Rochfort.   You incourage
A bold Petitioner, and 'tis not fit   265
Your fauours should be lost. Besides, 'tas beene
A custome many yeeres, at the surrendring
The place I now giue vp, to grant the President
One boone, that parted with it. And to confirme
Your grace towards me, against all such as may   270
Detract my actions, and life hereafter,

255 SD. CHARALOIS] *Gifford; not in* 32

I now preferre it to you.
  Du Croy.   Speake it freely.
  Rochfort. I then desire the liberty of *Romont*,
And that my Lord *Nouall*, whose priuate wrong
Was equall to the iniurie that was done
To the dignity of the Court, will pardon it,
And now signe his enlargement.
  Nouall Senior.   Pray you demand
The moyety of my estate, or any thing
Within my power, but this.
  Rochfort.   Am I denyed then—
My first and last request?
  Du Croy.   It must not be.
  2 President. I haue a voyce to giue in it.
  3 President.   And I.
And if perswasion will not worke him to it,
We will make knowne our power.
  Nouall Senior.   You are too violent,
You shall haue my consent—But would you had
Made tryall of my loue in any thing
But this, you should haue found then——But it skills not.
You haue what you desire.
  Rochfort.   I thanke your Lordships.
  Du Croy. The court is vp, make way.
        Exeunt omnes, præter ROCHFORT *and* BAUMONT.
  Rochfort.   I follow you—
Baumont!
  Baumont. My Lord.
  Rochfort.   You are a scholler, *Baumont*,
And can search deeper into th' intents of men,
Then those that are lesse knowing—How appear'd
The piety and braue behauiour of
Young *Charaloyes* to you?
  Baumont.   It is my wonder,
Since I want language to expresse it fully;
And sure the Collonell——
  Rochfort.   Fie! he was faulty—
What present mony haue I?
  Baumont.   There is no want
Of any summe a priuate man has vse for.

Rochfort. 'Tis well:
I am strangely taken with this *Charaloyes*;
Methinkes, from his example, the whole age 300
Should learne to be good, and continue so.
Vertue workes strangely with vs: and his goodnesse
Rising aboue his fortune, seemes to me
Princelike, to will, not aske a courtesie.   *Exeunt.*

Actus secundus. Scæna prima.

Enter PONTALIER, MALOTIN, BAUMONT.

Malotin. Tis strange.
Baumont.   Me thinkes so.
Pontalier.   In a man, but young,
Yet old in iudgement, theorique, and practicke,
In all humanity (and to increase the wonder)
Religious, yet a Souldier, that he should
Yeeld his free liuing youth a captiue, for   5
The freedome of his aged fathers Corpes,
And rather choose to want lifes necessaries,
Liberty, hope of fortune, then it should
In death be kept from Christian ceremony.
    Malotin. Come, 'tis a golden president in a Sonne, 10
To let strong nature haue the better hand,
(In such a case) of all affected reason.
What yeeres sits on this *Charolois*?
    Baumont.   Twenty eight,
For since the clocke did strike him 17 old,
Vnder his fathers wing, this Sonne hath fought, 15
Seru'd and commanded, and so aptly both,
That sometimes he appear'd his fathers father,
And neuer lesse then's sonne; the old mans vertues
So recent in him, as the world may sweare,
Nought but a faire tree, could such fayre fruit beare. 20
    Pontalier. But wherefore lets he such a barbarous law,
And men more barbarous to execute it,
Preuaile on his soft disposition,
That he had rather dye aliue for debt

II. i. 2. iudgement,] *32*; ~; *Gifford*   3. (and to] *32*; and (to *Coxeter*

Of the old man in prison, then he should 25
Rob him of Sepulture, considering
These monies borrow'd bought the lenders peace,
And all their meanes they inioy, nor was diffus'd
In any impious or licencious path?
   Baumont. True: for my part, were it my fathers trunke, 30
The tyrannous Ram-heads, with their hornes should gore it,
Or, cast it to their curres (than they) less currish,
Ere prey on me so, with their Lion-law,
Being in my free will (as in his) to shun it.
   Pontalier. Alasse! he knowes himselfe (in pouerty) lost: 35
For in this parciall auaricious age
What price beares Honor? Vertue? Long agoe
It was but prays'd, and freez'd, but now a dayes
'Tis colder far, and has, nor loue, nor praise,
Very prayse now freezeth too: for nature 40
Did make the heathen, far more Christian then,
Then knowledge vs (lesse heathenish) Christian.
   Malotin. This morning is the funerall.
   Pontalier.   Certainely!
And from this prison 'twas the sonnes request 44
That his deare father might interment haue.   *Recorders*
See, the young sonne interd in liuely graue.   *Musique.*
   Baumont. They come, obserue their order.

Enter Funerall. Body borne by 4. Captaines and Souldiers. Mourners,
[PRIEST]. *Scutchions, and very good order.* CHARALOIS, *and*
ROMONT *meet it.* CHARALOIS *speakes,* ROMONT *weeping. Solemne
Musique.* 3 CREDITORS, [*Iaylors*].

   Charalois. How like a silent streame shaded with night,
And gliding softly with our windy sighes,
Moues the whole frame of this solemnity! 50
Teares, sighes and blackes, filling the simily,
Whilst I the onely murmur in this groue
Of death, thus hollowly break forth! Vouchsafe
To stay a while. Rest, rest in peace, deare earth,

    40. Very] *32*; The very *Gifford*   44. request] *32*; ~. *Symons*   45. haue.]
32; ~ˆ *Symons*   46. interd in liuely] *editor*; interd a liuely *32*; enters alive the
conj. Mason; enter'd a lively *Gifford*   47 SD. PRIEST] *Gifford*; not in *32*
Iaylors] *Gifford*; not in *32*   54. while.] *Coxeter*; ~, *32*

Thou that brought'st rest to their vnthankfull lyues, 55
Whose cruelty deny'd thee rest in death:
Heere stands thy poore Executor thy sonne,
That makes his life prisoner, to bale thy death;
Who gladlier puts on this captiuity,
Then Virgins long in loue, their wedding weeds: 60
Of all that euer thou hast done good to,
These onely haue good memories, for they
Remember best, forget not gratitude.
I thanke you for this last and friendly loue.
And tho this Country, like a viperous mother, 65
Not onely hath eate vp vngratefully
All meanes of thee her sonne, but last thy selfe,
Leauing thy heire so bare and indigent,
He cannot rayse thee a poore Monument,
Such as a flatterer, or a vsurer hath, 70
Thy worth, in euery honest brest buyldes one,
Making their friendly hearts thy funerall stone.
   Pontalier. Sir.
   Charalois.   Peace, O peace, this sceane is wholy mine.
What, weepe ye, souldiers? Blanch not, *Romont* weepes.
Ha, let me see, my miracle is eas'd, 75
The iaylors and the creditors do weepe;
Euen they that make vs weepe, do weepe themselues.
Be these thy bodies balme: these and thy vertue
Keepe thy fame euer odoriferous,
Whilst the great, proud, rich, vndeseruing man, 80
Aliue stinkes in his vices, and being vanish'd,
The golden calfe that was an Idoll dect
With Marble pillars, Iet, and Porphyrie,
Shall quickly both in bone and name consume,
Though wrapt in lead, spice, Searecloth and perfume. 85
   1 *Creditor.* Sir.
   Charalois.   What! Away for shame: you prophane rogues
Must not be mingled with these holy reliques:
This is a Sacrifice, our showre shall crowne
His sepulcher with Oliue, Myrrh and Bayes,
The plants of peace, of sorrow, victorie, 90

57. thy poore] *32²*; the poore *32¹*

Your teares would spring but weedes.
 1 *Creditor.*   Would they but so?
Wee'll keepe them to stop bottles then.
 Romont.   No; keepe 'em
For your owne sins, you Rogues, till you repent:
You'll dye else and be damn'd.
 2 *Creditor.*   Damn'd! ha, ha, ha.
 Romont. Laugh yee?
 3 *Creditor.*   Yes faith. Sir, wee'ld be very glad 95
To please you eyther way.
 1 *Creditor.*   Y'are ne're content,
Crying nor laughing.
 Romont.   Both with a birth, shee rogues!
 2 *Creditor.* Our wiues, Sir, taught vs.
 Romont. Looke, looke you slaues, your thanklesse cruelty
And sauage manners, of vnkind *Dijon*, 100
Exhaust these flouds, and not his fathers death.
 1 *Creditor.* Slid, Sir, what would yee, ye'are so cholericke?
 2 *Creditor.* Most souldiers are so yfaith, let him alone:
They haue little else to liue on, we haue not had
A penny of him, haue wee?
 3 *Creditor.*   Slight, wo'd you haue our hearts? 105
 1 *Creditor.* We haue nothing but his body heere in durance
For all our mony.
 Priest. On.
 Charalois.   One moment more,
But to bestow a few poore legacyes,
All I haue left in my dead fathers rights,
And I haue done. Captaine, weare thou these spurs 110
That yet ne're made his horse runne from a foe.
Lieutenant, thou, this Scarfe, and may it tye
Thy valor, and thy honestie together:
For so it did in him. Ensigne, this Curace,
Your Generalls necklace once. You gentle Bearers, 115
Deuide this purse of gold, this other, strow
Among the poore: tis all I haue. *Romont*,
(Weare thou this medall of himselfe) that like
A hearty Oake, grew'st close to this tall Pine,

  91. they but so?] *conj. Adams;* they not so? *32;* they so? *Coxeter;* they? Not so; *Symons*

Euen in the wildest wildernesse of war, 120
Whereon foes broke their swords, and tyr'd themselues;
Wounded and hack'd yee were, but neuer fell'd.
For me, my portion prouide in Heauen:
My roote is earth'd, and I a desolate branch
Left scattered in the high way of the world, 125
Trod vnder foot, that might haue bin a Columne,
Mainely supporting our demolish'd house.
This would I weare as my inheritance,
And what hope can arise to me from it,
When I and it are both heere prisoners? 130
Onely may this, if euer we be free,
Keepe, or redeeme me from all infamie. *Musicke.*

Song.

Fie, cease to wonder,
Though you heare Orpheus *with his Iuory Lute,*
Moue Trees and Rockes, 135
Charme Buls, Beares and men more sauage to be mute,
Weake foolish singer, here is one,
Would haue transform'd thy selfe, to stone.

1 *Creditor.* No farther, looke to 'em at your owne perill.
2 *Creditor.* No, as they please: their Master's a good man. 140
I would they were ith' *Burmudas.*
Jaylor. You must no further.
The prison limits you, and the Creditors
Exact the strictnesse.
Romont. Out you wooluish mungrells!
Whose braynes should be knockt out, like dogs in Iuly,
Lest your infection poyson a whole towne. 145
Charalois. They grudge our sorrow: your ill wills perforce
Turnes now to Charity: they would not haue vs
Walke too farre mourning, vsurers reliefe
Grieues, if the Debtors haue too much of griefe. *Exeunt.*

Enter BEAUMELLE, FLORIMEL, BELLAPERT.

Beaumelle. I prithee tell me, *Florimell,* why do women marry?
Florimel. Why truly Madam, I thinke, to lye with their husbands.

136. Buls, Beares] *32*; Buls, and Beares *McIlwraith*   141. ith'] *editor*; the *32*;
at the *Coxeter*; ath' *McIlwraith*

Bellapert. You are a foole. She lyes, Madam, women marry husbands to lye with other men. 4

Florimel. Faith, eene such a woman wilt thou make. By this light, Madam, this wagtaile will spoyle you, if you take delight in her licence.

Beaumelle. Tis true, *Florimell*: and thou wilt make me too good for a yong Lady. What an electuary found my father out for his daughter, when hee compounded you two my women! for thou, *Florimell*, art eene a graine too heauy, simply for a wayting Gentlewoman. 12

Florimel. And thou *Bellapert*, a graine too light.

Bellapert. Well, go thy wayes goody wisdom, whom no body regards. I wonder whether be elder, thou or thy hood: you thinke, because you seru'd my Ladyes mother, are 32 yeeres old, which is a peepe out, you know— 17

Florimel. Well sayd, wherligig.

Bellapert. You are deceyu'd: I want a peg ith' middle. Out on these Prerogatiues! you thinke to be mother of the maydes heere, and mortifie em with prouerbs: goe, goe, gouern the sweet meates, and waigh the Suger, that the wenches steale none: say your prayers twice a day, and as I take it, you have performd your function.

Florimel. I may bee euen with you.

Bellapert. Harke, the Court's broke vp. Goe helpe my old Lord out of his Caroch, and scratch his head till dinner time. 26

Florimel. Well. *Exit.*

Bellapert. Fy Madam, how you walke! By my mayden-head you looke 7 yeeres older then you did this morning: why, there can be nothing vnder the Sunne valuable, to make you thus a minute. 30

Beaumelle. Ah my sweete *Bellapert*, thou Cabinet
To all my counsels, thou dost know the cause
That makes thy Lady wither thus in youth.

Bellapert. Vd's-light, enioy your wishes: whilst I liue,
One way or other you shall crowne your will. 35
Would you haue him your husband that you loue,
And can't not bee? he is your seruant though,
And may performe the office of a husband.

Beaumelle. But there is honor, wench.

II. ii. 14. goody] *Gifford*; goodly *32*   15. wonder] *Gifford*; ~, *32*   elder,] *Coxeter*; ~∧ *32*   16. seru'd] *Gifford*; serue *32*   17. know—] *Gifford*; ~. *32*   19. on] *conj. F. P. Wilson*; of *32*

Bellapert. Such a disease
There is in deed, for which ere I would dy—
Beaumelle. Prethee, distinguish me a mayd and wife.
Bellapert. Faith, Madam, one may beare any mans children, Tother must beare no mans.
Beaumelle. What is a husband?
Bellapert. Physicke, that tumbling in your belly, will make you sicke ith' stomacke: the onely distinction betwixt a husband and a seruant is: the first will lye with you, when hee please; the last shall lye with you when you please. Pray tell me, Lady, do you loue, to marry after, or would you marry, to loue after?
Beaumelle. I would meete loue and marriage both at once.
Bellapert. Why then you are out of the fashion, and wilbe contemn'd: for (Ile assure you) there are few women i'th world, but either they haue married first, and loue after, or loue first, and marryed after: you must do as you may, not as you would: your fathers will is the Goale you must fly to: if a husband approch you, you would haue further off, is he you loue, the lesse neere you? A husband in these dayes is but a cloake to bee oftner layde vpon your bed, then in your bed.
Beaumelle. Humpe.
Bellapert. Sometimes you may weare him on your shoulder, now and then vnder your arme: but seldome or neuer let him couer you: for 'tis not the fashion.

Enter YOUNG NOVALL, PONTALIER, MALOTIN, LILADAM, AYMER.

Nouall Iunior. Best day to natures curiosity,
Starre of *Dijum*, the lustre of all *France*,
Perpetuall spring dwell on thy rosy cheekes,
Whose breath is perfume to our Continent,
See *Flora* turn'd in her varieties.
Bellapert. Oh diuine Lord!
Nouall Iunior. No autumne, nor no age euer approach
This heauenly piece, which nature hauing wrought,
She lost her needle and did then despaire,
Euer to worke so liuely and so faire.
Liladam. Vds light, my Lord, one of the purles of your band is (without all discipline) falne out of his ranke.

55. he you] *Gifford;* he your *32*   loue,] *32 catchword;* ~? *32 text*   you?] Mason; ~. *32*   58. Beaumelle.] *Coxeter;* Baum. *32*

Nouall Iunior. How? I would not for a 1000 crownes she had seen't. Deare *Liladam*, reforme it. 75

Bellapert. Oh Lord *per se*, Lord, quintessence of honour, shee walkes not vnder a weede that could deny thee any thing.

Beaumelle. Prethy peace, wench, thou dost but blow the fire, that flames too much already.

LILADAM, AYMER *trim* NOVALL, *whilst* BELLAPERT *her Lady.*

Aymer. By gad, my Lord, you haue the diuinest Taylor of Christendome; he hath made you looke like an Angell in your cloth of Tissue doublet. 82

Pontalier. This is a three-leg'd Lord, ther's a fresh assault, oh that men should spend time thus! See see, how her blood driues to her heart, and straight vaults to her cheekes againe.

Malotin. What are these?

Pontalier. One of 'em there the lower is a good, foolish, knauish, sociable gallimaufry of a man, and has much caught my Lord with singing, hee is master of a musicke house: the other is his dressing blocke, vpon whom my Lord layes all his cloathes, and fashions, ere he vouchsafes 'em his owne person; you shall see him i'th morning in the Gally-foyst, at noone in the Bullion, i'th euening in Quirpo, and all night in—— 93

Malotin. A Bawdy house.

Pontalier. If my Lord deny, they deny, if hee affirme, they affirme: they skip into my Lords cast skins some twice a yeere, and thus they liue to eate, eate to liue, and liue to prayse my Lord.

Malotin. Good sir, tell me one thing.

Pontalier. What's that?

Malotin. Dare these men euer fight, on any cause? 100

Pontalier. Oh no, 'twould spoyle their cloathes, and put their bands out of order.

Nouall Iunior. Mistress, you heare the news: your father has resign'd his Presidentship to my Lord my father.

Malotin. And Lord *Charolois* vndone foreuer. 105

Pontalier. Troth, 'tis pity, sir.
A brauer hope of so assur'd a father
Did neuer comfort *France.*

Liladam. A good dumbe mourner.

Aymer. A silent blacke. 110

76. Lord *per se*,] *Gifford*; Lord: *Per se, 32*   78. *Beaumelle.*] *Coxeter; Baum. 32*
88 caught] *Mason*; taught *32.*

Nouall Iunior. Oh fie vpon him, how he weares his cloathes!
As if he had come this Christmas from St. *Omers*,
To see his friends, and return'd after Twelfetyde.
  Liladam. His Colonell lookes fienely like a drouer,
  Nouall Iunior. That had a winter ly'n perdieu i'th rayne.   115
  Aymer. What, he that weares a clout about his necke,
His cuffes in's pocket, and his heart in's mouth?
  Nouall Iunior. Now out vpon him!
  Beaumelle.   Seruant, tye my hand.
How your lips blush, in scorne that they should pay
Tribute to hands, when lips are in the way!   120
  Nouall Iunior. I thus recant, yet now your hand looks white,
Because your lips robd it of such a right.
Mounsieur Aymour, I prethy sing the song
Deuoted to my Mistress.   *Musicke.*

Cantat.

A Dialogue betweene NOVALL, *and* BEAUMELLE.

Man.   Set Phœbus, *set, a fayrer sunne doth rise*,   125
           From the bright Radience of my Mistress eyes,
           Then euer thou begat'st. I dare not looke,
           Each haire a golden line, each word a hooke,
           The more I striue, the more still I am tooke.
Woman. *Fayre seruant, come, the day these eyes doe lend*   130
           To warme thy blood, thou doest so vainely spend.
           Come strangle breath.
Man.   *What noate so sweet as this,*
           That calles the spirits to a further blisse?
Woman. *Yet this out-savours wine, and this Perfume.*   135
Man.   *Let's die, I languish, I consume.*

After the Song, Enter ROCHFORT, *and* BAUMONT.

  Baumont. Romont will come, sir, straight.
  Rochfort. 'Tis well.
  Beaumelle. My Father.
  Nouall Iunior. My honorable Lord.   140
  Rochfort. My Lord *Nouall*, this is a vertue in you.
So early vp and ready before noone,
That are the map of dressing through all *France*.

    124 SD. *Cantat.*] editor; *Cant. 32*   132. strangle] Mason; strangled *32*

Nouall Iunior. I rise to say my prayers, sir, heere's my Saint.
Rochfort. Tis well and courtly: you must giue me leaue, 145
I haue some priuate conference with my daughter,
Pray vse my garden, you shall dine with me.
Liladam. Wee'l waite on you.
Nouall Iunior. Good morne vnto your Lordship,
Remember what you haue vow'd—— *To his Mistress.*
Beaumelle. Performe I must.
Exeunt omnes, præter ROCHFORT, DAUGHTER.
Rochfort. Why how now *Beaumelle*, thou look'st not well. 150
Th'art sad of late, come cheere thee, I haue found
A wholesome remedy for these mayden fits,
A goodly Oake whereon to twist my vine,
Till her faire branches grow vp to the starres.
Be neere at hand, successe crownes my intent, 155
My businesse fills my little time so full,
I cannot stand to talke: I know, thy duty
Is handmayd to my will, especially
When it presents nothing but good and fit.
Beaumelle. Sir, I am yours. Oh if my feares proue true, 160
Fate hath wrong'd loue, and will destroy me too. *Exit* DAUGHTER.

Enter ROMONT, *Keeper.*

Romont. Sent you for me, sir?
Rochfort. Yes.
Romont. Your Lordships pleasure?
Rochfort. Keeper, this prisoner I will see forthcomming,
Vpon my word—Sit downe good Colonell, *Exit Keeper.*
Why I did wish you hither, noble sir, 165
Is to aduise you from this yron carriage,
Which, so affectedly, *Romont*, you weare,
To pity and to counsell yee submit
With expedition to the great *Nouall*:
Recant your sterne contempt, and slight neglect 170
Of the whole Court, and him, and opportunity,
Or you will vndergoe a heauy censure
In publique very shortly.

160. feares] *Gifford*; teares *32* 163. forthcomming,] *Gifford*; ~ ˄ *32*
167. affectedly] *Symons*; affected *32* 171. opportunity] *32*; opportunely *Mason*

Romont.   Hum hum: reuerend sir,
I haue obseru'd you, and doe know you well,
And am now more affraid you know not me,   175
By wishing my submission to *Nouall*,
Then I can be of all the bellowing mouthes
That waite vpon him to pronounce the censure,
Could it determine me torments, and shame.
Submit, and craue forgiuenesse of a beast?   180
Tis true, this bile of state weares purple Tissue,
Is high fed, proud: so is his Lordships horse,
And beares as rich Caparisons. I know,
This Elephant carries on his backe not onely
Towres, Castles, but the ponderous republique,   185
And neuer stoops for't, with his strong breath trunk
Snuffes others titles, Lordships, Offices,
Wealth, bribes, and lyues, vnder his rauenous iawes,
Whats this vnto my freedome? I dare dye;
And therfore aske this Cammell, if these blessings   190
(For so they would be vnderstood by a man)
But mollifie one rudenesse in his nature,
Sweeten the eager relish of the law,
At whose great helme he sits: helps he the poore
In a iust businesse? nay, does he not crosse   195
Euery deserued souldier and scholler,
As if when nature made him, she had made
The generall Antipathy of all vertue?
How sauagely, and blasphemously hee spake
Touching the Generall, the graue Generall dead,   200
I must weepe when I thinke on't.
  Rochfort.   Sir.
  Romont.   My Lord,
I am not stubborne, I can melt, you see,
And prize a vertue better then my life:
For though I be not learnd, I euer lou'd
That holy Mother of all issues good,   205
Whose white hand (for a Scepter) holdes a File
To pollish roughest customes, and in you
She has her right: see, I am calme as sleepe,
But when I thinke of the grosse iniuries,

                205. issues] *Mason*; ~, 32

The godlesse wrong done, to my Generall dead, 210
I raue indeed, and could eate this *Nouall*,
A soule-lesse Dromodary.
  Rochfort.   Oh bee temperate.
Sir, though I would perswade, I'le not constraine:
Each mans opinion freely is his owne,
Concerning anything or any body; 215
Be it right or wrong, tis at the Iudges perill.

          Enter BAUMONT.

  Baumont. These men, Sir, waite without, my Lord is come too.
  Rochfort. Pay'em those summes vpon the table, take
Their full releases: stay, I want a witnesse:
Let mee intreat you Colonell, to walke in, 220
And stand but by, to see this money pay'd,
It does concerne you and your friend, it was
The better cause you were sent for, though sayd otherwise.
The deed shall make this my request more plaine.
  Romont. I shall obey your pleasure Sir, though ignorant 225
To what it tends.   *Exit* BAUMONT, ROMONT.

          Enter CHARALOIS.

  Rochfort.   Worthiest Sir,
You are most welcome: fye, no more of this:
You haue out-wept a woman, noble *Charolois*.
No man but has, or must bury a father.
  Charalois. Graue Sir, I buried sorrow, for his death, 230
In the graue with him. I did neuer thinke
Hee was immortall, though I vow I grieue,
And see no reason why the vicious,
Vertuous, valiant and vnworthy men
Should dye alike.
  Rochfort.   They do not.
  Charalois.   In the manner 235
Of dying, Sir, they do not, but all dye,
And therein differ not: but I haue done.
I spy'd the liuely picture of my father,
Passing your gallery, and that cast this water

<small>215. body;] *Gifford*; ~, 32   222. friend] *Mason*; friends 32   226 SD. BAUMONT] *Gifford*; Seruant 32   234. men] 32²; man 32¹</small>

Into mine eyes: see, foolish that I am, 240
To let it doe so.
   Rochfort.   Sweete and gentle nature,
How silken is this will comparatiuely
To other men! I haue a suite to you Sir.
   Charalois. Take it, tis granted.
   Rochfort.   What?
   Charalois.   Nothing, my Lord.
   Rochfort. Nothing is quickly granted.
   Charalois.   Faith, my Lord, 245
That nothing granted, is euen all I haue,
For (all know) I haue nothing left to grant.
   Rochfort. Sir, ha' you any suite to me? I'll grant
You some thing, any thing.
   Charalois.   Nay surely, I that can
Giue nothing, will but sue for that againe. 250
No man will grant mee any thing I sue for,
But begging nothing, euery man will giue't.
   Rochfort. Sir, the loue I bore your father, and the worth
I see in you, so much resembling his,
Made me thus send for you. And tender heere 255
                                  Drawes a Curtayne.
What euer you will take, gold, Iewels, both,
All, to supply your wants, and free your selfe.
Where heauenly vertue in high blouded veines
Is lodg'd, and can agree, men should kneele downe,
Adore, and sacrifice all that they haue; 260
And well they may, it is so seldome seene.
Put off your wonder, and heere freely take,
Or send your seruants. Nor, Sir, shall you vse
In ought of this, a poore mans fee, or bribe,
Vniustly taken of the rich, but what's 265
Directly gotten, and yet by the Law.
   Charalois. How ill, Sir, it becomes those haires to mocke!
   Rochfort. Mocke? thunder strike mee then.
   Charalois.   You doe amaze mee:
But you shall wonder too, I will not take
One single piece of this great heape: why should I 270
Borrow, that haue not meanes to pay, nay am

        242. will] *McIlwraith*; well *32*

A very bankerupt, euen in flattering hope
Of euer raysing any? All my begging,
Is *Romonts* libertie.

  Enter ROMONT, CREDITORS *loaden with mony*, BAUMONT.

 Rochfort.   Heere is your friend,
Enfranchist ere you spake. I giue him you,   275
And *Charolois*, I giue you to your friend
As free a man as hee; your fathers debts
Are taken off.
 Charalois. How?
 Romont.   Sir, it is most true.
I am the witnes.
 1 *Creditor.* Yes faith, wee are pay'd.   279
 2 *Creditor.* Heauen blesse his Lordship, I did thinke him wiser.
 3 *Creditor.* He a states-man! he an asse. Pay other mens debts?
 1 *Creditor.* That hee was neuer bound for.
 Romont.   One more such
Would saue the cost of pleaders.
 Charalois.   Honord *Rochfort.*
Lye still my toung and blushes, scald my cheekes,
That offer thankes in words, for such great deeds. 285
 Rochfort. Call in my daughter: still I haue a suit to you,
            Exit BAUMONT.
Would you requite mee.
 Romont.   With his life, assure you.
 Rochfort. Nay, would you make me now your debter, Sir—

  Enter BAUMONT, BEAUMELLE.

This is my onely child: what shee appeares,
Your Lordship well may see: her education   290
Followes not any: for her mind, I know it
To be far fayrer then her shape, and hope
It will continue so: if now her birth
Be not too meane for *Charolois*, take here
This virgin by the hand, and call her wife,   295
Indowd with all my fortunes: blesse mee so,

  283. cost] *editor*; rest *32*   284. blushes, scald] *Coxeter*; bushes, cal'd *32*
  290. see:] *Mason*; ~∧ *32* 294. take here] *McIlwraith*; take her *32*; take her, take *Gifford*

^{E4r} Requite mee thus, and make mee happier,
In ioyning my poore empty name to yours,
Then if my state were multiplied ten fold.
  Charalois. Is this the payment, Sir, that you expect?   300
Why, you participate me more in debt,
That nothing but my life can euer pay.
This beautie being your daughter, in which yours
I must conceiue necessitie of her vertue,
Without all dowry is a Princes ayme,   305
Then, as shee is, for poore and worthlesse I,
How much too worthy! Waken me, *Romont*,
That I may know I dreamt, and find this vanisht.
  Romont. Sure, I sleepe not.
  Rochfort.   Your sentence, life or death.
  Charalois. Faire *Beaumelle*, can you loue me?
  Beaumelle.   Yes, my Lord.   310

   Enter YOUNG NOVALL, PONTALIER, MALOTIN, LILADAM,
                AYMER. *All salute.*

  Charalois. You need not question me, if I can you.
You are the fayrest virgin in *Digum*,
And *Rochfort* is your father.
  Nouall Iunior.   What's this change?
  Rochfort. You meet my wishes, Gentlemen.
  Romont.   What make
These dogs in doublets heere?
  Beaumelle.   A Visitation, Sir.   315
  Charalois. Then thus, Faire *Beaumelle*, I write my faith,
Thus seale it in the sight of Heauen and men.
Your fingers tye my heart-strings with this touch
In true-loue knots, which nought but death shall loose.
And let these teares (an Embleme of our loues)   320
Like Cristall riuers indiuidually
Flow into one another, make one source,
Which neuer man distinguish, lesse deuide:
Breath, marry breath, and kisses, mingle soules.
Two hearts, and bodies, heere incorporate: 325

   301. participate] *32*; precipitate *Coxeter*   308. dreamt] *Coxeter* (dream'd);
dream't *32*   314. meet] *Gifford*; met *32*   320. let] *Mason*; yet *32*   teares]
Coxeter; eares *32*

And though with little wooing I haue wonne,
My future life shall bee a wooing tyme.
And euery day, new as the bridall one.
Oh Sir, I groane vnder your courtesies, 330
More then my fathers bones vnder his wrongs;
You *Curtius*-like, haue throwne into the gulfe,
Of this his Countries foule ingratitude,
Your life and fortunes, to redeeme their shames.

 Rochfort. No more, my glory, come, let's in and hasten
This celebration.

 Romont, Malotin, Pontalier, Baumont. All faire blisse vpon it. 335

   Exeunt ROCHFORT, CHARALOIS, ROMONT,
      BAUMONT, MALOTIN.

 Nouall Iunior. Mistresse.
 Beaumelle.   Oh seruant, vertue strengthen me.
Thy presence blowes round my affections vane:
You will vndoe me, if you speake againe.   *Exit* BEAUMELLE.

 Liladam, Aymer. Here will be sport for you. This workes.

       Exeunt LILADAM, AYMER.

 Nouall Iunior.   Peace, peace.
 Pontalier. One word, my Lord *Nouall*.
 Nouall Iunior.   What, thou wouldst mony;
There.

 Pontalier. No, Ile none, Ile not be bought a slaue, 341
A Pander, or a Parasite, for all
Your fathers worth; though you haue sau'd my life,
Rescued me often from my wants, I must not
Winke at your follyes: that will ruine you. 345
You know my blunt way, and my loue to truth:
Forsake the pursuit of this Ladies honour,
Now you doe see her made another mans,
And such a mans, so good, so popular,
Or you will plucke a thousand mischiefes on you. 350
The benefits you haue done me, are not lost,
Nor cast away, they are purs'd heere in my heart,
But let me pay you, sir, a fayrer way
Then to defend your vices, or to sooth 'em.

 Nouall Iunior. Ha, ha, ha, what are my courses vnto thee? 355
Good Cousin *Pontalier*, meddle with that

   343. worth;] *Coxeter;* ~, 32

That shall concerne thy selfe. *Exit* NOVALL.
 Pontalier.   No more but scorne?
Moue on then, starres, worke your pernicious will.
Onely the wise rule, and preuent your ill.   *Exit.*
                Hoboyes.
Here a passage ouer the Stage, while the Act is playing, for the Marriage of CHARALOIS *with* BEAUMELLE, *&c.*

Actus tertius. Scæna prima.

Enter NOVALL IUNIOR, BELLAPERT.

 Nouall Iunior. FLIE not to these excuses: thou hast bin
False in thy promise, and when I haue said
Vngratefull, all is spoke.
 Bellapert.   Good my Lord,
But heare me onely.
 Nouall Iunior.   To what purpose, trifler?
Can any thing that thou canst say, make voyd   5
The marriage? or those pleasures but a dreame,
Which *Charaloyes* (oh *Venus*) hath enioyd?
 Bellapert. I yet could say that you receiue aduantage,
In what you thinke a losse, would you vouchsafe me,
That you were neuer in the way till now   10
With safety to arriue at your desires,
That pleasure makes loue to you vnattended
By danger or repentance.
 Nouall Iunior.   That I could
But apprehend one reason how this might be,
Hope would not then forsake me.
 Bellapert.   The enioying   15
Of what you most desire, I say th' enioying
Shall, in the full possession of your wishes,
Confirme that I am faithfull.
 Nouall Iunior.   Giue some rellish
How this may appeare possible.
 Bellapert.   I will

  359 SD. *playing,*] *McIlwraith;* ~∧ *32*   III. i. 3. spoke] *32*; spoken *Gifford*
9. me,] *Coxeter* (~;); ~∧ *32*   13. repentance.] *Gifford;* ~? *32*   19. will] *32*; ~. *Coxeter*

Rellish, and taste, and make the banquet easie:
You say my Ladie's married. I confesse it.
That *Charalois* hath inioyed her, 'tis most true.
That with her, hee's already Master of
The best part of my old Lords state. Still better.
But that the first, or last, should be your hindrance,
I vtterly deny: for but obserue me:
While she went for, and was, I sweare, a Virgin,
What courtesie could she with her honour giue
Or you receiue with safety—take me with you,
When I say courtesie, doe not thinke I meane
A kisse, the tying of her shoo or garter,
An houre of priuate conference: those are trifles.
In this word courtesy, we that are gamesters point at
The sport direct, where not alone the louer
Brings his Artillery, but vses it.
Which word expounded to you, such a courtesie
Doe you expect, and sudden.
   Nouall Iunior.   But he tasted
The first sweetes, *Bellapert.*
   Bellapert.   He wrong'd you shrewdly,
He toyl'd to climbe vp to the *Phœnix* nest,
And in his prints leaues your ascent more easie.
I doe not know, you that are perfect Crittiques
In womens bookes, may talke of maydenheads—
   Nouall Iunior. But for her marriage.
   Bellapert.   'Tis a faire protection
'Gainst all arrests of feare, or shame for euer.
Such as are faire, and yet not foolish, study
To haue one at thirteene; but they are mad
That stay till twenty. Then sir, for the pleasure,
To say Adulterie's sweeter, that is stale.
This onely, is not the contentment more,
To say, This is my Cuckold, then my Riuall?
More I could say——but briefely, she doates on you,
If it proue otherwise, spare not, poyson me
With the next gold you giue me.

   21. confesse it.] *editor*; ~, *32*; ~: *Coxeter*   22. true.] *editor*; ~ₐ *32*; ~:
Coxeter   24. better.] *Gifford*; ~, *32*   53. With the] *Coxeter*; With *32*

Enter BEAUMELLE.

Beaumelle. Hows this, seruant,
Courting my woman?
  Bellapert. As an entrance to
The fauour of the mistris: you are together
And I am perfect in my qu.
  Beaumelle. Stay *Bellapert.*
  Bellapert. In this, I must not with your leaue obey you.
Your Taylor and your Tire-woman waite without
And stay my counsayle, and direction for
Your next dayes dressing. I haue much to doe,
Nor will your Ladiship, now time is precious,
Continue idle: this choise Lord will finde
So fit imployment for you. *Exit* BELLAPERT.
  Beaumelle. I shall grow angry.
  Nouall Iunior. Not so, you haue a iewell in her, Madam.

Enter againe.

  Bellapert. I had forgot to tell your Ladiship
The closet is priuate and your couch ready;
And if you please that I shall loose the key,
But say so, and tis done. *Exit* BELLAPERT.
  Beaumelle. You come to chide me, seruant, and bring with you
Sufficient warrant, you will say and truely,
My father found too much obedience in me,
By being won too soone; yet if you please
But to remember, all my hopes and fortunes
Had reference to this likening: you will grant
That though I did not well towards you, I yet
Did wisely for my selfe.
  Nouall Iunior. With too much feruor
I haue so long lou'd and still loue you, Mistresse,
To esteeme that an iniury to me
Which was to you conuenient: that is past
My helpe, is past my cure. You yet may, Lady,
In recompence of all my dutious seruice,
(Prouided that your will answere your power)
Become my Creditresse.

61. Ladiship,] *Coxeter*; ~∧ *32* now] *Gifford*; know, *32*; now, *Coxeter*   69. *Beaumelle.*] *Coxeter*; *Baum. 32*   74. reference] *Mason*; reuerence *32* this likening] *32*; his liking *Mason*

Beaumelle. I vnderstand you,
And for assurance, the request you make
Shall not be long vnanswered, pray you sit,
And by what you shall heare, you'l easily finde,
My passions are much fitter to desire,
Then to be sued to.

Enter ROMONT *and* FLORIMEL.

Florimel. Sir, tis not enuy
At the start my fellow has got of me in
My Ladies good opinion, thats the motiue
Of this discouery; but due payment
Of what I owe her Honour.
   Romont. So I conceiue it.
   Florimel. I haue obseru'd too much, nor shall my silence
Preuent the remedy——yonder they are,
I dare not bee seene with you. You may doe
What you thinke fit, which wilbe, I presume,
The office of a faithfull and tryed friend
To my young Lord.   *Exit* FLORIMEL.
   Romont. This is no vision: ha!
   Nouall Iunior. With the next opportunity.
   Beaumelle. By this kisse,
And this, and this.
   Nouall Iunior. That you would euer sweare thus.
   Romont. If I seeme rude, your pardon, Lady; yours
I do not aske: come, do not dare to shew mee
A face of anger, or the least dislike.
Put on, and suddainly, a milder looke,
I shall grow rough else.
   Nouall Iunior. What haue I done, Sir,
To draw this harsh vnsauory language from you?
   Romont. Done, Popinjay? why, dost thou thinke that if
I ere had dreamt that thou hadst done me wrong,
Thou shouldest outliue it?
   Beaumelle. This is something more
Then my Lords friendship giues commission for.
   Nouall Iunior. Your presence and the place, makes him presume
Vpon my patience,

       85. vnanswered, pray] *Coxeter*; vnanswered. Pray 32

III. i. 112–43 *The Fatal Dowry* 51

Romont. As if thou ere wer't angry
But with thy Taylor, and yet that poore shred
Can bring more to the making vp of a man,
Then can be hop'd from thee: thou art his creature, 115
And did hee not each morning new create thee
Thou wouldst stinke and be forgotten. Ile not change
On sillable more with thee, vntill thou bring
Some testimony vnder good mens hands,
Thou art a Christian. I suspect thee strongly, 120
And wilbe satisfied: till which time, keepe from me.
The entertainment of your visitation
Has made what I intended on, a businesse.
 Nouall Iunior. So wee shall meete—Madam.
 Romont.   Vse that legge againe,
And Ile cut off the other.
 Nouall Iunior.   Very good.   *Exit* NOVALL.
 Romont. What a perfume the Muske-cat leaues behind him! 126
Do you admit him for a property,
To saue you charges, Lady?
 Beaumelle.   Tis not vselesse,
Now you are to succeed him.
 Romont.   So I respect you,
Not for your selfe, but in remembrance of 130
Who is your father, and whose wife you now are,
That I choose rather not to vnderstand
Your nasty scoffe then,——
 Beaumelle.   What, you will not beate mee,
If I expound it to you? Heer's a Tyrant
Spares neyther man nor woman.
 Romont.   My intents 135
Madam, deserue not this; nor do I stay
To bee the whetstone of your wit: preserue it
To spend on such, as know how to admire
Such coloured stuffe. In me there is now speaks to you
As true a friend and seruant to your Honour, 140
And one that will with as much hazzard guard it,
As euer man did goodnesse.——But then Lady,
You must endeauour not alone to bee,

116. create thee] *Coxeter*; create . . . . *32* [failure to ink] 123. on,] *Gifford*
(one,); ~∧ *32*   139. there is] *32*; there *Gifford*

But to appeare worthy such loue and seruice.
   Beaumelle. To what tends this?
   Romont.   Why, to this purpose, Lady,   145
I do desire you should proue such a wife
To *Charaloys* (and such a one hee merits)
As *Cæsar*, did hee liue, could not except at,
Not onely innocent from crime, but free
From all taynt and suspition.
   Beaumelle.   They are base   150
That iudge me otherwise.
   Romont.   But yet bee carefull.
Detraction's a bold monster, and feares not
To wound the fame of Princes, if it find
But any blemish in their liues to worke on.
But Ile bee plainer with you: had the people   155
Bin learnd to speake but what euen now I saw,
Their malice out of that would raise an engine
To ouerthrow your honor. In my sight
(With yonder pointed foole I frighted from you)
You vs'd familiarity beyond   160
A modest entertaynment: you embrac'd him
With too much ardor for a stranger, and
Met him with kisses neyther chaste nor comely:
But learne you to forget him, as I will
Your bounties to him, you will find it safer   165
Rather to bee vncourtly, then immodest.
   Beaumelle. This prety rag about your necke shews well,
And being coorse and little worth, it speakes you,
As terrible as thrifty.
   Romont.   Madam.
   Beaumelle.   Yes.
And this strong belt in which you hang your honor   170
Will out-last twenty scarfs.
   Romont.   What meane you, Lady?
   Beaumelle. And all else about you Cap a pe,
So vniforme in spite of handsomnesse,
Shews such a bold contempt of comelinesse,
That tis not strange your Laundresse in the Leaguer,   175
Grew mad with loue of you.

            159. pointed] *32*; painted *Coxeter*

III. i. 176–210 *The Fatal Dowry* 53

Romont. Is my free counsayle
Answerd with this ridiculous scorne?
  Beaumelle. These obiects
Stole very much of my attention from me,
Yet something I remember, to speake truth,
Deliuer'd grauely, but to little purpose, 180
That almost would haue made me sweare, some Curate
Had stolne into the person of *Romont*,
And in the praise of goodwife honesty,
Had read an homely.
  Romont. By this hand.
  Beaumelle. And sword,
I will make vp your oath, twill want weight else. 185
You are angry with me, and poore I laugh at it.
Do you come from the Campe, which affords onely
The conuersation of cast suburbe whores,
To set downe to a Lady of my ranke,
Lymits of entertainment? 190
  Romont. Sure a Legion has possest this woman.
  Beaumelle. One stamp more would do well: yet I desire not
You should grow horne-mad, till you haue a wife.
You are come to warme meate, and perhaps cleane linnen:
Feed, weare it, and bee thankfull. For me, know, 195
That though a thousand watches were set on mee,
And you the Master-spy, I yet would vse
The liberty that best likes mee. I will reuell,
Feast, kisse, imbreace, perhaps grant larger fauours:
Yet such as liue vpon my meanes, shall know 200
They must not murmur at it. If my Lord
Bee now growne yellow, and has chose out you
To serue his Iealouzy that way, tell him this,
You haue something to informe him. *Exit* BEAUMELLE.
  Romont. And I will.
Beleeue it wicked one I will. Heare, Heauen, 205
But hearing pardon mee: if these fruts grow
Vpon the tree of marriage, let me shun it,
As a forbidden sweete. An heyre and rich,
Young, beautifull, yet adde to this a wife,
And I will rather choose a Spittle sinner 210

180. Deliuer'd] *Coxeter*; Deceyued 32   184. this] *Coxeter*; thy 32

Carted an age before, though three parts rotten,
And take it for a blessing, rather then
Be fettered to the hellish slauery
Of such an impudence.

Enter BAUMONT *with writings.*

Baumont. Collonell, good fortune
To meet you thus: you looke sad, but Ile tell you
Something that shall remoue it. Oh how happy
Is my Lord *Charaloys* in his faire bride!
 Romont. A happy man indeede!—pray you in what?
 Baumont. I dare sweare, you would thinke so good a Lady,
A dower sufficient.
 Romont. No doubt. But on.
 Baumont. So faire, so chaste, so vertuous: so indeed
All that is excellent.
 Romont. Women haue no cunning
To gull the world.
 Baumont. Yet to all these, my Lord
Her father giues the full addition of
All he does now possesse in *Burgundy*:
These writings to confirme it, are new seal'd,
And I most fortunate to present him with them;
I must goe seeke him out, can you direct mee?
 Romont. You'l finde him breaking a young horse.
 Baumont. I thanke you.
            Exit BAUMONT.
 Romont. I must do something worthy *Charaloys* friendship.
If she were well inclin'd, to keepe her so,
Deseru'd not thankes: and yet to stay a woman
Spur'd headlong by hot lust, to her owne ruine,
Is harder then to prop a falling towre
With a deceiuing reed.

Enter ROCHFORT.

 Rochfort. Some one seeke for me,
As soone as he returnes.
 Romont. Her father! ha?
How if I breake this to him? sure it cannot
Meete with an ill construction. His wisedome

Made powerfull by the authority of a father,
Will warrant and giue priuiledge to his counsailes.
It shall be so—my Lord.
   Rochfort.   Your friend *Romont*:
Would you ought with me?
   Romont.   I stand so ingag'd
To your so many fauours, that I hold it
A breach in thankfulnesse, should I not discouer,
Though with some imputation to my selfe,
All doubts that may concerne you.
   Rochfort.   The performance
Will make this protestation worth my thanks.
   Romont. Then with your patience lend me your attention,
For what I must deliuer, whispered onely,
You will with too much griefe receiue.

        Enter BEAUMELLE, BELLAPERT.

   Beaumelle.   See wench!
Vpon my life as I forespake, hee's now
Preferring his complaint: but be thou perfect,
And we will fit him.
   Bellapert.   Feare not me, pox on him:
A Captaine turne Informer against kissing?
Would he were hang'd vp in his rusty Armour:
But if our fresh wits cannot turne the plots
Of such a mouldy murrion on it selfe,
Rich cloathes, choyse fare, and a true friend at a call,
With all the pleasures the night yeelds, forsake vs.
   Rochfort. This in my daughter? doe not wrong her.
   Bellapert.   Now
Begin. The games afoot, and wee in distance.
   Beaumelle. Tis thy fault, foolish girle, pinne on my vaile,
I will not weare those iewels. Am I not
Already matcht beyond my hopes? yet still
You prune and set me forth, as if I were
Againe to please a suyter.
   Bellapert.   Tis the course
That our great Ladies take.
   Romont.   A weake excuse.

      267. Romont.] 32 (*Rom.*); Beaumel. *Gifford*

Beaumelle. Those that are better seene, in what concernes
A Ladies honour and faire fame, condemne it.
You waite well, in your absence, my Lords friend
The vnderstanding, graue and wise *Romont*—
Romont. Must I be still her sport?
Beaumelle. Reprou'd me for it.
And he has traueld to bring home a iudgement
Not to be contradicted. You will say
My father, that owes more to yeeres then he,
Has brought me vp to musique, language, Courtship,
And I must vse them. True, but not t'offend,
Or render me suspected.
   Rochfort. Does your fine story
Begin from this?
   Beaumelle. I thought a parting kisse
From young *Nouall*, would haue displeasd no more
Then heretofore it hath done; but I finde
I must restrayne such fauours now; looke therefore
As you are carefull to continue mine,
That I no more be visited. Ile endure
The strictest course of life that iealousie
Can thinke secure enough, ere my behauiour
Shall call my fame in question.
   Romont. Ten dissemblers
Are in this subtile deuill. You beleeue this?
   Rochfort. So farre that if you trouble me againe
With a report like this, I shall not onely
Iudge you malicious in your disposition,
But study to repent what I haue done
To such a nature.
   Romont. Why, 'tis exceeding well.
   Rochfort. And for you, daughter, off with this, off with it:
I haue that confidence in your goodnesse, I,
That I will not consent to haue you liue
Like to a Recluse in a cloyster: goe
Call in the gallants, let them make you merry,
Vse all fit liberty.
   Bellapert. Blessing on you.
If this new preacher with the sword and feather

272. Reprou'd] *Mason;* Reproue 32

Could proue his doctrine for Canonicall,
We should haue a fine world. *Exit* BELLAPERT.
 Rochfort.   Sir, if you please
To beare your selfe as fits a Gentleman,
The house is at your seruice: but if not,
Though you seeke company else where, your absence
Will not be much lamented— *Exit* ROCHFORT.
 Romont.   If this be
The recompence of striuing to preserue
A wanton gigglet honest, very shortly
'Twill make all mankinde Panders—Do you smile,
Good Lady Loosenes? your whole sex is like you,
And that man's mad that seekes to better any:
What new change haue you next?
 Beaumelle.   Oh, feare not you, sir,
Ile shift into a thousand, but I will
Conuert your heresie.
 Romont. What heresie? Speake.
 Beaumelle. Of keeping a Lady that is married,
From entertayning seruants.

  Enter NOVALL IUNIOR, MALOTIN, LILADAM, AYMER, PONTALIER.

      O, you are welcome.
Vse any meanes to vexe him,
And then with welcome follow me. *Exit* BEAUMELLE.
 Nouall Iunior.   You are tyr'd
With your graue exhortations, Collonell.
 Liladam. How is it? Fayth, your Lordship may doe well,
To helpe him to some Church-preferment: 'tis
Now the fashion, for men of all conditions,
How euer they haue liu'd, to end that way.
 Aymer. That face would doe well in a surplesse.
 Romont.   Rogues,
Be silent—or—
 Pontalier. S'death will you suffer this?
 Romont. And you, the master Rogue, the coward rascall,
I shall be with you suddenly.
 Nouall Iunior. *Pontallier,*
If I should strike him, I know I shall kill him:

And therefore I would haue thee beate him, for
Hee's good for nothing else.
   Liladam.   His backe
Appeares to me, as it would tire a Beadle,
And then he has a knotted brow, would bruise
A courtlike hand to touch it.
   Aymer.   Hee lookes like
A Curryer when his hides growne deare.
   Pontalier.   Take heede
He curry not some of you.
   Nouall Iunior.   Gods me, hee's angry.
   Romont. I breake no Iests, but I can breake my sword
About your pates.

           Enter CHARALOIS *and* BAUMONT.

   Liladam.   Heres more.
   Aymer.   Come let's bee gone.
Wee are beleaguerd.
   Nouall Iunior.   Looke they bring vp their troups.
   Pontalier. Will you sit downe with this disgrace?
You are abus'd most grosely.
   Lildam. I grant you, Sir, we are, and you would haue vs
Stay and be more abus'd.
   Nouall Iunior.   My Lord, I am sorry,
Your house is so inhospitable, we must quit it.   *Exeunt.*
                     Manent CHARALOIS, ROMONT.
   Charalois. Prethee *Romont*, what caus'd this vprore?
   Romont.   Nothing.
They laugh'd and vs'd their scuruy wits vpon mee.
   Charalois. Come, tis thy iealous nature: but I wonder
That you which are an honest man and worthy,
Should foster this suspition: no man laughes;
No one can whisper, but thou apprehend'st
His conference and his scorne reflects on thee:
For my part they should scoffe their thin wits out,
So I not heard 'em, beate me, not being there.
Leaue, leaue these fits, to conscious men, to such
As are obnoxious to those foolish things
As they can gibe at.
   Romont.   Well, Sir.

Charalois.   Thou art known
Valiant without defect, rightly defin'd,
Which is (as fearing to doe iniury,
As tender to endure it) not a brabbler,
A swearer.
  Romont. Pish, pish, what needs this my Lord?
If I bee knowne none such, how vainly, you
Do cast away good counsaile? I haue lou'd you,
And yet must freely speake: so young a tutor,
Fits not so old a Souldier as I am.
And I must tell you, t'was in your behalfe
I grew inraged thus, yet had rather dye,
Then open the great cause a syllable further.
  Charalois. In my behalfe? wherein hath *Charalois*
Vnfitly so demean'd himselfe, to giue
The least occasion to the loosest tongue,
To throw aspersions on him, or so weakely
Protected his owne honor, as it should
Need a defence from any but himselfe?
They are fooles that iudge me by my outward seeming;
Why should my gentlenesse beget abuse?
The Lion is not angry that does sleepe,
Nor euery man a Coward that can weepe.
For Gods sake speake the cause.
  Romont.   Not for the world.
Oh it will strike disease into your bones
Beyond the cure of physicke, drinke your blood,
Rob you of all your rest, contract your sight,
Leaue you no eyes but to see misery,
And of your owne, nor speach but to wish thus:
Would I had perish'd in the prisons iawes
From whence I was redeem'd! twill weare you old,
Before you haue experience in that Art,
That causes your affliction.
  Charalois.   Thou dost strike
A deathfull coldnesse to my harts high heate,
And shrinkst my liuer like the *Calenture*.
Declare this foe of mine, and lifes, that like

356. defect] *Coxeter;* detect *32*   rightly] *Coxeter;* right *32*   382. thus:] *after Coxeter;* ~∧ *32*

A man I may encounter and subdue it, 390
It shall not haue one such effect in mee,
As thou denouncest: with a Souldiers arme,
If it be strength, Ile meet it: if a fault
Belonging to my mind, Ile cut it off
With mine owne reason, as a Scholler should. 395
Speake, though it make mee monstrous.
  Romont.   Ile dye first.
Farewell, continue merry, and high Heauen
Keepe your wife chaste.
  Charalois.   Hump, stay and take this wolfe
Out of my brest, that thou hast lodg'd there, or
For euer lose mee.
  Romont.   Lose not, Sir, your selfe, 400
And I will venture—So the dore is fast. *Locke the dore.*
Now noble *Charaloys*, collect your selfe,
Summon your spirits, muster all the strength
That can belong to man, sift passion,
From euery veine, and whatsoeuer ensues, 405
Vpbraid not me heereafter, as the cause of
Iealousy, discontent, slaughter and ruine:
Make me not parent to sinne: you will know
This secret that I burne with.
  Charalois.   Diuell on't,
What should it be? *Romont*, I heard you wish 410
My wifes continuance of Chastity.
  Romont. There was no hurt in that.
  Charalois.   Why? do you know
A likelyhood or possibility
Vnto the contrarie?
  Romont. I know it not, but doubt it, these the grounds: 415
The seruant of your wife now, young *Nouall*,
The sonne vnto your fathers Enemy
(Which aggrauates my presumption the more)
I haue bin warnd of, touching her, nay, seene them
Tye heart to heart, one in anothers armes, 420
Multiplying kisses, as if they meant
To pose Arithmeticke, or whose eyes would
Bee first burnt out, with gazing on the others.

  403. the] *conj. McIlwraith*; you *32*; your *Coxeter* 410. heard] *Gifford*; heare *32*

I saw their mouthes engender, and their palmes
Glew'd, as if Loue had lockt them, their words flow   425
And melt each others, like two circling flames,
Where chastity, like a Phœnix (me thought) burn'd,
But left the world nor ashes, nor an heire.
Why stand you silent thus? what cold dull flegme,
As if you had no drop of choller mixt   430
In your whole constitution, thus preuailes,
To fix you now, thus stupid hearing this?
  Charalois. You did not see 'em on my Couch within,
Like George a horse-backe, on her, nor a bed?
  Romont. Noe.
  Charalois. 	Ha, ha.
  Romont. 		Laugh yee? eene so did your wife, 435
And her indulgent father.
  Charalois. 		They were wise.
Wouldst ha me be a foole?
  Romont. 		No, but a man.
  Charalois. There is no dramme of manhood to suspect,
On such thin ayrie circumstance as this,
Meere complement and courtship. Was this tale   440
The hydeous monster which you so conceal'd?
Away, thou curious impertinent
And idle searcher of such leane nice toyes.
Goe, thou sedicious sower of debate:
Fly to such matches, where the bridegroome doubts   445
He holdes not worth enough to counteruaile
The vertue and the beauty of his wife.
Thou buzzing drone that 'bout my eares dost hum,
To strike thy rankling sting into my heart,
Whose venom, time, nor medicine could asswage,   450
Thus doe I put thee off, and confident
In mine owne innocency, and desert,
Dare not conceiue her so vnreasonable,
To put *Nouall* in ballance against me,
An vpstart cran'd vp to the height he has.   455
Hence busiebody, thou'rt no friend to me,
That must be kept to a wiues iniury.
  Romont. Ist possible? farewell, fine, honest man,

433. 'em] *32*; him *Gifford*

Sweet temper'd Lord adieu: what Apoplexy
Hath knit sence vp? Is this *Romonts* reward?
Beare witnes the great spirit of thy father,
With what a healthfull hope I did administer
This potion that hath wrought so virulently,
I not accuse thy wife of act, but would
Preuent her præcipice, to thy dishonour,
Which now thy tardy sluggishnesse will admit.
Would I had seene thee grau'd with thy great Sire,
Ere liue to haue mens marginall fingers point
At *Charaloys*, as a lamented story.
An Emperour put away his wife for touching
Another man, but thou wouldst haue thine tasted
And keepe her (I thinke.) Puffe. I am a fire
To warme a dead man, that waste out my selfe.
Bleed—what a plague, a vengeance is't to mee,
If you will be a Cuckold? heere I shew
A swords point to thee, this side you may shun,
Or that, the perrill: if you will runne on,
I cannot helpe it.
    Charalois.   Didst thou neuer see me
Angry, *Romont*?
    Romont.   Yes, and pursue a foe
Like lightening.
    Charalois.   Prethee see me so no more.
I can be so againe. Put vp thy sword,
And take thy selfe away, lest I draw mine.
    Romont. Come fright your foes with this: sir, I am your friend,
And dare stand by you thus.
    Charalois.   Thou are not my friend,
Or being so, thou art mad; I must not buy
Thy friendship at this rate; had I iust cause,
Thou knowst I durst pursue such iniury
Through fire, ayre, water, earth, nay, were they all
Shuffled againe to *Chaos*; but ther's none.
Thy skill, *Romont*, consists in camps, not courts.
Farewell, vnciuill man, let's meet no more.
Heere our long web of friendship I vntwist.

461. thy] *Coxeter*; my *32*   462. I did] *Mason*; I *32*   477. that, the perrill:] *Coxeter*; that: the perrill, *32*

Shall I goe whine, walke pale, and locke my wife
For nothing, from her births free liberty,
That open'd mine to me? yes; if I doe,   495
The name of cuckold then, dog me with scorne.
I am a *Frenchman*, no *Italian* borne.   *Exit*.
  Romont. A dull *Dutch* rather; fall and coole (my blood)
Boyle not in zeale of thy friends hurt, so high,
That is so low, and cold himselfe in't. Woman,   500
How strong art thou, how easily beguild!
How thou dost racke vs by the very hornes!
Now wealth I see change manners and the man:
Something I must do mine owne wrath to asswage,   504
And note my friendship to an after-age.   *Exit*.

Actus quartus. Scæna prima.

Enter NOVALL IUNIOR, *as newly dressed, a* TAYLOR, BARBER,
PERFUMER, LILADAM, AYMER, PAGE. NOVALL *sits in a chaire,
Barber orders his haire, Perfumer giues powder, Taylor sets his clothes.*

  Nouall Iunior. MEND this a little: pox! thou hast burnt me. Oh fie
vpon't, O Lard, hee has made me smell (for all the world) like a
flaxe, or a red headed womans chamber: powder, powder, powder.
  Perfumer. O sweet Lord!
  Page. That's his Perfumer.   5
  Taylor. Oh deare Lord!
  Page. That's his Taylor.
  Nouall Iunior. Monsieur *Liladam*, *Aymour*, how allow you the
modell of these clothes?
  Aymer. Admirably, admirably, oh sweet Lord! assuredly it's pitty
the wormes should eate thee.   11
  Page. Here's a fine Cell; a Lord, a Taylor, a Perfumer, a Barber,
and a paire of *Mounsieurs*: 3 to 3, as little wit in the one, as honesty in
the other. S'foote ile into the country againe, learne to speake truth,
drinke Ale, and conuerse with my fathers Tenants; here I heare
nothing all day, but vpon my soule as I am a Gentleman, and an
honest man.   17

  IV. i. SD. NOVALL *sits ... clothes.*] *editor; at l. 5 in* 32   13. wit] *Coxeter*;
will *32*

Aymer. I vow and affirme, your Taylor must needs be an expert Geometrician, he has the Longitude, Latitude, Altitude, Profundity, euery Demension of your body, so exquisitely; here's a lace layd as directly, as if truth were a Taylor.

Page. That were a miracle.

Liladam. With a haire breadth's errour, ther's a shoulder piece cut, and the base of a pickadille in *puncto*.

Aymer. You are right, Mounsieur, his vestaments sit as if they grew vpon him, or art had wrought 'em on the same loome, as nature fram'd his Lordship: as if your Taylor were deepely read in Astrology, and had taken measure of your honourable body, with a *Iacobs* staffe, an *Ephimerides*.

Taylor. I am bound t'ee Gentlemen.

Page. You are deceiu'd, they'l be bound to you, you must remember to trust 'em none.

Nouall Iunior. Nay, fayth, thou art a reasonable neat Artificer, giue the diuell his due.

Page. I, if hee would but cut the coate according to the cloth still.

Nouall Iunior. I now want onely my mistres approbation, who is indeed, the most polite punctuall Queene of dressing in all *Burgundy*. Pah, and makes all other young Ladies appeare, as if they came from boord last weeke out of the country. Is't not true, *Liladam*?

Liladam. True my Lord, as if any thing your Lordship could say, could be otherwise then true.

Nouall Iunior. Nay, a my soule, 'tis so, what fouler obiect in the world, then to see a young faire, handsome beauty, vnhandsomely dighted and incongruently accoutred; or a hopefull *Cheualier*, vnmethodically appointed, in the externall ornaments of nature? For euen as the Index tels vs the contents of stories, and directs to the particular Chapters, euen so does the outward habit and superficiall order of garments (in man or woman) giue vs a tast of the spirit, and demonstratiuely poynt (as it were a manuall note from the margin) all the internall quality, and habiliment of the soule, and there cannot be a more euident, palpable, grosse manifestation of poore degenerate dunghilly blood, and breeding, then rude, vnpolish'd, disordered and slouenly outside.

Page. An admirable lecture. Oh all you gallants, that hope to be saued by your cloathes, edify, edify.

Aymer. By the Lard, sweet Lard, thou deseru'st a pension o'the State.

Page. Oth' Taylors, two such Lords were able to spread Taylors ore the face of a whole kingdome.

Nouall Iunior. Pox a this glasse! it flatters, I could find in my heart to breake it.

Page. O saue the glasse my Lord, and breake their heads, they are the greater flatterers I assure you.

Aymer. Flatters? detracts, impayres, yet put it by,
Lest thou deare Lord (*Narcissus*-like) should doate
Vpon thy selfe, and dye; and rob the world
Of natures copy, that she workes forme by.

Liladam. Oh that I were the Infanta Queene of Europe,
Who (but thy selfe sweete Lord) shouldst marry me?

Nouall Iunior. I marry? were there a Queene oth' world, not I.
Wedlocke? no, padlocke, horslocke, I weare spurrs   *He capers.*
To keepe it off my heeles; yet my *Aymour*,
Like a free wanton iennet i'th meddows,
I looke about, and neigh, take hedge and ditch,
Feed in my neighbours pastures, picke my choyce
Of all their faire-maind mares: but married once,
A man is stak'd, or pown'd, and cannot graze
Beyond his owne hedge.

Enter PONTALIER, *and* MALOTIN.

Pontalier.   I haue waited, sir,
Three houres to speake w'ee, and not take it well,
Such magpies, are admitted, whilst I daunce
Attendance.

Liladam. Magpies? what d'ee take me for?

Pontalier. A long thing with a most vnpromising face.

Aymer. I'll ne're aske him, what he takes me for?

Malotin.   Doe not, sir,
For hee'l goe neere to tell you.

Pontalier.   Art not thou
A Barber Surgeon?

Barber.   Yes sira, why?

Pontalier. My Lord is sorely troubled with two scabs.

Liladam. Aymer.   Humph——

Pontalier. I prethee cure him of 'em.

Nouall Iunior.   Pish: no more,

65. should] *32*; shouldst *Gifford*   69. shouldst] *32*; should *Coxeter*

Thy gall sure's ouerthrowne; these are my Councell,
And we were now in serious discourse.
    Pontalier. Of perfume and apparell. Can you rise   90
And spend 5 houres in dressing talke, with these?
    Nouall Iunior. Thou'ldst haue me be a dog: vp, stretch and shake,
And ready for all day.
    Pontalier.   Sir, would you be
More curious in preseruing of your honours
Trim, 'twere more manly. I am come to wake   95
Your reputation, from this lethargy
You let it sleepe in, to perswade, importune,
Nay, to prouoke you, sir, to call to account
This Collonell *Romont*, for the foule wrong
Which like a burthen, he hath layd on you,   100
And like a drunken porter, you sleepe vnder.
'Tis all the townes talke, and beleeue it, sir,
If your tough sence persist thus, you are vndone,
Vtterly lost, you will be scornd and baffled
By euery Lacquay; season now your youth,   105
With one braue thing, and it shall keep the odour
Euen to your death, beyond, and on your Tombe,
Sent like sweet oyles and Frankincense; sir, this life
Which once you sau'd, I ne're since counted mine,
I borrow'd it of you; and now will pay it;   110
I tender you the seruice of my sword
To beare your challenge, if you'l write: your fate
Ile make mine owne: what ere betide you, I
That haue liu'd by you, by your side will dye.
    Nouall Iunior. Ha, ha, would'st ha' me challenge poore *Romont*?
Fight with close breeches? thou mayst thinke I dare not.   116
Doe not mistake me (cooze) I am very valiant,
But valour shall not make me such an Asse.
What vse is there of valour (now a dayes?)
'Tis sure, or to be kill'd, or to be hang'd.   120
Fight thou as thy minde moues thee, 'tis thy trade,
Thou hast nothing else to doe; fight with *Romont*?
No, i'le not fight vnder a Lord.

    94–5. honours / Trim] *editor*; honour. / Trim *32*; honour / Trim *Coxeter*; honour trim, / *Gifford*   102. townes talke] *McIlwraith*; towne talkes *32*; town-talk *Coxeter* beleeue it]*Gifford*; beleeue *32*   112. write: your fate] *Mason*; write, your fate: *32*

Pontalier. Farewell, sir, I pitty you.
Such louing Lords walke, their dead honours graues,
For no companions fit, but fooles and knaues. 125
Come *Malotin*. *Exeunt* PONTALIER, MALOTIN.

Enter ROMONT.

Liladam. 'Sfoot, *Colbran*, the low gyant.
Aymer. He has brought a battaile in his face, let's goe.
Page. Colbran d'ee call him? hee'l make some of you smoake,
I beleeue.
Romont. By your leaue, sirs. 130
Aymer. Are you a Consort?
Romont. D'ee take me for
A fidler? y'are deceiu'd: looke. Ile pay you. *Kickes 'em.*
Page. It seemes he knows you one, he bumfiddles you so.
Liladam. Was there euer so base a fellow? 135
Aymer. A rascall!
Liladam. A most vnciuill Groome!
Aymer. Offer to kicke a Gentleman, in a Noblemans chamber?
A pox of your manners.
Liladam. Let him alone, let him alone, thou shalt lose thy aime,
fellow: if wee stirre against thee, hang vs. 141
Page. S'foote, I thinke they haue the better on him, though they
be kickd, they talke so.
Liladam. Let's leaue the mad Ape.
Nouall Iunior. Gentlemen. 145
Liladam. Nay, my Lord, we will not offer to dishonour you so
much as to stay by you, since hee's alone.
Nouall Iunior. Harke you.
Aymer. We doubt the cause, and will not disparage you, so much
as to take your Lordships quarrell in hand. Plague on him, how he
has crumpled our bands. 151
Page. Ile eene away with 'em, for this souldier beates man,
woman, and child. *Exeunt. Manent* NOVALL, ROMONT.
Nouall Iunior. What meane you, sir? My people!
Romont. Your boye's gone,
Lockes the door.
And the doore's lockt, yet for no hurt to you, 155

140. aime] *Mason*; arme *32* 155. the doore's] *editor*; doore's *32, Dunn*; your door's *Gifford*

But priuacy: call vp your blood againe, sir,
Be not affraid, I do beseech you, sir,
(And therefore come) without more circumstance
Tell me how farre the passages haue gone
'Twixt you, and your faire Mistresse *Beaumelle*. 160
Tell me the truth, and by my hope of Heauen
It neuer shall goe further.
   Nouall Iunior.   Tell you, why sir?
Are you my confessor?
   Romont. I will be your confounder, if you doe not.   *Drawes a*
Stirre not, nor spend your voyce.   *pocket dag.*
   Nouall Iunior.   What will you doe? 165
   Romont. Nothing but lyne your brayne-pan, sir, with lead,
If you not satisfie me suddenly,
I am desperate of my life, and command yours.
   Nouall Iunior. Hold, hold, ile speake. I vow to heauen and you,
Shee's yet vntouch't, more then her face and hands: 170
I cannot call her innocent; for I yeeld
On my sollicitous wooings she consented
Where time and place met oportunity
To grant me all requests.
   Romont.   But may I build
On this assurance?
   Nouall Iunior.   As vpon your fayth. 175
   Romont. Write this, sir, nay you must.
                               Drawes Inkehorne and paper.
   Nouall Iunior.   Pox of this Gunne.
   Romont. Withall, sir, you must sweare, and put your oath
Vnder your hand, (shake not) ne're to frequent
This Ladies company, nor euer send
Token, or message, or letter, to incline 180
This (too much prone already) yeelding Lady.
   Nouall Iunior. 'Tis done, sir,
   Romont.   Let me see, this first is right,
And here you wish a sudden death may light
Vpon your body, and hell take your soule,
If euer more you see her, but by chance, 185
Much lesse allure her. Now, my Lord, your hand.

   162. you,] *Coxeter* (~?); ~∧ *32*   172. wooings] *Symons*; wrongs *32*;
Wooing *Mason*

Nouall Iunior. My hand to this?
Romont. Your heart else I assure you.
Nouall Iunior. Nay, there 'tis.
Romont. So, keepe this last article
Of your fayth giuen, and stead of threatnings, sir,
The seruice of my sword and life is yours: 190
But not a word of it, 'tis Fairies treasure;
Which but reueal'd, brings on the blabbers, ruine.
Vse your youth better, and this excellent forme
Heauen hath bestowed vpon you. So good morrow to your Lordship.
Exit.
Nouall Iunior. Good diuell to your rogueship. No man's safe: 195
Ile haue a Cannon planted in my chamber,
Against such roaring roagues.

Enter BELLAPERT.

Bellapert. My Lord away,
The Coach stayes: now haue your wish, and iudge,
If I haue beene forgetfull.
Nouall Iunior. Ha?
Bellapert. D'ee stand
Humming and hawing now? *Exit.*
Nouall Iunior. Sweete wench, I come. 200
Hence feare,
I swore, that's all one, my next oath i'le keepe
That I did meane to breake, and then 'tis quit.
No paine is due to louers periury.
If *Ioue* himselfe laugh at it, so will I. *Exit* NOVALL.

Scæna 2.

Enter CHARALOIS, BAUMONT.

Baumont. I grieue for the distaste, though I haue manners,
Not to inquire the cause, falne out betweene
Your Lordship and *Romont*.
Charalois. I loue a friend,
So long as he continues in the bounds
Prescrib'd by friendship, but when he vsurpes 5

<small>194. *Exit.*] *Coxeter*; at l. 196 in 32   205. *Ioue*] *Coxeter*; loue 32</small>

Too farre on what is proper to my selfe,
And puts the habit of a Gouernor on,
I must and will preserue my liberty.
But speake of something else, this is a theame
I take no pleasure in: what's this *Aymeire*, 10
Whose voyce for Song, and excellent knowledge in
The chiefest parts of Musique, you bestow
Such prayses on?
    Baumont.   He is a Gentleman,
(For so his quality speakes him) well receiu'd
Among our greatest Gallants; but yet holds 15
His maine dependance from the young Lord *Nouall*:
Some trickes and crotchets he has in his head,
As all Musicians haue, and more of him
I dare not author: but when you haue heard him,
I may presume, your Lordship so will like him, 20
That you'l hereafter be a friend to Musique.
    Charalois. I neuer was an enemy to't, *Baumont*,
Nor yet doe I subscribe to the opinion
Of those old Captaines, that thought nothing musicall,
But cries of yeelding enemies, neighing of horses, 25
Clashing of armour, lowd shouts, drums, and trumpets:
Nor on the other side in fauour of it,
Affirme the world was made by musicall discord,
Or that the happinesse of our life consists
In a well varied note vpon the Lute: 30
I loue it to the worth of it, and no further.
But let vs see this wonder.
    Baumont.   He preuents
My calling of him.

                Enter AYMER.

    Aymer.   Let the Coach be brought
To the backe gate, and serue the banquet vp:
My good Lord *Charalois*, I thinke my house 35
Much honor'd in your presence.
    Charalois.   To haue meanes,
To know you better, sir, has brought me hither
A willing visitant, and you'l crowne my welcome
In making me a witnesse to your skill,

IV. ii. 40-66 　　　　　*The Fatal Dowry* 　　　　　　　　　71

Which crediting from others I admire. 　　　　　　　　　40
　Aymer. Had I beene one houre sooner made acquainted
With your intent my Lord, you should haue found me
Better prouided: now such as it is,
Pray you grace with your acceptance.
　Baumont. 　　　　　　　　You are modest.
　Aymer. Begin the last new ayre.
　Charalois. 　　　　　　　Shall we not see them? 　　45
　Aymer This little distance from the instruments
Will to your eares conuey the harmony
With more delight.
　Charalois. 　　Ile not contend.
　Aymer. 　　　　　　　　　Y'are tedious.
By this meanes shall I with one banquet please 　　　*[Aside.]*
Two companies, those within and these Guls heere. 　　50

　　　　　　Song aboue. Musique.
　　　　　Cittizens Song of the Courtier.
　　　　Courtier, if thou needs wilt wiue,
　　　　From this lesson learne to thriue.
　　　　If thou match a Lady, that
　　　　Passes thee in birth and state,
　　　　Let her curious garments be 　　　　　　　　55
　　　　Twice aboue thine owne degree;
　　　　This will draw great eyes vpon her,
　　　　Get her seruants and thee honour.

　Beaumelle (*within*). Ha, ha, ha. 　　　　　　　　　59
　Charalois. How's this? It is my Ladies laugh! most certaine!
When I first pleas'd her, in this merry language, 　　　*[Aside.]*
She gaue me thanks.
　Baumont. 　　How like you this?
　Charalois. 　　　　　　　　　　'Tis rare—
Yet I may be deceiu'd, and should be sorry 　　　　　*[Aside.]*
Vpon vncertaine suppositions, rashly
To write my selfe in the blacke list of those 　　　　　65
I haue declaym'd against, and to *Romont*.

　　IV. ii. 48. *Charalois*] *32 ; Beaumelle. conj. Gifford.* 　　contend] *Coxeter*; consent
32, Dunn 　　49. *Aside.] Symons; not in 32* 　　50-9. *Song aboue. . . . Ha, ha,
ha.] editor; Song aboue. | Musique and a Song, Beaumelle within—ha, ha, ha. 32*
60. *Aside.] Symons; not in 32* 　　63. *Aside.] Symons; not in 32*

Aymer. I would he were well of——Perhaps your Lordship
Likes not these sad tunes, I haue a new Song
Set to a lighter note, may please you better;
'Tis cal'd The happy husband.
  Charalois.   Pray sing it.   70

     Song below.
   Courtiers Song of the Citizen.

Poore Citizen, if thou wilt be
A happy husband, learne of me
To set thy wife first in thy shop,
A faire wife, a kinde wife, a sweet wife, sets a poore man vp.
What though thy shelues be ne're so bare: 75
A woman still is currant ware:
Each man will cheapen, foe, and friend,
But whilst thou art at tother end,
What ere thou seest, or what dost heare,
Foole, haue no eye to, nor an eare;   80
And after supper for her sake,
When thou hast fed, snort, though thou wake:
What though the Gallant call thee mome?
Yet with thy lanthorne light him home:
Then looke into the towne and tell,   85
If no such Tradesmen there doe dwell.
    At the end of the Song, BEAUMELLE *within.*

  Beaumelle. Ha, ha, 'tis such a groome.
  Charalois.   Doe I heare this,
And yet stand doubtfull?   *Exit* CHARALOIS.
  Aymer.   Stay him, I am vndone,
And they discouered.
  Baumont. Whats the matter?
  Aymer.   Ah!
That women, when they are well pleas'd, cannot hold, 90
But must laugh out.

Enter NOVALL IUNIOR, CHARALOIS, BEAUMELLE, BELLAPERT.

  Nouall Iunior. Help, saue me, murther, murther.
  Beaumelle. Vndone foreuer.

78. *whilst*] 32; *whistle Bodleian MS. Don. c. 57* 83. *Gallant*] Bodl. MS. Don. c. 57; *Gallants* 32 84. *him*] Bodl. MS. Don. c. 57; *her* 32

Charalois.   Oh, my heart!
Hold yet a little——Doe not hope to scape
By flight, it is impossible: though I might
On all aduantage take thy life, and iustly;
This sword, my fathers sword, that nere was drawne,
But to a noble purpose, shall not now
Doe th' office of a hangman, I reserue it
To right mine honour, not for a reuenge
So poore, that though with thee, it should cut off
Thy family, with all that are allyed
To thee in lust, or basenesse, 'twere still short of
All termes of satisfaction. Draw.
  Nouall Iunior.   I dare not,
I haue already done you too much wrong,
To fight in such a cause.
  Charalois.   Why, darest thou neyther
Be honest, coward, nor yet valiant, knaue?
In such a cause come doe not shame thy selfe:
Such whose bloods wrongs, or wrong done to themselues
Could neuer heate, are yet in the defence
Of their whores, daring; looke on her againe.
You thought her worth the hazard of your soule,
And yet stand doubtfull in her quarrell, to
Venture your body.
  Baumont.   No, he feares his cloaths,
More then his flesh.
  Charalois.   Keepe from me, garde thy life,
Or as thou hast liu'd like a goate, thou shalt
Dye like a sheepe.
  Nouall Iunior.   Since ther's no remedy
Despaire of safety now in me proue courage.
                        They fight, NOVALL *is slaine.*
  Charalois. How soone weak wrong's o'rthrowne! lend me your
Beare this to the Caroach—come, you haue taught me   hand,
To say you must and shall; I wrong you not,
Y'are but to keepe him company you loue.
                 [*They take out the body, then enter again.*]

117 SD. *They fight...*] Coxeter; *at l. 115 in 32*   121 SD. *They take... enter again.*] editor; *not in 32*; *Exeunt Beaumont and Bellapert, with the Body of Novall; followed by Beaumelle.* [at l. 119] *Re-enter* Beaumont. Gifford

Is't done? 'tis well. Raise officers, and take care,
All you can apprehend within the house
May be forth comming. Do I appeare much mou'd?
   Baumont. No, sir.
   Charalois.   My griefes are now, thus to be borne.   125
Hereafter ile finde time and place to mourne.   *Exeunt.*

Scæna 3.

Enter ROMONT, PONTALIER.

   Pontalier. I was bound to seeke you, sir.
   Romont.   And had you found me
In any place, but in the streete, I should
Haue done,—not talk'd to you. Are you the Captaine?
The hopefull *Pontalier*? whom I haue seene
Doe in the field such seruice, as then made you   5
Their enuy that commanded, here at home
To play the parasite to a gilded knaue,
And it may be the Pander?
   Pontalier.   Without this
I come to call you to account, for what
Is past already. I by your example   10
Of thankfulnesse to the dead Generall
By whom you were rais'd, haue practis'd to be so
To my good Lord *Nouall*, by whom I liue;
Whose least disgrace that is, or may be offred,
With all the hazzard of my life and fortunes,   15
I will make good on you, or any man,
That has a hand in't; and since you allowe me
A Gentleman and a souldier, there's no doubt
You will except against me. You shall meete
With a faire enemy, you vnderstand   20
The right I looke for, and must haue.
   Romont.   I doe,
And with the next dayes sunne you shall heare from me.
                                                              Exeunt.

Scæna 4.

Enter CHARALOIS *with a casket,* BEAUMELLE, BAUMONT.

Charalois. Pray beare this to my father, at his leasure
He may peruse it: but with your best language
Intreat his instant presence: you haue sworne
Not to reueale what I haue done.
   Baumont.   Nor will I—
But—
   Charalois. Doubt me not, by Heauen, I will doe nothing   5
But what may stand with honour: pray you leaue me
To my owne thoughts. [*Exit* BAUMONT.] If this be to me, rise;
I am not worthy the looking on, but onely
To feed contempt and scorne, and that from you
Who with the losse of your faire name haue caus'd it,   10
Were too much cruelty.
   Beaumelle.   I dare not moue you
To heare me speake. I know my fault is farre
Beyond qualification, or excuse,
That 'tis not fit for me to hope, or you
To thinke of mercy; onely I presume   15
To intreate, you would be pleas'd to looke vpon
My sorrow for it, and beleeue, these teares
Are the true children of my griefe and not
A womans cunning.
   Charalois.   Can you *Beaumelle*,
Hauing deceiued so great a trust as mine,   20
Though I were all credulity, hope againe
To get beleefe? no, no, if you looke on me
With pity or dare practise any meanes
To make my sufferings lesse, or giue iust cause
To all the world, to thinke what I must doe,   25
Was cal'd vpon by you, vse other waies:
Deny what I haue seene, or iustifie
What you haue done, and as you desperately
Made shipwracke of your fayth to be a whore,
Vse th' armes of such a one, and such defence,   30
And multiply the sinne, with impudence;

       IV. iv. 7 SD. *Exit* BAUMONT.] *Coxeter; not in* 32

Stand boldly vp, and tell me to my teeth,
You haue done but what's warranted,
By great examples, in all places, where
Women inhabit, vrge your owne deserts, 35
Or want in me of merit; tell me how,
Your dowre from the low gulfe of pouerty,
Weighd vp my fortunes, to what now they are:
That I was purchas'd by your choyse, and practise,
To shelter you from shame, that you might sinne 40
As boldly as securely: that poore men
Are married to those wiues that bring them wealth,
One day their husbands, but obseruers euer:
That when by this proud vsage you haue blowne
The fire of my iust vengeance to the height, 45
I then may kill you: and yet say 'twas done
In heate of blood, and after die my selfe,
To witnesse my repentance.
  Beaumelle.   O my fate,
That neuer would consent that I should see
How worthy thou wert both of loue and duty 50
Before I lost you; and my misery made
The glasse, in which I now behold your vertue:
While I was good, I was a part of you,
And of two, by the vertuous harmony
Of our faire mindes, made one: but since I wandred 55
In the forbidden Labyrinth of lust,
What was inseparable, is by me diuided.
With iustice therefore you may cut me off,
And from your memory, wash the remembrance
That ere I was, like to some vicious purpose 60
Within your better iudgement, you repent of
And study to forget.
  Charalois.   O Beaumelle,
That you can speake so well, and doe so ill!
But you had bin too great a blessing, if
You had continued chast: see how you force me 65
To this, because mine honour will not yeeld
That I againe should loue you.
  Beaumelle.   In this life

    36. in me of] *Coxeter;* of me in *32*

It is not fit you should: yet you shall finde,
Though I was bold enough to be a strumpet.
I dare not yet liue one: let those fam'd matrones
That are canoniz'd worthy of our sex,
Transcend me in their sanctity of life,
I yet will equall them in dying nobly,
Ambitious of no honour after life,
But that when I am dead, you will forgiue me.
  Charalois. How pity steales vpon me! should I heare her
But ten words more, I were lost—one knocks, go in. *Knock within.*
                                            Exit BEAUMELLE.
That to be mercifull should be a sinne!

Enter ROCHFORT.

O, sir, most welcome. Let me take your cloake,
I must not be denyed—here are your robes,
As you loue iustice once more put them on:
There is a cause to be determind of
That does require such an integrity,
As you haue euer vs'd—ile put you to
The tryall of your constancy, and goodnesse:
And looke that you that haue beene Eagle-eyd
In other mens affaires, proue not a Mole
In what concernes your selfe. Take you your seate:
I will be for you presently.   *Exit.*
  Rochfort.   Angels guard me,
To what strange Tragedy does this distraction
Serue for a Prologue?

Enter CHARALOIS [*and Attendants*] *with* NOVALL'S *body.*
BEAUMELLE, BAUMONT.

  Charalois.   So, set it downe before
The Iudgement seate, and stand you at the bar:
For me? I am the accuser.
  Rochfort.   *Nouall* slayne,
And *Beaumelle* my daughter in the place
Of one to be arraign'd!
  Charalois.   O, are you touch'd?
I finde that I must take another course.

    90. distraction] *Dunn, conj. McIlwraith;* destruction *32;* induction *conj. Mason*

Feare nothing. I will onely blinde your eyes,
For Iustice should do so, when 'tis to meete
An obiect that may sway her equall doome
From what it should be aim'd at.——Good my Lord,
A day of hearing.
    Rochfort.   It is granted, speake—
You shall haue iustice.
    Charalois.   I then here accuse,
Most equall Iudge, the prisoner your faire Daughter,
For whom I owed so much to you: your daughter,
So worthy in her owne parts: and that worth
Set forth by yours, to whose so rare perfections,
Truth witnesse with me, in the place of seruice
I almost pay'd Idolatrous sacrifice,
To be a false adultresse.
    Rochfort.   With whom?
    Charalois. With this *Nouall* here dead.
    Rochfort.   Be wel aduis'd
And ere you say adultresse againe,
Her fame depending on it, be most sure
That she is one.
    Charalois.   I tooke them in the act.
I know no proofe beyond it.
    Rochfort.   O my heart!
    Charalois. A Iudge should feele no passions.
    Rochfort.   Yet remember
He is a man, and cannot put off nature.
What answere makes the prisoner?
    Beaumelle.   I confesse
The fact I am charg'd with, and yeeld my selfe
Most miserably guilty.
    Rochfort.   Heauen take mercy
Vpon your soule then: it must leaue your body.
Now free mine eyes, I dare vnmou'd looke on her,
And fortifie my sentence, with strong reasons.
Since that the politique law prouides that seruants,
To whose care we commit our goods, shall die,
If they abuse our trust: what can you looke for,
To whose charge this most hopefull Lord gaue vp
All hee receiu'd from his braue Ancestors,

Or he could leaue to his posterity?—
His Honour, wicked woman, in whose safety
All this lifes ioyes, and comforts were locked vp,
Which thy lust, like a theefe hath now stolne from him,
And therefore——
   Charalois.   Stay, iust Iudge, may not what's lost
By her one fault, (for I am charitable,
And charge her not with many) be forgotten
In her faire life hereafter?
   Rochfort.   Neuer, Sir.
The wrong that's done to the chaste married bed,
Repentant teares can neuer expiate,
And be assured, to pardon such a sinne,
Is an offence as great as to commit it.
   Charalois. I may not then forgiue her?
   Rochfort.   Nor she hope it.
Nor can shee wish to liue; no sunne shall rise,
But ere it set, shall shew her vgly lust
In a new shape, and euery on more horrid:
Nay, euen those prayers, which with such humble feruor
She seemes to send vp yonder, are beate backe,
And all suites, which her penitence can proffer,
As soone as made, are with contempt throwne down
Off all the courts of mercy.
   Charalois.   Let her die then.   *He kils her.*
Better prepar'd I am sure I could not take her,
Nor she accuse her father, as a Iudge
Partiall against her.
   Beaumelle.   I approue his sentence,
And kisse the executioner: my lust
Is now run from me in that blood, in which
It was begot and nourished.
   Rochfort.   Is she dead then?
   Charalois. Yes, sir, this is her heart blood, is it not?
I thinke it be.
   Rochfort.   And you haue kild her?

---

131. Which] *Mason*; With *32*   lust, like a theefe] *McIlwraith*; lust, a theefe *32*;
hot *or* foul lust, a theefe *conj. Gifford*   133. one] *Mason*; owne *32*   147. throwne
down / Off] *editor*; throwne / Off *32*; throwne out / Of *Gifford*   148. *He kils her.*]
Coxeter; follows mercy. *in 32*

Charalois. True,
And did it by your doome.
   Rochfort. But I pronounc'd it
As a Iudge onely, and friend to iustice,
And zealous in defence of your wrong'd honour,
Broke all the tyes of nature, and cast off
The loue and soft affection of a father.
I in your cause, put on a Scarlet robe
Of red died cruelty, but in returne,
You haue aduanc'd for me no flag of mercy:
I look'd on you, as a wrong'd husband, but
You clos'd your eyes against me, as a father.
O *Beaumelle*, my daughter.
   Charalois. This is madnesse.
   Rochfort. Keep from me—could not one good thought rise up,
To tell you that she was my ages comfort,
Begot by a weake man, and borne a woman,
And could not therefore, but partake of frailety?
Or wherefore did not thankfulnesse step forth,
To vrge my many merits, which I may
Obiect vnto you, since you proue vngratefull,
Flinty-hearted *Charaloys*?
   Charalois. Nature does preuaile
Aboue your vertue.
   Rochfort. No: it giues me eyes,
To pierce the heart of the designe against me.
I finde it now, it was my state was aym'd at,
A nobler match was sought for, and the houres
I liu'd, grew teadious to you: my compassion
Towards you hath rendred me most miserable,
And foolish charity vndone my selfe:
But ther's a Heauen aboue, from whose iust wreake
No mists of policy can hide offendors.
   Nouall Senior [*within*]. Force ope the doors——

        Enter NOVALL SENIOR *with Officers.*

        O monster, caniball,
Lay hold on him, my sonne, my sonne.—O *Rochfort,*

   177. the designe] *McIlwraith*; designe *32*; your design *Coxeter*   185. [*within*]] *Gifford*; not in *32*   SD. Enter ... Officers] *Gifford*; at l. *184* in *32*

'Twas you gaue liberty to this bloody wolfe
To worry all our comforts,——But this is
No time to quarrell; now giue your assistance
For the reuenge.
  Rochfort. Call it a fitter name—
Iustice for innocent blood.
  Charalois.   Though all conspire
Against that life which I am weary of,
A little longer yet ile striue to keepe it,
To shew in spite of malice, and their lawes,
His plea must speed that hath an honest cause. *Exeunt.*

Actus quintus. Scæna prima.

Enter LILADAM, TAYLOR, OFFICERS.

 Liladam. WHY 'tis both most vnconscionable, and vntimely
T'arrest a gallant for his cloaths, before
He has worne them out: besides you sayd you ask'd
My name in my Lords bond but for forme onely,
And now you'l lay me vp for't. Do not thinke
The taking measure of a customer
By a brace of varlets, though I rather wait
Neuer so patiently, will proue a fashion
Which any Courtier or Innes of court man
Would follow willingly.
  Taylor.   There I beleeue you.
But sir, I must haue present moneys, or
Assurance to secure me, when I shall.——
Or I will see to your comming forth.
  Liladam.   Plague on't,
You haue prouided for my enterance in:
That comming forth you talke of, concernes me.
What shall I doe? you haue done me a disgrace
In the arrest, but more in giuing cause
To all the street, to thinke I cannot stand
Without these two supporters for my armes:
Pray you let them loose me: for their satisfaction
I will not run away.

    V. i. 4. forme] *Mason*; me 32

Taylor. For theirs you will not,
But for your owne you would; looke to him fellows.
　Liladam. Why doe you call them fellows? doe not wrong
Your reputation so; as you are meerely
A Taylor, faythfull, apt to beleeue in Gallants,
You are a companion at a ten crowne supper
For cloth of bodkin, and may with one Larke
Eate vp three manchets, and no man obserue you,
Or call your trade in question for't. But when
You study your debt-booke, and hold correspondence
With officers of the hanger, and leane swordmen,
The learned conclude, the Taylor and Sergeant
In the expression of a knaue or thief
To be *Synonima.* Looke therefore to it,
And let vs part in peace, I would be loth
You should vndoe your selfe.
　Taylor. To let you goe
Were the next way.

Enter OLD NOVALL, *and* PONTALIER.

But see! heeres your old Lord,
Let him but giue his word I shall be paide,
And you are free.
　Liladam. S'lid, I will put him to't:
I can be but denied: or what say you?
His Lordship owing me three times your debt,
If you arrest him at my suite, and let me
Goe run before to see the action entred.
'Twould be a witty iest.
　Taylor. I must haue ernest:
I cannot pay my debts so.
　Pontalier. Can your Lordship
Imagine, while I liue and weare a sword,
Your sonnes death shall be vnreueng'd?
　Nouall Senior. I know not
One reason why you should not doe like others:
I am sure, of all the herd that fed vpon him,

22. him] *Coxeter*; them *32*　　31. leane] *conj. Lockert*; leaue *32*　　33. or thief] *Mason*; are these *32*　　37 SD. *Enter . . .* PONTALIER] *editor ; at l. 36 in 32 ; after* your selfe *Coxeter*　　47. vnreueng'd] *Coxeter*; reueng'd *32*

I cannot see in any, now hee's gone,
In pitty or in thankfulnesse one true signe
Of sorrow for him.
   Pontalier.   All his bounties yet
Fell not in such vnthankefull ground: 'tis true
He had weakenesses, but such as few are free from,
And though none sooth'd them lesse then I—for now
To say that I foresaw the dangers that
Would rise from cherishing them, were but vntimely—
I yet could wish the iustice that you seeke for
In the reuenge, had bin trusted to me,
And not the vncertaine issue of the lawes:
'Tas rob'd me of a noble testimony
Of what I durst doe for him: but howeuer,
My forfait life redeem'd by him, though dead,
Shall doe him seruice.
   Nouall Senior.   As farre as my griefe
Will giue me leaue, I thanke you.
   Liladam.   Oh my Lord,
Oh my good Lord, deliuer me from these furies.
   Pontalier. Arrested? This is one of them whose base
And abiect flattery helpt to digge his graue:
He is not worth your pitty, nor my anger.
Goe to the basket and repent.
   Nouall Senior.   Away,
I onely know now to hate thee deadly:
I will doe nothing for thee.
   Liladam.   Nor you, Captaine?
   Pontalier. No, to your trade againe, put off this case,
It may be the discouering what you were,
When your vnfortunate master tooke you vp,
May moue compassion in your creditor.
Confesse the truth.   *Exit* NOVALL SENIOR, PONTALIER.
   Liladam.   And now I thinke on't better,
I will; brother, your hand, your hand, sweet brother.
I am of your sect, and my gallantry but a dreame,
Out of which these two fearefull apparitions
Against my will haue wak'd me. This rich sword
Grew suddenly out of a taylors bodkin;

      68. abiect] *Coxeter*; obiect *32*   71. know] *32*; know thee *Gifford*

These hangers from my vailes and fees in Hell:
And where as now this beauer sits, full often
A thrifty cap compos'd of broad cloth lists, 85
Nere kin vnto the cushion where I sate
Crosse-leg'd, and yet vngartred, hath beene seene;
Our breakefasts famous for the buttred loaues,
I haue with ioy bin oft acquainted with;
And therefore vse a conscience, though it be 90
Forbidden in our hall towards other men,
To me that as I haue beene, will againe
Be of the brotherhood.
   Officer.   I know him now:
He was a prentice to *Le Robe* at *Orleance.*
   Liladam. And from thence brought by my young Lord, now dead,
Vnto *Dijon,* and with him till this houre 96
Hath bin receiu'd here for a compleate Mounsieur.
Nor wonder at it: for but tythe our gallants,
Euen those of the first ranke, and you will finde
In euery ten, one: peraduenture two, 100
That smell ranke of the dancing schoole, or fiddle,
The pantofle or pressing yron: but hereafter
Weele talke of this. I will surrender vp
My suites againe: there cannot be much losse,
'Tis but the turning of the lace, with one 105
Addition more you know of, and what wants
I will worke out.
   Taylor.   Then here our quarrell ends.
The gallant is turn'd Taylor, and all friends.   *Exeunt.*

Scæna 2.

Enter ROMONT, BAUMONT.

   Romont. You haue them ready?
   Baumont.   Yes, and they will speake
Their knowledge in this cause, when thou thinkst fit
To haue them cal'd vpon.
   Romont.   'Tis well, and something
I can add to their euidence, to proue

85. cap] *Coxeter*; cape *32*   105-6. one / Addition] *Coxeter*; ones / Additions *32*

V. ii. 5–34　　　　　*The Fatal Dowry*　　　　　85

　　This braue reuenge, which they would haue cal'd murther,　　5
A noble Iustice.
　　Baumont.　　　In this you expresse
(The breach by my Lords want of you, new made vp)
A faythfull friend.
　　Romont.　　　　That friendship's rays'd on sand,
Which euery sudden gust of discontent,　　　　　　　　　　10
Or flowing of our passions can change,
As if it nere had bin: but doe you know
Who are to sit on him?
　　Baumont.　　　　　　　Mounsieur *Du Croy*
Assisted by *Charmi.*
　　Romont.　　　　The Aduocate
That pleaded for the Marshalls funerall,
And was checkt for it by *Nouall*?
　　Baumont.　　　　　　　　　The same.　　　　15
　　Romont. How fortunes that?
　　Baumont.　　　　　　　Why, sir, my Lord *Nouall*
Being the accuser, cannot be the Iudge,
Nor would grieu'd *Rochfort*, but Lord *Charaloys*
(How-euer he might wrong him by his power,)
Should haue an equall hearing.
　　Romont.　　　　　　　By my hopes　　　　20
Of *Charaloys* acquitall, I lament
That reuerent old mans fortune.
　　Baumont.　　　　　　　Had you seene him,
As to my griefe I haue, now promise patience,
And ere it was beleeu'd, though spake by him
That neuer brake his word, inrag'd againe　　　　　　　25
So far as to make warre vpon those haires,
Which not a barbarous Scythian durst presume
To touch, but with a superstitious feare,
As something sacred, and then curse his daughter,
But with more frequent violence himselfe,　　　　　　　30
As if he had bin guilty of her fault,
By being incredulous of your report,
You would not onely iudge him worthy pitty,
But suffer with him.

　　V. ii. 18. grieu'd] *Mason*; grieue *32*　　　23. haue, now promise] *Coxeter*; haue now promis'd *32*　　26. haires] *Coxeter*; heires *32*

Enter CHARALOIS, *with Officers.*

But heere comes the prisoner,
I dare not stay to doe my duty to him,
Yet rest assur'd, all possible meanes in me
To doe him seruice, keepes you company.
 Romont. It is not doubted.   *Exit* BAUMONT.
 Charalois.   Why, yet as I came hither,
The people, apt to mocke calamity,
And tread on the oppress'd, made no hornes at me,
Though they are too familiar I deserue them.
And knowing what blood my sword hath drunke
In wreake of that disgrace, they yet forbare
To shake their heads, or to reuile me for
A murtherer: they rather all put on
(As for great losses the old *Romans* vs'd)
A generall face of sorrow, waighted on
By a sad murmur breaking through their silence,
And no eye but was readier with a teare
To witnesse 'twas shed for me, then I could
Discerne a face made vp with scorne against me.
Why should I then, though for vnusuall wrongs
I chose vnusuall meanes to right those wrongs,
Condemne my selfe, as ouer-partiall
In my owne cause?——*Romont*!
 Romont.   Best friend, well met,
By my hearts loue to you, and ioyne to that,
My thankfulnesse that still liues to the dead,
I looke vpon you now with more true ioy,
Then when I saw you married.
 Charalois.   You haue reason
To giue you warrant for't; my falling off
From such a friendship with the scorne that answered
Your too propheticke counsell, may well moue you
To thinke, your meeting me going to my death,
A fit encounter for that hate which iustly
I haue deseru'd from you.
 Romont.   Shall I still then

38 SD. *Exit* BAUMONT.] *Symons*; *at l. 37 in 32*   41. familiar] *Mason*; ∼: *32*
55. cause?——*Romont*!] *Gifford*; cause *Romont*? *32*

Speake truth, and be ill vnderstood?
  Charalois.   You are not.
I am conscious, I haue wrong'd you, and allow me
Onely a morall man; to looke on you,
Whom foolishly I have abus'd and iniur'd,
Must of necessity be more terrible to me,   70
Then any death the Iudges can pronounce
From the tribunall which I am to plead at.
  Romont. Passion transports you.
  Charalois.   For what I haue done
To my false Lady, or *Nouall*, I can
Giue some apparent cause: but touching you,   75
In my defence, childlike, I can say nothing,
But I am sorry for't, a poore satisfaction:
And yet mistake me not: for it is more
Then I will speake, to haue my pardon sign'd
For all I stand accus'd of.
  Romont.   You much weaken   80
The strength of your good cause, should you but thinke
A man for doing well could entertaine
A pardon, were it offred: you haue giuen
To blinde and slow-pac'd iustice, wings, and eyes
To see and ouertake impieties,   85
Which from a cold proceeding had receiu'd
Indulgence or protection.
  Charalois.   Thinke you so?
  Romont. Vpon my soule; nor should the blood you chaleng'd
And tooke to cure your honour, breed more scruple
In your soft conscience, then if your sword   90
Had bin sheath'd in a Tygre, or she Beare,
That in their bowels would haue made your tombe.
To iniure innocence is more then murther:
But when inhumane lusts transforme vs, then
As beasts we are to suffer, not like men   95
To be lamented. Nor did *Charalois* euer
Performe an act so worthy the applause
Of a full theater of perfect men,
As he hath done in this: the glory got
By ouerthrowing outward enemies,   100

         88. chaleng'd] *Gifford*; chalenge 32

  Since strength and fortune are maine sharers in it,
We cannot but by pieces call our owne:
But when we conquer our intestine foes,
Our passions breed within vs, and of those
The most rebellious tyrant powerfull loue,   105
Our reason suffering vs to like no longer
Then the faire obiect being good deserues it,
That's a true victory, which, were great men
Ambitious to atchieue, by your example
Setting no price vpon the breach of fayth,   110
But losse of life, 'twould fright adultery
Out of their families, and make lust appeare
As lothsome to vs in the first consent,
As when 'tis wayted on by punishment.
  Charalois. You haue confirm'd me. Who would loue a woman 115
That might inioy in such a man, a friend?
You haue made me know the iustice of my cause,
And mark't me out the way, how to defend it.
  Romont. Continue to that resolution constant,
And you shall, in contempt of their worst malice,   120
Come off with honour. Heere they come.
  Charalois.   I am ready.

  Enter DU CROY, CHARMI, ROCHFORT, NOVALL SENIOR,
      PONTALIER, BAUMONT.

  Nouall Senior. See, equall Iudges, with what confidence
The cruell murtherer stands, as if he would
Outface the Court and Iustice!
  Rochfort.   But looke on him,
And you shall finde, for still methinks I doe,   125
Though guilt hath dide him black, something good in him,
That may perhaps worke with a wiser man
Then I haue beene, againe to set him free
And giue him all he has.
  Charmi.   This is not well.
I would you had liu'd so, my Lord, that I,   130
Might rather haue continu'd your poore seruant.
Then sit here as your Iudge.

  104. breed] *32*; bred *Coxeter*   121 SD. Enter...] *Gifford*; Scæna 3.
Enter... *32*

Du Croy. I am sorry for you.
 Rochfort. In no act of my life I haue deseru'd
This iniury from the court, that any heere
Should thus vnciuilly vsurpe on what
Is proper to me only.
 Du Croy.   What distaste
Receiues my Lord?
 Rochfort.   You say you are sorry for him:
A griefe in which I must not haue a partner:
'Tis I alone am sorry, that I rays'd
The building of my life for seuenty yeeres
Vpon so sure a ground, that all the vices
Practis'd to ruine man, though brought against me,
Could neuer vndermine, and, no way left
To send these gray haires to the graue with sorrow,
Vertue that was my patronesse, betrayd me:
For entring, nay, possessing this young man,
It lent him such a powerfull Maiesty
To grace what ere he vndertooke, that freely
I gaue my selfe vp with my liberty,
To be at his disposing; had his person,
Louely I must confesse, or far fam'd valour,
Or any other seeming good, that yet
Holds a neere neyghbour-hood with ill, wrought on me,
I might haue borne it better; but when goodnesse
And piety it selfe in her best figure
Were brib'd to my destruction, can you blame me,
Though I forget to suffer like a man,
Or rather act a woman?
 Baumont.   Good my Lord.
 Nouall Senior. You hinder our proceeding.
 Charmi.   And forget
The parts of an accuser.
 Baumont.   Pray you remember
To vse the temper which to me you promis'd.
 Rochfort. Angels themselues must breake, *Baumont*, that promise
Beyond the strength and patience of Angels.

---

139. that] *32*; that when *Gifford*   143. and,] *editor*; ~∧ *32*   144. sorrow,] *Gifford*; ~. *32*   151. fam'd] *Coxeter*; fain'd *32*   153. neyghbour-hood with ill,] *Coxeter*; neyghbour-hood, with ill ∧ *32*   156. my] *32²*; by *32¹*

But I haue done, my good Lord, pardon me
A weake old man, and pray adde to that 165
A miserable father, yet be carefull
That your compassion of my age, nor his,
Moue you to any thing, that may dis-become
The place on which you sit.
    Charmi.   Read the Inditement.
    Charalois. It shall be needelesse, I my selfe, my Lords, 170
Will be my owne accuser, and confesse
All they can charge me with, nor will I spare
To aggrauate that guilt with circumstance
They seeke to loade me with: onely I pray,
That as for them you will vouchsafe me hearing, 175
I may not be denide it for my selfe,
When I shall vrge by what vnanswerable reasons
I was compel'd to what I did, which yet
Till you haue taught me better, I repent not.
    Rochfort. The motion's honest.
    Charmi.   And 'tis freely granted. 180
    Charalois. Then I confesse my Lords, that I stood bound,
When with my friends, euen hope it selfe had left me,
To this mans charity for my liberty,
Nor did his bounty end there, but began:
For after my enlargment, cherishing 185
The good he did, he made me master of
His onely daughter, and his whole estate:
Great ties of thankfulnesse I must acknowledge,—
Could any one feed by you, presse this further?
But yet consider, my most honourd Lords, 190
If to receiue a fauour, make a seruant,
And benefits are bonds to tie the taker
To the imperious will of him that giues,
Ther's none but slaues will receiue courtesies,
Since they must fetter vs to our dishonours. 195
Can it be cal'd magnificence in a Prince,
To powre downe riches, with a liberall hand,
Vpon a poore mans wants, if that must bind him

    168. dis-become] *32²*; mis-become *32¹*   169. sit.] *Coxeter*; fit ‸ *32*   172. nor] *Coxeter*; or *32*   180. motion's] *Coxeter*; motion *32*   189. feed] *Mason*; freed *32*   194. courtesies] *Coxeter*; courtesie. *32*

To play the soothing parasite to his vices?
Or any man, because he sau'd my hand,
Presume my head and heart are at his seruice?
Or did I stand ingag'd to buy my freedome
(When my captiuity was honourable)
By making my selfe here and fame hereafter,
Bondslaues to mens scorne and calumnious tongues?
Had his faire daughters mind bin like her feature,
Or for some little blemish I had sought
For my content elsewhere, wasting on others
My body and her dowry; my forhead then
Deseru'd the brand of base ingratitude:
But if obsequious vsage, and faire warning
To keepe her worth my loue, could not preserue her
From being a whore, (and that no cunning one,
So to offend, and yet the fault kept from me)
What should I doe? let any freeborne spirit
Determine truly, if that thankfulnesse,
Choise forme, with the whole world giuen for a dowry,
Could strengthen so an honest man with patience,
As with a willing necke to vndergoe
The insupportable yoake of slaue or wittoll.
    Charmi. What proofe haue you she did play false, besides
Your oath?
    Charalois. Her owne confession to her father.
I aske him for a witnesse.
    Rochfort.   'Tis most true.
I would not willingly blend my last words
With an vntruth.
    Charalois.   And then to cleere my selfe,
That his great wealth was not the marke I shot at,
But that I held it, when faire *Beaumelle*
Fell from her vertue, like the fatall gold
Which *Brennus* tooke from *Delphos*, whose possession
Brought with it ruine to himselfe and Army,
Heer's one in Court, *Baumont*, by whom I sent
All graunts and writings backe, which made it mine,
Before his daughter dy'd by his owne sentence,

---

212. could not] *Coxeter*; could *32*   213. (and] *McIlwraith*; ˆ~ *32*   that] *McIlwraith*; yet *32*   214. me)] *McIlwraith*; ~? *32*

As freely as vnask'd he gaue it to me.
  Baumont. They are here to be seene.
  Charmi.   Open the casket.   235
Peruse that deed of gift.
  Romont.   Halfe of the danger
Already is discharg'd: the other part
As brauely, and you are not onely free,
But crownd with praise for euer.
  Du Croy.   'Tis apparent.
  Charmi. Your state, my Lord, againe is yours.
  Rochfort.   Not mine,   240
I am not of the world; if it can prosper,
(And yet being iustly got, Ile not examine
Why it should be so fatall) doe you bestow it
On pious vses. Ile goe seeke a graue.
And yet for proofe, I die in peace, your pardon   245
I aske, and as you grant it me, may Heauen,
Your conscience, and these Iudges free you from
What you are charg'd with. So farewell for euer.— *Exit* ROCHFORT.
  Nouall Senior. Ile be mine owne guide. Passion, nor example,
Shall be my leaders. I haue lost a sonne,   250
A sonne, graue Iudges, I require his blood
From his accursed homicide.
  Charmi.   What reply you
In your defence for this?
  Charalois.   I but attended
Your Lordships pleasure. For the fact, as of
The former, I confesse it, but with what   255
Base wrongs I was vnwillingly drawne to it,
To my few words there are some other proofes
To witnesse this for truth. When I was married,
For there I must begin, the slayne *Nouall*
Was to my wife, in way of our French courtship,   260
A most deuoted seruant, but yet aym'd at
Nothing but meanes to quench his wanton heate,
His heart being neuer warm'd by lawfull fires
As mine was (Lords:) and though on these presumptions,
Ioyn'd to the hate betweene his house and mine,   265
I might with opportunity and ease

242. yet] *32*; it *McIlwraith*

Haue found a way for my reuenge, I did not;
But still he had the freedome as before
When all was mine, and told that he abus'd it
With some vnseemely licence, by my friend, 270
My approu'd friend *Romont*, I gaue no credit
To the reporter, but reprou'd him for it,
As one vncourtly and malicious to him.
What could I more, my Lords? yet after this
He did continue in his first pursute 275
Hoter then euer, and at length obtaind it;
But how it came to my most certaine knowledge,
For the dignity of the court and my owne honour
I dare not say.
 Nouall Senior. If all may be beleeu'd
A passionate prisoner speakes, who is so foolish 280
That durst be wicked, that will appeare guilty?
No, my graue Lords: in his impunity
But giue example vnto iealous men
To cut the throats they hate, and they will neuer
Want matter or pretence for their bad ends. 285
 Charmi. You must finde other proofes to strengthen these
But meere presumptions.
 Du Croy.   Or we shall hardly
Allow your innocence.
 Charalois.   All your attempts
Shall fall on me, like brittle shafts on armor,
That breake themselues; or like waues against a rocke, 290
That leaue no signe of their ridiculous fury
But foame and splinters; my innocence like these
Shall stand triumphant, and your malice serue
But for a trumpet to proclaime my conquest;
Nor shall you, though you doe the worst fate can, 295
How ere condemne, affright an honest man.
 Romont. May it please the Court, I may be heard.
 Nouall Senior.   You come not
To raile againe? but doe, you shall not finde
Another *Rochfort*.
 Romont.   In *Nouall* I cannot.
But I come furnished with what will stop 300

287. meere] *32²*; more *32¹*

The mouth of his conspiracy against the life
Of innocent *Charaloys.* Doe you know this Character?
  Nouall Senior. Yes, 'tis my sonnes.
  Romont.   May it please your Lordships, reade it,
And you shall finde there, with what vehemency
He did sollicite *Beaumelle,* how he had got   305
A promise from her to inioy his wishes,
How after he abiur'd her company,
And yet, but that 'tis fit I spare the dead,
Like a damnd villaine, assoone as recorded,
He brake that oath; to make this manifest,   310
Produce his bawds and hers.
        Enter AYMER, FLORIMEL, BELLAPERT.
  Charmi.   Haue they tooke their oathes?
  Romont. They haue; and rather then indure the racke,
Confesse the time, the meeting, nay the act;
What would you more? onely this matron made
A free discouery to a good end;   315
And therefore I sue to the Court, she may not
Be plac'd in the blacke list of the delinquents.
  Pontalier. I see by this, *Nouals* reuenge needs me,
And I shall doe.
  Charmi.   'Tis euident.
  Nouall Senior.   That I
Till now was neuer wretched, here's no place   320
To curse him or my stars.   *Exit* NOVALL SENIOR.
  Charmi.   Lord *Charalois,*
The iniuries you haue sustain'd, appeare
So worthy of the mercy of the Court,
That notwithstanding you haue gone beyond
The letter of the Law, they yet acquit you.   325
  Pontalier. But in *Nouall,* I doe condemne him thus. [*Stabs him.*]
  Charalois. I am slayne.
  Romont.   Can I looke on? Oh murderous wretch,
Thy challenge now I answere. So die with him. [*Stabs* PONTALIER.]
  Charmi. A guard: disarme him.
  Romont.   I yeeld vp my sword
Vnforc'd. Oh *Charaloys.*

    311. bawds] *Coxeter*; bands *32*   326 SD. *Stabs him.*] *Coxeter; not in 32*
328 SD. *Stabs* PONTALIER.] *Coxeter; not in 32*

 Charalois.   For shame, *Romont*, 330
Mourne not for him that dies as he hath liu'd,
Still constant and vnmou'd: what's falne vpon me,
Is by Heauens will, because I made my selfe
A Iudge in my owne cause without their warrant:
But he that lets me know thus much in death, 335
With all good men forgiue mee.   [*Dies.*]
 Pontalier.   I receiue
The vengeance, which my loue, not built on vertue,
Has made me worthy, worthy of.   [*Dies.*]
 Charmi.   We are taught
By this sad president, how iust soeuer
Our reasons are to remedy our wrongs, 340
We are yet to leaue them to their will and power,
That to that purpose haue authority.
For you, *Romont*, although in your excuse
You may plead, what you did, was in reuenge
Of the dishonour done vnto the Court: 345
Yet since from vs you had not warrant for it,
We banish you the State: for these, they shall,
As they are found guilty, or innocent,
Be set free, or suffer punishment.   *Exeunt omnes.*

FINIS.

  336, 338. *Dies.*] *Coxeter; not in 32*
  349. Be] *32*; Or be *Coxeter*

APPENDIX A

VERSE REARRANGEMENT

Unless it is otherwise indicated, it is to be understood that the divisions noted below are not made in *32*.

I. i

46–7 euer / Hope] *Gifford*

93–4 these / Can] *Gifford*

103–4 patience— / Offer't] *Gifford*

136–7 as / The] *Gifford*

154–5 Rascals? / I] *Gifford*

I. ii

2–3 good / Of] *Gifford*

82–3 Sir / Practis'd] *Gifford*

85–6 cause / In] *Gifford*

186–7 fault / To] *Coxeter*

187–8 state / Sufficient] *Coxeter*

264–5 incourage / A] *Gifford*

279–80 then— / My] *Gifford*

288–9 you— / *Baumont*] *Gifford*

295–6 faulty— / What] *Gifford*

II. i

13–14 eight, / For] *Coxeter*

92–4 *rearranged by Gifford; 32 reads* No . . . Rogues, / Till . . . damn'd.

II. ii

126–8 *rearranged by Coxeter; 32 reads From . . . begat'st. / I . . . line, / Each*

201–2 Lord, / I] *Gifford*

282–3 such / Would] *Coxeter*

340–1 mony; / There] *McIlwraith*

III. i

3–4 Lord, / But] *Gifford*

37–8 tasted / The] *Gifford*

53–4 seruant, / Courting] *Gifford*

99–100 kisse, / And] *Gifford*

124–5 againe, / And] *Gifford*

150–1 base / That] *Gifford*

222–3 cunning / To] *Gifford*

241–2 *Romont*: / Would] *Coxeter*

260–1 *rearranged by Gifford; 32 reads* Now begin. / The

278–9 story / Begin] *Gifford*

324–5 Rogues, / Be] *Gifford*

334–5 heede / He] *Gifford*

412–13 know / A] *Coxeter*

IV. i

84–5 thou / A] *Gifford*

156–8 *rearranged by Coxeter; 32 reads* But priuacy . . . I do / Beseech . . . circumstance

174–5 build / On] *Coxeter*

IV. ii

32–3 preuents / My] *Gifford*

53–4 *that / Passes*] *McIlwraith*

86–7 this, / And] *Coxeter*

112–13 cloaths, / More] *Coxeter*

IV. iv

4–5 I— / But] *McIlwraith*

Appendix A

101–2	speake— / You] *Gifford*		V. ii
156–7	True, / And] *Gifford*	80–1	*rearranged by Coxeter; 32*
175–6	preuaile / Aboue] *Gifford*		*reads* You . . . cause, /
190–1	name— / Iustice] *Coxeter*		Should
		336–8	*rearranged by Coxeter; 32*
	V. i		*reads* I receiue . . . loue /
70–1	Away, / I] *Gifford*		Not . . . worthy of.

APPENDIX B (Music)

THE COURTIER'S SONG OF THE CITIZEN

Music for 'The Courtier's Song of the Citizen', or 'The Happy Husband' (IV. ii. 71–86), exists in Bodleian MS. Don. c. 57, among a collection of some 160 seventeenth-century songs (see the Commentary; note to IV. ii. 71–86). The setting appears on fols. 96^v, 97^r, and is written as a melody line for a bass singer, with an accompaniment in tablature notation; the composer may have been Robert Johnson. J. P. Cutts, who first identified the song, printed it in *La Musique de scène de la troupe de Shakespeare*, Paris, 1959, pp. 78–80, together with a realization of the tablature. The present edition has been prepared from a photostat of the Bodleian manuscript, and differs in several points from Cutts's transcription.

No time-signature or key-signature is supplied at the beginning of the original manuscript; at bar 32 there is a change to triple-time in minims, indicated by the signature C 3. It has not been thought necessary to introduce a modern key-signature, but an initial $\frac{4}{4}$ signature has been supplied, and the triple-time movement in minims has been halved and barred in $\frac{3}{4}$. Bars have been numbered for ease of reference. A plain realization of the tablature notation is given, with editorial emendations in square brackets.

The song-text is given exactly as in the manuscript, with one exception. In bars 37–40 the words are printed out in full, where the scribe indicated the five-fold repetition of the phrase 'no such' by using the sign :∥:.

poore Cit-ti-zen if yu wilt be a hap-py— hus-band
5
learne of me to set thy wife first in thy shop a
faire wife a sweet wife a kinde wife setts a

poore man up w^t though thy shelves be nere so bare a wo-man still is cur-rant ware all men will cheapen foe & friend but whistle y^u at th' oth-er end

20
wt ere yu seest or wt yu heare foole have no eye to
nor an eare & af-ter sup-per for her sake
25
wn yu hast fed snort snort though yu wake

30
wt though ye gallant call yee Mome yet wth yie lanthorne
light him home
Then looke in -
35
to the towne & tell if

Notes

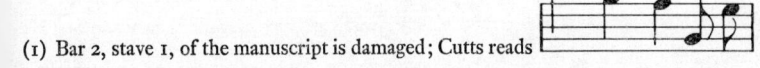

(1) Bar 2, stave 1, of the manuscript is damaged; Cutts reads

(2) On the third beat in bar 21, stave 1, the manuscript gives a G crochet, which is dissonant against the accompaniment and inconsistent with other instances of the same musical phrase.

(3) In bar 42, stave 3, the manuscript omits the required F♯ resolution of the previous chord.

(4) In the final bar, the original closes with a semibreve chord.

THE MAID OF HONOUR

INTRODUCTION

(a) *Date*

There is no firm evidence for the dating of *The Maid of Honour* except its publication in 1632. Malone, however, specifically said that it was 'not entered for the stage in Sir Henry Herbert's book'.[1] Bentley comments (iv. 798), 'Of course Malone may have missed the licence, or it may have been in a decayed part of the manuscript ... but the fact remains that *The Maid of Honour* is one of the very few plays which Malone ever says he did *not* find in Herbert's list of licences.' There is a good case, then, that *The Maid of Honour* is before 1622, when Herbert's Office Book (started by his predecessor, Sir John Astley) begins. We know from the title-page and from the list of plays protected by the Lord Chamberlain in 1639[2] that *The Maid of Honour* was a Phoenix play, and a date of 1621–2 would make it one of the series of his own plays which Massinger wrote for Beeston's companies at the Phoenix at the same time that he was collaborating with Fletcher for the King's men at the Blackfriars and the Globe.[3] The other plays, *The Bondman*, *The Renegado*, *The Parliament of Love*, and *A New Way to Pay Old Debts*, seem to belong to the period 1623–5. In its moral severity and its pronounced religious tone *The Maid of Honour* has kinship with both *The Bondman* and *The Renegado*. S. R. Gardiner and Eva Bryne have both attempted to use topical allusions to assist dating,[4] but the former finds 1631 indicated, and the latter 1623; their disagreement shows the vagueness of the parallels. The general situation of a king and a favourite concerned in the matter of intervention in a foreign war is not easily attached to a single historical episode. The impartiality

---

[1] *Variorum Shakespeare*, 1821, iii. 230; Adams, *Herbert*, p. 31.
[2] Bentley, i. 330–1.
[3] See General Introduction, vol. i, p. xxi.
[4] S. R. Gardiner, 'The Political Element in Massinger', New Shakespere Society's *Transactions*, 1875–6, pp. 326 ff.; E. A. W. Bryne, edition of *The Maid of Honour*, 1927, p. xxxv.

with which Massinger handles the motives and responses of the personalities, the expediency of the proposals, and the principles involved, make the idea that he was conducting political propaganda an absurdity.

Dated 1621-2, *The Maid of Honour* is with *The Duke of Milan* the earliest of Massinger's ventures in writing plays on his own.[1]

(b) *Source*

The source of *The Maid of Honour* was pointed out by Koeppel in 1897[2] as Boccaccio's story of Camiola and Roland as told by William Painter in the thirty-second novel of Tome II of his *Palace of Pleasure* (first published 1567).[3] The head-piece summary is as follows:

> A Gentlewoman and Wydow called Camiola of hir owne minde Raunsomed Roland the Kyng's Sonne of Sicilia, of purpose to haue him to hir Husband, who when he was redeemed vnkindly denied hir, agaynst whom very Eloquently, she Inueyed, and although the Law proued him to be hir Husband, yet for his vnkindnes, shee vtterly refused him.

Camiola lives in Messina and is 'an heyre of very great wealth and ritchesse'. A great army under Count John, containing 'many Barons and Gentlemen [who] willingly went vpon their own proper costes, and charges . . . onely for fame, and to be renoumed in armes', went to the aid of the people of Lippary, which was besieged by Godefroy. John's troops raised the siege, but in a pitched battle were defeated by Godefroy, who took many prisoners. One of these was Roland (who is now first introduced), the natural son of the late king. He 'not being redeemed, taried alone in prison very sorrowful to see all others discharged after they had payd their Raunsome and himselfe not to haue wherewith to furnish the same. For king Pietro . . . for that his warres had no better successe, and done contrary to his commaundement, conceyued displeasure so wel agaynst him, as all others which were at that battell'. Camiola is sorry for him and remembers the old king's kindness to her father; she resolves to set him at liberty, 'for the accomplishment whereof without preiudice to hir honour, she sawe none other wayes but take him to husband'. She sends a deputy, Roland happily accepts the terms, and the

---
[1] See the chronological table, vol. i, p. xxx.
[2] *Quellen-Studien*, pp. 121-4. [3] Ed. Jacobs, 1890, iii. 354-62.

ransom is paid. But when he gets back to Messina, he denies the contract. Summoned before a judge, however, he gives in. She makes a very long speech in which she says she assumes that he thought her ambitious for a husband of the royal blood, and that he despised her comparatively humble birth. In the end she says she will marry neither him nor anyone else. And he is so ashamed that he also remains unmarried.

The lack of motive in Painter's Camiola for acting as she does is astonishing. The previous love-relationship between her and Bertoldo, which Massinger adds, seems essential. Massinger's other additions are to make Bertoldo a Knight of Malta (to provide an extra reason for Camiola refusing to marry him in the first place, and an extra sign of his weakness in breaking his vow by making war upon a woman); and to provide, in Aurelia, some reason for his forgetting his contract with Camiola. Camiola's entrance into a religious life is also an addition, though in Painter Camiola's vow not to marry is called 'hir holy intent'.

Eva Bryne is right to suggest that the relationship between Helena and Bertram in Shakespeare's *All's Well That Ends Well* may have been in Massinger's mind as he wrote his play. She also notes resemblances between *The Maid of Honour* and themes and episodes in Massinger's collaborative plays, *The Double Marriage*, and *The Prophetess* in particular.[1]

(c) *Text*

The Maid of Honour was entered in the Stationers' Register on 16 January 1632:

M[r]. Waterson Iun'   Entred for his Copy vnder the hands of S[r] Henry Herbert & m[r] Islip warden a play called The maid of Honor by Phil: Messinger   vj[d].

(Register D 236; Greg, *Bibliography*, i. 40; Arber, iv. 270.)

Waterson did not publish the play, however; it appeared in the same year (1632), 'Printed by *I. B.* for *Robert Allot*'; this is the principal edition and will be referred to as *32* (see p. 117 for title-page); Greg, *Bibliography*, no. 470; ii. 619. As Greg remarks, since

---

[1] *The Maid of Honour*, ed. E. A. W. Bryne, 1927, p. xv. A further comparison of Massinger and Painter, besides those of Bryne and Koeppel, is that of K. Raebel, *Massinger's Drama 'The Maid of Honour' in seinem Verhältnis zu Painter's 'Palace of Pleasure'* . . ., Halle, 1901 [dissertation].

there is no reason to suppose that Allot's edition was surreptitious, 'Waterson probably made over the copy privately'. 'I. B.' (John Beale) printed also about this time Ford's *The Broken Heart* (1633), Mabbe's *The Spanish Bawd* (1631, also for Allot) and, again for Allot, the three plays dated 1631 which went into the second, 1640, volume of Jonson's *Works*: *Bartholomew Fair*, *The Devil is an Ass*, and *The Staple of News*. The ornamental head-piece to A1ᵛ in *32* may be seen again frequently in the Jonson plays, in *The Broken Heart* (A2ʳ) and in *The Spanish Bawd* (A6ʳ). The same ornamental headpiece precedes the text in both *32* and *The Broken Heart*.[1]

There are two issues of *32*, which we may call *32*(a) and *32*(b).

32(a) is in quarto, [A]², B–L⁴ (42 leaves). [A]² is misprinted B². K is wrongly perfected, running 1ʳ, 3ᵛ, 4ʳ, 2ᵛ, 3ʳ, 1ᵛ, 2ʳ, 4ᵛ. Five copies of *32*(a) are known. An error in perfecting (that is to say in completing a sheet by printing the four pages of the outer forme on the reverse side of the paper which already contains the four pages of the inner forme) may be caused by turning the sheet in the wrong way, or by placing the outer forme the wrong way on the bed of the press. In either error, the first recto of the sheet will be backed by the third instead of the first verso. It is evident that, with sheet K of *32*(a), the whole impression was perfected and the type for the sheet distributed before the error was discovered; it is more reasonable to suppose that the forme was put down wrong than that the sheets were incorrectly turned for the entire impression. The evidence that the error was not discovered until the type was distributed lies in the fact that sheet K of *32*(b) is, quite clearly, entirely reset; there are very many variant readings and changes in punctuation and type.[2]

32(b) then is as *32*(a) save that it holds a cancel for sheet K, whose pages now run in the correct order.

The contents are: [A]1ʳ, *title*; [A]1ᵛ, 'The Actors names.'; [A]2ʳ ('B2'), *dedication*, 'To my most honour'd friends, Sir FRANCIS FOLIAMBE, Knight, and Baronet, and to Sir THOMAS BLAND Knight.', *signed* '*Philip Massinger.*'; [A]2ᵛ, *verse epistle*, 'TO MY WORTHY FRIEND THE AVTHOR VPON HIS TRAGÆ-COMÆDY, THE MAID OF HONOVR.', *signed* 'ASTON COKAYNE.'; B1ʳ, *text*

---

[1] All these works are printed by 'I. B.' or 'J. B.'; but the identification of Beale is certain. McIlwraith noted that the *Maid of Honour* ornaments were to be found in Dilke's *Comfortable Sermons* (1635) printed by 'Iohn Beale'.

[2] Cf. A. K. McIlwraith, 'Some Bibliographical Notes on Massinger' *The Library*, 4th Series, xi (1930), 91–2.

Introduction

begins; L4ᵛ, *text ends*, '*The END*.'. The text is in roman, 20 lines measuring approximately 79 mm. The type is worn, and the impression of individual letters very often blurred.

Although the text of *The Maid of Honour* has been, on the whole, carefully and intelligently set up by the compositors, it is evident that their work was hampered by some strange irregularities in the printing house, of which the incorrect perfecting of K is the chief example. McIlwraith was able to distinguish the work of two compositors, α and β, and, though his account must be modified in certain ways, his main argument, establishing these two workmen and showing their stint to be a half-sheet (1–2ᵛ or 3–4ᵛ), still stands.[1]

The most obvious irregularities in *32*, after the errors of K, are (*a*) the variation in the number of lines to the page (from 35 to 39), and (*b*) the inconsistency in setting new speeches beginning with a half-line (sometimes printed continuously, sometimes given a new line in the way more usual with Massinger's plays). It seems evident that the copy was cast off by half-sheets, and so inaccurately cast off that the compositors were often forced to crowd as much as they could on to a page, or, (though this is rare) were left with too much space. Compositor α tried to solve his difficulties by printing new 'half-line' speeches continuously across the page; β by inserting an extra line to the page. While it is difficult to ascertain the order in which the pages in each sheet were composed, it is of interest that the 23 'crowded' pages (continuous speeches or extra lines) are as follows: in the inner formes, the crowded pages are 3ᵛ and 4ʳ on 8 of the 13 occasions, in the outer formes, the crowded pages are 3ʳ and 4ᵛ on 10 out of the 12 occasions.

The crowding gets worse towards the end of the play. Sheet B, as a comparison, is printed regularly with 36 lines to a page and with no continuous speeches. From H3 to I4ᵛ, 8 out of 12 pages are 37 lines to a page, in K and L 38 is normal, with 39 twice, and many 'continuous' speeches. If an initial calculation of 10 sheets had been made in casting off, it was evidently becoming more difficult to meet it.

McIlwraith's α and β were not, I believe, the only compositors; they were assisted by a third who may well be called γ. The press work of *32*(**a**) is from the beginning rather irregular: two skeletons were used through the inner and outer formes of sheets B, C, D as follows: 1, 2, 1, 2, 2, 1, 2. The inner forme of E is printed on 1, but

[1] Ibid., pp. 87–91.

for the outer forme, a new skeleton, 3, is used: the order for the remainder of the working running in this order. 3, 2, 1, 3, 1, 3, 2, 2, 3, 2, 3. Possibly for a time an extra press was brought in, but certainly there is every sign that the bringing in of an extra skeleton is coupled with the introduction of a third compositor in sheet E. Compositor γ began with misreadings of copy and misprints; 'Madiens' for 'Maidens' (II. ii. 173), 'magnious' for 'mignions' (174), 'pen-pence' for 'ten-pence' (185). The quantity of turned and omitted letters, faulty and omitted punctuation, rises steeply. It seems that γ was responsible for the greater part of E, and also for a large part of sheet H.

This matter of the compositors is not examined for the interest it has in itself, but for the light which I believe it sheds on the nature of the copy.

McIlwraith remarked on the different habits of compositors α and β in handling stage directions, especially punctuation between names and the use of italic and roman.[1] He found anomalies and exceptions, but they are wider than he thought and of course he did not take account of γ. Once the stints of those compositors are established,[2] one interesting feature of the stage-directions is observed to be common to all three compositors, namely a use of larger roman type used almost exclusively for information of a particularly theatrical kind. 'A Florish.' (I. i. 107) (β); 'The chambers discharg'd: A flourish, as to an assault', (II. iii) (γ); 'above.' (II. iv) (γ); 'A long charge[;] after[,] a Flourish for Victory.' (II. v) (γ); '. . . divers servants with presents:' (III. iii) (β); '. . . *Aurelia* (under a Canopie) *Astutio* presents her with letters, lowd musicke, shee reads the letters.' (IV. ii) (γ); '*Bertoldo* with a small booke in fetters, *Iaylor*.' (IV. iii) (γ); 'A Flourish.' (IV. iv) (α); 'At severall doores.' (IV. v) (α); 'Lowd Musicke . . . with Attendants.' (V. ii) (α).

There is one 'larger roman' direction by β at I. ii, '*Signior Sylli*. walking fantastically before . . .' which seems distinctly authorial

[1] A. K. McIlwraith, 'Some Bibliographical Notes on Massinger', *The Library*, 4th Series, xi (1930), 88–9.

[2] The tentative pattern is as follows:

	B	C	D	E	F	G	H	I	K	L
α	1–2^v	3–4^v	3–4^v	4–4^v	3–4^v	3–4^v	3–4	3–4^v	3–4^v	3–4^v
β	3–4^v	1–2^v	1–2^v		1–2^v	1–2^v		1–2^v	1–2^v	1–2^v
γ				1–3^v			1–2^v, 4^v			

and Massingerian. But it seems possible from the character of these directions, from the spread of their special type through the three compositors, from their greater frequency in the less discerning γ, together with a feeling of illogical order in, for example, 'presents her with letters, lowd musicke, shee reads the letters', that the compositors have (γ most of all) incorporated directions added to an author's manuscript to fit it for stage use, like the directions added to Massinger's autograph of *Believe As You List*. The bolder roman type may represent the bolder hand of the stage adapter. If we accept this, we may see a further theatre-insertion among the stage-directions at the close of IV. ii, though here the fount is italic. Gonzaga's 'Make way there.' is followed by '*Exeunt*.'; then, grouped in the margin is the additional direction, '*A Guard made: Aurelia. passes thorow 'em. lowd musicke.*

32 seems to be based on Massinger's own manuscript. His spellings are preserved in 'ghesse' (IV. v. 24; V. ii. 239); 'sclanders' (IV. v. 79); 'mistrisse' (II. v. 25; V. i. 109); 'mignions' (misprinted 'mignious') (II. ii. 174); 'waight' and 'waigh'd' (several times); 'alleage' (IV. iii. 36; V. ii. 181); 'battaile' (I. ii. 169); 'Affoord' (IV. v. 19). His characteristic 'ck' forms appear in 'Shrincke' (I. i. 218), 'twinckle' (I. ii. 49), 'truncks' (IV. iii. 104). There are also several examples of his conventional scene-headings in which the names of the characters appear divided by full stops without 'Enter'.

McIlwraith's collations revealed a large number of press-corrections; every forme has variants except inner E and F. Some of the changes are so radical as to suggest that (as can be shown from the corrections in other plays) Massinger was present in the printing house. For example, 'braines' is altered to 'beames' (I. i. 172); 'whole' to 'absolute' (I. i. 268); 'divine' to 'dimne' (I. ii. 164); 'gentleman' to 'gentlewoman' (II. ii. 39); 'butcher' to 'brother' (II. ii. 186); 'summon' to 'sounde' (III. i. 120). As McIlwraith remarks (Thesis, i. 187), the rejected reading is always self-evidently wrong and could have roused the attention of the printer's reader and caused him to consult the manuscript; but the likelier explanation is that the author himself spotted the errors.

A final point about the printing is that the compositors have adopted or been told to adopt the modern usage of v, u, j, i, but habit, perhaps, has led them often to keep the older form of common words, e.g. 'giue' and 'haue'. In the present text the clear intentions of the printer have been carried out, and the remnants of the consonantal 'u' and 'i' have been silently modernized.

Copies of *32*(a) are located at the Bodleian Library, Malone 178 (6) and Malone 236 (8); the Chapin Library, Williamstown; the Folger Shakespeare Library, and the Pierpont Morgan Library.

There are copies of *32*(b) at the following libraries and institutions: Bodleian Library (2 copies, Malone Q 21 and Malone Q 22); British Museum (3 copies); Cambridge University Library; University of Chicago; Christ Church, Oxford; Library of Congress; Folger Shakespeare Library; Guildhall Library, London; Harvard College Library (2 copies); Huntington Library; University of Illinois; King's College, Cambridge; University of Leeds; University of Liverpool; Merton College, Oxford; University of Michigan; Newberry Library; Ohio State University; University of Pennsylvania; Princeton University (3 copies); Royal Library, The Hague; Royal Library, Stockholm; John Rylands Library, Manchester; University of Sheffield; University of Texas (3 copies); Trinity College, Cambridge; Victoria and Albert Museum (3 copies); Wadham College, Oxford; Worcester College, Oxford; Yale University.

The text of the present edition has been prepared from the Bodleian Library copy of *32*(a), Malone 236 (8), with the pages of sheet K placed in the proper narrative order.

A copy of *32*(b), now in the Folger Library, formed one of the eight quartos bound up about 1632–3 in the Harbord volume (see General Introduction, p. xxxii). Massinger's corrections do not, however, extend to *The Maid of Honour*.

The play was not reprinted in the seventeenth century. Apart from appearing in the standard collected editions, *The Maid of Honour* was printed in expurgated form in *The Mirror of Taste* in Philadelphia in 1810 and in Harness's selection, 1830. The edition in Cumberland's *British Theatre* (?1831) is mentioned below under Stage-history. Dicks published the play in 1865 as volume v of *The British Drama: Illustrated*, and there is an undated later edition (?1883) in *Dicks' Standard Plays*. Symons included it in volume i of his Mermaid selection (1887), and L. A. Sherman in his *Masterpieces of English Drama* (New York, 1912). The fullest edition to date, with introduction and notes, was published in 1927 by Eva A. W. Bryne; it had been submitted for a Ph.D. at Bryn Mawr College. This edition is referred to in the text-notes as *Bryne*. In 1933,

Maurice Chelli's translation was published posthumously in Paris: *La Fille d'honneur* (Théâtre anglais de la renaissance); it is referred to as *Chelli*. A further French translation by P. Messiaen was published at Brussels in 1948.

(d) *Stage History*

As we have seen, the title page of the 1632 edition of *The Maid of Honour* states that it had been acted by the Queen's Majesty's servants (Queen Henrietta's Men) at the Phoenix in Drury Lane. This makes *The Maid of Honour* a Beeston play: which one of Beeston's companies originally performed it depends upon the date of its first production (see above); it might be either Prince Charles's Men or Lady Elizabeth's. The play is named with Massinger's other Beeston plays in the list of plays protected for the younger Beeston and his boys' company by the Lord Chamberlain in 1639 (Bentley, i. 330–1). It seems that *The Maid of Honour* may have remained in the repertory of successive companies at the Phoenix or Cockpit for about 18 years. But after 1639 there is a silence for 150 years. On 27 January, 1785, John Philip Kemble revived the play at the Theatre Royal, Drury Lane, apparently because of the opportunity that he thought the part of Camiola would give his sister, Mrs. Siddons.[1] The prologue praises Massinger's serious and moral strain, but the epilogue, by the elder Colman, is facetious:

> Yet sure Camiola thy Fate was hard
> Severe the Sentence of our Rigid Bard

and congratulates a modern age on the suits for breach of promise that maids of honour may bring. According to Boaden, Mrs. Siddons could not achieve the comic tone which the epilogue needed (how could she be expected to?). The revival was not a success: Genest said it ran for three nights.[2] Though Mrs. Siddons acted Camiola 'with grace and sweetness', says Boaden, he thought the part too declamatory for her. Kemble did his best as Adorni, and 'Bertoldo was a fine showy part for Palmer'. But, goes on Boaden, 'The audience, I remember, was cold to it—to the great bulk of them it must have been utterly unintelligible.' They were especially perplexed by Camiola's decision to enter a convent when she had

[1] James Boaden, *Memoirs of the Life of John Philip Kemble, Esq.*, 1825, i. 239.
[2] *Some Account of the English Stage*, vi. 335.

won back her lover (see D. J. Rulf's article in *Studies in Philology*, xlvi (1949), 54-69).

Kemble's version was never printed, but the manuscript submitted for the Lord Chamberlain's approval is now in the Huntington Library with the Larpent plays (number 687). The play is much shortened; most of the speeches are at least partly rewritten; scenes are transposed or even omitted. The most striking change is that Sylli's part is cut out altogether,[1] and Adorni's part as Bertoldo's rival is much increased. An attempt is made to avoid the surprise of Camiola's marriage-bargain when she sends the ransom. To elevate her sufferings when told of Bertoldo's betrayal, she is allowed some of Aspatia's famous lines from *The Maid's Tragedy*:

> And the trees about me
> Let them be dry and leafless, let the Rocks
> Groan with continual Surges, and behind me
> Make all a Desolation.

On 31 October of the same year, 1785, 'Messrs. Austin and Whitlock's Company of Comedians' presented *The Maid of Honour* in a season at Chester ('never acted here'); Mrs. Whitlock was Camiola, and the Bertoldo was G. F. Cooke (later a notable Overreach).[2]

In 1830 Fanny Kemble was reading Massinger in the Family Library, which for some reason she supposed 'my friend the Reverend Alexander Dyce' had edited. 'I was so enchanted with these plays . . . but more especially with the one called "The Maid of Honour", that I never rested till I had obtained from the management its revival on the stage. The part of Camiola is the only one that I ever selected for myself.'[3] George Daniel wrote enthusiastically about the consequent revival at Covent Garden in 1831. 'The representation . . . was beheld with deep interest—the audience honoured *themselves* by their applause. Miss Kemble, in Camiola, added another wreath to her brow; and Mr. [Charles] Kemble, in Bertoldo, acted with great effect. The coxcomb, Sylli, found an appropriate representative in Mr Keeley: he fluttered round the Maid of Honour like a gaudy butterfly. . .'.[4] Fanny Kemble herself said that the production 'succeeded on its first representation, but failed to attract audiences.'[5] Both *The Morning Chronicle* and *The*

---

[1] This was not known to Genest who tries to name an actor for the part.
[2] See M. St. Clare Byrne, *Theatre Notebook*, xv (1960), 23.
[3] Frances A. Kemble, *Records of a Girlhood*, 1878, ii. 117-18.
[4] *The Maid of Honour* (Cumberland), 1831, p. 7.   [5] Op. cit.

Literary Gazette were critical of the play itself, the latter remarking that Aurelia's passion for Bertoldo 'revolts all our present notions of feminine propriety' (see D. J. Rulf's essay cited above). Cumberland's text of the play, 'printed from the Acting Copy, with Remarks, Biographical and Critical, by D—— G.', is adorned with a steel engraving of Keeley as Sylli, notes on costumes, and the cast-list. The text is a shortened version of Massinger's text, possibly taken from Harness's Family Library edition, with some of the scenes renumbered.

Nicoll cites *Maid of Honour* licensed by the Lord Chamberlain on 10 October 1841, and produced at the Adelphi theatre on 25 October.[1] This was not Massinger's as is made clear by a press-cutting in the Enthoven collection at the Victoria and Albert Museum. At least three other dramatic efforts of the nineteenth century bore the same title.

[1] *History of English Drama*, iv. 499.

THE MAID OF HONOVR.

AS IT HATH BEENE OFTEN PRESENTED

with good allowance at the *Phœnix* in DRVRIE-LANE, by the Queenes Majesties SERVANTS.

Written by PHILIP MASSINGER.

LONDON,
Printed by I. B. for *Robert Allot*, and are to be sold at his Shop at the signe of the blacke Beare in *Pauls* Church-yard, 1632.

The Actors names.

Roberto,	King of *Sicilie*.
Ferdinand,	Duke of *Vrbin*.
Bertoldo,	The Kings naturall brother, a knight of *Malta*.
Gonzaga,	A knight of *Malta*, General to the Duchesse of *Siena*.
Astutio,	A counsellor of state.
Fulgentio,	The mignion of *Roberto*.
Adorni,	A follower of *Camiolas* father.
Embassador,	From the Duke of *Urbin*.
Signior Sylli,	A foolish selfe-lover.
Anthonio, *Gasparo*, }	Two rich heyres, Citty-bred.
Pierio,	A Colonel to *Gonzaga*.
Roderigo, *Iacomo*, }	Captaines to *Gonzaga*.
Druso, *Livio*, }	Captaines to Duke *Ferdinand*.
Paulo,	A priest, *Camiolas* confessor.
Scout,	
Souldiers,	
Servants,	
[*Bishop*,]	
Jaylor,	
Dwarfe,	
Mutes,	
Aurelia,	Duchesse of *Siena*.
Camiola,	The Maid of Honour.
Clarinda,	Her woman.

22. Bishop,] *after Gifford; not in* 32.

To my most honour'd friends, Sir FRANCIS FOLIAMBE, Knight, and Baronet, and to Sir THOMAS BLAND Knight.

THAT you have beene, and continued so for many yeeres (since you vouchsafed to owne me) Patrons to me and my despised studies, I cannot but with all humble thankefulnesse acknowledge: And living, as you have done, inseparable in your friendship (notwithstanding all differences, and suites in Law arising betweene you) I held it as impertinent, as absurd, in the presentment of my service in this kinde, to divide you. A free confession of a debt in a meaner man, is the amplest satisfaction to his superiours, and I heartily wish, that the world may take notice, and from my selfe, that I had not to this time subsisted, but that I was supported by your frequent courtesies, and favours. When your more serious occasions will give you leave, you may please to peruse this trifle, and peradventure find somthing in it that may appeare worthy of your protection. Receive it, I beseech you, as a testimony of his duty, who, while he lives, resolves to be

Truly, and sincerely devoted
to your service,

Philip Massinger.

TO
MY WORTHY FRIEND
THE AUTHOR UPON
HIS TRAGÆ-COMÆDY,
THE MAID OF HONOUR.

Was not thy Emperor *enough before*
For thee to give, that thou dost give vs more?
I would be just, but cannot: that I know
I did not slander, this I feare I doe.
But pardon mee, if I offend: Thy fire   5
Let equall Poets praise, while I admire.
If any say that I enough have writ,
They are thy foes, and envy at thy wit.
Believe not them, nor mee, they know thy lines
Deserve applause, but speake against their mindes.   10
I, out of iustice, would commend thy Play,
But (friend forgive mee) 'tis above my way.
One word, and I have done (and from my heart
Would I could speake the whole truth, not the part):
Because 'tis thine, it henceforth will be said,   15
Not the Maid of Honour, but the Honour'd Maid.
ASTON COKAYNE.

The Maide of Honour

A Tragæ-Comedy

Act I. Secne I.

ASTUTIO. ADORNI.

Adorni. Good day to your Lordship.
Astutio. Thanks *Adorni.*
Adorni. May I presume to aske if the Embassador
Imploy'd by *Ferdinand*, the Duke of *Urbin*,
Hath audience this morning?

Enter FULGENTIO.

Astutio. 'Tis uncertaine,
For though a counsaylor of state, I am not
Of the Cabinet counsaile. But ther's one if he please
That may resolve you.
Adorni. I will move him Sir.
Fulgentio. If you have a suite, shew water, I am blinde else.
Adorni. A suite, yet of a nature, not to prove
The quarrie that you hawke for: if your words
Are not like Indian wares, and every scruple
To be waigh'd and rated, one poore sillable
Vouchsaf'd in answer of a faire demand,
Cannot deserve a fee.
Fulgentio. It seemes you are ignorant,
I neither speake, nor hold my peace for nothing;
And yet for once, I care not if I answer
One single question, *gratis*.
Adorni. I much thanke you.
Hath the Embassador audience Sir to day?
Fulgentio. Yes.
Adorni. At what houre?

Fulgentio. I promis'd not so much.
A sillable you begg'd, my Charity gave it.
Move me no further. *Exit* FULGENTIO.
   Astutio. This you wonder at?
With me 'tis usuall.
   Adorni. Pray you Sir, what is he?
   Astutio. A Gentleman, yet no lord. He hath some drops
Of the Kings blood running in his veines, deriv'd
Some ten degrees off. His revenue lyes
In a narrow compasse, the Kings eare, and yeelds him
Every houre a fruitfull harvest. Men may talke
Of three croppes in a yeare in the fortunate Islands,
Or profit made by wooll. But while there are sutors,
His sheepe sheering, nay shaving to the quicke
Is in every quarter of the Moone, and constant;
In the time of trussing a point, he can undoe
Or make a man. His play or recreation
Is to raise this up, or pull downe that, and though
He never yet tooke orders, makes more Bishops
In Sicilie, then the Pope himselfe.

   Enter BERTOLDO, GASPARO, ANTHONIO, *a Servant.*

   Adorni. Most strange!
   Astutio. The presence fils. He in the Malta habit
Is the naturall brother of the King, a byblow.
   Adorni. I understand you.
   Gasparo. Morrow to my Uncle.
   Anthonio. And my late Guardian. But at length I have
The reines in my owne hands.
   Astutio. Pray you use 'em well,
Or you'll too late repent it.
   Bertoldo. With this Jewell
Presented to *Camiola*, prepare
This night a visit for me. I shall have *Exit Servant.*
Your company Gallants I perceive, if that
The King will heare of war.
   Anthonio. Sir, I have horses
Of the best breed in Naples, fitter far
To breake a ranke, then cracke a lance, and are
In their carere of such incredible swiftnes

They out-strip swallowes.
Bertoldo. And such may bee usefull
To run away with, should we be defeated.
You are well provided Signior.
Anthonio. Sir, excuse me.
All of their race by instinct know a Coward,
And scorne the burthen. They come on like lightning,
Founder'd in a retreat.
Bertoldo. By no meanes backe 'em,
Unlesse you know your courage sympathize
With the daring of your horse.
Anthonio. My lord, this is bitter.
Gasparo. I will rayse me a company of foote,
And when at push of pike I am to enter
A breach, to shew my valour, I have bought mee
An armor cannon proofe.
Bertoldo. You will not leape then
Ore an out-worke in your shirt?
Gasparo. I do not like
Activity that way.
Bertoldo. You had rather stand
A marke to try their muskets on?
Gasparo. If I doe
No good, I'll doe no hurt.
Bertoldo. 'Tis in you Signior
A Christian resolution, and becomes you,
But I will not discourage you.
Anthonio. You are Sir
A knight of Malta, and as I have heard,
Have serv'd against the Turke.
Bertoldo. 'Tis true.
Anthonio. Pray you shew us
The difference betweene the city valour,
And service in the field.
Bertoldo. 'Tis somewhat more
Then roaring in a taverne, or a brothell,
Or to steale a Constable from a sleeping watch;
Then burne their halberds; or safe guarded by
Your tenants sonnes, to carry away a Maypole
From a neighbour village; you will not finde there

Your Masters of Dependencies to take up
A drunken brawle, or to get you the names
Of valiant Cheivaleirs, fellowes that will bee
For a cloake with thrice died velvet, and a cast suite   80
Kick'd down the stairs. A knave with halfe a britch there,
And no shirt (being a thing superfluous,
And worne out of his memorie) if you beare not
Your selves both in, and upright, with a provant sword
Will slash your skarlets, and your plush a new way;   85
Or with the hilts thunder about your eares
Such musicke as will make your worships dance
To the dolefull tune of *Lachrymæ*.
   Gasparo.   I must tell you,
In private, as you are my princely friend,
I doe not like such Fidlers.
   Bertoldo.   No? they are usefull   90
For your initiation; I remember you
When you came first to the Court, and talkt of nothing
But your rents, and your entradas; ever chiming
The golden bells in your pockets, you believ'd
The taking of the wall, as a tribute due to   95
Your gaudy clothes; and could not walke at mid-night
Without a causelesse quarrell, as if men
Of courser outsides were in duty bound
To suffer your affronts: but when you had beene
Cudgell'd well, twice or thrice, and from the doctrine   100
Made profitable uses, you concluded
The soveraigne meanes to teach irregular heyres
Civility, with conformity of manners,
Were two or three sound beatings.
   Anthonio.   I confesse
They did much good upon mee.
   Gasparo.   And on mee—   105
The principles that they read were sound.
   Bertoldo.   You'll finde
The like instructions in the Campe.
   Astutio.   The King.

I. i. 84. upright,] *Gifford*; ~ ∧ *32*   88. *Lachrymæ.*] *Gifford*; Lachryma, *32*
91. initiation] *Mason*; imitation *32*   93. your] *Coxeter*; you *32*   105-6. mee—/ The] *Gifford*; undivided *32*

A Florish.

Enter ROBERTO, FULGENTIO, EMBASSADOR, *Attendants.*

Roberto. Wee sit prepar'd to heare.
   Embassador.   Your Majesty
Hath beene long since familiar, I doubt not,
With the desperate fortunes of my Lord, and pitty
Of the much that your confederate hath suffer'd
(You being his last refuge) may perswade you
Not alone to compassionate, but to lend
Your royall aydes to stay him in his fall
To certaine ruine. Hee too late is conscious,
That his ambition to incroach upon
His neighbours territories, with the danger of
His liberty, nay his life, hath brought in question
His owne inheritance: but youth and heat
Of blood, in your interpretation, may
Both plead, and mediate for him. I must grant it
An error in him, being deni'd the favours
Of the faire Princesse of *Siena* (though
He sought her in a noble way) t'endeavour
To force affection, by surprisall of
Her principall seat *Siena.*
   Roberto.   Which now proves
The seat of his captivity, not triumph.
Heaven is still just.
   Embassador.   And yet that justice is
To be with mercy temper'd, which heav'ns Deputies
Stand bound to minister. The injur'd Duchesse
By reason taught, as nature, could not with
The reparation of her wrongs, but aime at
A brave revenge, and my Lord feeles too late
That innocence will finde friends. The great *Gonzaga,*
The honor of his Order (I must praise
Vertue, though in an enemy) hee whose fights
And conquests hold one number, rallying up
Her scatter'd troopes, before wee could get time
To victuall, or to man the conquer'd City,

135–6. (I . . . enemy) hee] *after Coxeter*; , I . . . enemy. Hee 32

Sate downe before it, and presuming that 140
'Tis not to be releev'd, admits no parley,
Our flags of truce hung out in vaine, nor will hee
Lend an eare to composition, but exacts
With the rendring up the towne, the goods, and lives
Of all within the walls, and of all Sexes 145
To be at his discretion.
  Roberto.   Since injustice
In your Duke, meets this correction, can you presse us
With any seeming argument of reason,
In foolish pitty to decline his dangers,
To draw 'em on our selfe? Shall we not be 150
Warn'd by his harmes? The league proclaim'd between us,
Bound neither of us farther then to ayde
Each other, if by forraigne force invaded,
And so farre in my honour I was tied.
But since without our counsell, or allowance, 155
He hath tooke armes, with his good leave, he must
Excuse us, if wee steere not on a rocke
We see, and may avoyd. Let other Monarchs
Contend to be made glorious by proud warre,
And with the blood of their poore subjects purchase 160
Increase of Empire, and augment their cares
In keeping that which was by wrongs extorted;
Guilding unjust invasions with the trimne
Of glorious conquests; wee that would be knowne
The father of our people in our study, 165
And vigilance for their safety, must not change
Their plough-shares into swords, or force them from
The secure shade of their owne vines to be
Scorch'd with the flames of warre, or for our sport
Expose their lives to ruine.
  Embassador.   Will you then 170
In his extremity forsake your friend?
  Roberto. No, but preserve our selfe.
  Bertoldo.   Cannot the beames
Of honour thaw your icie feares?
  Roberto.   Who's that?
  Bertoldo. A kinde of brother, Sir, how e'er your subject,

172. beames] *32²*; braines *32¹*

Your father's Sonne, and one who blushes that
You are not heire to his brave spirit, and vigour,
As to his Kingdome.
   Roberto.   How's this?
   Bertoldo.   Sir, to be
His living Chronicle, and to speake his praise
Cannot deserve your anger.
   Roberto.   Where's your warrant
For this presumption?
   Bertoldo.   Here, Sir, in my heart.
Let Sycophants, that feed upon your favours,
Stile coldnesse in you caution, and preferre
Your ease before your honour; and conclude
To eate and sleepe supinely, is the end
Of humane blessings: I must tell you Sir,
Vertue, if not in action, is a vice,
And when wee move not forward, we goe backeward;
Nor is this peace (the nurse of drones, and cowards)
Our health, but a disease.
   Gasparo.   Wel urg'd my Lord.
   Anthonio. Perfit what is so well begunne.
   Embassador.   And binde,
My Lord, your servant.
   Roberto.   Hare-braind foole! what reason
Canst thou inferre to make this good?
   Bertoldo.   A thousand
Not to be contradicted. But consider
Where your command lies? 'Tis not, Sir, in *France*,
Spaine, *Germany*, *Portugall*, but in *Sicilie*,
An Island, Sir. Here are no mines of gold,
Or silver to enrich you, no worme spinnes
Silke in her wombe to make distinction
Betweene you, and a Peasant, in your habits.
No fish lives neere our shores, who's blood can dy
Scarlet, or purple; all that wee possesse
With beasts, wee have in common: Nature did
Designe us to be warriours, and to breake through
Our ring the sea, by which we are inviron'd;
And we by force must fetch in what is wanting,
Or precious to us. Adde to this, wee are

A populous nation, and increase so fast,
Cr That if we by our providence, are not sent
Abroad in colonies, or fall by the sword,
Not *Sicilie* (though now, it were more fruitfull,　　　210
Then when 'twas stil'd the granary of great *Rome*)
Can yeeld our numerous frie bread, we must starve,
Or eat up one another.
  Adorni.   The King heares
With much attention.
  Astutio.   And seemes mov'd with what
Bertoldo hath deliver'd.
  Bertoldo.   May you live long, Sir,　　　215
The King of peace, so you deny not us
The glory of the warre; let not our nerves
Shrincke up with sloth, nor for want of imployment
Make younger brothers theves; 'tis their swordes, Sir,
Must sow and reape their harvest; if examples　　　220
May move you more then arguments, looke on *England*,
The Empresse of the European Isles,
And unto whom alone ours yeelds precedence;
When did she flourish so, as when she was
The Mistress of the Ocean, her navies　　　225
Putting a girdle round about the world;
When the *Iberian* quak'd, her worthies nam'd;
And the faire flowre Deluce grew pale, set by
The red Rose and the white? Let not our armour
Hung up, or our unrig'd *Armada* make us　　　230
Ridiculous to the late poore snakes our neighbours
Warm'd in our bosomes, and to whom againe
We may be terrible: while wee spend our houres
Without variety, confinde to drinke,
Dice, Cards, or whores. Rowze us, Sir, from the sleepe　　　235
Of idlenesse, and redeeme our morgag'd honours.
Your birth, and justly, claimes my fathers Kingdome;
But his Heroique minde descends to mee,
I will confirme so much.
  Adorni.   In his lookes he seemes
Cr^v To breake ope *Janus* Temple.

  219. swordes] *32*²; sworde *32*¹ 225. Ocean,] *Gifford*; ~. *32* 229. white?] *Gifford*; ~: *32*

I. i. 240-70   *The Maid of Honour*   129

 Astutio.   How these younglings   240
Take fire from him!
 Adorni.   It works an alteration
Upon the King.
 Anthonio. I can forbeare no longer:
Warre, warre, my Soveraigne.
 Fulgentio.   The King appeares
Resolv'd, and does prepare to speake.
 Roberto.   Thinke not
Our counsel's built upon so weake a base,   245
As to be overturn'd, or shaken with
Tempestuous windes of words. As I, my Lord,
Before resolv'd you, I will not ingage
My person in this quarrell; neyther presse
My Subjects to maintaine it: yet to shew   250
My rule is gentle, and that I have feeling
Of your Masters sufferings, since these Gallants weary
Of the happinesse of peace, desire to taste
The bitter sweets of warre, wee doe consent
That as Adventurers, and Voluntiers   255
(No way compell'd by us) they may make tryall
Of their boasted valours.
 Bertoldo.   Wee desire no more.
 Roberto. 'Tis well, and but my grant in this, expect not
Assistance from mee. Governe as you please
The Province you make choice of, for I vow   260
By all things sacred, if that thou miscarry
In this rash undertaking, I will heare it
No otherwise then as a sad disaster,
Falne on a stranger: nor will I esteeme
That man my Subject, who in thy extremes   265
In purse or person ayds thee. Take your fortune:
You know mee, I have said it. So my Lord
You have my absolute answer.
 Embassador.   My Prince payes
In me his duty.
 Roberto. Follow me, *Fulgentio,*
And you, *Astutio.*
     Exeunt ROBERTO, FULGENTIO, ASTUTIO, *Attendants.*

255. Adventurers] *Coxeter*; Adventures *32* 268 absolute] *32²*; whole *32¹*

130   *The Maid of Honour*   I. i. 270–ii. 18

 Gasparo.   What a frowne he threw   270
At his departure, on you.
 Bertoldo.   Let him keepe
His smiles for his state Catamite, I care not.
 Anthonio. Shall wee aboord to night?
 Embassador.   Your speed, my Lord,
Doubles the benefit.
 Bertoldo.   I have a businesse   274
Requires dispatch, some two houres hence I'll meet you. *Exeunt.*

[I. ii]
      Act I. Scene II.

SIGNIOR SYLLI, *walking fantastically before, followed
by* CAMIOLA *and* CLARINDA.

 Camiola. Nay *Signior*, this is too much ceremony
In my owne house.
 Sylli.   What's gratious abroad,
Must be in private practis'd.
 Clarinda.   For your mirth-sake
Let him alone, he has beene all this morning
In practice with a perugd Gentleman usher,   5
To teach him his true amble and his postures,
When he walkes before a Lady.
       SYLLI *walking by, and practising his postures.*
 Sylli.   You may, Madame,
Perhaps, beleeve that I in this use art,
To make you dote upon mee by exposing
My more then most rare features to your view.   10
But I as I have ever done, deale simply,
A marke of sweet simplicity ever noted
I' the family of the *Syllies*. Therefore Lady,
Looke not with too much contemplation on mee,
If you doe, you are i' the suds.
 Camiola.   You are no Barber?   15
 Sylli. Fie no, not I, but my good parts have drawne
More loving hearts out of faire Ladies bellies,
Then the whole trade have done teeth.
 Camiola.   Is't possible?

  I. ii. 2–3. abroad, / Must] *Coxeter*; *undivided* 32   6. amble] 32²; Camble 32¹

Sylli. Yes, and they live too, marry much condoling
The scorne of their *Narcissus*, as they call mee,
Because I love my selfe.
 Camiola. Without a rivall;
What philtres or love-powders doe you use
To force affection? I see nothing in
Your person, but I dare looke on, yet keepe
My owne poore heart still.
 Sylli. You are warn'd, be arm'd,
And doe not lose the hope of such a husband
In being too soone enamour'd.
 Clarinda. Hold in your head,
Or you must have a martingale.
 Sylli. I have sworne
Never to take a wife, but such a one
(O may your Ladiship prove so strong) as can
Hold out a moneth against mee.
 Camiola. Never feare it,
Though your best taking part, your wealth, were trebl'd
I would not wooe you. But since in your pitty
You please to give me caution, tell me what
Temptations I must flye from?
 Sylli. The first is
That you never heare mee sing, for I am a *Syren*.
If you observe, when I warble, the dogs howle
As ravish'd with my Ditties, and you will
Runne mad to heare mee.
 Camiola. I will stop my eares,
And keepe my little wits.
 Sylli. Next when I dance
And come aloft thus, cast not a sheepes eye
Upon the quivering of my calfe.
 Camiola. Proceed, Sir.
 Sylli. But on no termes, for 'tis a maine point, dreame not
Of the strength of my back, though it will beare a burthen
With any porter.
 Camiola. I meane not to ride you.
 Sylli. Nor I your little Ladiship, 'till you have

36. Syren] *Coxeter*; Syri 32 38. Ditties] *Coxeter*; D tties 32 46. *Sylli.*]
Coxeter; Cam. 32

Perform'd the Covenants. Be not taken with
My prettie spider fingers, nor my eyes,
That twinckle on both sides.
    Camiola.   Was there ever such   *One knocks.*
A piece of motlie heard of! who's that? you may spare
The Catalogue of my dangers.   *Exit* CLARINDA.
    Sylli.   No good Madam,
I have not told you halfe.
    Camiola.   Enough good Signior,
If I eate more of such sweete meats, I shall surfet.

                Enter CLARINDA.

Who is't?
    Clarinda. The brother of the King.
    Sylli.   Nay start not,
The brother of the King! is he no more?
Were it the King himselfe, I'll give him leave
To speake his mind to you, for I am not jealous,
And to assure your Ladyship of so much,
I'll usher him in, and that done, hide my selfe.   *Exit* SYLLI.
    Camiola. Camiola if ever, now be constant:
This is indeed a sutor, whose sweet presence,
Courtship and loving language would have stagger'd
The chast *Penelope.* And to increase
The wonder, did not modestie forbid it,
I should aske that from him, he sues to me for;
And yet my reason like a tyran, tells me
I must nor give, nor take it.

           Enter SYLLI, *and* BERTOLDO.

    Sylli.   I must tell you
You loose your labour. 'Tis enough to prove it,
Signior Sylli came before you, and you know
First come first serv'd; yet you shall have my countenance
To parley with her and I'l take speciall care
That none shal interrupt you.
    Bertoldo.   You are courteous.
    Sylli. Come wench wilt thou heare wisedome?
    Clarinda.   Yes from you Sir.   *Steps aside.*
    Bertoldo. If forcing this sweet favour from your lips *Kisseth her.*

        60. constant:] *Coxeter;* ~∧ 32

Faire Madam, argue me of too much boldnesse,
When you are pleas'd to understand, I take
A parting kisse, if not excuse, at least
'Twill qualifie the offence.
  Camiola.   A parting kisse Sir?
What Nation envious of the happinesse
Which *Sicilie* enjoyes in your sweet presence,
Can buy you from her? or what Climate yeeld
Pleasures transcending those which you injoy here,
Being both belov'd and honor'd, the North-star
And guider of all hearts, and to summe up
Your full accompt of happinesse in a word,
The brother of the King?
  Bertoldo.   Doe you alone,
And with an unexampl'd cruelty,
Inforce my absence, and deprive me of
Those blessings, which you with a polish'd phrase
Seeme to insinuate, that I doe possesse,
And yet tax me as being guilty of
My wilfull exile? what are Titles to me?
Or popular suffrage? or my neerenesse to
The King in blood? or fruitfull *Sicilie*,
Though it confess'd no Soveraigne but my selfe,
When you that are the essence of my being,
The anchor of my hopes; the reall substance
Of my felicity, in your disdaine
Turne all to fading and deceiving shaddowes?
  Camiola. You tax me without cause.
  Bertoldo.   You must confesse it.
But answer love with love, and seale the contract
In the uniting of our soules, how gladly
(Though now I were in action, and assur'd,
Following my fortune, that plum'd victory
Would make her glorious stand upon my tent)
Would I put off my armour, in my heate
Of conquest, and like *Anthonie* pursue
My *Cleopatra*! will you yet looke on me
With an eye of Favour?
  Camiola.   Truth beare witnesse for me,
That in the Judgement of my Soule, you are

A man so absolute, and circular
In all those wish'd-for rarities, that may take
A Virgin captive, that though at this instant
All sceptr'd Monarches of our Westerne world
Were rivalls with you, and *Camiola* worthy 115
Of such a competition, you alone
Should weare the ghirlond.
   Bertoldo.   If so, what diverts
Your Favour from me?
   Camiola.   No mulct in your selfe,
Or in your person, mind or fortune.
   Bertoldo.   What then?
   Camiola. The Consciousnesse of mine owne wants. Alas Sir, 120
We are not parallells, but like lines divided
Can nere meete in one Centre. Your Birth Sir
(Without addition) were an ample Dowrie
For one of fairer Fortunes, and this shape,
Were you ignoble, far above all value; 125
To this, so cleare a mind, so furnish'd with
Harmonious faculties, moulded from heaven,
That though you were *Thersites* in your features,
Of no descent, and *Irus* in your fortunes,
Ulisses like you would force all eyes, and eares 130
To love, but seene, and when heard, wonder at
Your matchlesse story. But all these bound up
Together in one Volume, give me leave
With admiration to looke upon 'em,
But not presume in my owne flattering hopes, 135
I may or can injoy 'em.
   Bertoldo.   How you ruine
What you would seeme to build up. I know no
Disparitie betweene us, you are an heyre
Sprung from a noble familie, faire, rich, young,
And every way my equall.
   Camiola.   Sir excuse me, 140
One aerie with proportion, nere discloses
The eagle and the wren: tissue, and freese
In the same garment monstrous: But suppose
That what's in you excessive, were diminish'd,
And my desert supply'd, the strongest bar, 145

Religion stops our Entrance, you are Sir
A Knight of Malta, by your order bound
To a single life, you cannot marrie me,
And I assure my selfe you are too noble
To seek me (though my frailtie should consent)   150
In a base path.
   Bertoldo.   A dispensation Lady
Will easiely absolve me.
   Camiola.   O take heed Sir,
When, what is vow'd to heaven, is dispens'd with,
To serve our ends on earth, a curse must follow,
And not a blessing.
   Bertoldo.   Is there no hope left me?   155
   Camiola. Nor to my selfe, but is a neighbour to
Impossibility: true love should walke
On equall feete, in us it does not Sir.
But rest assur'd, excepting this, I shall be
Devoted to your service.
   Bertoldo.   And this is your   160
Determinate sentence?
   Camiola.   Not to be revok'd.
   Bertoldo. Farewell then fairest cruell. All thoughts in me
Of Women perish. Let the glorious light
Of noble war extinguish loves dimne taper
That onely lends me light to see my follie;   165
Honor, be thou my everliving Mistresse,
And fond affection as thy bond-slave serve thee. *Exit* BERTOLDO.
   Camiola. How soone my Sun is set, he being absent,
Never to rise againe! what a fierce battaile
Is fought betweene my passions! me thinkes   170
We should have kiss'd at parting.
   Sylli.   I perceive
He has his answer, now must I step in
To comfort her; you have found, I hope, sweet Lady,
Some difference betweene a youth of my pitch,
And this bug-beare *Bertoldo*, men are men,   175
The Kings brother is no more: good parts will doe it,
When Titles faile, despaire not, I may be
In time intreated.

            164. dimne] *32²*; divine *32¹*

Camiola.   Be so now to leave mee,
Lights for my chamber, O my heart!
                              Exeunt CAMIOLA, *and* CLARINDA.
    Sylli.   She now
I know is going to bed to ruminate   180
Which way to glut her selfe upon my person,
But for my oath-sake I will keepe her hungry,
And to grow full my selfe, I'll straight to supper.   *Exit.*

            The end of the first Act.

Act II. Scene I.

ROBERTO, FULGENTIO, ASTUTIO.

Roberto. EMBARQU'D tonight doe you say?
Fulgentio.   I saw him aboord, Sir,
Roberto. And without taking of his leave?
Astutio.   'Twas strange!
Roberto. Are we growne so contemptible?
Fulgentio.   'Tis far
From me Sir, to adde fuell to your anger,
That in your ill opinion of him, burnes   5
Too hot already, else I should affirme
It was a grosse neglect.
    Roberto.   A wilfull scorne
Of duty and alleageance, you give it
Too faire a name. But we shall think on't: can you
Guesse what the numbers were that follow'd him   10
In his desperate action?
    Fulgentio.   More then you thinke, Sir.
All ill affected spirits in *Palermo*,
Or to your government, or person, with
The turbulent sword-men, such whose poverty forc'd 'em
To wish a change, are gone along with him,   15
Creatures devoted to his undertakings
In right or wrong, and to expresse their zeale,
And readinesse to serve him, ere they went

II. i. 3–4. far / From] *Gifford*; *undivided* 32   11. Fulgentio.] *Coxeter*;
Roberto. 32

Prophanely tooke the sacrament on their knees,
To live and dye with him.
 Roberto.   O most impious!
Their loyalty to us forgot?
 Fulgentio.   I feare so.
 Astutio. Unthankfull as they are.
 Fulgentio.   Yet this deserves not
One troubled thought in you, Sir, with your pardon,
I hold that their remove from hence makes more
For your security, then danger.
 Roberto.   True;
And as I'll fashion it, they shall feele it too.
Astutio, you shall presently be dispatch'd
With letters writ, and sign'd with our owne hand,
To the Duchesse of *Siena*, in excuse
Of these forces sent against her. If you spare
An oath to give it credit, that, wee never
Consented to it, swearing for the King,
Though false, it is no perjury.
 Astutio.   I know it.
They are not fit to be state agents, Sir,
That without scruple of their conscience, cannot
Be prodigall in such trifles.
 Fulgentio.   Right, *Astutio*.
 Roberto. You must beside from us take some instructions
To be imparted, as you judge 'em usefull,
To the Generall *Gonzaga*. Instantly
Prepare you for your journey.
 Astutio.   With the wings
Of loyalty and duty.   *Exit* ASTUTIO.
 Fulgentio.   I am bold
To put your Majesty in mind—
 Roberto.   Of my promise,
And ayds, to further you in your amorous project
To the faire, and rich *Camiola*: there's my ring;
Whatever you shall say that I intreat

---

19. knees] *32²*; kindes *32¹*   20-1. impious! / Their] *Coxeter; undivided 32*
23. One troubled] *32²*; Oou trouble *32¹*   25-6. True; / And] *Coxeter; undivided 32*   41-2 bold / To] *Gifford; undivided 32*   42. your] *32²*; you *32¹*   mind—] *Coxeter*; ~. *32*

Or can command by power, I will make good.
 Fulgentio. Ever your Majesties creature.
 Roberto.   *Venus* prove
Propitious to you.   *Exit* ROBERTO.
 Fulgentio.   All sorts to my wishes:
Bertoldo was my hindrance. Hee remov'd,
I now will court her in the conquerours stile,   50
Come, see, and overcome. Boy.

Enter PAGE.

 Page.   Sir, your pleasure.
 Fulgentio. Haste to *Camiola*, bid her prepare
An entertainment sutable to a fortune,
She could not hope for. Tell her, I vouchsafe
To honour her with a visit.
 Page.   'Tis a favour   55
Will make her proud.
 Fulgentio.   I know it.
 Page.   I am gone, Sir.   *Exit* PAGE.
 Fulgentio. Intreaties fit not me, a man in grace,
May challenge awe, and priviledge by his place. *Exit* FULGENTIO.

Act II. Scene II.

SYLLI, ADORNI, CLARINDA.

 Adorni. So melancholy say you?
 Clarinda.   Never given
To such retirement.
 Adorni.   Can you guesse the cause?
 Clarinda. If it hath not it's birth, and being from
The brave *Bertoldo's* absence, I confesse
It is pass'd my apprehension.
 Sylli.   You are wide,   5
The whole field wide. I in my understanding
Pitty your ignorance: yet if you will
Sweare to conceale it, I will let you know
Where her shooe ringes her.

  47–8. prove / Propitious] *Gifford; undivided* 32   50. in the] 32²; in 32¹

Clarinda.   I vow, *Signior*,
By my virginity.
    Sylli.   A perillous oath
In a waiting-woman of fifteene, and is indeed
A kinde of nothing.
    Adorni.   I'll take one of something
If you please to minister it.
    Sylli.   Nay, you shall not sweare,
I had rather take your word, for should you vow:
Damne mee, I'll doe this, you are sure to breake.
    Adorni. I thanke you *Signior*, but resolve us.
    Sylli.   Know then,
Here walkes the cause. She dares not looke upon me,
My beauties are so terrible, and inchaunting,
Shee cannot endure my sight.
    Adorni.   There I believe you.
    Sylli. But the time will come, be comforted, when I will
Put off this vizor of unkindnesse to her,
And shew an amorous, and yeelding face:
And untill then, though *Hercules* himselfe
Desire to see her, hee had better eate
His clubbe then passe her threshold, for I'll be
Her *Cerberus* to guard her.
    Adorni.   A good dogge.
    Clarinda. Worth twenty porters.

                    Enter PAGE.

    Page.   Keepe you open house here?
No groome to attend a Gentleman? O, I spie one.
    Sylli. Hee meanes not mee, I am sure.
    Page.   You sirrha Sheepes-head,
With a face cut on a cat-sticke, Doe you heare?
You yeoman phewterer, conduct mee to
The Lady of the mansion, or my poniard
Shall disemboge thy soule.
    Sylli.   O terrible!
Disemboge! I talke of *Hercules*, and here is one
Bound up in *decimo sexto*.
    Page.   Answer wretch.

_{II. ii. 29. sirrha] *Gifford*; ~; 32}

Sylli. Pray you little gentleman, be not so furious,
The Lady keepes her chamber.
 Page.   And we present?
Sent in an Embassie to her? But here is
Her gentlewoman, Sirrah hold my cloake,
While I take a leape at her lips, do it and neatly;   40
Or having first tripp'd up thy heeles, I'll make
Thy backe my footstoole.   PAGE *kisses* CLARINDA.
 Sylli.   *Tamberlaine* in little!
Am I turn'd Turke? what an office am I put to!
 Clarinda. My Lady, gentle youth, is indispos'd.
 Page. Though she were dead and buried, only tell her,   45
The great man in the Court, the brave *Fulgentio*
Descends to visit her, and it will raise her
Out of the grave for joy.

      Enter FULGENTIO.

 Sylli.   Here comes another!
The divell I feare in his holi-day clothes.
 Page.   So soone,
My part is at an end then, cover my shoulders,   50
When I grow great, thou shalt serve me.
 Fulgentio.   Are you Sirrah
An implement of the house?
 Sylli.   Sure he will make
A joyne-stoole of me!
 Fulgentio.   Or if you belong
To the Lady of the place, command her hither.
 Adorni. I do not weare her livery, yet acknowledge   55
A duty to her. And as little bound
To serve your peremptorie will, as she is
To obey your summons. 'Twill become you Sir,
To waite her leisure, then her pleasure knowne
You may present your duty.
 Fulgentio.   Duty? Slave,   60
I'll teach you manners.
 Adorni.   I am past learning, make not
A tumult in the house.

 39. gentlewoman] *32²*; gentleman *32¹*   53. joyne-stoole] *editor*; joynes-stoole *32*; Joint-stool *Coxeter*

Fulgentio. Shall I be brav'd thus? *They draw.*
Sylli. O I am dead! and now I sowne. *Fals on his face.*
Clarinda. Helpe, murther!

Enter CAMIOLA.

Page. Recover Sirrah, the Ladies here.
Sylli. Nay then
I am alive againe, and I'll be valiant.
Camiola. What insolence is this? *Adorni*, hold,
Hold I command you.
Fulgentio. Sawcy groome.
Camiola. Not so Sir,
However in his life, he had dependance
Vpon my Father, he is a gentleman
As well borne as your selfe. Put on your hat.
Fulgentio. In my presence, without leave?
Sylli. He has mine Madam.
Camiola. And I must tell you Sir, and in plaine language,
How e'r your glittring out-side promise gentry,
The rudenesse of your carriage and behaviour
Speakes you a courser thing.
Sylli. She meanes a clowne Sir,
I am her interpreter for want of a better.
Camiola. I am a Queene in mine owne house, nor must you
Expect an Empire here.
Sylli. Sure I must love her
Before the day, the prettie Soule's so valiant.
Camiola. What are you? and what would you with me?
Fulgentio. Proud one,
When you know what I am, and what I came for,
And may on your submission proceed to,
You in your reason must repent the coursenesse
Of my entertainement.
Camiola. Why fine man? what are you?
Fulgentio. A kinsman of the Kings.
Camiola. I cry you mercy,
For his sake, not your owne. But grant you are so,
'Tis not impossible, but a king may have
A foole to his kinsman, no way meaning you Sir.

75. courser] *Coxeter* (coarser); couser *32* 82. to] *Mason*; fo *32*; so *Coxeter*

Fulgentio. You have heard of *Fulgentio*?
Camiola.   Long since Sir,
A suit-broker in Court. He has the worst
Report among good men I ever heard of,
For briberie and extortion. In their prayers
Widdowes and Orphans curse him for a canker,
And caterpiller in the state. I hope Sir,
You are not the man, much lesse imploy'd by him
As a smocke-agent to me.
   Fulgentio.   I reply not
As you deserve, being assur'd you know me,
Pretending ignorance of my person, onely
To give me a tast of your wit; 'Tis well and courtly,
I like a sharpe wit well.
   Sylli.   I cannot indure it,
Nor any of the *Syllies.*
   Fulgentio.   More I know too,
This harsh induction must serve as a foyle
To the well tun'd observance and respect
You will hereafter pay me, being made
Familiar with my credit with the King,
And that, containe your joy, I daine to love you.
   Camiola. Love me? I am not rap'd with't.
   Fulgentio.   Hear't againe.
I love you honestly, now you admire me.
   Camiola. I doe indeed, it being a word so seldome
Heard from a courtiers mouth. But pray you deale plainly,
Since you finde me simple. What might be the motives
Inducing you to leave the freedome of
A batchelers life, on your soft necke to weare
The stubborne yoake of marriage? And of all
The beauties in *Palermo,* to choose me,
Poore me? that is the maine point you must treate of.
   Fulgentio. Why I will tell you. Of a little thing
You are a prettie peate, indifferently faire too;
And like a new-rigg'd shippe both tite, and yare,
Well truss'd to beare. Virgins of Gyant size
Are sluggards at the sport: but for my pleasure,
Give me a neat well timbred gamster like you,

      101. More] *32*; ~; *Gifford*   119. yare,] *Mason*; y'are ∧ *32*

Such neede no spurres, the quickenes of your eye
Assures an active spirit.
 Camiola.   You are pleasant Sir,
Yet I presume, that there was one thing in me
Unmention'd yet, that tooke you more then all
Those parts you have remembred.
 Fulgentio.   What?
 Camiola.   My wealth Sir.
 Fulgentio. You are i' the right, without that beautie is
A flower worne in the morning, at night trod on:
But beautie, youth, and fortune meeting in you,
I will vouchsafe to marrie you.
 Camiola.   You speake well,
And in return excuse me Sir, if I
Deliver reasons why upon no tearmes
I'll marrie you: I fable not.
 Sylli.   I am glad
To heare this, I began to have an ague.
 Fulgentio. Come, your wise reasons.
 Camiola.   Such as they are, pray you take them.
First I am doubtfull whether you are a man,
Since for your shape trimmd up in a Ladies dressing
You might passe for a woman: now I love
To deale on certainties. And for the fairenes
Of your complexion, which you thinke will take me,
The colour I must tell you in a man
Is weake and faint, and never will hold out
If put to labour, give me the lovely browne,
A thicke curl'd hayre of the same dye, broad shoulders,
A brawnie arme full of veines, a legge without
An artificiall calfe, I suspect yours,
But let that passe.
 Sylli.   She meanes me all this while,
For I have every one of those good parts,
O *Sylli*, fortunate *Sylli*!
 Camiola.   You are mov'd Sir.
 Fulgentio. Fie no, go on.
 Camiola.   Then as you are a courtier,
A grac'd one too, I feare you have beene too forward,
And so much for your person. Rich you are,

Divelish rich, as 'tis reported, and sure have
The aides of Satans little fiends to get it,　　　　　155
And what is got upon his backe, must be
Spent you know where, the proverb's stale, one word more
And I have done.
　　Fulgentio.　　I'll ease you of the trouble,
Coy, and disdainefull.
　　Camiola.　　　Save me, or else he'll beat me.
　　Fulgentio. No, your owne folly shall, and since you put mee　160
To my last charme, look upon this, and tremble.
　　　　　　　　　　　　　　　Shewes the Kings ring.
　　Camiola. At the sight of a faire ring? the Kings, I take it.
I have seene him weare the like; if he hath sent it
As a favour to mee—
　　Fulgentio.　　　Yes, 'tis verie likely,
His dying mothers gift, priz'd at his crowne.　　　165
By this hee does command you to be mine,
By his gift you are so: you may yet redeme all.
　　Camiola. You are in a wrong account still. Though the King may
Dispose of my life and goods, my mind's mine owne,
And shall be never yours. The King (Heaven blesse him)　170
Is good and gracious, and being in himselfe
Abstemious from base and goatish loosenesse,
Will not compell against their wills, chaste Maidens,
To dance in his mignions circles. I believe
Forgetting it, when he washed his hands, you stole it　175
With an intent to awe me. But you are coozin'd,
I am still my selfe, and will be.
　　Fulgentio.　　　　A proud haggard,
And not to be reclaim'd, which of your groomes,
Your coach-man, foole, or foot-man, ministers
Night phisicque to you?
　　Camiola.　　　You are foule-mouth'd,
　　Fulgentio.　　　　　Much fairer　180
Then thy black soule, and so I will proclaime thee.
　　Camiola. Were I a man, thou durst not speake this.
　　Fulgentio.　　　　　　Heav'n
So prosper mee, as I resolve to doe it

　　161 SD. *placed as Coxeter; opposite l. 163 in 32*　　173. Maidens] *32²*; Madiens
32¹　174. mignions] *Coxeter* (minion's); magnious *32¹*; mignious *32²*

To all men, and in every place; scorn'd by
A tit of ten-pence? *Exit* FULGENTIO *and his* PAGE.
 Sylli.   Now I begin to be valiant, 185
Nay, I will draw my sword. O for a brother!
Doe a friends part, 'pray you carry him the length of 't.
I give him three yeeres, and a day to match my Toledo,
And then wee'll fight like Dragons.
 Adorni.   Pray have patience.
 Camiola. I may live to have vengeance; My *Bertoldo* 190
Would not have heard this.
 Adorni.   Madam.
 Camiola.   'Pray you spare
Your language; Pre'thee foole, and make me merry.
 Sylli. That is my Office ever.
 Adorni.   I must doe,
Not talke, this glorious gallant shall heare from me. *Exeunt.*

Act II. Scene III.

The chambers discharg'd: A flourish, as to an assault.

GONZAGA, PIERIO, RODERIGO, IACOMO, *Souldiers.*

 Gonzaga. Is the breach made assaultable?
 Pierio.   Yes, and the moate
Fill'd up, the Canonier hath don his parts,
We may enter six a brest.
 Roderigo.   There's not a man
Dares shew himselfe upon the wall.
 Iacomo.   Defeate not
The souldiers hop'd-for spoile.
 Pierio.   If you, Sir, 5
Delay the assault, and the Citie be given up
To your discretion, you in honour cannot
Use the extremitie of warre, but in
Compassion to 'em, you to us prove cruell.
 Iacomo. And an enemy to your selfe.
 Roderigo.   A hindrance to 10
The brave revenge you have vow'd.

  185. ten-pence] Coxeter; pen-pence 32 186. brother] 32²; butcher 32¹

Gonzaga.   Temper your heat,
And loose not by too sudden rashnesse, that
Which be but patient, will be offer'd to you.
Security ushers ruine; proud contempt
Of an enemy three parts vanquish'd, with desire
And greedinesse of spoyle, have often wrested
A certaine victory from the Conquerours gripe.
Discretion is the tutor of the warre,
Valour the pupill, and when we command
With lenity and your directions follow'd
With cheerefulnesse, a prosperous end must crowne
Our workes well undertaken.
   Roderigo.   Ours are finish'd—
   Pierio. If we make use of fortune.
   Gonzaga.   Her false smiles
Deprive you of your judgements. The condition
Of our affaires exacts a double care,
And like bifronted *Janus*, wee must looke
Backward, as forward: though a flattering calme
Bids us urge on, a sudden tempest rais'd,
Not fear'd, much lesse expected, in our reere,
May foully fall upon us, and distract us

                          Enter SCOUT.

To our confusion. Our scout! what brings
Thy ghastly lookes, and sudden speede?
   Scout.   Th'assurance
Of a new enemy.
   Gonzaga.   This I fore-saw, and fear'd.
What are they, know'st thou?
   Scout.   They are by their colours
Sicilians, bravely mounted, and the brightnesse
Of their rich armours doubly guilded with
Reflection of the Sunne.
   Gonzaga.   From *Sicilie*?
The King in league! no warre proclaimed! 'tis foule,
But this must be prevented, not disputed.
Ha, how is this? your Estridge plumes, that but
E'n now like quills of Porcupines seem'd to threaten
The starres, drop at the rumor of a shower?

And like to captive colours sweep the earth?
Beare up, but in great dangers, greater mindes
Are never proud. Shall a few loose troopes untrain'd 45
But in a customary ostentation,
Presented as a sacrifice to your valours
Cause a dejection in you?
   Pierio. No dejection.
   Roderigo. However startl'd, where you lead, we'll follow.
   Gonzaga. 'Tis bravely said. We will not stay their charge, 50
But meet 'em man to man, and horse to horse.
Pierio in our absence hold our place,
And with our foot-men, and those sickely troupes,
Prevent a sally. I in mine owne person,
With part of the cavallery, will bid 55
These hunters welcome to a bloody breakefast,
But I lose time.
   Pierio. I'll to my charge. *Exit* PIERIO.
   Gonzaga. And wee
To ours. I'll bring you on.
   Iacomo. If we come off
It is not amisse, if not, my state is settl'd. *Exeunt, alarme.*

Act II. Scene IIII.

FERDINAND. DRUSO. LIVIO. above.

Ferdinand. No aydes from *Sicilie*? Hath hope forsooke us?
And that vaine comfort to affliction, pitty
By our vow'd friend deni'd us? we can nor live,
Nor die with honor: like beasts in a toyle
Wee waite the leasure of the bloody hunter, 5
Who is not so farre reconcil'd unto us,
As in one death to give a period
To our calamities, but in delaying
The fate wee cannot flie from, starv'd with wants,
Wee die this night to live againe tomorrow, 10
And suffer greater torments.
   Druso. There is not
Three dayes provision for every soldiour,

II. iii. 45. proud] *32*; prov'd *McIlwraith*

At an ounce of bread a day, left in the Citty.
   Livio. To dye the beggers death with hunger, made
Anatomies while we live, cannot but cracke 15
Our heart-strings with vexation.
   Ferdinand.   Would they would breake,
Breake altogether, how willingly like *Cato*
Could I teare out my bowells, rather then
Looke on the conquerors insulting face,
But that religion, and the horrid dreame 20
To be suffer'd in the other world denyes it.

                Enter SOULDIER.
What newes with thee?
   Souldier.   From the turret of the fort
By the rising clouds of dust, through which, like lightning
The splendor of bright armes sometimes brake through,
I did descry some forces making towards us, 25
And from the campe, as emulous of their glory,
The Generall, (for I know him by his horse)
And bravely seconded, encounter'd 'em.
Their greetings were to rough for friends, their swords
And not their tongues exchanging courtesies. 30
By this the maine Battalias are joyn'd,
And if you please to be spectators of
The horrid issue, I will bring you where
As in a Theater you may see their fates
In purple gore presented.
   Ferdinand.   Heaven, if yet 35
Thou art appeas'd for my wrong done to *Aurelia*,
Take pitty of my miseries. Lead the way, friend.   [*Exeunt.*]

Act II. Scene V.

A long charge; after, a Flourish for Victory.

GONZAGA, IACOMO, RODERIGO *wounded.* BERTOLDO,
GASPARO, ANTHONIO *prisoners.*

   Gonzaga. We have 'em yet, though they cost us deer. This was
Charg'd home, and bravely follow'd. Be to your selves

II. iv. 37 SD. *Exeunt.*] Coxeter; not in 32

True mirrors to each others worth, and looking
With noble Emulation on his wounds,
(The glorious Livery of triumphant war)　　　　　　　5
Imagine these with equall grace appeare
　　　　　　　　　　To IACOMO *and* RODERIGO.
Upon your selfe. The bloody sweat you have suffer'd
In this laborious, nay toylesome harvest,
Yeelds a rich crop of conquest, and the spoyle,
Most precious balsum to a souldiers hurts,　　　　　　10
Will ease and cure 'em. Let me looke upon
The prisoners faces. O how much transform'd
　　　　　　　　　　To GASPARO *and* ANTHONIO.
From what they were. O *Mars*! were these toyes fashion'd
To undergoe the burthen of thy service?
The weight of their defensive armor bruiz'd　　　　　　15
Their weak, effeminate limbes, and would have forc'd 'em
In a hot day without a blow to yeeld.
　Anthonio. This insultation shewes not manly in you.
　Gonzaga. To men I had forborne it, you are women,
Or at the best loose carpet knights, what fury　　　　　20
Seduc'd you to exchange your ease in Court
For labour in the field? Perhaps you thought,
To charge through dust, and blood, an armed foe,
Was but like gracefull running at the ring
For a wanton mistrisse glove, and the encounter　　　　25
A soft impression on her lips. But you
Are gawdie butterflies, and I wrong my selfe
In parling with you.
　Gasparo.　　　　*Væ victis.* Now we prove it.
　Roderigo. But here's one fashion'd in another mould,
And made of tougher mettall.
　Gonzaga.　　　　　　True, I owe him　　　　　　30
For this wound bravely given.
　Bertoldo.　　　　　O that mountaines
Were heap'd upon me, that I might expire
A wretch no more remembered.
　Gonzaga.　　　　　　　Look up Sir,
To be orecome deserves no shame. If you
Had falne ingloriously, or could accuse　　　　　　　35
Your want of courage in resistance, 'twere

To be lamented: But since you perform'd
As much as could be hop'd for from a man,
(Fortune his enemy) you wrong your selfe
In this direction. I am honor'd in 40
My victory ore you: but to have these
My prisoners, is in my true judgement rather
Captivitie then a triumph; you shall finde
Faire quarter from me, and your many wounds
(Which I hope are not mortall) with such care 45
Lookt to, and cur'd, as if your nearest friend
Attended on you.
    Bertoldo.   When you know me better,
You will make void this promise: Can you call me
Into your memory?
    Gonzaga.   The brave *Bertoldo*!
A brother of our order! By Saint *John*, 50
(Our holy patron) I am more amaz'd,
Nay thunderstrooke, with thy Apostacy,
And præcipice from the most solemne vowes
Made unto heaven, when this, the glorious badge
Of our redeemer was conferr'd upon thee, 55
By the great master, then if I had seene
A reprobate Jew, an Atheist, Turke, or Tartar
Baptiz'd in our religion.
    Bertoldo.   This I look'd for,
And am resolv'd to suffer.
    Gonzaga.   Fellow Souldiers,
Behold this man, and taught by his example 60
Know that 'tis safer far to play with lightning,
Then trifle in things sacred. In my rage   *Weepes.*
I shed these at the funerall of his vertue,
Faith and religion; why I will tell you
He was a gentleman, so trayn'd up, and fashion'd 65
For noble uses, and his youth did promise
Such certainties, more then hopes, of great atchievments,
As if the Christian world had stood oppos'd
Against the Ottoman race to trie the fortune
Of one encounter, this *Bertoldo* had beene 70
For his knowledge to direct, and matchles courage

    II. v. 40. direction] *32*; dejection *Coxeter*   62. rage] *32²*; rag *32¹*

To execute, without a rivall, by
The votes of good men chosen generall,
As the prime souldier, and most deserving,
Of all that weare the crosse, which now in justice 75
I thus teare from him.
   Bertoldo.   Let me dye with it,
Upon my breast.
   Gonzaga.   No, by this thou wer't sworne
On all occasions, as a knight to guard
Weake Ladies from oppression, and never
To draw thy sword against 'em, where as thou 80
In hope of gaine or glory, when a Princesse
And such a Princesse as *Aurelia* is,
Was dispossess'd by violence, of what was
Her true inheritance, against thine oth,
Hast to thy uttermost labour'd to uphold 85
Her falling enemie. But thou shalt pay
A heavy forfeiture, and learne too late,
Valour, imploy'd in an ill quarrell, turnes
To cowardice, and vertue then puts on
Foule vices vizard. This is that which cancells 90
All friendships bands between us. Beare 'em off,
I will heare no replie. And let the ransome
Of these, for they are yours, be highly rated.
In this I doe but right, and let it be 94
Stil'd justice, and not wilfull cruelty.   *Exeunt.*

The end of the second Act.

Act III. Scene I.

GONZAGA, ASTUTIO, RODERIGO, IACOMO.

   Gonzaga. What I have done Sir by the law of armes
I can, and will make good.
   Astutio.   I have no commission
To expostulate the act. These letters speake
The King my Masters love to you, and his
Vow'd service to the Duchesse, on whose person 5
I am to give attendance.

Gonzaga. At this instant
Shee's at *Pienza*; you may spare the trouble
Of riding thither: I have advertized her
Of our successe, and on what humble termes
Siena stands: though presently I can
Possesse it I deferre it, that shee may
Enter her owne, and as she please dispose of
The prisoners and the spoyle.
   Astutio. I thanke you, Sir.
I' the meane time, if I may have your licence,
I have a Nephew, and one once my ward
For whose liberties and ransomes, I would gladly
Make composition.
   Gonzaga. They are, as I take it,
Call'd *Gasparo*, and *Anthonio*.
   Astutio. The same, Sir.
   Gonzaga. For them you must treat with these, but for *Bertoldo*,
He is mine owne, if the King will ransom him,
He payes downe fifty thousand crownes, if not
He lives, and dies my slave.
   Astutio. Pray you a word.
The King will rather thanke you to detaine him,
Then give one crowne to free him.
   Gonzaga. At his pleasure.
I'll send the prisoners under guard, my businesse
Calls me another way.   *Exit* GONZAGA.
   Astutio. My service waits you.
Now Gentlemen do not deale like Merchants with me,
But noble Captaines, you know in great mindes
Posse, et nolle nobile.
   Roderigo. Pray you speake
Our language.
   Iacomo. I finde not in my commission
An officers bound to speake or understand
More then his Mother tongue.
   Roderigo. If hee speake that
After midnight 'tis remarkable.
   Astutio. In plaine termes then,
Anthonio is your prisoner, *Gasparo* yours.
   Iacomo. You are i' the right.

Astutio. At what summe doe you rate
Their severall ransomes?
   Roderigo. I must make my market
As the commodity cost me.
   Astutio. As it cost you?
You did not buy your Captainship? your desert
I hope advanc'd you.
   Roderigo. How? it well appeares
You are no souldier. Desert in these daies?
Desert may make a Serjeant to a Colonel,
And it may hinder him from rising higher,
But if it ever get a company,
A company, pray you marke mee, without money
Or private service done for the Generalls Mistresse,
With a commendatory Epistle from her,
I will turne Lansprizadoe.
   Iacomo. Pray you observe, Sir:
I serv'd two prenticeships, just foureteene yeere,
Trayling the puissant pike; and halfe so long
Had the right hand file, and I fought well, 'twas said too:
But I might have serv'd, and fought, and serv'd til doomsday,
And never have carryed a flagge, but for the legacy
A buxsome widdow of threescore, bequeath'd mee,
And that too, my backe knowes, I labour'd hard for,
But was beter paid.
   Astutio. You are merry with your selves,
But this is from the purpose.
   Roderigo. To the point then.
Prisoners are not tane every day, and when
We have 'em we must make the best use of 'em.
Our pay is little to the part we should beare,
And that so long a comming, that 'tis spent
Before we have it, and hardly wipes off scores
At the Taverne, and the Ordinary.
   Iacomo. You may adde to,
Our sport tooke up on trust.
   Roderigo. Peace, thou smocke vermin.
Discover commanders secrets! In a word, Sir,
We have requir'd, and find our prisoners rich:

   III. i. 54. labour'd] *Mason*; labour 32   65. requir'd] 32; enquired *Coxeter*

Two thousand crownes a piece, our companies cost us,
And so much each of us will have, and that
In present pay.
  Iacomo. It is too little; yet
Since you have said the word, I am content,
But will not goe a gazet lesse.
  Astutio.   Since you are not   70
To be brought lower, there is no evading,
I'll be your pay-master.
  Roderigo.   Wee desire no better.
Astutio. But not a word of what's agreed between us,
'Till I have schoold my gallants.
  Iacomo.   I am dumb, Sir.

Enter a guard: BERTOLDO, ANTHONIO, GASPARO, *in yrons.*

Bertoldo. And where remov'd now? hath the Tyrant found out 75
Worse usage for us?
  Anthonio. Worse it cannot be.
My grewhound has fresh straw, and scraps in his kennell,
But wee have neyther.
  Gasparo. Did I ever thinke
To weare such garters on silke stockings? or
That my too curious appetite, that turn'd   80
At the sight of godwits, pheasant, partridge, quales,
Larkes, wood-cocks, calverd sammon, as course diet,
Would leape at a mouldy crust?
  Anthonio.   And goe without it
So oft as I doe; O how have I jeer'd
The City entertainment. A huge shoulder   85
Of glorious fat Ramme Mutton, seconded
With a paire of tame cats, or conies, a crabbe tart
With a worthy loyne of veale, and valiant Capon,
Mortifi'd to grow tender. These I scorn'd
From their plentifull horne of abundance, though invited: 90
But now I could carry my owne stoole to a tripe,
And call their chitterlings charity, and blesse the founder.
  Bertoldo. O that I were no farther sensible
Of my miseries then you are! you like beasts
Feele onely stings of hunger, and complaine not   95

    77. scraps] *32²*; scrapes *32¹*

III. i. 96–126   *The Maid of Honour*   155

But when you are empty: but your narrow soules
(If you have any) cannot comprehend
How insupportable the torments are,
Which a free and noble soule made captive, suffers:
Most miserable men! and what am I then,   100
That envy you? Fetters though made of gold,
Expresse base thraldome, and all delicates
Prepar'd by *Median* cookes for Epicures,
When not our owne, are bitter; quilts fill'd high
With gossamire and roses, cannot yeeld   105
The body soft repose, the mind kep't waking
With anguish and affliction.
   Astutio.   My good Lord.
   Bertoldo. This is no time, nor place for flaterry Sir,
Pray you stile me as I am, a wretch forsaken
Of the world, as my selfe.
   Astutio.   I would it were   110
In me to helpe you.
   Bertoldo.   In that you want power Sir,
Lip comfort cannot cure me, pray you leave mee
To mine owne private thoughts.   *Walkes by.*
   Astutio.   My valiant Nephew!
And my more then warlike ward! I am glad to see you
After your glorious conquests. Are these chaines   115
Rewardes for your good service? If they are
You should weare 'em on your necks (since they are massie)
Like Aldermen of the war.
   Anthonio.   You jeere us to!
   Gasparo. Good uncle name not (as you are a man of honor)
That fatall word of war, the very sounde of't   120
Is more dreadfull then a Cannon.
   Anthonio.   But redeeme us
From this Captivitie, and I'll vow hereafter
Never to weare a sword, or cut my meate
With a knife, that has an edge or point. I'll starve first.
   Gasparo. I will crie broome or cats meate in *Palermo*;   125
Turne porter, carrie burthens; any thing,

---

104. bitter;] *Coxeter*; ~∧ *32*   111. In] *editor*; I if *32*; If *Coxeter*
113 SD. *opposite* 'Nephew' *in 32*   120. sounde] *32*²; summon *32*¹   125. broome] *32*;
Brooms *Coxeter*

Rather then live a souldier.
 Astutio.   This should have
Beene thought upon before. At what price thinke you
Your two wise heads are rated?
 Anthonio.   A calves head is
More worth then mine, I am sure it has more braines in't 130
Or I had never come here.
 Roderigo.   And I will eate it
With bacon, if I have not speedy ransome.
 Anthonio. And a little garlick too, for your own sake Sir,
'Twill boyle in your stomacke else.
 Gasparo.   Beware of mine
Or the hornes may choake you. I am married Sir. 135
 Anthonio. You shall have my row of houses neare the pallace.
 Gasparo. And my villa, all.
 Anthonio.   All that we have. *To* ASTUTIO.
 Astutio. Well, have more wit hereafter, for this time
You are ransom'd.
 Iacomo.   Off with their irons.
 Roderigo.   Do do.
If you are ours again, you know your price. 140
 Anthonio. Pray you dispatch us: I shall nere beleeve
I am a freeman, till I set my foote
In *Sicilie* agen, and drinke *Palermo,*
And in *Palermo* too.
 Astutio.   The wind sits faire,
You shall aboord tonight, with the rising Sun 145
You may touch upon the coast. But take your leaves
Of the late Generall first.
 Gasparo.   I will be briefe.
 Anthonio. And I, my lord heaven keepe you.
 Gasparo.   Yours to use
In the way of peace, but as your souldiers never.
 Anthonio. A pox of war, no more of war.
      Exeunt RODERIGO, IACOMO, ANTHONIO, GASPARO.
 Bertoldo.   Have you 150
Authority to loose their bonds, yet leave
The brother of your King, whose worth disdaines

  130. has] *Gifford*; had *32* 138–40 *rearranged by Coxeter; 32 reads* Well ... hereafter / For ... irons / Do ... price.

Comparison with such as these, in irons?
If ransome may redeeme them, I have landes,
A patrimony of mine owne assign'd me
By my deceased sire, to satisfie
What ere can be demanded for my freedome.
 Astutio. I wish you had Sir, but the king who yeelds
No reason for his will, in his displeasure
Hath seas'd on all you had; nor will *Gonzaga*,
Whose prisoner now you are, accept of lesse
Then fiftie thousand crownes.
 Bertoldo.   I finde it now
That misery nere comes alone. But grant
The King is yet inexorable, time
May worke him to a feeling of my sufferings.
I have friends, that swore their lives and fortunes were
At my devotion, and among the rest
Your selfe my lord, when forfeited to the Law
For a foule murther, and in cold blood done,
I made your life my gift, and reconcil'd you
To this incensed king, and got your pardon.
Beware ingratitude. I know you are rich
And may pay downe the Sum.
 Astutio.   I might my lord,
But pardon me.
 Bertoldo. And will *Astutio* prove then
To please a passionate man, the kings no more,
False to his maker and his reason? which
Commandes more then I aske? O summer friendship,
Whose flattering leaves that shaddowed us in our
Prosperity, with the least gust drop off
In th' Autumne of adversity! How like
A prison is to a grave! when dead we are
With solemne Pompe brought thither; and our heires,
(Masking their joy in false dissembled teares)
Weepe ore the hearse, but earth no sooner covers
The earth brought thither, but they turne away
With inward smiles, the dead no more remembred.
So enter'd in a prison—
 Astutio.   My occasions

  178–9 *rearranged by Gifford; 32 reads* Whose ... in / Our ... off

Command me hence my lord.
  Bertoldo.   Pray you leave me, doe;
And tell the cruell king, that I will weare
These fetters 'till my flesh, and they are one   190
Incorporated substance. In my selfe,
As in a glasse, I'll looke on humane frailty,
And curse the height of Royall blood: since I
In being borne neare to *Jove*, am neare his thunder.
Cedars once shaken with a storme, their owne *Exit* ASTUTIO.
Waight grubs their rootes out. Lead me where you please; 196
I am his, not fortunes martyr, and will dye
The great example of his cruelty.   *Exit cum suis.*

Act III. Scene II.

ADORNI.

 Adorni. He undergoes my challenge, and contemnes it,
And threatens me with the late Edict made
'Gainst duellists, the altar cowards flie to.
But I that am ingag'd, and nourish in me
A higher aime then faire *Camiola* dreames of,   5
Must not sit down thus. In the court I dare not
Attempt him; and in publike, hee's so guarded
With a heard of Parasites, Clients, fooles and sutors,
That a musket cannot reach him; my designes
Admit of no delay. This is her birth-day,   10
Which with a fit and due solemnitie
Camiola celebrates; and on it, all such
As love or serve her, usually present
A tributary duty. I'll have something
To give, if my intelligence prove true,   15
Shall find acceptance. I am told, neare this grove
Fulgentio every morning makes his markets
With his petitioners. I may present him
With a sharpe petition. Ha, 'tis he: my fate
Be ever bless'd for't.

  III. ii. 3. the] *conj. Davies (in Coxeter²);* then *32* 17. every] *Coxeter;* very *32* makes] *32²;* markes *32¹* markets] *Coxeter;* makets *32*

Enter FULGENTIO [*and* PAGE].

Fulgentio. Command such as waite me 20
Not to presume at the least for halfe an houre
To presse on my retirements.
  Page. I will say, Sir,
You are at your prayers.
  Fulgentio. That will not finde beliefe,
Courtiers have something else to do, be gon, Sir. [*Exit* PAGE.]
Challeng'd! 'tis well! and by a grome! still better! 25
Was this shape made to fight? I have a tongue yet,
How e'r no sword to kill him, and what way
This morning, I'll resolve of. *Exit* FULGENTIO.
  Adorni. I shall crosse
Your resolution, or suffer for you. *Exit* ADORNI.

Act III. Scene III.

CAMIOLA: *divers* SERVANTS *with presents*: SYLLI, CLARINDA.

  Sylli. What are all these?
  Clarinda. Servants with severall presents,
And rich ones too.
  1. *Servant.* With her best wishes, Madam,
Of many such daies to you, the Lady *Petula*
Presents you with this fanne.
  2. *Servant.* This Diamond
From your Aunt *Honoria.*
  3. *Servant.* This piece of plate 5
From your Uncle, old *Vincentio*, with your armes
Graven upon it.
  Camiola. Good friends, they are too
Munificent in their love, and favour to me.
Out of my cabinet returne such jewells
As this directs you, for your paines; and yours; 10
Nor must you be forgotten. Honour mee
With the drinking of a health.

20 SD. *Enter*] *Coxeter; Exit 32 and* PAGE] *Gifford; not in 32* 22–3. Sir,/
You] *Gifford; undivided 32* 24 SD. *Exit* PAGE.] *Gifford; not in 32*
III. iii. 7. friends,] *Coxeter;* ~∧ *32* too] *Coxeter;* ~. *32*

1. Servant. Gold on my life!
2. Servant. She scornes to give base silver.
3. Servant. Would she had beene
Borne every moneth in the yeere!
1. Servant. Moneth? every day.
2. Servant. Shew such another maid.
3. Servant. All happinesse wait you.
Sylli. I'll see your will done. *Exeunt* SYLLI, CLARINDA,
SERVANTS.

Enter ADORNI *wounded.*

Camiola. How, *Adorny* wounded?
Adorni. A scratch got in your service, else not worth
Your observation; I bring not Madame
In honour of your birth-day, anticque plate,
Or pearle, for which the savage Indian dives
Into the bottome of the Sea; nor Diamonds
Hewne from steepe rockes with danger: such as give
To those that have what they themselves want, aime at
A glad returne with profit: yet despise not
My offering at the altar of your favour;
Nor let the lownesse of the giver lessen
The height of whats presented: since it is
A pretious jewell, almost forfeyted,
And dimn'd with clouds of infamy, redeem'd
And in its naturall splendor, with addition,
Restor'd to the true owner.
Camiola. How is this?
Adorni. Not to hold you in suspence, I bring you, Madame,
Your wounded reputation cur'd, the sting
Of virulent malice, festring your faire name,
Pluck'd out and trode on. That proud man, that was
Deny'd the honour of your bed, yet durst
With his untrue reports, strumpet your fame,
Compell'd by mee, hath given himselfe the lye,
And in his owne blood wrote it, you may read
Fulgentio subscrib'd.
Camiola. I am amaz'd!
Adorni. It does deserve it, Madam. Common service
Is fit for hindes, and the reward proportion'd

To their conditions. Therefore looke not on mee
As a follower of your fathers fortunes, or
One that subsists on yours. You frowne! my service   45
Merits not this aspect.
    Camiola.   Which of my favours,
I might say bounties, hath begot, and nourish'd
This more then rude presumption? since you had
An itch to try your desperate valour, wherefore
Went you not to the warre? couldst thou suppose   50
My innocence could ever fall so low,
As to have need of thy rash sword to guard it
Against malicious slander? O how much
Those Ladies are deceiv'd and cheated, when
The clearnesse and integrity of their actions   55
Doe not defend themselves, and stand secure
On their owne bases! Such as in a colour
Of seeming service give protection to 'em,
Betray their owne strengthes. Malice scorn'd, puts out
It selfe, but argu'd, gives a kinde of credit   60
To a false accusation. In this
This your most memorable service, you beleev'd
You did me right, but you have wrong'd mee more
In your defence of my undoubted honour,
Then false *Fulgentio* could.
    Adorni.   I am sorry, what   65
Was so well intended, is so ill receiv'd,

                Enter CLARINDA.

Yet under your correction you wish'd
Bertoldo had beene present.
    Camiola.   True I did:
But he and you, Sir, are not parallells,
Nor must you thinke your selfe so.
    Adorni.   I am what   70
You'll please to have mee.
    Camiola.   If *Bertoldo* had
Punish'd *Fulgentio's* insolence, it had showne
His love to her, whom in his judgement hee
Vouchsaf'd to make his wife. A height I hope

       74. Vouchsaf'd] *Mason*; Vouchsafe 32

Which you dare not aspire to. The same actions
Sute not all men alike: but I perceive
Repentance in your lookes. For this time leave me:
I may forgive, perhaps forget your folly.
Conceale your selfe till this storme be blowne over.
You will be sought for, yet, for my estate
Can hinder it, shall not suffer in my service.
Gives him her hand to kisse.
Adorni. This is something yet, tho I mist the mark I shot at.
Exit ADORNI.
 Camiola. This Gentleman is of a noble temper,
And I too harsh, perhaps in my reproofe,
Was I not *Clarinda*?
 Clarinda. I am not to censure
Your actions Madame: but there are a thousand
Ladies, and of good fame, in such a cause,
Would be proud of such a servant.
 Camiola. It may be;

Enter a SERVANT.

Let me offend in this kinde. Why uncall'd for?
 Servant. The Signiors, Madame, *Gasparo* and *Anthonio*,
(Selected friends of the renowned *Bertoldo*)
Put ashore this morning.
 Camiola. Without him?
 Servant. I thinke so.
 Camiola. Never thinke more then.
 Servant. They have beene at Court,
Kiss'd the Kings hand; and their first duties done
To him, appeare ambitious to tender
To you their second service.
 Camiola. Waite 'em hither. *Exit* SERVANT.
Feare doe not racke me, reason, now if ever,
Haste with thy ayds, and tell me such a wonder,
As my *Bertoldo* is, with such care fashion'd,
Must not, nay cannot, in hev'ns providence,

---

80. yet, for] *Coxeter*; ~ˌ~ *32*; yet, if *Mason*; yet soe *conj.* McIlwraith   94. their] *Coxeter*; there *32*   95. ambitious] *Coxeter*; ambitions *32*   96 SD. *Exit*] *Mason*; *Eexeunt 32*

III. iii. 101–27   *The Maid of Honour*   163

Enter ANTHONIO, GASPARO, SERVANT.

So soone miscarry; pray you forbeare, ere you
Take the priviledge, as strangers to salute mee,
(Excuse my manners) make me first understand,
How it is with *Bertoldo*?
   Gasparo.   The relation
Will not I feare deserve your thankes.
   Anthonio.   I wish
Some other should informe you.
   Camiola.   Is he dead?
You see, though with some feare, I dare enquire it.
   Gasparo. Dead! Would that were the worst, a debt were pay'd then,
Kings in their birth owe nature.
   Camiola.   Is there ought
More terrible then death?
   Anthonio.   Yes to a spirit
Like his. Cruell imprisonment, and that
Without the hope of freedome.
   Camiola.   You abuse me,
The royall King cannot in love to vertue,
(Though all springs of affection were dri'd up)
But pay his ransome.
   Gasparo.   When you know what 'tis
You will thinke otherwise; No lesse will do it
Then fifty thousand crownes.
   Camiola.   A pettie sum,
The price waigh'd, with the purchase, 50. thousand?
To the King 'tis nothing. He that can spare more
To his minion for a masque, cannot but ransome
Such a brother at a million, you wrong
The Kings magnificence.
   Anthonio.   In your opinion,
But 'tis most certaine. He does not alone
In himselfe refuse to pay it, but forbids
All other men.
   Camiola.   Are you sure of this?
   Gasparo.   You may reade
The edict to that purpose, publish'd by him,
That will resolve you.

     104. Gasparo.] *Coxeter;* Ber. *32*   117. pettie] *Coxeter;* prettie *32*

Camiola. Possible! pray you stand off,
If I doe not mutter treason to my selfe
My heart will breake; yet I will not curse him,
He is my king. The newes you have delivered,
Makes me wearie of your company, wee'll salute
When we meete next. I'll bring you to the dore,
Nay pray you no more complements.
    Gasparo.   One thing more
And that's substantiall. Let your *Adorni*
Looke to himselfe.
    Anthonio.   The king is much incens'd
Against him for *Fulgentio.*
    Camiola.   As I am
For your slownesse to depart.
    Both.   Farewell sweet Lady.
                            Exeunt GASPARO, ANTHONIO.
    Camiola. O more then impious times! when not alone
Subordinate Ministers of justice are
Corrupted, and seduc'd, but kings themselves,
(The greater wheeles by which the lesser move)
Are broken or disjointed; could it be else
A king, to sooth his politique ends, should so far
Forsake his honor, as at once to breake
Th'Adamant chaines of nature and religion,
To binde up Atheisme, as a defence
To his darke counsailes? will it ever be
That to deserve too much is dangerous,
And vertue, when too eminent, a crime?
Must she serve fortune still? or when stripp'd of
Her gay, and glorious favours, loose the beauties
Of her owne naturall shape? O my *Bertoldo!*
Thou onely Sun in honors Spheare, how soone
Art thou eclipsed and darkened! not the nearnesse
Of blood prevailing on the king; nor all
The benefits to the generall good dispens'd
Gayning a retribution! But that
To owe a courtesie to a simple Virgin
Would take from the deserving, I finde in me

---

    154. the] *32*; thy *McIlwraith*   156. The] *32*; Thy *McIlwraith*   159. the] *32*; thy *Mason*

Som sparks of fire, which fann'd with honors breath
Might rise into a flame, and in men darken
Their usurp'd splendor. Ha! my aime is high,
And for the honor of my sex to fall so,
Can never prove inglorious. 'Tis resolv'd:
Call in *Adorni*.
  Clarinda.   I am happy in
Such imployment, Madam.   *Exit* CLARINDA.
  Camiola.   Hee's a man,
I know that at a reverend distance loves me,
And such are ever faithfull: What a Sea
Of melting ice I walke on! what strange censures
Am I to undergoe! but good intents
Deride all future rumors.

      Enter CLARINDA *and* ADORNI.
  Adorni.   I obey
Your summons, Madam.
  Camiola.   Leave the place *Clarinda*,
One woman, in a secret of such waight,   [*Exit* CLARINDA.]
Wisemen may thinke too much, nearer *Adorni*.
I warrant it with a smile.
  Adorni.   I cannot aske
Safer protection, what's your will?
  Camiola.   To doubt
Your ready desire to serve me, or prepare you
With the repetition of former merits,
Would in my diffidence wrong you. But I will
And without circumstance, in the trust that I
Impose upon you, free you from suspition.
  Adorni. I foster none of you.
  Camiola.   I know you do not.
You are *Adorni* by the love you owe me—
  Adorni. The surest conjuration.
  Camiola.   Take me with you,
Love borne of duty, but advance noe further.
You are Sir as I sayd to do me service,
To undertake a taske, in which your faith,
Judgement, discretion, in a word, your all
That's good, must be ingag'd, nor must you studie

171 SD. *Enter*] *Coxeter; Exit* 32   173 SD. *Exit* CLARINDA.] *Coxeter; not in* 32

In the execution, but what may make 190
For the ends I aime at.
    Adorni.   They admit no rivalls.
    Camiola. You answer well, you have heard of *Bertoldo's*
Captivity? and the kings neglect? the greatnesse
Of his ransome, fiftie thousand crownes, *Adorni*,
Two parts of my estate.
    Adorni.   To what tends this? 195
    Camiola. Yet I so love the gentleman (for to you
I will confesse my weaknesses) that I purpose
Now, when he is forsaken by the king,
And his owne hopes, to ransome him, and receive him
Into my bosome as my lawfull husband,   ADORNI *starts and*
Why change you colour?   *seems troubl'd.*
    Adorni.   'Tis in wonder of 201
Your vertue, Madam.
    Camiola.   You must therefore to
Siena for mee, and pay to *Gonzaga*
This ransome for his liberty, you shall
Have bills of exchange along with you. Let him sweare 205
A solemne contract to me, for you must be
My principall witnesse, if he should—But why
Do I entertaine these jealousies? you will do this?
    Adorni. Faithfully, Madam. But not live long after.   *Aside.*
    Camiola. One thing I had forgot. Besides his freedome 210
He may want accomodations, furnish him
According to his birth. And from *Camiola*
Deliver this kisse, printed on your lips,   *Kisses him.*
Seal'd on his hand! you shall not see my blushes,
I'll instantly dispatch you.   *Exit* CAMIOLA.
    Adorni.   I am halfe 215
Hang'd out of the way already, was there ever
Poore lover so imploy'd against himselfe
To make way for his rivall? I must doe it,
Nay more, I will. If loyalty can finde
Recompence beyond hope, or imagination, 220
Let it fall on mee in the other world
As a reward, for in this I dare not hope it.   *Exit.*
              The end of the third Act.
                207. should—] *Coxeter*; ~. 32

Act IIII. Scene I.

GONZAGA, PIERIO, RODERIGO, IACOMO.

Gonzaga. YOU have seaz'd upon the Citadell, and disarm'd
All that could make resistance?
   Pierio.   Hunger had
Done that before wee came; nor was the souldiour
Compell'd to seeke for prey; the famish'd wretches,
In hope of mercy, as a sacrifice offer'd
All that was worth the taking.
   Gonzaga.   You proclaim'd,
On paine of death, no violence should be offer'd
To any woman?
   Roderigo.   But it needed not,
For famine had so humbl'd 'em and tooke off
The care of their sexes honour, that there was not
So coy a beauty in the towne, but would
For halfe a mouldy bisket sell her selfe
To a poore besognion, and without shrieking.
   Gonzaga. Where is the Duke of *Urbin*?
   Iacomo.   Under guard,
As you directed.
   Gonzaga.   See the Souldiers set
In ranke, and file, and as the Dutchesse passes
Bid 'em vaile their ensignes, and charge 'em on their lives
Not to cry whores.
   Iacomo.   The divell cannot fright 'em
From their military licence, though they know
They are her subjects, and will part with being,
To do her service; yet since she is a woman,
They will touch at her britch with their tongues, and that is all
That they can hope for.

A shout, and a generall cry within, whores, whores.

   Gonzaga.   O the divell! they are at it.
Hell stoppe their bawling throats; again! make up
And cudgell them into jelly.
   Roderigo.   To no purpose,
Though their mothers were there,
They would have the same name for 'em.   *Exeunt.*

       IV. i. 26. mothers] *Coxeter*; mouthes 32

Act IIII. Scene II.

RODERIGO, IACOMO, PIERIO, GONZAGA, AURELIA (*under a Canopie*), ASTUTIO *presents her with letters, lowd musicke, shee reads the letters.*

   Gonzaga. I doe beseech your highnesse not to ascribe
To the want of disciplin, the barbarous rudenes
Of the souldier in his prophanation of
Your sacred name, and vertues.
   Aurelia.   No, Lord Generall,
I have heard my father say oft, 'twas a custome,
Usuall in the campe, nor are they to be punish'd
For words, that have in fact deserv'd so well.
Let the one excuse the other.
   All.   Excellent Princesse!
   Aurelia. But for these aides from *Sicily* sent against us
To blast our spring of conquest in the bud:
I cannot find, my Lord Embassadour,
How we should entertaine't but as a wrong,
With purpose to detaine us from our owne.
How e'r the King endeavours in his letters
To mitigate the affront.
   Astutio.   Your grace hereafter
May heare from me such strong assurances
Of his unlimitted desires to serve you,
As will, I hope, drowne in forgetfulnesse
The memory of what's past.
   Aurelia.   Wee shall take time
To search the depth of't further, and proceed
As our counsell shall direct us.
   Gonzaga.   Wee present you
With the keyes of the Citty, all lets are remov'd,
Your way is smooth and easie, at your feet
Your proudest enemy falls.
   Aurelia.   Wee thanke your valoures;
A victory without blood is twice atchiev'd,
And the disposure of it to us tender'd,

The greatest honor; worthy captains thanks.
My love extends itselfe to all.
    A Guard made: AURELIA *passes thorow 'em. Lowd musicke.*
Gonzaga.   Make way there.   *Exeunt.*

Act IIII. Scene III.

BERTOLDO, *with a small booke, in fetters*, JAYLOR.

Bertoldo. Tis here determin'd (great examples arm'd
With arguments produc'd to make it good)
That neither tyrants, nor the wrested lawes,
The peoples franticke rage, sad exile, want,
Nor that which I endure, captivity,   [*Exit* JAYLOR.]
Can doe a wise man any injury: 6
Thus *Seneca*, when he wrot it, thought. But then
Felicity courted him; his wealth exceeding
A private man's; happy in the embraces
Of his chaste wife *Paulina*; his house full   10
Of children, clyents, servants, flattering friends
Soothing his lip-positions, and created
Prince of the Senate, by the generall voyce,
At his pupill *Neroes* suffrage: then no doubt
He held, and did believe this. But no sooner   15
The Princes frownes, and jealosies had throw'n him
Out of securities lappe, and a centurion
Had offer'd him what choyce of death he pleas'd,
But told him dye he must: when straight the armour
Of his so boasted fortitude, fel off,   *Throwes away the booke.*
Complaining of his frailtie. Can it then   21
Be censur'd womanish weaknesse in mee, if
Thus clog'd with yrons, and the period
To close up all calamities, deni'd mee,
(Which was presented *Seneca*) I wish   25
I ne'r had being, at least, never knew
What happines was, or argue with heavens justice?
Tearing my locks, and in defiance throwing
Dust in the ayre? or falling on the ground, thus

    IV. iii. 5 SD. *Exit* JAYLOR.] *editor; not in* 32   14. At] *Mason;* As 32   pupill
Neroes] *McIlwraith, Chelli;* pupill newes 32; new pupil's *Mason;* pupills new *Bryne*

With my nayles, and teeth to digge a grave or rend 30
The bowells of the earth, my stepmother,
And not a naturall parent? or thus practise
To dye, and as I were insensible,
Believe I had no motion? *Lies on his face.*

Enter GONZAGA, ADORNI, JAYLOR.

Gonzaga. There he is:
Ile not enquire by whom his ransome's paid, 35
I am satisfi'd that I have it: nor alleage
One reason to excuse his cruell usage,
As you may interpret it, let it suffice
It was my will to have it so, he is yours now,
Dispose of him as you please. *Exit* GONZAGA.
Adorni. How e'r I hate him, 40
As one preferr'd before me, being a man,
He does deserve my pitty. Sir, he sleepes:
Or is he dead? Would hee were a Saint in heaven;
'Tis all the hurt I wish him. But I was not *Kneeles by him.*
Borne to such happinesse. No, he breaths, come neer, 45
And if't be possible, without his feeling
Take off his yrons, so, now leave us private.
 His yrons taken of. Exit JAYLOR.
He does begin to stir, and as transported
With a joyfull dreame, how he stares! and feeles his legges!
As yet uncertaine, whether it can be 50
True or phantasticall.
Bertoldo. Ministers of mercy,
Mocke not calamitie. Ha! 'tis no vision!
Or if it be, the happiest that ever
Appear'd to sinfull flesh! who's here? His face
Speakes him *Adorni*! but some glorious Angell 55
Concealing its divinity in his shape,
Hath done this miracie, it being not an act
For wolvish man. Resolve me, if thou look'st for
Bent knees in adoration?
Adorni. O forbeare Sir,
I am *Adorni*, and the instrument 60
Of your deliverance; but the benefit

44. 'Tis] *Coxeter;* 'Tis is 32   I was] *Coxeter;* was 32

You owe another.
  Bertoldo.   If he has a name,
Assoone as spoken, 'tis writ on my heart,
I am his bond-man.
  Adorni.   To the shame of men,
This great act is a womans.
  Bertoldo.   The whole sex   65
For her sake must be deifi'd. How I wander
In my imagination, yet cannot
Ghesse who this *Phœnix* should be!
  Adorni.   'Tis *Camiola.*
  Bertoldo. Pray you speake't againe, there's musicke in her name,
Once more I pray you Sir.
  Adorni.   *Camiola,*   70
The Maid of honor.
  Bertoldo.   Curs'd Atheist that I was,
Onely to doubt it could be any other,
Since she alone in the abstract of her selfe,
That small, but ravishing substance comprehends
Whatever is, or can be wished, in the   75
Idea of a woman. O what service,
Or sacrifice of duty can I pay her!
If not to live, and dye her charities slave,
Which is resolv'd already.
  Adorni.   She expects not
Such a dominion ore you: yet ere I   80
Deliver her demands, give me your hand:
On this, as she enjoyn'd me, with my lips
I print her love and service by me sent you.
  Bertoldo. I am orewhelm'd with wonder!
  Adorni.   You must now
(Which is the sum of all that she desires)   85
By a solemne contract bind your selfe, when she
Requires it as a debt, due for your fredome,
To marrie her.
  Bertoldo.   This does ingage me further,
A payment! an increase of obligation!
To marry her! 'twas my *nil ultra* ever!   90
The end of my ambition! O that now

       75. is] *Coxeter*; it *32*   76. Idea] *32²*; Iudea *32¹*

The holy man, she present, were prepar'd
To joyne our hands; but with that speed, my heart
Wishes, mine eyes might see her.
   Adorni.   You must sweare this.
   Bertoldo. Swear it? Collect all oaths, and imprecations   95
Whose least breach is damnation, and those
Ministred to me in a forme more dreadfull,
Set heaven, and hell before me, I will take 'em:
False to *Camiola*? Never. Shall I now
Begin my vowes to you?
   Adorni.   I am no Church-man,   100
Such a one must file it on record, you are free,
And that you may appeare like to your selfe
(For so she wish'd) there's gold with which you may
Redeeme your truncks and servants, and what ever
Of late you lost. I have found out the Captaine   105
Whose spoyle they were. His name is *Roderigo*.
   Bertoldo. I know him.
   Adorni.   I have done my parts.
   Bertoldo.   So much Sir
As I am ever your's for't, now me thinkes
I walke in ayre! divine *Camiola*,
But words cannot expresse thee. I'll build to thee   110
An altar in my soule, on which I'll offer
A still increasing sacrifice of duty.   *Exit* BERTOLDO.
   Adorni. What will become of me now is apparant!
Whether a poniard, or a halter be
The nearest way to hell (for I must thither,   115
After I have kill'd my selfe) is somewhat doubtfull.
This Roman resolution of selfe-murther,
Will not hold water, at the high Tribunall,
When it comes to be argu'd; my good Genius
Prompts me to this consideration. He   120
That kills himselfe, to avoid misery, feares it,
And at the best shewes but a bastard valour;
This lifes a fort committed to my trust,
Which I must not yeeld up, till it be forc'd,
Nor will I: Hee's not valiant that dares dye,   125
But he that boldly beares calamitie.   *Exit.*

       109. in] *32*; on *McIlwraith*

Act IV. Scene IV.

A Flourish.

PIERIO. RODERIGO. IACOMO. GONZAGA. AURELIA.
FERDINAND. ASTUTIO. *Attendants.*

Aurelia. A seat here for the Duke. It is our glory
To overcom with courtesies, not rigor;
The Lordly Roman, who held it the height
Of humane happinesse, to have kings and Queenes
To wait by his triumphant chariot wheeles, 5
In his insulting pride, depriv'd himselfe
Of drawing neare the nature of the gods,
Best known for such, in being mercifull;
Yet give me leave, but still with gentle language,
And with the freedome of a friend to tell you, 10
To seeke by force, what courtship could not win,
Was harsh, and never taught in loves milde schoole.
Wise Poets faine that Venus coach is draw'n
By doves, and sparrowes, not by beares, and tygres.
I spare the application.
    Ferdinand. In my fortune, 15
Heav'ns justice hath confirm'd it, yet great Lady,
Since my offence grew from excesse of love,
And not to be resisted, having paid too,
With the losse of liberty, the forfeyture
Of my presumption, in your clemency 20
It may finde pardon.
    Aurelia. You shall have just cause
To say it hath. The charge of the long siege
Defraid, and the losse my subjects have sustain'd
Made good, since so farre I must deale with caution,
You have your liberty.
    Ferdinand. I could not hope for 25
Gentler conditions.
    Aurelia. My Lord *Gonzaga.*
Since my comming to *Siena*, I have heard much

IV. iv. 3. The 32²; To 32¹   12. Was harsh] *Coxeter*; was not harsh 32
15. I] 32²; Ferd. I 32¹   Ferdinand. In] 32² (*Ferd.* In); In 32¹   25–6. for /
Gentler] *Coxeter; undivided* 32

Of your prisoner; brave *Bertoldo*.
 Gonzaga.   Such an one,
Madam, I had.
 Astutio.   And have still, Sir, I hope.
 Gonzaga. Your hopes deceive you. He is ransom'd, Madame.
 Astutio. By whom, I pray you, Sir?
 Gonzaga.   You had best enquire
Of your intelligencer. I am no informer.
 Astutio. I like not this.
 Aurelia.   He is, as 'tis reported,
A goodly gentleman, and of noble parts,
A brother of your order.
 Gonzaga.   Hee was, Madam,
Till he against his oath wrong'd you, a princesse,
Which his religion bound him from.
 Aurelia.   Great mindes
For tryall of their valours oft maintaine
Quarrells that are unjust, yet without malice,
And such a faire construction I make of him.
I would see that brave enemy.
 Gonzaga.   My duty
Commands me to seeke for him.
 Aurelia.   Pray you doe:
And bring him to our presence.   *Exit* GONZAGA.
 Astutio.   I must blast
His entertainment; may it please your excellency,
He is a man debauch'd, and for his riots
Cast off by the King my Master, and that, I hope, is
A crime sufficient.
 Ferdinand.   To you his subjects,
That like as your king likes.

  Enter GONZAGA, BERTOLDO, *richly habited*: ADORNI.

 Aurelia.   But not to us;
We must waigh with our owne scale. This is he, sure!
How soone mine eye had found him! what a port
He beares! how well his bravery becomes him!
A prisoner! nay, a princely sutor rather!
But I am too sudden.

   28-9 one, / Madam,] *Coxeter; undivided* 32

Gonzaga.   Madame, 'twas his suite,
Unsent for, to present his service to you,
Ere his departure.
    Aurelia.   With what Majesty
He beares himselfe!
    Astutio.   The divell I thinke supplies him,
Ransom'd, and thus rich too!
    Aurelia.   You ill deserve
            BERTOLDO *kneeling, kisses her hand.*
The favour of our hand; we are not well,
Give us more ayre.   *She descends suddenly.*
    Gonzaga.   What sudden qualme is this?
    Aurelia. That lifted yours against mee.
    Bertoldo.   Thus once more,
I sue for pardon.
    Aurelia.   Sure his lips are poyson'd,
And through these veines, force passage to my heart   *Aside.*
Which is already seaz'd upon.
    Bertoldo.   I wait, Madam,
To know what your commands are; my designes
Exact me in another place.
    Aurelia.   Before
You have our licence to depart? if manners,
Civility of manners cannot teach you
T'attend our leasure, I must tell you, Sir,
That you are still our prisoner, nor had you
Commission to free him.
    Gonzaga.   How's this, Madam?
    Aurelia. You were my substitute, and wanted power
Without my warrant to dispose of him.
I will pay backe his ransome ten times over,
Rather then quit my interest.
    Bertoldo.   This is
Against the law of armes.
    Aurelia.   But not of love: *Aside.*
Why, hath your entertainment, Sir, beene such
In your restraint, that with the wings of feare
You would flie from it?

57 SD. BERTOLDO] *Coxeter;* Ferdinand *32*   66. depart?] *Coxeter;* ~; *32*

Bertoldo.   I know no man, Madame,
Enamour'd of his fetters, or delighting
In cold or hunger, or that would in reason
Preferre straw in a dungeon, before
A downe bed in a Palace.
   Aurelia.   How, come neerer;
Was his usage such?
   Gonzaga.   Yes, and it had beene worse,
Had I foreseene this.
   Aurelia.   O thou mis-shap'd monster!
In thee it is confirm'd, that such as have
No share in natures bounties, know no pitty
To such as have 'em. Looke on him with my eyes,
And answer then, whether this were a man,
Whose cheekes of lovely fulnesse should be made
A prey to meagre famine? or these eyes
Whose every glance store *Cupids* empti'd quiver,
To be dimm'd with tedious watching? or these lips,
These rudie lips, of whose fresh colour, cherries
And roses were but coppies, should grow pale
For want of Nectar? or these legges that beare
A burthen of more worth, then is supported
By *Atlas* wearied shoulders, should be cramp'd
With the weight of yron? O I could dwell ever
On this description!
   Bertoldo.   Is this in dirision
Or pitty of me?
   Aurelia.   In your charity
Beleeve me innocent. Now you are my prisoner
You shall have fairer quarter, you will shame
The place where you have beene, should you now leave it
Before you are recover'd. I'll conduct you
To more convenient lodgings, and it shall be
My care to cherish you. Repine who dare;
It is our will. You'll follow mee?
   Bertoldo.   To the centre,
Such a *Sybilla* guiding me.   *Exeunt* AURELIA, BERTOLDO.
   Gonzaga.   Who speakes first?   *All amaz'd.*
   Ferdinand. We stand, as we had seen *Medusas* head!
   Pierio. I know not what to thinke, I am so amaz'd!

Roderigo. Amaz'd! I am thunderstrooke!
Iacomo.   Wee are inchaunted,
And this is some illusion.
Adorni.   Heav'n forbid!
In darke despaire, it shewes a beame of hope.
Containe thy joy, *Adorni.*
Astutio.   Such a Princesse,
And of so long experienc'd reservednesse
Breake forth, and on the sudden, into flashes
Of more then doubted loosenesse!

[*Enter* AURELIA *and* BERTOLDO.]

Gonzaga.   They come againe,
Smiling, as I live: his arme circling her wast:
I shall runne mad: some fury hath possess'd her.
If I speake, I may be blasted. Ha, I'll mumble
A prayer or two, and crosse my selfe, and then
Though the divell fart fire, have at him.
Aurelia.   Let not, Sir,
The violence of my passions nourish in you
An ill opinion; or grant my carriage
Out of the rode, and garbe of private women,
'Tis still done with decorum. As I am
A Princesse, what I doe, is above censure,
And to be imitated.
Bertoldo.   Gracious Madam,
Vouchsafe a little pawse, for I am so rapt
Beyond my selfe, that 'till I have collected
My scatter'd faculties, I cannot tender
My resolution.
Aurelia.   Consider of it,
I will not be long from you.   BERTOLDO *walking by musing.*
Gonzaga.   Pray I cannot!
This cursed object strangles my devotion!
I must speake, or I burst. Pray you faire Lady,
If you can in courtesie, direct mee to
The chaste *Aurelia.*
Aurelia.   Are you blinde? who are wee?
Gonzaga. Another kind of thing. Her blood was govern'd

117 SD. *Enter* ... BERTOLDO.] *Bryne; not in* 32

By her discretion, and not rul'd her reason:
The reverence and Majesty of *Juno* 140
Shinde in her lookes, and comming to the campe,
Appear'd a second *Pallas*. I can see
No such divinities in you. If I
Without offence may speake my thoughts, you are,
As it were, a wanton *Helen*.
  Aurelia.   Good, ere long 145
You shall know mee better.
  Gonzaga.   Why, if you are *Aurelia*,
How shall I dispose of the Souldier?
  Astutio.   May it please you
To hasten my dispatch?
  Aurelia.   Prefer your suites
Unto *Bertoldo*, we will give him hearing,
And you'll finde him your best advocate. *Exit* AURELIA.
  Astutio.   This is rare! 150
  Gonzaga. What are we come to?
  Roderigo.   Grown up in a moment
A favorite!
  Ferdinand. He does take state already.
  Bertoldo. No, no, it cannot be, yet but *Camiola*,
There is no stop betweene me and a crowne.
Then my ingratitude! a sinne in which 155
All sinnes are comprehended! Aide me vertue,
Or I am lost.
  Gonzaga. May it please your excellence—
Second me, Sir.
  Bertoldo. Then my so horrid oathes,
And hell-deepe imprecations made against it.
  Astutio. The king your brother will thank you, for th' advancement
Of his affaires—
  Bertoldo. And yet who can hold out 161
Against such batteries, as her power and greatnesse
Raise up against my weake defences!
  Gonzaga.   Sir,
     Enter AURELIA.
Doe you dreame waking? Slight, shee's here againe.

 160. you,] *editor;* ~∧ 32 161. affaires—] *editor;* ~∧ 32; ~. *Gifford*

Walkes she on woollen feete?
    Aurelia.   You dwell too long
In your deliberation, and come
With a criples pace to that which you should fly to.
    Bertoldo. It is confess'd, yet why should I to winne
From you, that hazzard all to my poore nothing,
By false play send you off a looser from me?
I am already too too much ingag'd
To the king my brothers anger; and who knowes
But that his doubts, and politick feares, should you
Make me his equall, may draw war upon
Your territories? Were that breach made up
I should with joy embrace, what now I feare
To touch but with due reverence.
    Aurelia.   That hinderance
Is easily remov'd. I owe the king
For a royall visit, which I straight will pay him,
And having first reconcil'd you to his favour,
A dispensation shall meete with us.
    Bertoldo. I am wholly yours.
    Aurelia.   On this booke seale it.
    Gonzaga. What hand and lip too, then the bargaine's sure.
You have no imployment for me?
    Aurelia.   Yes *Gonzaga*,
Provide a royall ship.
    Gonzaga.   A ship? Saint *John*,
Whither are we bound now?
    Aurelia.   You shall know hereafter,
My lord your pardon, for my too much trenching
Upon your patience.
    Adorni.   *Camiola.*   *Whispers to* BERTOLDO.
    Aurelia. How doe you?
    Bertoldo.   Indisposed, but I attend you.   *Exeunt.*
    Adorni. The heavie curse that waites on perjurie,
And foule ingratitude, pursue thee ever.
Yet why from me this? In this breach of faith
My loyalty findes reward! what poysons him
Proves Mithridate to me! I have perform'd
All she commanded punctually, and now

    165. Walkes] *Mason;* Ber. Walkes 32

In the cleare mirrour of my truth, she may
Behold his falsehood. O that I had wings
To beare me to *Palermo*! This once knowne,
Must change her love into a just disdaine,
And worke her to compassion of my paine. *Exit.*

Act IV. Scene V.

SYLLI. CAMIOLA. CLARINDA. At severall doores.

Sylli. Undone! undone! poore I that whilome was
The top and ridge of my house, am on the sudden
Turn'd to the pittifullest animal
Of the lignage of the *Syllies*!
   Camiola. What's the matter?
   Sylli. The king! breake gyrdle, breake!
   Camiola. Why? what of him?
   Sylli. Hearing how far you doted on my person,
Growing envious of my happines, and knowing
His brother, nor his favorite *Fulgentio*,
Could get a sheepes eie from you, I being present,
Is come himselfe a suitor, with the awle
Of his authoritie to bore my nose,
And take you from me, Oh, oh, oh.
   Camiola. Do not rore so;
The king!
   Sylli. The king! yet loving *Sylli* is not
So sorrie for his owne, as your misfortune,
If the king should carrie you, or you beare him,
What a looser should you be? He can but make you
A queene, and what a simple thing is that
To the being my lawful spouse. The world can never
Affoord you such a husband.
   Camiola. I beleeve you,
But how are you sure the king is so inclin'd?
Did not you dreame this?
   Sylli. With these eyes I saw him
Dismisse his traine, and lighting from his coach,
Whispering *Fulgentio* in the eare.
   Camiola. If so
I ghesse the businesse.

IV. v. 24–52   *The Maid of Honour*   181

   Sylli.   It can be no other
But to give me the bob, that being a matter   25
Of maine importance, yonder they are, I dare not

              Enter ROBERTO, FULGENTIO.

Be seene, I am so desperate; if you forsake me,
Send me word that I may provide a willow ghyrlond
To weare when I drowne my selfe. O *Sylli*, O *Sylli*!   *Exit crying.*
   Fulgentio. It will be worth your paines Sir to observe   30
The constancie and bravery of her spirit,
Though great men tremble at your frownes, I dare
Hazzard my head, your majesty set off
With terror, cannot fright her.
   Roberto.   May she answer
My expectation.
   Fulgentio.   There she is.
   Camiola.   My knees thus   35
Bent to the earth (while my vowes are sent upward
For the safety of my Soveraigne) pay the duty
Due for so great an honor, in this favour
Done to your humblest hand-maid.
   Roberto.   You mistake me,
I come not (Lady) that you may report,   40
The king to do you honor, made your house
(He being there) his court, but to correct
Your stubborne disobedience. A pardon
For that, could you obtaine it, were well purchas'd
With this humility.
   Camiola.   A pardon Sir?   45
'Till I am conscious of an offence,
I will not wrong my innocence to begge one,
What is my crime Sir?
   Roberto.   Look on him I favour,
By you scorn'd and neglected.
   Camiola.   Is that all Sir?
   Roberto. No minion, though that were too much. How can you   50
Answer the setting on your desperate bravo
To murther him?
   Camiola.   With your leave, I must not kneele Sir,

        IV. v. 27 SD. *Enter*] Coxeter; *Exit* 32

  While I replie to this: but thus rise up
In my defence, and tell you as a man
(Since when you are unjust, the deity   55
K1ʳ Which you may challenge as a King, parts from you)
'Twas never read in holy writ, or morall,
That subjects on their loyalty were oblig'd
To love their Soveraignes vices; your grace, Sir,
To such an undeserver is no vertue.   60
  Fulgento. What thinke you now Sir?
  Camiola.   Say you should love wine,
You being the king, and cause I am your subject,
Must I be ever drunke? Tyrants, not Kings,
By violence, from humble vassals force
The liberty of their soules. I could not love him,   65
And to compell affection, as I take it,
Is not found in your prerogative.
  Roberto.   Excellent virgin!
How I admire her confidence!   *Aside.*
  Camiola.   Hee complaines
Of wrong done him: but be no more a King,
Unlesse you doe me right. Burne your decrees,   70
And of your lawes, and statutes make a fire,
To thaw the frozen numnesse of delinquents,
If he escape unpunish'd. Doe your edicts
Call it death in any man that breakes into
Anothers house to rob him, though of trifles,   75
And shall *Fulgentio*, your *Fulgentio* live?
Who hath committed more then sacriledge
In the pollution of my cleare fame
By his malicious sclanders.
  Roberto.   Have you done this?
Answer truely on your life.
  Fulgentio.   In the heat of blood   80
Some such thing I reported.
  Roberto.   Out of my sight.
For I vow, if by true penitence thou win not
This injur'd virgin to sue out thy pardon,
Thy grave is digg'd already.

   53. While I replie] *32²*;   replie *32¹*   rise up] *32²*; ris *32¹*   83. virgin]
*32*a; *not in 32*b¹; *Lady 32*b²

Fulgentio. By my owne folly,
I have made a faire hand of 't. *Exit* FULGENTIO.
  Roberto. You shall know Lady 85
While I weare a crowne, justice shall use her sword
To cut offenders off, though neerest to us.
  Camiola. I, now you shew whose Deputy you are.
If now I bath your feete with teares, it cannot
Be censur'd superstition.
  Roberto. You must rise. 90
Rise in our favour, and protection ever. *Kisses her.*
  Camiola. Happy are subjects! when the prince is still
Guided by justice, not his passionate will. *Exeunt.*

The end of the fourth Act.

Act V. Scene I.

CAMIOLA, SYLLI.

  Camiola. You see how tender I am of the quiet
And peace of your affection, and what great ones
I put off in your favour.
  Sylli. You doe wisely.
Exceeding wisely! and when I have said,
I thanke you for't, be happy.
  Camiola. And good reason, 5
In having such a blessing.
  Sylli. When you have it:
But the baite is not yet ready. Stay the time,
While I triumph by my selfe. King, by your leave,
I have wip'd your royall nose, without a napkin,
You may cry willow, willow; for your brother, 10
I'll onely say goe by; for my fine favourite,
He may graze where he please, his lips may water
Like a puppies ore a fermenty pot, while *Sylli*
Out of his two-leav'd cherry-stone dish drinkes Nectar!
I cannot hold out any longer; heav'n forgive me, 15
'Tis not the first oath, I have broke, I must take
A little for a preparative. *Offers to kisse and embrace her.*

89. your] *32*a, *32*b^2; my *32*b^1

Camiola. By no meanes.
If you forsweare your selfe wee shall not prosper.
I'll rather lose my longing.
　　Sylli. Pretty soule!
How carefull it is of me! let me busse yet
Thy little dainty foot for't: that I am sure
Is out of my oath.
　　Camiola. Why, if thou canst dispense with't
So farre, I'll not be scrupulous; such a favour
My amorous shoomaker steales.
　　Sylli. O most rare leather!

Kisses her shooe often.

I doe begin at the lowest, but in time
I may grow higher.
　　Camiola. Fie, you dwell too long there.
Rise, prethee rise.

Enter CLARINDA *hastily.*

　　Sylli. O I am up already.
　　Camiola. How I abuse my houres! what newes with thee now?
　　Clarinda. Off with that gowne, 'tis mine, mine by your promise.
Signior *Adorni* is return'd! now upon entrance:
Off with it, off with it Madam.
　　Camiola. Be not so hasty,
When I goe to bed 'tis thine.
　　Sylli. You have my grant too;
But doe you heare Lady, though I give way to this,
You must heareafter aske my leave before
You part with things of moment.
　　Camiola. Very good.
When I am your's, I will be govern'd.
　　Sylli. Sweet obedience!

Enter ADORNI.

　　Camiola. You are well return'd.
　　Adorni. I wish that the successe
Of my service had deserv'd it.
　　Camiola. Lives *Bertoldo?*
　　Adorni. Yes, and return'd with safety.
　　Camiola. 'Tis not then
In the power of fate to adde to, or take from

My perfit happinesse: and yet he should
Have made me his first visit.
 Adorni.   So I thinke too:
But hee—
 Sylli. Durst not appeare, I being present,
That's his excuse, I warrant you.
 Camiola.   Speake, where is hee?
With whom? who hath deserv'd more from him? or
Can be of equall merit? I in this
Doe not except the King.
 Adorni.   Hees at the Palace
With the Dutchesse of *Siena*. One coach brought 'em hither,
Without a third. Hee's very gracious with her,
You may conceive the rest.
 Camiola.   My jealous feares
Make me to apprehend.
 Adorni.   Pray you dismisse
Signior wisedome, and I'll make relation to you
Of the particulars.
 Camiola.   Servant, I would have you
To haste unto the Court.
 Sylli.   I will out-runne
A foote-man for your pleasure.
 Camiola.   There observe
The Duchesse traine and entertainment.
 Sylli.   Feare not,
I will discover all that is of waight
To the liveries of her Pages, and her footemen.
This is fit imployment for mee.   *Exit* SYLLI.
 Camiola.   Gracious with
The Duchesse! sure you said so?
 Adorni.   I will use
All possible brevity to enforme you Madam,
Of what was trusted to mee, and discharg'd
With faith, and loyall duty.
 Camiola.   I believe it;
You ransom'd him, and suppli'd his wants; imagine
That is already spoken; and what vowes
Of service he made to mee is apparent;
His joy of mee, and wonder too perspicuous;

Does not your story end so?
   Adorni.   Would the end
Had answered the beginning, in a word,
Ingratitude, and perjurie at the height   70
Cannot expresse him.
   Camiola.   Take heed.
   Adorni.   Truth is arm'd
And can defend it selfe. It must out, Madam.
I saw, the presence full, the amorous Dutchesse
Kisse and embrace him, on his part accepted
With equall ardor, and their willing hands   75
No sooner joyn'd, but a remove was publish'd,
And put in execution.
   Camiola.   The proofes are
Too pregnant. O *Bertoldo*!
   Adorni.   Hee's not worth
Your sorrow, Madam.
   Camiola.   Tell mee, when you saw this
Did not you greive as I doe now to heare it?   80
   Adorni. His precipice from goodnesse raising mine,
And serving as a foyle to set my faith off,
I had little reason.
   Camiola.   In this you confesse
The divellish malice of your disposition.
As you were a man, you stood bound to lament it,   85
And not in flattery of your false hopes,
To glory in it: when good men pursue
The path mark'd out by vertue, the bless'd Saints
With joy looke on it, and Seraphique Angells
Clap their celestiall wings in heavenly plaudits,   90
To see a scene of grace so well presented,
The fiends and men made up of envy mourning;
Where as now on the contrary as far
As their divinitie can partake of passion,
With me they weepe, beholding a faire Temple   95
Built in *Bertoldo's* loyalty turn'd to ashes
By the flames of his inconstancy, the damn'd
Rejoycing in the object. 'Tis not well

     V. i. 86. your false] *32*a; false *32*b¹; false your *32*b²   87. good men] *32*a;
good *32*b¹   91. see] *Coxeter*; be *32*

In you *Adorni*.
   Adorni.   What a temper dwells
In this rare Virgin, can you pitty him
That hath shown none to you?
   Camiola.   I must not be
Cruell by his example; you perhaps
Expect I now should seeke recovery
Of what I have lost by teares, and with bent knees
Beg his compassion. No; my towring vertue
From the assurance of my merit scornes
To stoope so low. I'll take a nobler course,
And confident in the justice of my cause,
The king his brother, and new mistrisse, judges,
Ravish him from her armes; you have the contract
In which he swore to marrie me?
   Adorni.   'Tis here, Madam.
   Camiola. He shal be then against his wil my husband
And when I have him, I'll so use him—Doubt not,
But that your honesty being unquestion'd,
This writing with your testimony cleares all.
   Adorni. And buries me, in the dark mists of error.
   Camiola. I'll presently to court, pray you give order
For my caroch.
   Adorni.   A cart for me were fitter
To hurrie me to the gallowes.   *Exit* ADORNI.
   Camiola.   O false men!
Inconstant! perjur'd! my good Angell helpe me
In these extreamities!

               Enter SYLLI.

   Sylli.   If you ever will see brave sight,
Loose it not now. *Bertoldo*, and the Dutchesse
Are presently to be married. There's such pompe
And preparation.
   Camiola.   If I marry, 'tis
This day, or never.
   Sylli.   Why with all my heart,
Though I break this, I'll keep the next oath I make

103. I now] *32a*; now I *32b*   104. and with] *32a, 32b²*; and *32b¹*   111. me] *32a*; her *32b*   113. him—Doubt] *Coxeter*; him, doubt *32*   121. these] *32a*; those my *32b¹*; these my *32b²*

And then it is quit.
    Camiola. Follow me to my Cabinet,
You know my confessor, Father *Paulo*?
    Sylli. Yes. Shall he
Doe the feate for us?
    Camiola. I will give in writing
Directions to him, and attire my selfe   130
Like a Virgin-bride, and something I will doe
That shall deserve mens prayse, and wonder too.
    Sylli. And I to make all know, I am not shallow,
Will have my points of Cucchineale and yellow.   *Exeunt.*

Act V. Scene II.

Lowd Musicke.

ASTUTIO. GONZAGA. RODERIGO. IACOMO. PIERIO. ROBERTO.
BERTOLDO. AURELIA. BISHOP. With Attendants.

  Roberto. Had our division beene greater, Madam,
Your clemency, the wrong being done to you,
In pardon of it, like the rod of concord
Must make a perfect union. Once more
With a brotherly affection we receive you   5
Into our favour. Let it be your study
Hereafter to deserve this blessing, farre
Beyond your merit.
    Bertoldo. As the Princesse grace
To me is without limit, my endeavours
With all obsequiousnesse to serve her pleasures   10
Shall know no bounds, nor will I being made
Her husband, ere forget the duty that
I owe her as a servant.
    Aurelia. I expect not
But faire equality, since I well know
If that superiority be due   15
'Tis not to mee. When you are made my consort,
All the prerogatives of my high birth cancell'd

    V. ii. 4. make a] *32*a; make *32*b¹   12. ere forget] *32*a; forget *32*b

I'll practise the obedience of a wife,
And freely pay it. Queenes themselves, if they
Make choice of their inferiors, onely aiming
To feed their sensuall appetites, and to raigne
Over their husbands, in some kinde commit
Authoriz'd whoredome, nor will I be guilty
In my intent of such a crime.
 Gonzaga.   This done,
As it is promis'd, Madam, may well stand for
A president to great women: but when once
The griping hunger of desire is cloyd,
(And the poore foole advanc'd, brought on his knees)
Most of your Eagle breed, I'll not say all
(Ever excepting you) challenge againe,
What in hot blood they parted from.
 Aurelia.   You are ever
An enemy of our sex, but you I hope Sir
Have better thoughts.
 Bertoldo.   I dare not entertaine
An ill one of your goodnesse.
 Roberto.   To my power
I will enable him to prevent all danger
Envy can raise against your choice. One word more
Touching the articles.

   Enter FULGENTIO, CAMIOLA, SYLLI, ADORNI.

 Fulgentio.   In you alone
Lye all my hopes, you can or kill or save me,
But pitty in you, will become you better,
(Though I confesse in justice 'tis deni'd me)
Then too much rigor.
 Camiola.   I will make your peace
As far as it lyes in me, but must first
Labour to right my selfe.
 Aurelia.   Or adde or alter
What you thinke fit. In him I have my all,
Heaven make me thankfull for him.
 Roberto.   On to the Temple.
 Camiola. Stay royall Sir, and as you are a king
Erect one here, in doing justice to

An injur'd mayde.
    Aurelia.   How's this?
    Bertoldo.   O I am blasted!
    Roberto. I have given some proofe, sweet Lady, of my promptnes
To doe you right, you need not therfore doubt me,   50
And rest assur'd, that this great worke dispatch'd,
You shall have audience and satisfaction
To all you can demand.
    Camiola.   To doe mee justice
Exacts your present care, and can admit
Of no delay. If, e'r my cause be heard,   55
In favour of your brother, you goe on Sir,
Your scepter cannot right mee. Hee's the man,
The guilty man, whom I accuse, and you
Stand bound in duty, as you are Supreame,
To be impartiall. Since you are a Judge,   60
As a Delinquent, looke on him, and not
As on a brother; justice painted blinde
Inferres, her Ministers are oblig'd to heare
The cause and truth, the Judge, determine of it,
And not sway'd, or by favour, or affection,   65
By a false glosse, or wrested comment alter
The true intent, and letter of the law.
    Roberto. Nor will I Madam.
    Aurelia.   You seeme troubl'd, Sir.
    Gonzaga. His colour changes too.
    Camiola.   The alteration
Growes from his guilt. The goodnesse of my cause   70
Begets such confidence in mee, that I bring
No hir'd tongue to plead for mee, that with gay
Rhetoricall flourishes may palliate
That, which stripp'd naked, will appeare deform'd.
I stand here, mine owne advocate; and my truth   75
Deliver'd in the plainest language, will
Make good it selfe, nor will I, if the King
Give suffrage to it, but admit of you,
My greatest enemy, and this stranger Prince,
To sit assistants with him.
    Aurelia.   I ne'r wrong'd you.   80
    Camiola. In your knowledge of the injury, I believe it,

Now will you in your justice, when you are
Acquainted with my interest in this man
Which I lay claime to.
    Roberto.   Let us take our seats,
What is your title to him?
    Camiola.   By this contract
Seal'd solemnely before a reverend man,
I challenge him for my husband.
    Sylli.   Ha! was I
Sent for the Frier, for this? O *Sylli*! *Sylli*!
Some cordiall, or I faint.
    Roberto.   This writing is
Authenticall.
    Aurelia.   But done in heat of blood,
(Charm'd by her flatteries, as no doubt he was)
To be dispens'd with.
    Ferdinand.   Adde this, if you please,
The distance and disparity betweene
Their births and fortunes.
    Camiola.   What can inocence hope for
When such as sit her judges, are corrupted!
Disparity of birth, or fortune urge you?
Or *Syren* charmes? or at his best, in mee
Wants to deserve him? Call some few daies backe,
And as he was, consider him, and you
Must grant him my inferiour. Imagine
You saw him now in fetters with his honour,
His liberty lost; with her blacke wings despaire
Circling his miseries, and this *Gonzaga*
Trampling on his afflictions; the great summe
Propos'd for his redemption; the King
Forbidding payment of it; his neere kinsmen,
With his protesting followers, and friends,
Falling off from him; by the whole world forsaken;
Dead to all hope, and buried in the grave
Of his calamities, and then waigh duly
What she deserv'd (whose merits now are doubted)
That as his better Angell in her bounties
Appeard unto him, his great ransome paid,

    103. this] *Coxeter*; his *32*   106. his] *Coxeter*; this *32*

His wants, and with a prodigall hand suppli'd,
Whether then being my manumised slave,
Hee ow'd not himselfe to mee?
   Aurelia.   Is this true?
   Roberto. In his silence 'tis acknowledg'd.
   Gonzaga.   If you want
A witnesse to this purpose, I'll depose it.
   Camiola. If I have dwelt too long on my deservings
To this unthankfull man, pray you pardon me,
The cause requir'd it. And though now I adde
A little in my painting to the life
His barbarous ingratitude, to deterre
Others from imitation, let it meet with
A faire interpretation. This serpent,
Frozen to numnesse, was no sooner warm'd
In the bosome of my pitty, and compassion,
But in returne, he ruin'de his preserver,
The prints the yrons had made in his flesh
Still ulcerous; but all that I had done
(My benefits in sand, or water written)
As they had never beene, no more remembred.
And on what ground; but his ambitious hopes
To gaine this Duchesse favour?
   Aurelia.   Yes, the object,
Looke on it better (Lady) may excuse
The change of his affection.
   Camiola.   The object
In what? forgive mee, modesty, if I say
You looke upon your forme in the false glasse
Of flattery, and selfe-love, and that deceives you;
That you were a Duchesse, as I take it, was not
Character'd on your face, and that not seene,
For other feature, make all these that are
Experienc'd in women, judges of 'em,
And if they are not Parasites, they must grant
For beauty without art, though you storme at it,
I may take the right hand file.
   Gonzaga.   Well said i'faith;
I see faire women on no termes will yeeld

136. change] *Mason*; charge 32

Priority in beauty.
   Camiola.   Downe proud heart!
Why doe I rise up in defence of that,
Which, in my cherishing of it hath undone mee?
No Madam, I recant, you are all beauty,
Goodnesse, and vertue, and poore I not worthy
As a foyle to set you off; enjoy your conquest
But doe not tyranize. Yet as I am
In my lownesse from your height, you may looke on me,
And in your suffrage to me, make him know
That though to all men else I did appeare
The shame and scorne of women, hee stands bound
To hold me as her master-piece.
   Roberto.   By my life
You have show'n your selfe of such an abject temper,
So poore, and low condition'd, as I grieve for
Your neerenesse to mee.
   Ferdinand.   I am chang'd in my
Opinion of you Lady, and professe
The vertues of your minde, an ample fortune
For an absolute Monarch.
   Gonzaga.   Since you are resolv'd
To damne your selfe, in your forsaking of
Your noble order for a woman, doe it
For this. You may search through the world, and meet not
With such another *Phœnix*.
   Aurelia.   On the sudden
I feele all fires of love quench'd in the water
Of compassion; make your peace, you have
My free consent; for here I doe disclaime
All interest in you: and to further your
Desires, faire Maid, compos'd of worth and honour,
The dispensation procur'd by mee,
Freeing *Bertoldo* from his vow, makes way
To your embraces.
   Bertoldo.   Oh, how have I stray'd,
And wilfully, out of the noble tract

   153. foyle] *Coxeter*; soyle *32*   158. women] *32*; Nature *conj. Coxeter*
159. her] *32*; a *conj. Mason*; the *Gifford*; their *conj. Chelli*   171. Of]*32*; Of my *Gifford*

Mark'd mee by vertue! 'Till now, I was never
Truely a prisoner; to excuse my late
Captivity, I might alleage the malice
Of fortune; you that conquer'd me confessing
Courage in my defence was no way wanting;
But now I have surrendred up my strengths
Into the power of vice, and on my forehead
Branded with mine owne hand in capitall letters
Disloyall, and Ingratefull; though barr'd from
Humane society, and hiss'd into
Some desert nere yet haunted with the curses
Of men and women, sitting as a judge
Vpon my guilty selfe, I must confesse
It justly falls upon me, and one teare
Shed in compassion of my suffrings more
Then I can hope for.
 Camiola.   This compunction
For the wrong that you have done me, though you should
Fix here, and your true sorrow move no further,
Will in respect I lov'd once, make these eies
Two springs of sorrow for you.
 Bertoldo.   In your pittie
My cruelty shewes more monstrous, yet I am not,
Though most ingratfull, grown to such a height
Of impudence, as in my wishes onely
To aske your pardon. If as now I fall
Prostrate before your feete, you will vouchsafe
To act your owne revenge, treading upon me
As a viper eating through the bowels of
Your benefits, to whom with libertie
I owe my being, 'twill take from the burthen
That now is insupportable.
 Camiola.   Pray you rise,
As I wish peace, and quiet to my soule
I do forgive you heartily, yet excuse me
Though I deny my selfe a blessing that
By the favour of the Dutchesse seconded,
With your submission is offer'd to me.
Let not the reason I alleage for't grieve you,
You have been false once. I have done. And if

When I am married (as this day I will be)
As a perfit signe of your attonement with me
You wish me joy, I will receive it for
Full satisfaction of all obligations
In which you stand bound to me.
   Bertoldo.   I will doe it,
And what's more, in despite of sorrow, live
To see my selfe undone, beyond all hope
To be made up againe.
   Sylli.   My blood begins
To come to my heart againe.
   Camiola.   Pray you *Signior Sylli*,
Call in the holy Frier. Hee's prepar'd
For finishing the worke.
   Sylli.   I knew I was
The man. Heaven make mee thankfull.
   Roberto.   Who is this?
   Astutio. His Father was the banker of *Palermo*,
And this the heyre of his great wealth, his wisdome
Was not hereditarie.
   Sylli.   Though you know me not,
Your Majesty owes me a round Sum, I have
A seale, or two to witnesse, yet if you please
To weare my colours, and dance at my wedding,
I'll never sue you.
   Roberto.   And I'll grant your suite.
   Sylli. Gracious *Maddona*, Noble Generall,
Brave Captaines and my quondam rivalls, wear 'em
Since I am confident you dare not harbour
A thought, but that way currant.   *Exit.*
   Aurelia.   For my part
I cannot ghesse the issue.

    Enter SYLLI *with* PAULO.

   Sylli.   Do your duty,
And with all speed you can, you may despatch us.
   Paulo. Thus as a principal ornament to the Church
I sease her.
   All. How.

  239 SD. *with* PAULO.] *Coxeter* (the Friar); *with* 32

Roberto. So young and so religious.
Paulo. She has forsooke the world.
Sylli. And *Sylli* too,
I shall run mad.
Roberto. Hence with the foole, proceede Sir.   SYLLI *thrust off.*
Paulo. Looke on this maid of honor now   245
   Truely honor'd in her vow
   She payes to heaven, vaine delight
   By day, or pleasure of the night,
   She no more thinkes of, this faire haire
   (Favours for great kings to weare)   250
   Must now be shorn; her rich array
   Chang'd into a homely gray.
   The dainties with which she was fed
   And her proud flesh pampered,
   Must not be tasted; from the spring,   255
   For wine, cold water we will bring
   And with fasting mortifie
   The feasts of sensuality.
   Her jewells, beads, and she must looke
   Not in a glasse, but holy booke;   260
   To teach her the nere erring way
   To immortality. O may
   She as she purposes to be
   A Child new borne to piety,
   Persever in it, and good men   265
   With Saints and Angels say Amen.
Camiola. This is the marriage! this the port! to which
My vowes must steere me, fill my spreading sayles
With the pure wind of your devotions for me,
That I may touch the secure haven, where   270
Eternall happinesse keepes her residence,
Temptations to frailty never entring.
I am dead to the world, and thus dispose
Of what I leave behind me, and dividing
My state into three parts, I thus bequeath it. 275
The first to the faire Nunnery, to which
I dedicate the last, and better part
Of my fraile life; a second portion

251. Must] *Coxeter*; Muw 32

To pious uses; and the third to thee
Adorni, for thy true and faithfull service. 280
And ere I take my last farwel; with hope
To finde a grant, my suite to you is that
You would for my sake pardon this young man
And to his merits love him, and no further.
    Roberto. I thus confirme it.   *Gives his hand to* FULGENTIO.
    Camiola.   And as ere you hope 285
Like me to be made happy, I conjure you   *To* BERTOLDO.
To reassume your order; and in fighting
Bravely against the enemies of our faith
Redeeme your morgag'd honor.
    Gonzaga.   I restore this: *The white crosse.*
Once more brothers in armes,
    Bertoldo.   I'll live and die so. 290
    Camiola. To you my pious wishes. And to end
All differences, great Sir I beseech you
To be an arbitrator, and compound
The quarrell, long continuing betweene
The Duke and Dutchesse.
    Roberto.   I'll take it into 295
My speciall care.
    Camiola.   I am then at rest, now father
Conduct me where you please.   *Exeunt* PAULO *and* CAMIOLA.
    Roberto.   She well deserves
Her name, the Maid of Honor! May she stand
To all posterity, a faire example
For noble Maides to imitate. Since to live 300
In wealth and pleasure is common; but to part with
Such poyson'd baites is rare, there being nothing
Upon this Stage of life to be commended,
Though well begun, till it be fully ended.   *Exeunt.*

The END.

281. take my last] *Coxeter*; my take lust *32*   282. my] *Coxeter*; may *32*
289. Gonzaga.] *Mason;* Rob. *32*

THE DUKE OF MILAN

INTRODUCTION

(a) *Date*

In the absence of any record of a licence in the Astley–Herbert Office Book, the latest date for the writing of *The Duke of Milan* is set by the Stationers' Register entry dated 20 January 1623, which assigns the play to Edward Blackmore and George Norton (see p. 204).

Baldwin has argued that the play must have been completed before May 1622, when Herbert began his entries, but it is equally possible that the record of a licence granted at a later date has been lost.[1]

In 1891 Fleay threw off the suggestion that the imprisoned author mentioned in III. ii. 17–24 was George Wither,[2] and later scholars took Wither's imprisonment in 1621–2 as fixing the earliest date for the composition of the tragedy. However, Wither was twice imprisoned before 1623 on the charge of 'defaming of great Men' (from 20 March to 26 July 1614, and from 27 June 1621 to 15 March 1622), and neither term can easily be equated with the 'three dayes' mentioned in Massinger's text.[3]

In other respects the lines fit Wither well enough, and in the 1620s he was certainly a topical target. Jonson personified him as Chrono-mastix in the masque *Time Vindicated to Himself and to His Honours*, given at court on 19 January 1623, making him speak of ladies who 'sent me pensions, / To cherish, and to heighten my inventions' (ll. 130–1; cf. *Duke of Milan*, III. ii. 17–19). Davenant mocked him as Castruccio, in *The Cruel Brother* (1627), and Wither himself, in *Britain's Remembrancer* (1628), mentions *'publike*

[1] Bentley has drawn attention to the incompleteness of the extant records of the licences granted by Buc, Astley, and Herbert, in 'Authenticity and Attribution in the Jacobean and Caroline Drama', *English Institute Essays 1942* (1943), 101–18.
[2] *Biographical Chronicle of the English Drama (1559–1642)*, i. 212.
[3] See M. J. French, 'George Wither in Prison', *PMLA*, xlv (1930), 959–66; L. H. Kendall, 'George Wither in Prison' *NQ*, 3rd Series, cci (1956), 147–9; A. Pritchard, '*Abuses Stript and Whipt* and Wither's Imprisonment', *RES*, N.S. xiv (1963), 337–45.

Masques, *and* Playes, *to* [*my*] *disgrace* / ... *set abroach*; *till justly they became*, / *To those that made, and favour'd them, a shame*'. In 1614 Wither had incurred the wrath of Henry Howard, Earl of Northampton; in 1621 he offended James and others with his satirical poem *Wither's Motto*. He was restored to favour through the offices of William Herbert, Earl of Pembroke, and in the fourth book of his *Collection of Emblems* (1634), dedicated to Pembroke's brother Philip, he says that when James

> tooke offence
> At my Free *Lines*; HEE [William Herbert], foun'd such *Meanes* and *Place*
> To bring, and reconcile mee to his *Grace*;
> That, therewithall, his *Majestie* bestow'd
> A gift upon mee, which his *Bountie* show'd:[1]

If the parallels here with Massinger's poet-prisoner, 'Discharged by another that set him on ... and his stripes wash'd of / With oyle of Angels' (*Duke of Milan*, III. ii. 22–4), establish an allusion to Wither's imprisonment in 1621–2, then Massinger must have written *The Duke of Milan* for the 1622 winter season at Blackfriars, but the identification cannot be considered conclusive.

In the same scene two other prisoners are mentioned: one an obstinate 'Sectarie', who afterwards became 'a fine Pulpet man, and was benefic'd'; the other a 'she waiter' involved in a court scandal. Gifford suspected topical allusions, and there are contemporary references to the imprisonment, in July 1621, of two notable preachers with puritan sympathies. 'Dr. Baylie, bishop of Bangor, was committed to the Fleet for disputing (they say) somwhat malapertly with the King about the Sabbath, and Dr. Price is likewise clapt up for glauncing at somwhat in his sermon at Otelands on Sonday was sevenight.'[2] Price, known as 'the mawle of heretics' for his attacks on English Catholics and the Spaniards, is perhaps the likelier of the two men. The lady remains unidentified.

With Bentley, I reject Baldwin's metrical analyses, and his assumption that Massinger regularly wrote two plays a year, as further evidence for dating *The Duke of Milan*. In the absence of unambiguous factual evidence other than that of the Stationers' Register entry, the period 1621–2 must remain the probable date of composition of the tragedy.

---

[1] Signature * following p. 196.
[2] Chamberlain, *Letters*, ii. 387; the event is also discussed in letters from Joseph Mead (see *The Court and Times of James the First*, ed. R. F. Williams, 1848, ii. 265–7).

(b) Sources

The sources of Massinger's tragedy have been studied in a monograph, two theses, and a general study of plays based on the Herod–Mariamne story.[1] Seven dramatizations of that story were written before 1622, together with at least three plays founded on incidents from the life of Sforza, Duke of Milan. Massinger appears to be indebted to none of them, though Markham and Sampson's sensational chronicle play, *Herod and Antipater*, written before 1621 for the same company for whom Massinger and Dekker wrote *The Virgin Martyr* (1620),[2] may well have suggested the subject to him.

The major source for *The Duke of Milan* was Josephus's *Jewish Antiquities*, xv. §§ 183–242, together with his shorter version of the same story in *The Jewish War*, I. §§ 431–44. The dramatist may have been able to read the originals,[3] but it is most probable that he used the translations in Thomas Lodge's *The Famous and Memorable Workes of Iosephus*, 1602.[4]

From the *Jewish Antiquities* came the body of the plot in Acts I–IV, together with the theme of Sforza's obsessive and destructive passion for Marcelia. As well as idealizing to a degree the character of the duke and the duchess, Massinger compressed into one the two occasions in Josephus on which Herod left a secret command for the death of his wife Mariamne in the event of his failure to return first from a meeting with Antony, and later with Caesar, and formed a single character (Francisco) from the three men (Herod's uncle Joseph, Sohemus the Iturian, and Joseph the Treasurer) with whom the command is left. Graccho may have come from the 'Butler' who underwent torture for his part in a plot by Salome against Mariamne, though his counter-scheming against Francisco is Massinger's addition. In *The Jewish War*

---

[1] E. Koeppel, *Quellen-Studien*, pp. 90–5; E. Gerhardt, *Massinger's 'The Duke of Milan' und seine Quellen*, Halle, 1905; P. M. Smith, *Massinger's Use of Sources, with special reference to 'The Duke of Milan' and 'Believe as You List'*, unpublished University of Birmingham dissertation, 1963; M. J. Valency, *The Tragedies of Herod and Mariamne* (Columbia University Studies in English and Comparative Literature 145), New York, 1940. See also A. C. Dunstan, *An Examination of Two English Dramas: 'The Tragedy of Miriam' by Elizabeth Carew and 'The True Tragedy of Herod and Antipater' by Gervase Markham and William Sampson*, Koenigsberg, 1908.

[2] Bentley, iv. 734–5.

[3] See A. H. Cruickshank, *Philip Massinger*, 1920, 148–51. There were translations into Latin (1514), German (1531), and French (1534) available to Massinger.

[4] There were later editions in 1609 and 1620. The relevant passages are *The Antiquities of the Jews*, XV. IV, IX–XI, and *The Wars of the Jews*, I. XVII.

Massinger found a reference to the disasters which followed Herod's divorce from his first wife Doris, in favour of Mariamne. Out of this he developed Francisco's plot to revenge his sister Eugenia, but the lustful and scheming revenger who replaces Josephus's passive and innocent servants is almost entirely the dramatist's own invention.[1]

For Act V, Massinger abandoned Josephus's account of Herod's trial and condemnation of Mariamne, and substituted a more sensational ending derived from the final scene of *The Second Maiden's Tragedy*, which was licensed on 31 October 1611.[2] There are other Elizabethan and Jacobean plays in which a murder is brought about by physical contact with a poisoned corpse (for instance Kyd's *Soliman and Perseda*, and Tourneur's *The Revenger's Tragedy*), but Massinger's indebtedness to this tragedy is proved by the close correspondence of the action, and by several verbal parallels, which are noted in the Commentary. There is also a passage in the older play which may first have suggested its use to Massinger:

> I once read of a *Herod* whose affection
> pursued a virgins loue, as I did thine
> whoe for the hate she owd him kilde her self
>
> . . . . .
>
> yet he preserud her bodie dead in honie
> and kept her longe after her funerall[3]

Koeppel, Baldwin, and P. M. Smith have all recognized that Massinger kept in mind *Othello*, in developing the relationship between the fiercely jealous Sforza, his wife (a much more fiery Desdemona), and the treacherous favourite, Francisco; D. L. Frost, *The School of Shakespeare*, 1968, sees *The Duke of Milan* as Massinger's closest imitation of a Shakespearian play.[4] There are distant verbal echoes—'I know thee honest . . . While I found merit in my selfe to please her / I should beleeue her chast, and would not seeke / To find out my owne torment'[5]—but the influence of the

---

[1] B. T. Spencer, 'Philip Massinger', in *Seventeenth Century Studies*, edited by R. Shafer, Princeton, 1933, documents the Machiavellian villain element in Francisco.
[2] The play was never printed, and Bentley plausibly suggests (iv. 776) that Massinger was able to read it in the archives of the King's company.
[3] *The Second Maiden's Tragedy* (Malone Society Reprint, 1910), ll. 1856-61.
[4] It may be significant that *Othello* was first published in 1622.
[5] *Duke of Milan*, I. iii. 399, IV. iii. 103-5; *Othello*, III. iii. 122, 191-2.

Introduction

Shakespearian play is to be seen most clearly in Francisco's success in inflaming Sforza's jealousy to the point where he murders his innocent wife.

Perhaps to disguise his use of sources already exploited by Markham and Sampson, Massinger set his play in sixteenth-century Italy, freely adapting names, personalities, and events. His Duke of Milan bears the name of Ludovico Sforza, who intrigued against Charles VIII of France, but he is given the deeds and character of his son Francesco, who fought against the French at the battle of Pavia, but later made his peace with Charles after the Treaty of Cambrai. Pescara has the name of Charles's able lieutenant, the Marquis of Pescara, but something of the character of Francesco's chancellor, Jerome Moron.[1]

The standard history of Renaissance Italy, Geoffrey Fenton's translation of Guicciardini's *Historia d'Italia* (of which there were editions in 1579, 1599, and 1618), supplied most of Massinger's material. In Books XV and XIX in particular, the dramatist found the life of Ludovico already described in tragic terms (for instance, his death is 'the last act of his tragedie'), and the life of Francesco provided the basis for the confrontation between the Duke of Milan and the Emperor in III. i:

> When *Francis Sforce* was brought to the presence of the Emperour at *Bolognia*, and hauing thanked him for his benignitie in that he had admitted him vnto his presence, he told him, that he reposed so much in his iustice, that for all matters happened before the Marquis of *Pesquiero* restrained him within the Castle of *Millan*, he desired no other suretie or support then his owne innocence: and that therefore touching these things he frankly renounced the safeconduct, the escript whereof the Duke holding it in his hand, he cast it at the Emperours feete; which was a matter that contented him much. (Book XIX, p. 806.)

Massinger may also have consulted William Thomas's *The History of Italy* (1561). Thomas covers much the same ground as Guicciardini, though in less detail, and the names in Massinger's play have the form and spelling of those in Thomas rather than those in Fenton's translation of Guicciardini.[2]

---

[1] There is no equivalent to Pescara in Josephus, but P. M. Smith points out that in *The Duchess of Malfi* Duke Ferdinand has a loyal friend named Pescara.

[2] Cf. Thomas's *Millaine, Pauia, Pescara, Lodouico Sforza* with Fenton's *Millan, Pauie, Pesquiero, Lodowike Sforce*.

(c) *Text*

The Duke of Milan was entered in the Stationers' Register on 20 January 1623:[1]

Edw: Blackmore George Norton.   Entred for their Copie vnder the handes of Sr Iohn Ashley knight, M^r. of the Reuells and M^r. Gilmyn warden, A play called Sforza, Duke of Millaine, made by M^r. Messenger.   vj^d

(Register D 52; Greg, *Bibliography*, i. 33; Arber, iv. 90.)

On 5 May 1623, Norton assigned his rights in the play to Blackmore.[2] The Stationers' Register entry reads as follows:

Edw: Blackmore.   Assigned ouer vnto him by George Norton and consent of a full court holden this Daie all the estate, right and title the said George hath in the play called, The Duke of Millan   vj^d

(Register D 57; Greg, *Bibliography*, i. 33; Arber, iv. 95.)

Accordingly the first edition of Massinger's tragedy was published by Edward Blackmore in 1623. The printer was Bernard Alsop.[3] This edition is listed in the 'Catalogue of such Bookes as haue beene published, and (by authority) printed in English, since the last Autumne Mart, which was in September 1622. till this present Aprill 1623', added to John Brill's English edition of the *Catalogus Vniuersalis pro Nundinis Francofurtensibus Vernalibus de anno M.DC. XXIII*, 1623 (D4^r). It will be referred to from now on as *23*; the title-page is reproduced on page 213.

23 is in quarto, [A]², π², B–M⁴ (48 leaves); see Greg, *Bibliography*, no. 386 (ii. 533). The contents are: [A]1^r, *title*; [A]1^v, *blank*; [A]2^r, *dedication begins*, 'TO THE RIGHT HONOVRABLE AND MVCH ESTEEMED FOR HER HIGH BIRTH, BVT MORE ADMIred for her vertue, the Lady KATHERINE STANHOPE', *signed* 'PHILIP MASSINGER:'; [A]2^v, 'THE NAMES OF THE *ACTORS*.';

---

[1] The licenser 'Sr Iohn Ashley knight' is, of course, Herbert's predecessor as Master of the Revels. Herbert purchased the office from Ashley (or Astley) on 20 July 1623, but Ashley continued to license plays for printing only until 3 Sept. 1623; Herbert's first entry of this kind being on 12 Mar. 1624.

[2] See R. B. McKerrow, *A Dictionary of Printers and Booksellers* . . . (*1557–1640*), 1910, 203.

[3] There is little doubt of the interpretation of the initials '*B. A.*' on the title-page. Alsop printed Massinger and Dekker's *The Virgin Martyr* in 1622, and (with Thomas Fawcett) *The Roman Actor* in 1629. The (not very distinctive) initial *M* on A2^r of *The Duke of Milan* also appears on A4^r of Robert Sibthorpe's *A Counterplea to an Apostatæs Pardon* (1618), printed by 'Bar: Alsop' for Richard Fleming.

π1ʳ, *poem*, 'VPON THIS WORKE OF HIS *beloued friend the* AVTHOR.'; π1ᵛ, *poem ends*, signed 'W. B.'; π2, *blank* (*frequently missing*);¹ B1ʳ, 'THE DVKE OF MILLAINE.', *text begins*; M4ʳ, *text ends*, '*FINIS.*'; M4ᵛ, *blank*. The text is set in roman, 20 lines measuring approximately 100 mm. There are usually 35 lines to the page (36 on G1ᵛ, G3ᵛ, H3ᵛ and H4ᵛ). In sheet B only, the standard is 36 lines to the page (37 on B1ᵛ), and further space is saved by the omission of act and scene headings after the first one, in this sheet alone.²

Two skeletons were used in the printing, one for each inner forme and one for each outer forme. In sheet M alone, both formes were imposed by the inner skeleton, and some running titles were exchanged from one skeleton to another in sheets C, F, G, H, I, and L. In general the quarto is well printed, and there are comparatively few careless misprints. At two places in the text a blank space was left for a word which the compositor could not make out (IV. iii. 98 and 168). Though the evidence is not conclusive, differences in the style of composition suggest that one compositor was responsible for sheets A, C–G, and another for H–L.³ In sheet B the presence of a third compositor is indicated by a unique set of speech headings (*Gra.*, *Ma.*, *Fra.*, *Sfor.*), by the full forms of marginal stage directions which are almost invariably abbreviated elsewhere, by the omission of scene indications after the first one, and by a rash of italics. This compositor probably set up the half sheet containing W. B.'s poem as well; in these pages alone apostrophes and marks of elision are placed unusually, as in *Apoll'os* (π1ʳ) and *defor'md* (B3ᵛ). A fourth man may have set up sheet M, in which new speech headings appear (notably *Forza*, where the compositor has misread *ſſ* as *ff*), and a strong preference for *-y* to *-ie* is shown. *I'll* also appears for the first time, in place of *I'le* or *Ile*.

[1] In '"W. B." and Massinger', *RES*, iv (1928), 326–7, A. K. McIlwraith established that [A]1 and [A]2 form one half-sheet, and π1 and π2 another, and suggested that the verses were added after the edition was already in print.

[2] A. K. McIlwraith, 'Some Bibliographical Notes on Massinger', *The Library*, 4th Series, xi (1931), 82–3, plausibly suggests that this indicates the presence of a cancel, issued to make good some serious deficiency in the original printing. In all, sheet B holds 10 lines more than usual. There is a further discussion of the problem by Hiroshi Yamashita in 'The Printing of Philip Massinger's Plays', in *Shakespeare Studies*, x (1971–2), Tokyo, 1973.

[3] In sheets C–G capitalization is three times heavier than in the later sheets, there is a marked preference for *-ie* to *-y* forms (they appear in roughly equal numbers for H–L), and about twice as many instances of medial *y* for *i*. Act and scene headings, too, are less heavily abbreviated than in the later sheets.

Eleven of the twenty-six formes are variant. D(i) exists in three states; A (i) and (o), π (o), B (i), D (o), E (i) and (o), F (i), I (i) and (o) in two states. Thirty-six corrections have been noted; half of them in A (i) and B (i). That Massinger himself was responsible for some of these corrections is strongly suggested by several changes in spelling and some rewording (instances occur on the title-page,[1] and at I. i. 68, I. iii. 360, II. i. 274 and 305).

Greg thought that the printer's manuscript was probably in Massinger's hand, but from the evidence of misreadings and spelling in the text of 23 the printer's copy is more likely to have been a scribal transcript of Massinger's foul papers. From time to time Massinger's favourite w-spellings appear in the text (*lowd, showt, perswade*), and the erroneous *this* for *these* (Dedication 10) suggests an original Massinger spelling, *theis*. On the other hand, there are many spelling features not characteristic of the author. In a number of cases short words generally ending in a double consonant with or without a final *e* appear with a single consonant (*ad, al, kil, cal'd, shal, spels*); there are also words like *Starrs* and *shott* where the final consonant is doubled. The final *e* is frequently omitted from words in which it is usually present, as in *ther, wrot, hast, desperet, minuts*. The scribe's *e* and *o* seem to have been easily confused, too, as in *soldior, docter, dopraue, feruer*. Some of these spellings were corrected either during printing or by Massinger himself in the Foljambe copy. Such spellings are not frequent enough in the quarto to be a compositor's intentional spellings, and there is no pattern to their appearance. Stage properties are noted only occasionally ('*Graccho, Iouio, Giouanni, with Flagons*'; '*Song. Marcelia aboue in blacke*'), several exits and entrances are left unmarked, and there are vague directions for groups of minor characters ('*fidlers*'; '*Attendants*'; '*Graccho, & the rest*'; '*Doctors, Seruants*').[2] There is nothing in the few directions for music or actions beyond an author's range, and no positive evidence for a prompter's work on the manuscript. There are clear instances of alteration and addition to the text of the play; the major passages are discussed in the Commentary notes on II. i. 28–30; III. ii. 96–110; III. iii. 43–6;

---

[1] The readings *TRAGEDIE* and MESSENGER in 23[1] are corrected to *TRAGÆDIE* and MASSINGER in 23[2], and by Massinger himself in the Foljambe copy.

[2] The directions for '*three Gentlemen*' at I. iii. 1 and IV. iii. 1 are Massinger's rather than a prompter's: Baldwin has drawn attention to the dramatist's fondness for grouping minor characters in threes.

V. ii. 221–5. There are confusions and difficulties here which would have been intolerable in a text to be used in the theatre.

There are copies of *23* in the following libraries and institutions: the Bodleian Library (2 copies); the Boston Public Library; the British Museum (4 copies); the Chapin Library; the Library of Congress; the Folger Shakespeare Library (2 copies); the Henry E. Huntington Library; the University of Illinois; Innerpeffray Library; Magdalene College, Cambridge; the Newberry Library; the University of Pennsylvania; Princeton University; the National Library of Scotland; and the Victoria and Albert Museum (3 copies).

The present text has been prepared from the Bodleian Library copy, Malone 236 (1).

There are autograph corrections in the Harbord copy of *The Duke of Milan* (Folger Shakespeare Library, Gosse 5294). Two lines cut away by the binder are supplied in the margin, two defective letters are touched up, and in eight of the ten places in sheet M where Sforza's name is misprinted *Forza* an *S* is prefixed. More extensive and important autograph corrections are found in the Foljambe copy, now in the Victoria and Albert Museum, London (Dyce 6323).[1] The *Forza* error is set right, together with some minor mistakes in spelling and punctuation and more than forty misreadings in the text. These authorial corrections are recorded in the textual apparatus, with the siglum *Massinger MS*. Further manuscript corrections by an anonymous seventeenth-century hand are found in the Library of Congress copy of *23*. Of 33 substantive corrections, 22 agree (in substance but not always in accidentals) with Massinger's autograph corrections, one offers a new solution to a textual crux, and four agree with editorial emendations accepted into the present text. These corrections have no independent textual authority, but they are of considerable interest as the work of an intelligent contemporary reader, and the most important of them are recorded in the textual apparatus, with the siglum *Congress MS*.

A second edition of *The Duke of Milan* was printed by John Raworth in 1638 for the original publisher. It will be referred to from now on as *38*; see Greg, *Bibliography*, no. 386 (ii. 533). It is, presumably, this edition of the play which is named in booksellers'

---

[1] This copy is discussed in the introduction to 'To Sir Francis Foljambe' in vol. v. The corrections in both the Harbord and Foljambe copies were studied by W. W. Greg, in 'Massinger's Autograph Corrections in "The Duke of Milan," 1623,' *The Library*, 4th Series, iv (1923), 207–18, and 'More Massinger Corrections', *The Library*, 4th Series, v (1924), 59–91.

lists and catalogues of 1640/1, 1656, 1661, 1663, 1671, 1691 and 1700.[1] The wording of its title-page follows that of *23* as far as the author's name, and the text was set up from a copy of *23* which had the uncorrected state of two formes only (B (i) and D (i)). In the main it is a slightly modernized reprint, adopting (though not quite consistently) the later usage of lower-case 'i' and 'j', 'u' and 'v', altering old-fashioned spellings, toning down the exuberant capitals and rhetorical punctuation of *23*, and adding several necessary stops. *38* has little textual authority, for if Massinger had prepared the copy for it he could scarcely have overlooked the glaring errors in sheets A to L which he had already corrected in the Foljambe copy. Only in sheet M can a case be made for the authority of the second quarto,[2] and it may be that Massinger called in at the printing house only when the reprint was almost finished, or that in some copies of *23* there was a corrected state of sheet M no longer known.

The Duke of Milan was printed in the collected editions of Coxeter, Mason, Gifford, Coleridge, and Cunningham; for the alteration staged in 1816, and frequently reprinted, see page 210. A bowdlerized text was given in *The Plays of Philip Massinger, adapted for Family Reading*, edited by W. Harness for Murray in 1830; an American edition was published by Harper in 1831. The tragedy was also included in *The Works of the British Dramatists*, edited by J. S. Keltie, Edinburgh, 1870, and in the first volume of *The Best Plays of the Old Dramatists: Philip Massinger*, edited by Arthur Symons, 1887.

T. W. Baldwin's *An Edition of Philip Massinger's Duke of Milan*, Lancaster, Pa., 1918, was the first critical old-spelling edition of the play; it was followed by A. K. McIlwraith's unpublished doctoral thesis, 'The Life and Works of Philip Massinger', Oxford, 1931.

Selections from the play were printed in *The Beauties of the English Drama*, printed for G. Robinson in 1777, *Beauties of Massinger*, printed for John Porter in 1817, *Specimens of the British Poets*, edited by Thomas Campbell in 1819, and *Specimens of the Elizabethan Drama from Lyly to Shirley*, edited by W. H. Williams, 1905. Wolf Grafen von Baudissin published a German translation of *The Duke of Milan* in *Ben Jonson und seine Schule*, Leipzig, 1836, and M. Horn-Monval, *Répertoire bibliographique des traductions et*

---

[1] Greg, *Bibliography*, iii. 1146, 1187, 1318, 1323, 1332, 1342; iv. 1656.
[2] In this sheet *38* differs substantively from *23* in nineteen readings; in fifteen of these *38* agrees with Massinger's manuscript corrections.

adaptations françaises du théâtre étranger, Paris, 1963, v, no. 276, records an undated translation by Joseph de Smet, *Le Duc de Milan*, in manuscript. Brief selections from the tragedy were translated by A. J. F. Mézières in *Contemporains et successeurs de Shakspeare*, Paris, 1864. The story of *The Duke of Milan* was retold in a prose version by E. W. Macauley, in *Tales of the Drama*, 1822.

(d) *Stage History*

The only source of information about the original performances of *The Duke of Milan* is the statement on the title-page of 23 that the tragedy 'hath beene often acted by his Maiesties seruants, at the blacke Friers'. The suggestion that the play was a popular one is given some support by the existence of two seventeenth-century editions.

There is no evidence that Robert Gomersall drew on Massinger's work for his tragedy *Lodovick Sforza* (1628), but Gifford thought that in *The Lady's Trial* (1638), v. ii, where a jealous husband is convinced of his wife's faithfulness, Ford was imitating the close of *The Duke of Milan*, IV. iii, and McIlwraith found an imitation of the same scene in Davenant's *Albovine* (?1626), IV, where Paradine, on hearing a false confession by his wife Valdaura, stabs her.

'The Duke of Millan' is listed among the 108 plays allotted to Killigrew, the manager of the King's Majesty's Servants at the New Theatre, on 12 January 1668/9.[1] J. G. McManaway points out that a manager's interest in the acquisition of plays is seldom anything but practical, but if performances were given by Killigrew's company nothing is known of them.

On 10 November 1779, Richard Cumberland's adaptation of *The Duke of Milan* was staged at Covent Garden. The cast included Henderson (Sforza), Whitfield (Alphonso), Aickin (Francisco), L'Estrange (Pescara), Hull (Cardinal), Peile (Charles), Robson (Mederia), Fearon (Hernando), Booth (Lorenzo), Thompson (Lodovico), Miss Younge (Marcelia), and Miss Platt (Eugenia).[2] Cumberland attempted to blend Massinger's tragedy with Fenton's *Mariamne*, evidently with little success. Despite elaborate staging and costuming, the play was given only three performances; it excited 'neither Applause nor Disapprobation, but was received with a Degree of Languor which marked the Indifference of the

[1] Nicoll, *A History of Restoration Drama (1660–1700)*, 1923, 315–16.
[2] *The London Stage (1660–1800)*, Part 5, ed. C. B. Hogan, Carbondale, Illinois, 1968, i. 277, 295–6; see also 'The Dramas of Richard Cumberland, 1779–1785', S. T. Williams, *MLN*, xxxvi (1921), 403–8.

Audience as to the Fate of the Piece' (*Dublin Advertiser*, 11 November 1779). The text was never printed and is now lost; only the Prologue and Epilogue have been preserved among the Larpent collection (Larpent 495).

In 1816, after his enormous success as Overreach in *A New Way to Pay Old Debts*, Kean attempted a revival of *The Duke of Milan*. The play was given on 9, 12, 16, 19, 23 March, 1, 4 April, and 4 May at the Theatre Royal, Drury Lane. The cast included Kean himself as Sforza, Rae (Francisco), Wallack (Tiberio), Powell (Stephano), Oxberry (Graccho), Elrington (Charles), Holland (Pescara), Barnard (Hernando), Mrs. Bartley (Marcelia), Mrs. Brereton (Isabella), Miss Boyce (Mariana), and Mrs. Horn (Eugenia).[1] A reviewer thought that Kean gave 'throughout an equable uniform delineation of character; nor was he less successful in addressing the *Emperor*, on whom depend his life and fortune, than while dwelling with enthusiastic fondness on the charms of his *Marcelia*, or stabbing her to the heart in all the wild delirium of jealousy and rage ... many a Batchelor in the house, whilst listening to [Mrs. Bartley's] shrewish upbraidings and revilings, must have hugged himself when he reflected on his state of celibacy ... Mr. Rae afforded us little satisfaction; there was far too much of mouthing and noise. The play has been well brought out, and displays some pretty scenes ... [including] a beautiful view of the Cathedral at Milan.'[2] The Prologue is among the Larpent collection (Larpent 1914); the text, by an anonymous adapter, was printed for John Miller in 1816, *The Duke of Milan: A Tragedy in Five Acts. Revived at the Theatre Royal, Drury Lane, with Alterations and Additions*. The adapter has cut about 600 lines, removing archaic allusions and supposed 'coarseness' of any kind, and severely pruning some minor parts. The women's slanging match (II. i) and Graccho's exchange with the Officer (III. ii) are almost excised, and there is some rewriting in V. ii, where Eugenia, now dressed as the dead Marcelia and equipped with a poisoned flower, brings about Sforza's death.

This text was reprinted in *The London Theatre*, edited by T.

---

[1] Genest, viii. 527–9. Hazlitt's review in *The Examiner*, 17 Mar. 1816, is reprinted in the *Complete Works*, ed. P. P. Howe, v, 1930, 289–91. See also H. N. Hillebrand, *Edmund Kean*, New York, 1933, and G. W. Playfair, *Kean*, 1939.

[2] *The Theatrical Inquirer and Monthly Mirror*, viii (1816), 227–8. Other reviews are to be found in the *Times* and *Morning Herald* for 11 Mar., the *Champion* for 17 Mar., and the *Examiner* for 18 Mar. (see D. J. Rulfs, 'The Reception of the Elizabethan Playwrights on the London Stage 1776–1833', *Studies in Philology*, xlvi (1949), 54–69).

Dibdin, 1814–16, volume xviii; *The London Stage*, edited by G. Balne, 1824–7, ii. no. 77, and *The Select London Stage*, 1825, no. 77; *The British Theatre*, edited by O. Williams, Leipzig, 1828; *The British Drama*, edited by J. Dicks, 1864–72, volume vi, and *Dicks' Standard Plays*, 1883, no. 63.

The British Museum copy of the original 1816 publication (11771. e. 16) is a prompt copy for an unidentified performance, with a manuscript note, 'The Duke of Milan. Correctly marked according to the directions of M^r. Kean.' A few extra cuts are indicated, as are exits and entrances, stage movements and groupings, and characters required on stage. There are also directions for music (a trumpet, a piano, an orchestra), and hints of scenery (III. i. 1, '*From the Tent*'; V. ii. 1, '*an Archway cover'd by a Curtain*').

Kean is known to have repeated *The Duke of Milan* on 5 July, 1816, at the Bath Theatre, with Bengough as Francisco, Woulds as Graccho, Mrs. Weston as Marcelia, Mrs. West as Eugenia, and Stanley as Pescara (Genest, viii. 565). A benefit performance at the Sunderland Theatre during the 1815–16 season consisted of two plays, one of them *The Duke of Milan*.[1] There were also performances of an adaptation of the tragedy by Schroeder (under the title *Alfonso von Ferrara*) at Vienna in 1848, and at Berlin in 1879 (Baldwin, p. 10).

The Duke of Milan was given a tercentenary production at Merton College, Oxford, on 21, 22, 23, and 26 June 1923. A special Prologue was written by Professor G. S. Gordon, and the principal members of the cast were T. W. Sergeant (Sforza), G. R. G. Mure (Francisco), O. J. G. Welch (Tiberio), A. H. M. Morrell (Stephano), Lord Clonmore (Graccho), M. C. Petitpierre (Julio), F. L. Godfrey (Giovanni), L. M. Campbell (Charles), O. P. Stedall (Pescara), N. W. N. Davies (Hernando), P. B. Broadbent (Medina), H. F. N. Clarke (Alphonso), Sonia Seton (Marcelia), Clare Yates (Isabella), Frances Vine (Mariana), May Jenkin (Eugenia), and Bertha Phillips (Gentlewoman). The production was by Nigel Playfair, with music by F. Austin. The *TLS* reviewer commented that 'At times it was easy for *The Duke of Milan* to seem to modern eyes a trifle ridiculous, but on the whole the result was quite happy, and no superficialities can alter the fact that it is far too great a tragedy to have remained buried in comparative oblivion for more than a hundred years'.

[1] *The Theatrical Inquirer and Monthly Mirror*, ix (1816), 75.

THE DVKE OF MILLAINE.

A TRAGÆDIE.

As it hath beene often acted by his Maiesties seruants, at the blacke Friers.

Written by PHILIP MASSINGER *Gent.*

LONDON
Prinred by B. A. for *Edward Blackmore*, and are to be sold at his shop at the great South doore of Pauls. 1623.

TO THE RIGHT HONOVRABLE AND MVCH ESTEEMED FOR HER HIGH BIRTH,
but more admired for her vertue, the Lady KATHERINE STANHOPE, wife to PHILIP Lord STANHOPE, Baron of *Shelford*.

MADAM: *If I were not most assured that workes of this nature, haue found both patronage, and protection, amongst the greatest Princesses of Italie, and are at this day cherished by persons, most eminent in our kingdome, I should not presume to offer these my weake, and imperfect labours, at the altar of your fauour. Let the example of others more knowing, and more experienced in this kind (if my boldnesse offend) pleade my pardon, and the rather since there is no other meanes left mee (my misfortunes hauing cast me on this course) to publish to the world (if it hold the least good opinion of mee) that I am euer your Ladyships creature. Vouchsafe therefore, with the neuer fayling clemency of your Noble disposition, not to contemne the tender of his duty, who while hee is, will euer bee,*

An humble seruant to your
Ladyship, and yours.
PHILIP MASSINGER:

7. haue] 23², 38; hath 23¹   8. Princesses] 23; Princes 38   10. these] 23², 38; this 23¹   12. kind] 23; kindness Mason   21. MASSINGER] Massinger MS, 23², 38: MESSENGER 23¹

THE NAMES OF THE ACTORS.

Ludouico Sforza. *a supposed Duke of Millaine.*
Signior Francisco. *his especiall fauorite.*
Tiberio. ⎱
Stephano. ⎰ *two Lords of his Counsell.*
Pescara. *a Marquesse, and friend to* Sforza.
Graccho. *a creature of* Mariana, *sister to* Sforza.
[Iouio. ⎱
[Giouanni. ⎰ *Courtiers.*]
Charles. *the Emperour.*
Hernando. ⎫
Medina.   ⎬ *Captaines to the Emperour.*
[Alphonso.] ⎭

Marcelia. *the Dutches, wife to* Sforza.
Isabella. *mother to* Sforza.
Mariana. *wife to* Francisco, *and sister to* Sforza.
Eugenia. *sister to* Francisco.

2. Posts.
A Beadle.
Waiters.
Mutes.
[*3. Gentlemen.*]
[*Fiddlers.*]
[*A Guard.*]
[*2. Doctors.*]
[*A Gentlewoman.*]

9–10. Iouio ... Giouanni.] *Gifford; not in* 23   14. Alphonso.] *Coxeter; not in* 23
23–7. 3. Gentlemen ... Gentlewoman.] *Gifford; not in* 23

VPON THIS WORKE OF HIS
beloued friend the AVTHOR.

I am snap't already, and may goe my way;
The Poet-Critick's come; I heare him say,
This YOVTH'S *mistooke, The Authors* WORKE'S *a* PLAY.

 He could not misse it; he will strait appeare
At such a baite; Twas laid on purpose there   5
To take the vermine, *and I haue him here.*

 Sirra, you wilbe nibling; a small bitt,
(A sillable) when yo' are i' the hungry fitt,
Will serve to stay the stomacke of your witt.

 Foole; Knaue; *what's worse? for worse cannot depraue thee.*   10
And were the diuell *now instantly to haue thee,*
Thou canst not instance such a worke *to saue thee,*

 'Mongst all the ballets *which thou dost compose,*
And what thou stil'st thy Poems, *ill as those,*
And void of rime, and reason, thy worse Prose.   15

 Yet like a rude Iack-sauce *in* Poesie,
With thoughts vnblest, and hand vnmanerly,
Rauishing branches from Apollo's *tree,*

 Thou mak'st a garland (for thy touch vnfit)
And boldly deck'st thy pig-brain'd sconce with it,   20
As if it were the Supreme Head *of* wit.

 The blameles Muses *blush; who not allow*
That reuerend Order, *to each vulgar brow,*
Whose sinfull touch prophanes the holy Bough.

 Hence (shallow Prophet) *and admire the straine*   25
Of thine owne Pen, *or thy poore* Copesmat's *vaine.*
This PIECE *too curious is, for thy course* braine.

Here witt *(more fortunate) is ioyn'd with* Art,
And that most sacred Frenzie *beares a part*
Infus'd by Nature *in the* Poet's *heart*.   30

Here, may the Puny-wits *themselues direct,*
Here, may the Wisest *find what to affect;*
And Kings *may learne their proper* Dialect.

On then, deare friend, Thy Pen *thy* Name *shall spread;*
And should'st thou write, while thou shalt not be read,   35
Thy Muse *must labour, when thy* Hand *is dead.*

            W. B.

32. Wisest] *23*; Vilest *Hazlitt*   35. should'st . . . shalt] *23*; shal'st . . . shall *Hazlitt*

The Duke of Millaine

Actus Primus. Scæna Prima.

GRACCHO, IOVIO, GIOVANNI, *with Flagons.*

Graccho. TAKE euery man his flagon: giue the oath
To al you meet: I am this day, the state drunkard,
(I am sure against my will); And if you finde
A man at ten, that's sober, hee's a Traitor,
And in my name arrest him.
   Iouio.   Very good Sir:
But say hee be a Sexton?
   Graccho.   If the bells
Ring out of tune, as if the street were burning,
And he cry 'tis rare Musicke: bid him sleepe,
'Tis a signe he has tooke his liquour; And if you meet
An officer preaching of sobriety,
Vnlesse he read it in *Geneua* print,
Lay him by the heeles.
   Iouio.   But thinke you tis a fault
To be found sober?
   Graccho.   It is Capitall Treason,
Or if you mittigate it, Let such pay
Fortie Crownes to the poore; But giue a pention
To all the magistrates, you find singing catches,
Or their Wiues dauncing; For the Courtiers reeling,
And the *Duke* himselfe, (I dare not say distemperd,
But kind, and in his tottering chaire carousing)
They doe the countrie seruice. If you meet
One that eates bread, a child of Ignorance,
And bred vp in the darkenesse of no drinking,

I. i. SD. IOVIO] 23; Julio *Gifford*

Against his will you may initiate hym
In the true posture, though he die in the taking
His drench, it skilles not: What's a priuate man   25
For the publike honour? we haue nought else to thinke on.
And so deere friends, copartners in my trauailes
Drinke hard; and let the health run through the City,
Vntill it reele againe: and with me crie:
Long liue the *Dutches*.

Enter TIBERIO, STEPHANO.

Iouio.   Heere are two Lords; what thinke you?   30
Shall we giue the oath to them?
    Graccho.   Fie, no: I know them,
You neede not sweare 'em; your *Lord*, by his pattent
Stands bound to take his rouse. Long liue the *Dutches*.
             Exeunt GRACCHO, IOVIO, [GIOVANNI].
    Stephano. The cause of this? But yesterday the court
Wore the sad liuerie of distrust, and feare;   35
No smile, not in a buffon to bee seene,
Or common iester; The great *Duke* himselfe,
Had sorrow in his face: which waited on
By his mother, sister, and his fairest *Dutches*,
Dispers'd a silent mourning through all *Millaine*:   40
As if some great blow had been giuen the State,
Or were at least expected.
    Tiberio.   *Stephano*,
I know, as you are noble, you are honest,
And capable of secrets, of more weight
Then now I shall deliuer. If that *Sforza*,   45
The present *Duke*, (though his whole life hath beene
But one continued pilgrimage, through dangers,
Affrights, and horrors: which his Fortune, guided
By his strong Iudgement, still hath ouercome)
Appeares now shaken, it deserues no wonder.   50
All that his youth hath laboured for: the haruest
Sowen by his industry, readie to be reap'd, to,
Being now at stake; And all his hopes confirmd,

23. Against his will ... hym] *Massinger MS*; Against his will, ... him, 23   33 SD.
Exeunt ... GIOVANNI.] *Gifford; Exit Gra. Io.* 23   53. at] 23²; at the 23¹, 38

Or lost for euer.
 Stephano. I know no such hazard:
His guards are stronge, and sure, His coffers full,
The people well affected; And so wisely
His prouident care hath wrought: that though warre rages
In most parts of our westerne world, there is
No enemie neere vs.
 Tiberio.   Dangers that we see
To threaten ruine, are with ease preuented:
But those strike deadly, that come vnexpected;
The lightning is farre off: yet soone as seene,
We may behold the terrible effects,
That it produceth. But Ile helpe your knowledge,
And make his cause of feare familiar to you.
The warre so long continued betweene
The Emperour *Charles*, and *Francis* the French King
Haue interress'd in eithers cause, the most
Of the *Italian Princes*: Among which *Sforza*,
As one of greatest power, was sought by both,
But with assurance hauing one his frend,
The other liu'd his enemie.
 Stephano.   Tis true,
And 'twas a doubtfull choice.
 Tiberio.   But hee, well knowing,
And hatinge too, (it seemes) the *Spanish* pride,
Lent his assistance to the King of *France*:
Which hath so farre incens'd the *Emperor*,
That all his hopes, and honours are embark'd,
With his great Patrons Fortune.
 Stephano.   Which stands faire,
For ought I yet can heare.
 Tiberio.   But should it change,
The *Duke*'s vndon. They haue drawne to the field
Two royall armies, full of fierie youth,
Of equall spirit to dare, and power to doe:
So neere entrench'd, that 'tis beyond all hope,
Of humaine councell, they can er'e be seuerd,

---

 55. His ... full,] *Massinger MS* (full$_\wedge$); His ... strong, and sure, his Coffers full, *23*
 66. warre] *23*; wars *Mason* 68. interress'd] *23²*; interress'd *23¹, 38* eithers] *23*;
either *38* 74. hatinge] *Massinger MS, Mason*; hauing *23*

    Vntill it be determin'd by the sword, 85
Who hath the better cause. For the successe,
Concludes the victor innocent, and the vanquish'd
Most miserably guilty. How vncertaine,
The Fortune of the warre is, children know;
And, it being in suspence, on whose faire Tent, 90
Win'gd victory wil make her glorious stand;
You cannot blame the *Duke*, though he appeare
Perplex'd, and troubled.
  Stephano.   But why then,
In such a time when euery knee should bend,
For the successe, and safetie of his person, 95
Are these lowd triumphs? In my weake opinion,
They are vnseasonable.
  Tiberio.   I iudge so too;
But onely in the cause to be excus'd.
It is the *Dutchesse* Birth-day: once a yeere
Solemniz'd, with all pompe, and ceremony: 100
In which, the *Duke* is not his owne, but hers:
Nay, euery day indeed, he is her creature,
For neuer man so doted; But to tell
The tenth part of his fondnesse, to a stranger,
Would argue me of fiction.
  Stephano.   She's indeed, 105
A Lady of most exquisite forme.
  Tiberio.   She knowes it,
And how to prize it.
  Stephano.   I ne're heard her tainted,
In any point of honour.
  Tiberio.   On my life,
Shee's constant to his bed, and well deserues
His largest Fauours. But when beauty is 110
Stampt on great women, great in birth, and fortune,
And blowne by flatterers greater then it is,
'Tis seldome vnaccompanied with pride;
Nor is shee, that-way free. Presuming on
The *Dukes* affection, and her owne Desert, 115
Shee beares her selfe with such a Maiestie,
Looking with scorne on all, as things beneath her,
That *Sforzas* mother, (that would loose no part

Of what was once her owne), nor his faire Sister,
(A Lady too acquainted with her worth) 120
Will brooke it well; And howsoer'e their hate,
Is smother'd for a time, Tis more then feard,
It will at length breake out.
 Stephano.   Hee, in whose power 'tis,
Turne all to the best.
 Tiberio.   Come, let vs to the Court,
We there shall see, all brauery, and cost, 125
That art can boast of.
 Stephano.   Ile beare you company.   *Exeunt.*

   Enter FRANCISCO, ISABELLA, MARIANA.

 Mariana. I will not goe, I scorne to be a spot
In her proud traine.
 Isabella.   Shall I, that am his mother,
Be so indulgent, as to waite on her,
That owes me duty?
 Francisco.   Tis done to the *Duke*,
And not to her. And my sweet wife remember, 5
And Madam, if you please receiue my councell,
As *Sforza* is your sonne, you may command him,
And as a sister you may challenge from him,
A brothers loue, and Fauour: But this graunted,
Consider hee's the *Prince*, and you, his Subiects, 10
And not to question, or contend with her,
Whom hee is pleasd to honour. Priuate men
Preferre their wiues: and shall hee being a *Prince*,
And blest with one that is the *Paradice*
Of sweetnesse, and of beauty, to whose charge, 15
The stocke of womens goodnesse is giuen vp,
Not vse her, like her selfe?
 Isabella.   You are euer forward,
To sing her praises.
 Mariana.   Others are as faire,
I am sure as noble.
 Francisco.   I detract from none,
In giuing her what's due. Were she defor'md, 20

120. too] 23; ~, *Coxeter*   126 SD. *Exeunt.*] *Coxeter*; *follows* boast of. 23
I. ii. *Scene division Coxeter; undivided* 23

Yet being the *Dutches*, I stand bound to serue her,
But as she is, to admire her. Neuer wife
Met with a purer heate her husbands feruor;
A happie paire, one in the other blest:
She confident in her selfe, hee's wholy hers, 25
And cannot seeke for change: and he secure
That tis not in the power of man to tempt her.
And therefore, to contest with her that is
The stronger, and the better part of him,
Is more then folly; You know him of a nature 30
Not to be play'd with: and should you forget
To 'obey him as your *Prince*, hee'le not remember
The dutie that he owes you.
   Isabella.   Tis but trueth:
Come cleere our browes, and let vs to the banquet,
But not to serue his Idoll.
   Mariana.   I shall doe 35
What may become the sister of a *Prince*,
But will not stoope, beneath it.
   Francisco.   Yet be wise,
Sore not too high to fall, but stoope to rise.   *Exeunt*.

[I. iii]   *Enter three* GENTLEMEN *setting forth a banquet*.

   1. *Gentleman*. Quicke quicke for loues sake, let the court put on
Her choicest outside: Cost, and brauerie
Be onely thought of.
   2. *Gentleman*.   All that may be had
To please the eye, the eare, taste, touch, or smell,
Are carefully prouided.
   3. *Gentleman*.   Ther's a Masque, 5
Haue you heard what's the inuention?
   1. *Gentleman*.   No matter,
It is intended for the *Dutches* honour.
And if it giue her glorious attributes,
As the most faire, most vertuous, and the rest,
'Twill please the *Duke*. They come.
   3. *Gentleman*.   All is in order. 10

I. iii. *Scene division Coxeter; undivided* 23   7. intended] *23*; indeed *38*

I. iii. 11-42   *The Duke of Milan*   225

Enter TIBERIO, STEPHANO, FRANCISCO, SFORZA, MARCELIA,
ISABELLA, MARIANA, *Attendants*.

  Sforza. You are the Mistris of the feast, sit heere;
O my soules comfort: And when *Sforza* bowes
Thus low to doe you honour, let none thinke
The meanest seruice they can pay my loue,
But as a faire addition to those tytles,   15
They stand possest of. Let me glory in
My happinesse, and mightie Kings looke pale
With enuie, while I triumph in mine owne.
O mother looke on her, sister admire her:
And since this present age yeelds not a woman   20
Worthy to be her second, borrow of
Times past: and let imagination helpe
Of those canoniz'd Ladies *Sparta* boasts of,
And, in her greatnesse, *Rome* was proud to owe,
To fashion one, yet still you must confesse,   25
The *Phœnix* of perfection ner'e was seene,
But in my faire *Marcelia*.
  Francisco.   She's indeede
The wonder of all times.
  Tiberio.   Your excellence,
(Though I confesse you giue her but her owne)
Forces her modestie to the defence   30
Of a sweet blush.
  Sforza.   It neede not my *Marcelia*;
When most I striue to praise thee, I appeare
A poore detractor: For thou art indeed
So absolute in bodie, and in minde,
That, but to speake the least part to the height,   35
Would aske an Angels tongue: and yet then end
In silent admiration!
  Isabella.   You still court her,
As if she were a Mistris, not your wife.
  Sforza. A Mistris mother? she is more to me,
And euery day, deserues more to be su'de too.   40
Such as are cloyd with those they haue embrac'd,
May thinke their wooing done: No night to mee,

    25. one,] *Massinger MS*; and: *23*   30. Forces] *23²*; Enforces *23¹, 38*   32. most
I] *23*; I most *38*   34. absolute] *23*; perfect both *38*   40. too] *23*; to *38, Coxeter*

But is a brydall one, where *Himen* lights
His torches fresh, and new: And those delights,
Which are not to be cloth'd in ayrie sounds, 45
Inioyd, beget desires, as full of heat,
And Iouiall feruor, as when first I tasted
Her virgin fruit; Blest night, and be it numbred
Amongst those happy ones, in which a blessing
Was by the full consent of all the Starrs, 50
Confer'd vpon mankind.
   Marcelia.   My worthiest Lord,
The onely obiect I behold with pleasure:
My pride, my glory, in a word my all;
Beare witnesse *Heauen*, that I esteeme my selfe
In nothing worthy of the meanest praise 55
You can bestow, vnlesse it be in this,
That in my heart I loue, and honor you.
And but that it would smell of arrogance,
To speake my strong desire, and zeale to serue you:
I then could say, these eyes yet neuer saw 60
The rising Sun, but that my vowes, and prayers,
Were sent to Heauen, for the prosperitie
And safety of my Lord; Nor haue I euer
Had other studie, but how to appeare
Worthy your fauour: and that my embraces, 65
Might yeeld a fruitfull Haruest of content,
For all your noble trauaile, in the purchase
Of her, that's still your seruant; By these lips,
(Which pardon mee, that I presume to kisse)—
   Sforza. O sweare, for euer sweare.
   Marcelia.   I ne're will seeke 70
Delight, but in your pleasure: and desire,
When you are sated with all Earthly glories,
And age, and honours make you fit for Heauen,
That one Graue may receiue vs.
   Sforza.   'Tis belieu'd,
Belieu'd, my blest One.
   Mariana.   How she winds her selfe 75
Into his Soule!
   Sforza.   Sit all: Let others feed

70. O sweare] *23*; O sweet *38*   72. sated] *Coxeter*; seated *23*

On those grosse Cates, while *Sforza* banquets with
Immortall Viands, tane in at his Eyes.
I could liue euer thus. Command the Eunuch
To sing the Dittie that I last compos'd, 80
In prayse of my *Marcelia*.

Enter POST.

From whence?

Post. From *Pauie*, my dread Lord.
Sforza. Speake, is all lost?
Post. The Letter will informe you.
Francisco. How his Hand shakes,
As he receiues it!
Mariana. This is some allay
To his hot passion.
Sforza. Though it bring death, ile read it. 85

<blockquote>May it please your Excellence to vnderstand, that the verie houre I wrot this, I heard a bold defiance deliuered by a Herald from the Emperor, which was chearefully receiu'd by the King of France. The battailes being readie to ioyne, and the Vantguard committed to my charge, inforces me to end abruptly. 91

Your Highnesse humble Seruant,

Gaspero.</blockquote>

Readie to ioyne! By this, then I am nothing,
Or my Estate secure.
Marcelia. My Lord.
Sforza. To doubt, 95
Is worse then to haue lost: And to despaire,
Is but to antidate those miseries,
That must fall on vs. All my hopes depending
Vpon this battailes fortune, in my Soule
Me thinkes there should be that Imperious power, 100
By supernaturall, not vsuall meanes,
T'informe me what I am. The cause consider'd,
Why should I feare? The French are bold and strong,
Their numbers full, and in their counsels wise:
But then, the haughtie Spaniard is all Fire, 105

---

82. Pauie] 23 ; Pavia 38   89. battailes] 23; battle *Coxeter*   97. those] 23;
these 38   98. vs.] 23; ~; *Coxeter*   99. fortune,] *editor*; ~; 23; ~.— *Coxeter*

Hot in his executions; Fortunate
In his attempts; Married to victorie:
I, there it is that shakes me.
  Francisco.   Excellent Lady:
This day was dedicated to your Honor:
One gale of your sweet breath will easily   110
Disperse these Clouds: And, but your selfe, ther's none
That dare speake to him.
  Marcelia.   I will run the hazard.
My Lord?
  Sforza. Ha: Pardon me *Marcelia*, I am troubled;
And stand vncertaine, whether I am Master
Of ought that's worth the owning.
  Marcelia.   I am yours Sir; 115
And I haue heard you sweare, I being safe,
There was no losse could moue you. This day Sir,
Is by your guift made mine: Can you reuoke
A Grant made to *Marcelia*? Your *Marcelia*?
For whose loue, nay, whose honour (gentle Sir) 120
All deepe designes, and State affaires defer'd:
Be, as you purpos'd, merrie.
  Sforza.   Out of my sight,
And all thoughts that may strangle mirth forsake me.
Fall what can fall, I dare the worst of Fate;
Though the Foundation of the Earth should shrinke, 125
The glorious Eye of Heauen loose his Splendor:
Supported thus, I'le stand vpon the ruins,
And seeke for new life here. Why are you sad?
No other sports? By Heauen he's not my friend,
That weares one Furrow in his Face. I was told 130
There was a Masque.
  Francisco. They waite your Highnesse pleasure,
And when you please to haue it.
  Sforza.   Bid 'em enter:
Come, make me happie once againe. I am rap't,
'Tis not to day, to morrow, or the next,
But all my dayes, and yeeres shall be employed 135
To doe thee honour.
  Marcelia. And my life to serue you. *A Horne.*

133. once] *23*; yet once *38*

I. iii. 137-62   *The Duke of Milan*   229

   Sforza. Another Post? Goe hang him, hang him I say,
I will not interrupt my present pleasures,
Although his message should import my Head:
Hang him I say.
   Marcelia.   Nay, good Sir, I am pleas'd   140
To grant a little intermission to you;
Who knowes, but he brings newes, we wish to heare,
To heighten our delights.
   Sforza.   As wise as faire.

                Enter another POST.

From *Gaspero?*
   Post.   That was, my Lord.
   Sforza.   How, dead?
   Post. With the deliuerie of this, and prayers,   145
To guard your Excellencie from certaine dangers,
He ceast to be a Man.
   Sforza.   All that my feares
Could fashion to me, or my enemies wish
Is falne vpon me. Silence that harsh musicke,
'Tis now vnseasonable; A tolling Bell,   150
As a sad Harbinger to tell me, that
This pamper'd lumpe of Flesh, must feast the Wormes.
'Tis fitter for me, I am sick.
   Marcelia.   My Lord.
   Sforza. Sick to the death, *Marcelia.* Remoue
These signes of mirth, they were ominous, and but vsherd   155
Sorrow and ruine.
   Marcelia.   Blesse vs Heauen!
   Isabella.   My Sonne.
   Marcelia. What suddaine change is this?
   Sforza.   All leaue the roome;
Ile beare alone the burthen of my griefe,
And must admit no partner. I am yet
Your Prince, wher's your obedience? Stay *Marcelia:*   160
I cannot be so greedie of a sorrow,
In which you must not share.
                [*Exeunt all but* SFORZA *and* MARCELIA.]

   137. Sforza] *Congress MS* (Sfor:), *38; Franc. 23*   146. Excellencie] *23;* Excellence *38*   149. Silence] *Coxeter;* ~, *23*   162 SD. Exeunt ... MARCELIA.] *after Gifford; not in 23*

Marcelia. And chearefully,
I will sustaine my part. Why looke you pale?
Where is that wonted constancie, and courage,
That dar'd the worst of Fortune? Where is *Sforza*? 165
To whom all dangers that fright common men,
Appear'd but *Panicque* terrors? Why doe you eye me
With such fix'd lookes? Loue, counsell, dutie, seruice,
May flow from me, not danger.
Sforza. O *Marcelia*!
It is for thee I feare: For thee, thy *Sforza* 170
Shakes like a coward; For my selfe, vnmou'd,
I could haue heard my troupes were cut in peeces,
My Generall slaine; And he, on whom my hopes
Of Rule, of State, of Life, had their dependance,
The King of France, my greatest friend, made prisoner 175
To so proud enemies.
Marcelia. Then you haue iust cause
To show you are a Man.
Sforza. All this were nothing,
Though I ad to it, that I am assur'd
For giuing ayd to this vnfortunate King,
The Emperour incenc'd, layes his command 180
On his victorious Army, flesh'd with spoyle,
And bold of conquest, to march vp against me,
And sease on my Estates. Suppose that done too,
The Citie tane, the Kennels running blood,
The ransack'd Temples, falling on their Saints: 185
My Mother in my sight, toss'd on their Pikes,
And Sister rauish'd: And my selfe bound fast
In Chaines, to grace their Triumph: Or what else,
An Enemies insolence could load me with,
I would be *Sforza* still; But when I thinke, 190
That my *Marcelia* (to whom, all these
Are but as Atomes to the greatest Hill)
Must suffer in my cause: And for me suffer;
All Earthly torments; Nay, euen those the damn'd
Houl for in Hell, are gentle strokes, compar'd 195
To what I feele *Marcelia*.

171. vnmou'd,] *Mason*; ~: *23*; ~; *38* 174. dependance,] *Coxeter*; dependance; *23*; dependancy; *38* 193. suffer;] *Mason*; ~ₐ *23*

Marcelia.   Good Sir, haue patience:
I can as well partake your aduerse fortune,
As I thus long haue had an ample share
In your prosperitie. Tis not in the power
Of Fate to alter me: For while I am,
In spight of't, I am yours.
    Sforza.   But should that will
To be so be forc'd *Marcelia*! And I liue
To see those Eyes I prize aboue mine owne,
Dart fauours (though compel'd) vpon another!
Or those sweet Lips (yeelding Immortall Nectar)
Be gently touch'd by any but my selfe!
Thinke, thinke *Marcelia*, what a cursed thing
I were, beyond expression.
    Marcelia.   Doe not feed
Those iealous thoughts; The only blessing that
Heauen hath bestow'd on vs, more then on beasts,
Is, that 'tis in our pleasure when to dye.
Besides, were I now in anothers power,
There are so many wayes to let out life,
I would not liue, for one short minute, his;
I was borne only yours, and I will dye so.
    Sforza. Angels reward the goodnesse of this Woman:
All I can pay is nothing.

                     Enter FRANCISCO.

                 Why vncall'd for?
    Francisco. It is of waight, Sir, that makes me thus presse
Vpon your priuacies. Your constant friend
The Marquisse of Pescara, tyr'd with hast,
Hath businesse that concernes your life and fortunes,
And with speed to impart.
    Sforza.   Waite on him hether;   *Exit* FRANCISCO.
And deerest to thy Closet: Let thy prayers
Assist my counsels.
    Marcelia.   To spare imprecations
Against my selfe; without you I am nothing.   *Exit* MARCELIA.
    Sforza. The Marquisse of Pescara; A great Souldior:

---

201. should] *23*; were *Coxeter*   202. so be] *Gifford*[1,2]; so *23*; so— *Gifford*[2]

And though he seru'd vpon the aduerse partie,
Euer my constant friend.

Enter FRANCISCO, PESCARA.

 Francisco.   Yonder he walkes,
Full of sad thoughts.
 Pescara.   Blame him not good *Francisco*,
He hath much cause to grieue: Would I might end so,
And not ad this, to feare.
 Sforza.   My deere *Pescara*:
A miracle in these times, a friend and happie,
Cleaues to a falling fortune.
 Pescara.   If it were
As well in my weake power, in act to raise it,
As 'tis to beare a part of sorrow with you;
You then should haue iust cause to say, *Pescara*
Look'd not vpon your State, but on your Vertues,
When he made suit to be writ in the List
Of those you fauord. But my hast forbids
All complement. Thus then, Sir, to the purpose.
The cause that vnattended brought me hether,
Was not to tell you of your losse, or danger;
For Fame hath many Wings to bring ill tidings,
And I presume you haue heard it: But to giue you
Such friendly counsell, as perhaps may make
Your sad disaster lesse.
 Sforza.   You are all goodnesse,
And I giue vp my selfe to be dispos'd of,
As in your wisedome you thinke fit.
 Pescara.   Thus then, Sir.
To hope you can hold out against the Emperor,
Were flatterie in your selfe, to your vndooing;
Therefore, the safest course that you can take,
Is, to giue vp your selfe to his discretion,
Before you be compeld. For rest assur'd,
A voluntarie yeelding may find grace,
And will admit defence, at least excuse:
But should you linger doubtfull, till his Powers
Haue seas'd your Person, and Estates perforce,

244. giue you] *Massinger MS*; giue you such, *23*

You must expect extreames.
 Sforza.   I vnderstand you,
And I will put your counsell into act,
And speedilie; I only will take order
For some Domesticall affaires, that doe
Concerne me neerely, and with the next Sun
Ride with you; In the meane time, my best friend,
Pray take your rest.
 Pescara.   Indeed, I haue trauaild hard,
And will embrace your counsell.
 Sforza.   With all care, *Exit* PESCARA.
Attend my Noble friend. Stay you, *Francisco*,
You see how things stand with me?
 Francisco.   To my griefe:
And if the losse of my poore life could be
A Sacrifise, to restore them, as they were,
I willingly would lay it downe.
 Sforza.   I thinke so:
For I haue euer found you true, and thankful,
Which makes me loue the building I haue rays'd,
In your aduancement: And repent no grace,
I haue conferd vpon you: And beleeue me,
Though now I should repeate my fauours to you,
The Titles I haue giuen you, and the meanes
Sutable to your Honours, that I thought you
Worthy my Sister, and my Family,
And in my Dukedome made you next my selfe:
It is not to vpbraid you: But to tell you
I find you are worthy of them in your loue,
And seruice to me.
 Francisco. Sir, I am your Creature:
And any shape, that you would haue me weare,
I gladly will put on.
 Sforza.   Thus, then, *Francisco*;
I now am to deliuer to your trust,
A weightie secret: Of so strange a nature,
And 'twill I know appeare so monstrous to you,
That you will tremble in the execution,
As much as I am tortur'd, to command it:

   282. your] *Massinger touches up the defective* u

For 'tis a deed so horrid, that but to heare it, 290
Would strike into a Ruffian flesh'd in murthers,
Or an obdurate Hang-man, soft compassion;
And yet *Francisco* (of all Men the deerest,
And from me most deseruing) such my state,
And strange condition is, that thou alone, 295
Must know the fatall seruice, and performe it.
   Francisco. These preparations, Sir, to worke a stranger,
Or to one vnacquainted with your bounties,
Might appeare vsefull: But to me, they are
Needlesse impertinances: For, I dare doe, 300
What e're you dare command.
   Sforza.   But thou must sweare it,
And put into thy Oath, all ioyes, or torments
That fright the wicked, or confirme the good:
Not to conceale it only, that is nothing;
But whensoe're my will shall speake, strike now: 305
To fall vpon't like Thunder.
   Francisco.   Minister
The Oath, in any way, or forme you please,
I stand resolu'd to take it.
   Sforza.   Thou must doe then,
What no maleuolent Star will dare to looke on,
It is so wicked: For which, Men will curse thee, 310
For being the Instrument: And the blest Angels,
Forsake me at my need, for being the Author:
For 'tis a deed of Night, of Night *Francisco*,
In which the memorie of all good Actions
We can pretend too, shall be buried quick; 315
Or if we be remembred, it shall be
To fright posteritie, by our example:
That haue out-gone all presidents of Villaines,
That were before vs: And such as succeed,
Though taught in hels black schoole, shal ne're com nere vs. 320
Art thou not shaken yet?
   Francisco.   I grant you moue me:
But to a Man confirm'd;
   Sforza.   Ile try your temper:
What thinke you of my Wife?

    291. Ruffian] *Massinger touches up the defective* R   302. or] *23*; all *38*

Francisco.   As a thing Sacred:
To whose faire Name, and memorie, I pay gladly
These signes of dutie.
 Sforza.   Is she not the abstract
Of all that's rare, or to be wish't in Woman?
 Francisco. It were a kind of blasphemy to dispute it:
But to the purpose Sir.
 Sforza.   Ad to her goodnesse,
Her tendernesse of me, Her care to please me,
Her vnsuspected chastity, nere equall'd:
Her Innocence, her honor: O I am lost
In the Ocean of her vertues, and her graces,
When I thinke of them.
 Francisco.   Now I finde the end
Of all your coniurations: there's some seruice
To be done for this sweet Lady; If she haue enemies
That she would haue remou'd—
 Sforza.   Alas *Francisco,*
Her greatest enemy is her greatest louer,
Yet in that hatred, her Idolater.
One smile of hers would make a sauage tame;
One accent of that tongue would calme the Seas,
Though all the windes at once stroue there for Empire.
Yet I, for whom she thinks all this too little,
Should I miscarry in this present iourney,
(From whence it is all number to a cypher,
I ner'e returne with honor) by thy hand
Must haue her murthered.
 Francisco.   Murther'd? Shee that loues so,
And so deserues to be belou'd againe?
And I, (who sometimes you were pleas'd to fauor)
Pick'd out the instrument?
 Sforza.   Doe not flye off:
What is decreed, can neuer be recal'd.
'Tis more than loue to her, that markes her out,
A wish'd companion to me, in both fortunes:
And strong assurance of thy zealous faith,
That giues vp to thy trust a secret, that
Racks should not haue forc'd from me. O *Francisco*!

   328. to her] *23;* too, her *Gifford*

There is no heauen without her: nor a hell,
Where she recides. I aske from her but iustice,
And what I would haue payd to her: had sickenesse,
Or any other accident diuorc'd
Her purer soule, from her vnspotted body. 360
The slauish Indian Princes when they dye
Are cheerefully attended to the fire,
By the wife, and slaue, that liuing they lou'd best,
To doe them seruice in another world:
Nor will I be lesse honor'd, that loue more. 365
And therefore trifle not, but in thy lookes,
Expresse a ready purpose to performe
What I command, or by *Marcelias* soule,
This is thy latest minute.
   Francisco. 'Tis not feare
Of death, but loue to you, makes me embrace it; 370
But for mine owne security when 'tis done,
What warrant haue I? If you please to signe one,
I shall, though with vnwillingnesse and horror,
Perform your dreadfull charge.
   Sforza. I will *Francisco*;
But still remember, that a Princes secrets 375
Are balme, conceal'd, but poyson, if discouer'd.
I may come backe; then this is but a tryall,
To purchase thee, if it were possible,
A neerer place in my affection; but
I know thee honest.
   Francisco. 'Tis a Character 380
I will not part with.
   Sforza. I may liue to reward it. *Exeunt.*

Actus Secundus. Scæna Prima.

TIBERIO, STEPHANO.

Stephano. How? left the Court?
   Tiberio. Without guard or retinue
Fitting a Prince.

---

360. her] *Massinger MS*, 23²; his 23¹,², 38   376. conceal'd,] *Massinger MS*; ~: 23

Stephano. No enemy neere, to force him?
To leaue his owne strengths, yet deliuer vp
Himselfe, as 'twere in bonds, to the discretion
Of him that hates him? 'Tis beyond example:
You neuer heard the motiues that induc't him,
To this strange course?
   Tiberio. No, those are Cabinet councels,
And not to be communicated, but
To such as are his owne, and sure; Alas,
We fill vp emptie places, and in publique,
Are taught to giue our suffrages to that,
Which was before determin'd: And are safe so.
Signiour *Francisco* (vpon whom alone
His absolute power is with al strength confer'd,
During his absence) can with ease resolue you.
To me, they are Riddles.
   Stephano. Well, he shall not be
My *Oedipus*, Ile rather dwell in darkenesse.
But my good Lord *Tiberio*, this *Francisco*,
Is, on the suddaine, strangely rays'd.
   Tiberio. O Sir,
He tooke the thryuing course: He had a Sister,
A faire one too; With whom (as it is rumor'd)
The Duke was too familiar; But she cast off,
(What promises soeuer past betweene them)
Vpon the sight of this, forsooke the Court,
And since was neuer seene; To smother this,
(As Honors neuer faile to purchase silence)
Francisco first was grac'd, and step by step,
Is rais'd vp to this height.
   Stephano. But how is his absence borne?
   Tiberio. Sadly, it seemes
By the Dutches: For since he left the Court,
For the most part, she hath kept her priuate Chamber;
No visitants admitted. In the Church,
She hath been seene to pay her pure deuotions,
Season'd with teares: And sure her sorrow's trewe,
Or deeply counterfeited; Pompe, and State,
And brauerie cast off: And she that lately

II. i. 2. him?] *23*; ~, *Gifford*   34. trewe] *Massinger MS*; ttue *23*; true *38*

Riuald *Poppæa* in her varied shapes,
Or the Ægyptian Queene, now, widow-like,
In Sable colours (as her Husbands dangers
Strangled in her, the vse of any pleasure) 40
Mournes for his absence.
  Stephano.   It becomes her Vertue,
And does confirme, what was reported of her.
  Tiberio. You take it right; But on the other side,
The darling of his Mother, *Mariana*,
(As there were an Antipathy, betweene 45
Her, and the Dutches passions) And as
Sh'ad no dependance on her brothers fortune,
She ne're appear'd so full of mirth.
  Stephano.   'Tis strange.
But see, her fauorite: and accompani'd,
To your report.

           Enter GRACCHO *with* FIDDLERS.

  Graccho.   You shall scrape, and Ile sing, 50
A scuruie Dittie, to a scuruie tune,
Repine who dares.
  Fiddler.   But if we should offend,
The Dutches hauing silenc't vs: and these Lords,
Stand by to heare vs.
  Graccho.   They, in Name are Lords,
But I am one in Power: And for the Dutches, 55
But yester-day we were merrie for her pleasure,
We now'l be for my Ladies.
  Tiberio.   Signiour *Graccho*.
  Graccho. A poore Man, Sir, a Seruant to the Princes:
But you, great Lords, and Councellors of State,
Whom I stand bound to reuerence.
  Tiberio.   Come, we know 60
You are a Man in grace.
  Graccho.   Fye, no: I grant,
I beare my fortunes patiently: Serue the Princesse,
And haue accesse at all times to her closet,

45–6. (As ... passions)] *Massinger MS*; As ... passions: *23
38*; She had *23¹*   58. Princes] *23*; Princesse *38*   63. accesse] *Massinger MS*;
successe *23*

Such is my impudence: when your graue Lordships
Are masters of the modesty to attend 65
Three houres, nay sometimes foure; and then bid waite
Vpon her the next morning.
 Stephano.   He derides vs.
 Tiberio. Pray you, what newes is stirring? you know all.
 Graccho. Who, I? alas, I haue no intelligence
At home, nor abroad: I onely sometimes guesse 70
The change of the times. I should ask of your Lordships
Who are to keepe their Honors, who to loose 'em;
Who the Duchesse smil'd on last, or on whom frown'd,
You onely can resolue me: we poore waiters
Deale (as you see) in mirth, and foolish fyddles: 75
It is our element; and could you tell me,
What point of State 'tis, that I am commanded
To muster vp this musicke: on mine honesty,
You should much befriend me.
 Stephano.   Sirra, you grow sawcie.
 Tiberio. And would be layd by the heeles.
 Graccho.   Not by your Lordships,
Without a speciall warrant; looke to your owne stakes; 81
Were I committed, here come those would baile me:
Perhaps we might change places too.

Enter ISABELLA, MARIANA.

 Tiberio.   The Princesse;
We must be patient.
 Stephano.   There's no contending.
 Tiberio. See, the informing rogue.
 Stephano.   That we should stoope 85
To such a Mushrome.
 Mariana.   Thou dost mistake; they durst not
Vse the least word of scorne, although prouok'd,
To any thing of mine. Goe, get you home,
And to your seruants, friends, and flatterers, number
How many descents you are noble; Look to your wiues too, 90
The smooth-chin'd Courtiers are abroad.
 Tiberio. No way, to be a Free-man?

Exeunt TIBERIO, STEPHANO.

 71. of the] *23*; of *38*   90. descents] *Massinger MS, 38*; discents *23*

Graccho. Your Excellence hath the best guift to dispatch
These Arras pictures of Nobilitie,
I euer read of.
   Mariana.   I can speake sometimes.
   Graccho. And couer so your bitter Pills, with sweetnesse
Of Princely language to forbid reply,
They are greedily swallowed.
   Isabella.   But, the purpose Daughter,
That brings vs hither? Is it to bestow
A visit on this Woman? That, because
She only would be thoght truly to grieue
The absence, and the dangers of my Son,
Proclaimes a generall sadnesse?
   Mariana.   If to vexe her,
May be interpreted to doe her Honor,
She shall haue many of 'em! Ile make vse
Of my short Raigne: my Lord, now gouernes all:
And she shall know, that her Idolater,
My Brother, being not by now to protect her,
I am her equall.
   Graccho.   Of a little thing,   [*Aside.*]
It is so full of Gall: A Diuell of this size,
Should they run for a wager to be spitefull,
Gets not a Hors-head of her.
   Mariana.   On her Birth-day,
We were forc'd to be merrie: and now she's musty
We must be sad, on paine of her displeasure;
We will, we will. This is her priuate Chamber,
Where like an Hypocrite, not a true Turtle,
She seemes to mourne her absent Mate, her Seruants
Attending her like Mutes: But Ile speake to her
And in a high Key too. Play any thing
That's light and loud enough but to torment her,
And we will haue rare sport.

   Song. MARCELIA *aboue in blacke.*

   Isabella.   She frownes, as if
Her lookes could fright vs.
   Mariana.   May it please your greatnesse,

109 SD. *Aside.*] *Coxeter; not in* 23

We heard that your late Physicke hath not work'd,
And that breeds Melancholy, as your Doctor tells vs:
To purge which, we that are born your Highnesse Vassals,   125
And are to play the fooles to doe you seruice,
Present you with a fit of mirth: what thinke you
Of a new Anticke?
    Isabella.   'Twould show rare in Ladies.
    Mariana. Being intended for so sweet a creature,
Were she but pleas'd to grace it.
    Isabella.   Fye, she will,   130
Be it nere so meane: shee's made of courtesie.
    Mariana. The Mistresse of all hearts; one smile I pray you
On your poore seruants, or a Fidlers fee:
Comming from those faire hands, though but a Ducat,
We will inshrine it as a holy relique.   135
    Isabella. 'Tis Wormewood, and it workes.
    Marcelia.   If I lay by
My feares, and griefes (in which you should be sharers
If doting age could let you but remember,
You haue a sonne; or frontlesse impudence,
You are a sister) and in making answere,   140
To what was most vnfit for you to speake,
Or me to heare, borrow of my iust anger—
    Isabella. A set speech on my life.
    Mariana.   Pen'd by her Chaplaine.
    Marcelia. Yes, it can speake, without instruction speake;
And tell your want of manners, that y'are rude,   145
And sawcily rude, too.
    Graccho.   Now the game begins.
    Marcelia. You durst not else on any hire or hope,
(Remembring what I am, and whose I am)
Put on the desperate boldnesse, to disturbe
The least of my retirements.
    Mariana.   Note her now.   150
    Marcelia. For both shal vnderstand; though th'one presume
Vpon the priuiledge due to a Mother,
The Duke stands now on his owne legs, and needs
No nurse to leade him.
    Isabella.   How, a Nurse?

137–40. sharers ... sister)] *McIlwraith*; ~) ... ~; *23*   144. it] *23*; I *Coxeter*

Marcelia.   A dry one,
And vselesse too: But I am mercifull,
And dotage signes your pardon.
    Isabella.   I defie thee,
Thee, and thy pardons, proud one.
    Marcelia.   For you, Puppet.
    Mariana. What, of me? Pine-tree.
    Marcelia.   Little you are, I grant,
And haue as little worth, but much lesse wit,
You durst not else, the Duke being wholly mine,
His power and honour mine, and the alleageance,
You owe him, as a Subiect, due to me.
    Mariana. To you?
    Marcelia.   To me: And therefore as a Vassal,
From this houre learne to serue me, or, you'l feele,
I must make vse of my authoritie,
And as a Princesse punish it.
    Isabella.   A Princesse?
    Mariana. I had rather be a Slaue vnto a Moore,
Than know thee for my equall.
    Isabella.   Scornefull thing,
Proud of a white Face.
    Mariana.   Let her but remember
The Issue in her Legge.
    Isabella.   The charge, she puts
The State too, for Perfumes.
    Mariana.   And, howsoe're
She seemes, when she's made vp: As she's her selfe,
She stinkes aboue ground. O that I could reach you,
The little one you scorne so, with her nayles,
Would teare your painted Face, and scratch those Eyes out.
Doe but come downe.
    Marcelia.   Were there no other way,
But leaping on thy Neck, to breake mine owne,
Rather than be outbrau'd thus.   [*Exit* MARCELIA.]
    Graccho.   Fourtie Ducats
Vpon the little Hen: She's of the kind,
And will not leaue the Pit.
    Mariana.   That it were lawfull

178 SD. *Exit* MARCELIA.] *after Gifford; not in* 23

To meete her with a Ponyard, and a Pistoll;
But these weake hands shall shew my spleene.

Enter MARCELIA *below.*

Marcelia.   Where are you?
You Modicum, you Dwarfe.
Mariana.   Here, Giantesse, here.

Enter FRANCISCO, TIBERIO, STEPHANO.

Francisco. A tumult in the Court?
Mariana.   Let her come on.
Francisco. What winde hath rais'd this tempest?   185
Seuer 'em, I command you. What's the cause?
Speake *Mariana.*
Mariana.   I am out of breath;
But we shall meete, we shall. And doe you heare, Sir,
Or right me on this Monster (she's three foote
Too high for a Woman) or ne're looke to haue   190
A quiet houre with me.
Isabella.   If my Sonne were here,
And would endure this; May a Mothers curse
Persue, and ouertake him.
Francisco.   O forbeare,
In me he's present, both in power, and will;
And Madam, I much grieue, that in his absence,   195
There should arise the least distaste to moue you:
It being his principall, nay only charge,
To haue you in his absence seru'd, and honour'd,
As when himselfe perform'd the willing Office.
Mariana. This is fine, yfaith.
Graccho.   I would I were well off.   200
Francisco. And therefore, I beseech you Madam, frowne not
(Till most vnwittingly he hath deseru'd it)
On your poore Seruant; To your Excellence,
I euer was, and will be such: And lay
The Dukes authoritie, trusted to me,   205
With willingnesse at your feet.
Mariana.   O base.

182–4. *rearranged by Gifford*; 23 *reads* But . . . spleene. / Where . . . Dwarfe. / Here . . . here. / A . . . Court? / Let . . . on.

Isabella.   We are like
To haue an equall Iudge.
    Francisco.   But should I finde
That you are touchde in any point of Honor,
Or that the least neglect is falne vpon you,
I then stand vp a Prince.
    Fiddler.   Without reward,
Pray you dismisse vs.
    Graccho.   Would I were fiue Leagues hence.
    Francisco. I will be partial to none, not to my selfe,
Be you but pleas'd to shew me my offence,
Or if you hold me in your good opinion,
Name those that haue offended you.
    Isabella.   I am one,
And I will iustifie it.
    Mariana.   Thou art a base Fellow,
To take her part.
    Francisco.   Remember, she's the Dutchesse.
    Marcelia. But vs'd with more contempt, than if I were
A Peasants Daughter: Bayted, and hooted at
Like to a common Strumpet: With lowd noyses,
Forc'd from my prayers: And my priuate Chamber
(Which with all willingnesse I would make my Prison
During the absence of my Lord) deni'd me.
But if he e're returne—
    Francisco.   Were you an Actor,
In this lewd Comedie?
    Mariana.   I marrie was I,
And will be one againe.
    Isabella.   I'le ioyne with her,
Though you repine at it.
    Francisco.   Thinke not then, I speake
(For I stand bound to honour, and to serue you)
But that the Duke, that liues in this great Lady,
For the contempt of him, in her, commands you
To be close Prisoners.
    Isabella. Mariana.   Prisoners?
    Francisco.   Beare them hence.
This is your charge my Lord *Tiberio*,

                 208. touchde] *Massinger MS*; touc'd *23*; touch'd *38*

And *Stephano*, this is yours.
  Marcelia.   I am not cruell,
But pleas'd they may haue libertie.
  Isabella.   Pleas'd, with a mischiefe.
  Mariana. I'le rather liue in any loathsome Dungeon, 235
Than in a Paradice, at her intreatie:
And, for you vpstart—
  Stephano.   There is no contending.
  Tiberio. What shall become of these?
  Francisco.   See them well whip'd,
As you will answere it.
  Tiberio.   Now Signiour *Graccho*,
What thinke you of your greatnesse?
  Graccho.   I preach patience, 240
And must endure my fortune.
  Fiddler.   I was neuer yet
At such a hunts vp, nor was so rewarded.

    Exeunt omnes, preter FRANCISCO *and* MARCELIA.

  Francisco. Let them first know themselues, and how you are
To be seru'd, and honour'd: Which, when they confesse,
You may againe receiue them to your fauour: 245
And then it will shew nobly.
  Marcelia.   With my thankes,
The Duke shall pay you his, if he returne
To blesse vs with his presence.
  Francisco.   There is nothing
That can be added to your faire acceptance:
That is the prize, indeed: All else, are blankes, 250
And of no value. As in vertuous actions,
The vndertaker finds a full reward,
Although confer'd vpon vnthankefull Men;
So, any seruice done to so much sweetnesse,
(Howeuer dangerous, and subiect to 255
An ill construction) in your fauour finds
A wish'd, and glorious end.
  Marcelia.   From you, I take this
As loyall dutie, but in any other,
It would appeare grosse flatterie.

    240. What thinke you] *23*; What's become *38*

Francisco.   Flatterie, Madam?
You are so rare, and excellent in all things,   260
And rais'd so high vpon a Rock of goodnesse,
As that vice cannot reach you: who but looks on
This Temple built by Nature to Perfection,
But must bow to it: and out of that zeale,
Not only learne to adore it, but to loue it.   265
   Marcelia. Whither will this fellow?   [*Aside.*]
   Francisco.   Pardon therefore Madam,
If an excesse in me of humble dutie,
Teach me to hope (and though it be not in
The power of Man to merit such a blessing)
My pietie (for it is more than loue)   270
May find reward.
   Marcelia.   You haue it in my thankes:
And on my hand, I am pleas'd, that you shal take
A full possession of it. But take heed,
That you fix here, and feed no hope beyond this;
If you doe, 'twill proue fatall.
   Francisco.   Be it death,   275
And death with torments, Tyrants neuer found out:
Yet I must say I loue you.
   Marcelia.   As a Subiect,
And 'twill become you.
   Francisco.   Farewell circumstance:
And since you are not pleas'd to vnderstand me,
But by a plaine, and vsuall forme of speech: 280
All superstitious reuerence lay'd by,
I loue you as a Man, and as a Man
I would enioy you. Why do you start, and flye me?
I am no Monster, and you but a Woman:
A Woman made to yeeld, and by example   285
Told it is lawfull. Fauours of this nature,
Are, in our age, no miracles in the greatest:
And therefore Lady—
   Marcelia.   Keepe of. O you Powers!
Libidinous Beast, and ad to that vnthankfull
(A crime, which Creatures wanting reason, flye from)   290

262. As that] *23*; That *Coxeter*   266 SD. *Aside.*] *Gifford²; not in 23*   274. this] *23³, 38*; it *23¹, ²*

Are all the Princely bounties, fauours, honours,
Which (with some preiudice to his owne wisedome)
Thy Lord, and Rayser hath confer'd vpon thee,
In three dayes absence buried? Hath he made thee
(A thing obscure, almost without a name) 295
The enuie of great Fortunes? Haue I grac'd thee,
Beyond thy rancke? And entertain'd thee, as
A Friend, and not a Seruant? And is this,
This impudent attempt to taint mine Honour,
The faire returne of both our ventur'd fauours? 300
  Francisco. Heare my excuse.
  Marcelia.   The Diuell may plead mercie,
And with as much assurance, as thou yeeld one.
Burnes Lust so hot in thee? Or, is thy pride
Growne vp to such a height, that, but a Princesse,
No Woman can content thee? And ad to that, 305
His Wife, and Princesse, to whom thou art ti'de
In all the bonds of Dutie? Reade my life,
And finde one act of mine so loosely carried,
That could inuite a most selfe-louing Foole,
Set of, with all that fortune could throw on him, 310
To the least hope to find way to my fauour:
And (what's the worst mine enemies could wish me)
I'le be thy Strumpet.
  Francisco.   'Tis acknowledg'd Madam,
That your whole course of life hath been a patterne
For chast, and vertuous Women; In your beautie 315
(Which I first saw, and lou'd) as a faire Cristall,
I read your heauenly mind, cleere and vntainted;
And while the Duke did prize you to your valew
(Could it haue been in Man to pay that dutie)
I well might enuie him, but durst not hope 320
To stop you, in your full carreer of goodnesse.
But now I find that he's falne from his fortune,
And (howsoeuer he would appeare doting)
Growne cold in his affection: I presume,
From his most barbarous neglect of you, 325
To offer my true seruice: Nor stand I bound,
To looke back on the curtesies of him,

305. that] *23², 38*; it *23¹*

That, of all liuing Men, is most vnthankfull.
   Marcelia. Vnheard-of impudence!
   Francisco.   You'l say I am modest,
When I haue told the Storie. Can he taxe me
(That haue receiu'd some worldly trifles from him)
For being ingratefull? When he, that first tasted,
And hath so long enioy'd your sweet embraces
(In which, all blessings that our fraile condition
Is capable of, is wholy comprehended)
As cloy'd with happinesse, contemnes the giuer
Of his felicitie? And, as he reach'd not
The master-peice of mischiefe, which he aymes at,
Vnlesse he pay those fauours he stands bound to,
With fell and deadly hate? You thinke he loues you,
With vnexampled feruor: Nay, dotes on you,
As there were something in you more than Woman:
When on my knowledge, he long since hath wish'd,
You were among the dead: And I, you scorne so,
Perhaps, am your preseruer.
   Marcelia.   Blesse me good Angels,
Or I am blasted. Lyes so false, and wicked,
And fashion'd to so damnable a purpose,
Cannot be spoken by a humane tongue.
My Husband, hate me? Giue thy selfe the Lye,
False, and accurs'd; Thy Soule (if thou hast any)
Can witnesse, neuer Lady stood so bound,
To the vnfained affection of her Lord,
As I doe, to my *Sforza.* If thou would'st worke
Vpon my weake credulitie, Tell me rather,
That the Earth moues; The Sunne, and Starres, stand still;
The Ocean keeps nor Floods, nor Ebbes; Or that
Ther's peace betweene the Lyon, and the Lambe;
Or that the rauenous Eagle, and the Doue,
Keepe in one Ayery, and bring vp their yong:
Or any thing that is auerse to Nature:
And I will sooner credit it, than that
My Lord can thinke of me, but as a Iewell,
He loues more than himselfe, and all the World.
   Francisco. O Innocence, abus'd! Simplicitie cousen'd!
It were a sinne, for which we haue no name,

To keepe you longer in this wilfull errour.
Reade his affection here; And then obserue
How deere he holds you; Tis his Character,
Which cunning yet could neuer counterfeit.
   Marcelia. 'Tis his hand, I am resolu'd of 't.   370
I'le try what the Inscription is.
   Francisco.   Pray you doe so.
   Marcelia. You know my pleasure, and the houre of *Marcelias*
death, which faile not to execute, as you will answere the contrarie,
not with your Head alone, but with the ruine of your whole Famely.
And this written with mine owne Hand, and Signed with my
priuie Signet, shall be your sufficient Warrant.   *Lodouico Sforza.*
I doe obey it, euerie word's a Poynard,   377
And reaches to my Heart.   *She swones.*
   Francisco.   What haue I done?
Madam, for Heauens sake, Madam. O my Fate!
I'le bend her body: This is yet some pleasure,   380
I'le kisse her into a new life. Deare Lady:
She stirs: For the Dukes sake, for *Sforza's* sake.
   Marcelia. Sforzas? Stand off: Though dead, I will be his,
And euen my Ashes shall abhorre the touch
Of any other. O vnkind, and cruell.   385
Learne Women, learne to trust in one another;
There is no faith in Man: *Sforza* is false,
False to *Marcelia*.
   Francisco.   But I am true,
And liue to make you happie. All the Pompe,
State, and obseruance you had being his,   390
Compar'd to what you shall enioy when mine,
Shall be no more remembred. Loose his memory,
And looke with chearefull beames on your new Creature:
And know what he hath plotted for your good,
Fate cannot alter. If the Emperour,   395
Take not his life, at his returne he dyes,
And by my Hand: My Wife, that is his Heire,
Shall quickly follow; Then we Raigne alone,
For with this Arme I'le swim through Seas of blood,
Or make a Bridge, arch'd with the bones of Men,   400
But I will graspe my aymes in you my deerest,

           386. trust in] *23*; trust *38*

Deerest, and best of Women.
Marcelia.   Thou art a Villaine!
All attributes of Arch-Villaines made into one,
Cannot expresse thee. I preferre the hate
Of *Sforza*, though it marke me for the Graue,   405
Before thy base affection. I am yet
Pure, and vnspotted, in my true loue to him;
Nor shall it be corrupted, though he's tainted;
Nor will I part with Innocence, because
He is found guiltie. For thy selfe, thou art   410
A thing, that equall with the Diuell himselfe,
I doe detest, and scorne.
    Francisco.   Thou then art nothing:
Thy life is in my power, disdainefull Woman.
Thinke on't, and tremble.
    Marcelia.   No, though thou wert now
To play thy hangmans part. Thou well may'st be   415
My Executioner, and art only fit
For such employment; But ne're hope to haue
The least grace from me. I will neuer see thee,
But as the shame of Men: So, with my curses
Of horror to thy Conscience in this life,   420
And paines in Hell hereafter: I spit at thee,
And making hast to make my peace with heauen,
Expect thee as my Hangman.   *Exit* MARCELIA.
    Francisco.   I am lost,
In the discouerie of this fatall secret.
Curs'd hope that flatter'd me, that wrongs could make her   425
A stranger to her goodnesse; All my plots
Turne backe vpon my selfe; But I am in,
And must goe on: And since I haue put off
From the Shoare of Innocence, guilt be now my Pilot.
Reuenge first wrought me, Murther's his Twin-brother,   430
One deadly sin then helpe to cure another.   [*Exit.*]

       429. now] *23*; thou *38*   431 SD. *Exit.*] *Gifford*; *not in 23*

Actus Tercius. Scæna Prima.

Enter MEDINA, HERNANDO, ALPHONSO.

Medina. THE spoyle, the spoyle, 'tis that the soldior fights for;
Our victorie as yet affords vs nothing,
But wounds, and emptie honor. We haue past
The hazard of a dreadfull day, and forc'd
A passage with our Swords, through all the dangers,   5
That Page-like waite on the successe of warre;
And now expect reward.
    Hernando.   Hell put it in
The Enemies mind to be desperate, and hold out:
Yeeldings, and compositions will vndoe vs;
And what is that way giuen, for the most part,   10
Comes to the Emperours Coffers, to defray
The charge of the great action (as 'tis rumor'd)
When vsually, some Thing in Grace (that ne're heard
The Canons roring tongue, but at a Triumph)
Puts in, and for his intercession shares,   15
All that we fought for: The poore Soldior left
To starue, or fill vp Hospitalls.
    Alphonso.   But when
We enter Townes by force, and carue our selues,
Pleasure with pillage, and the richest Wines,
Open our shrunke-vp vaines, and poure into 'em   20
New blood, and feruor.
    Medina.   I long to be at it;
To see these Chuffes, that euerie day may spend
A Soldiors entertainement for a yeere,
Yet make a third meale of a bunch of Raysons;
These Spunges, that suck vp a Kingdomes fat   25
(Batning like *Scarabes* in the dung of Peace)
To be squees'd out by the rough hand of warre;
And all that their whole liues haue heap'd together,
By cous'nage, periurie, or sordid thrift,
With one gripe to be rauish'd.
    Hernando.   I would be towsing   30
Their faire *Madona's*, that in little Dogges,
Monkeis, and Paraquito's consume thousands;

III. i. 7. now] *23; now we 38*

Yet for the aduancement of a noble action,
Repine to part with a poore Peice of Eight.
Warres plagues vpon 'em: I haue seene 'em stop   35
Their scornefull noses first, then seeme to swone
At sight of a buffe Ierkin, if it were not
Perfum'd, and hid with Gold; Yet these nice wantons,
(Spurd on by Lust, couer'd in some disguise,
To meete some rough Court Stalion, and be leap'd)   40
Durst enter into any common Brothell,
Though all varieties of stinke contend there;
Yet prayse the entertainment.
   Medina.   I may liue,
To see the tatteredst Raskals of my troupe,
Drag 'em out of their Closets, with a vengeance: 45
When neither threatning, flattering, kneeling, howling,
Can ransome one poore Iewell, or redeeme
Themselues, from their blunt woing.
   Hernando.   My maine hope is,
To begin the sport at Millaine: Ther's enough,
And of all kinds of pleasure we can wish for,   50
To satisfie the most couetous.
   Alphonso.   Euerie day
We looke for a remoue.
   Medina.   For *Lodowick Sforza*
The Duke of Millaine, I, on mine owne knowledge,
Can say thus much; He is too much a Soldior,
Too confident of his owne worth, too rich to,   55
And vnderstands too well, the Emperor hates him,
To hope for composition.
   Alphonso.   On my life,
We need not feere his comming in.
   Hernando.   On mine,
I doe not wish it: I had rather that
To shew his valor, he'd put vs to the trouble   60
To fetch him in by the Eares.
   Medina.   The Emperor.

   Enter CHARLES *the Emperor,* PESCARA, *and Attendants.*
   Charles. You make me wonder (Nay it is no councell,

61 SD. *and*] Gifford; *&c.* 23

You may pertake it Gentlemen); who would haue thought,
That he that scorn'd our proffer'd amitie,
When he was sued to, should, ere he be summond, 65
(Whither perswaded to it by base feare,
Or flatter'd by false hope, which, 'tis vncertaine)
First kneele for mercie?
   Medina.   When your Maiestie,
Shall please to instruct vs, who it is, we may
Admire it with you.
   Charles.   Who, but the Duke of Millaine, 70
The right Hand of the French: Of all that stand
In our displeasure, whom necessitie
Compels to seeke our fauour, I would haue sworne
Sforza had been the last.
   Hernando.   And should be writ so,
In the list of those you pardon. Would his Citie 75
Had rather held vs out a Seidge like Troy,
Then by a fein'd submission, he should cheate you
Of a iust reuenge: Or vs, of those faire glories
We haue sweat blood to purchase.
   Medina.   With your honour
You cannot heare him.
   Alphonso.   The sack alone of Millaine 80
Will pay the Armie.
   Charles.   I am not so weake,
To be wrought on as you feare; Nor ignorant,
That Money is the sinew of the Warre;
And on what termes soeuer he seeke peace,
'Tis in our power to grant it, or denie it. 85
Yet for our glorie, and to shew him that
We haue brought him on his knees; It is resolu'd
To heare him as a Supplyant. Bring him in;
But let him see the effects of our iust anger,
In the Guard that you make for him.   *Exit* PESCARA.
   Hernando.   I am now 90
Familiar with the issue (all plagues on it).
He will appeare in some deiected habit,
His countenance sutable; And for his order,
A Rope about his neck; Then kneele, and tell

                 84. And on] *Massinger MS*; And 23

Old Stories, what a worthy thing it is 95
To haue power, and not to vse it; Then ad to that
A Tale of King *Tigranes*, and great *Pompey*,
Who said (forsooth, and wisely) 'Twas more honor
To make a King, then kill one: Which, applyed
To the Emperor, and himselfe, a Pardons granted 100
To him, an Enemie; and we his Seruants,
Condemn'd to beggerie.

Enter SFORZA [*and* PESCARA.]

 Medina.   Yonder he comes,
But not as you expected.
 Alphonso.   He lookes, as if
He would out-face his dangers.
 Hernando.   I am cousen'd:
A suitor in the Diuels name.
 Medina.   Heare him speake. 105
 Sforza. I come not (Emperor) to inuade thy mercie,
By fawning on thy fortune; Nor bring with me
Excuses, or denials. I professe
(And with a good Mans confidence, euen this instant,
That I am in thy power) I was thine enemie; 110
Thy deadly and vow'd enemie; One that wish'd
Confusion to thy Person and Estates;
And with my vtmost powers, and deepest counsels
(Had they been truely followed) further'd it:
Nor will I now, although my neck were vnder 115
The Hang-mans Axe, with one poore sillable
Confesse, but that I honor'd the French King,
More then thy selfe, and all Men.
 Medina.   By Saint *Iaques*,
This is no flatterie.
 Hernando. There is Fire, and Spirit in't;
But not long liu'd, I hope.
 Sforza.   Now giue me leaue, 120
(My hate against thy selfe, and loue to him
Freely acknowledg'd) to giue vp the reasons
That made me so affected. In my wants
I euer found him faithfull; Had supplyes

102 SD. *Enter* ... PESCARA.] *after Gifford*; *En. Sforza 23*

III. i. 125-60   *The Duke of Milan*   255

Of Men and Moneys from him; And my hopes   125
Quite sunke, were by his Grace, bouy'd vp againe:
He was indeed to me, as my good Angell,
To guard me from all dangers. I dare speake
(Nay must and will) his prayse now, in as high
And lowd a key, as when he was thy equall.   130
The benefits he sow'd in me, met not
Vnthankefull ground, but yeelded him his owne
With faire encrease, and I still glorie in it.
And though my fortunes (poore, compar'd to his,
And Millaine waigh'd with France, appeare as nothing)   135
Are in thy furie burnt: Let it be mentioned,
They seru'd but as small Tapers to attend
The solemne flame at this great Funerall:
And with them I will gladly wast my selfe,
Rather then vndergoe the imputation,   140
Of being base, or vnthankefull.
   Alphonso.   Nobly spoken.
   Hernando. I doe begin, I know not why, to hate him
Lesse then I did.
   Sforza.   If that then to be gratefull
For curtesies receiu'd; Or not to leaue
A friend in his necessities, be a crime   145
Amongst you Spaniards (which other Nations
That like you aym'd at Empire, lou'd, and cherish'd
Where e're they found it) *Sforza* brings his Head
To pay the forfeit; Nor come I as a Slaue,
Piniond and fetterd, in a squallid weed,   150
Falling before thy Feet, kneeling and howling,
For a forestal'd remission; That were poore,
And would but shame thy victorie: For conquest
Ouer base foes, is a captiuitie,
And not a triumph. I ne're fear'd to dye,   155
More then I wish'd to liue. When I had reach'd
My ends in being a Duke, I wore these Robes,
This Crowne vpon my Head, and to my side
This Sword was girt; And witnesse truth, that now
'Tis in anothers power when I shall part   160

  135. appeare] *23*; appears *38*   138. this] *23*; his *Mason*   147. you] *Coxeter*; your *23*

With them and life together, I am the same.
My Veines then did not swell with pride; nor now,
They shrinke for feare: Know Sir, that *Sforza* stands
Prepar'd for either fortune.
 Hernando.   As I liue,
I doe begin strangely to loue this fellow;
And could part with three quarters of my share
In the promis'd spoyle, to saue him.
 Sforza.   But if example
Of my fidelitie to the French (whose honours,
Titles, and glories, are now mixt with yours;
As Brookes deuowr'd by Riuers, loose their names)
Has power to inuite you to make him a friend,
That hath giuen euident proofe, he knowes to loue,
And to be thankefull; This my Crowne, now yours,
You may restore me: And in me instruct
These braue Commanders (should your fortune change,
Which now I wish not) what they may expect,
From noble enemies for being faithfull.
The charges of the warre I will defray,
And what you may (not without hazard) force,
Bring freely to you: I'le preuent the cryes
Of murther'd Infants, and of rauish'd Mayds,
Which in a Citie sack'd call on Heauens justice,
And stop the course of glorious victories.
And when I know the Captaines and the Soldiors,
That haue in the late battle, done best seruice,
And are to be rewarded; I, my selfe
(According to their quallitie and merrits)
Will see them largely recompenc'd. I haue said,
And now expect my sentence.
 Alphonso.   By this light,
'Tis a braue Gentleman.
 Medina.   How like a block
The Emperor sits!
 Hernando.   He hath deliuer'd reasons,
Especially in his purpose to enrich
Such as fought brauely (I my selfe am one,
I care not who knowes it) as, I wonder, that
He can be so stupid. Now he begins to stirre,

Mercie an't be thy will.
   Charles.   Thou hast so farre
Outgone my expectation, noble *Sforza*
(For such I hold thee), And true constancie,
Rais'd on a braue foundation, beares such palme,
And priuiledge with it; That where we behold it,
Though in an enemie, it does command vs
To loue and honour it. By my future hopes,
I am glad, for thy sake, that in seeking fauour,
Thou did'st not borrow of vice her indirect,
Crooked, and abiect meanes: And for mine owne,
That (since my purposes must now be chang'd
Touching thy life and fortunes) the world cannot
Taxe me of leuitie, in my setled councels;
I being neither wrought by tempting bribes,
Nor seruile flatterie; but forc'd vnto it,
By a faire warre of vertue.
   Hernando.   This sounds well.
   Charles. All former passages of hate be buried;
For thus with open armes I meete thy loue,
And as a friend embrace it: And so farre
I am from robbing thee of the least honor,
That with my hands, to make it sit the faster,
I set thy Crowne once more vpon thy head:
And doe not only stile thee, Duke of Millaine,
But vow to keepe thee so. Yet not to take
From others to giue only to my selfe,
I will not hinder your magnificence
To my Commanders, neither will I vrge it,
But in that, as in all things else I leaue you
To be your owne disposer.
                      Florish. Exeunt CHARLES [*and Attendants.*]
   Sforza.   May I liue
To seale my loyaltie, though with losse of life
In some braue seruice worthy *Cæsars* fauor,
And I shall dye most happy. Gentlemen,
Receiue me to your loues, and if henceforth
There can arise a difference betweene vs,

---

224 SD. *Exeunt ... Attendants.*] Gifford; *Ex. Charl.* 23   226. fauor] Massinger MS; fouor 23; favour 38

It shall be in a Noble emulation,
Who hath the fairest Sword, or dare go farthest,
To fight for *Charles* the Emperor?
   Hernando.   We embrace you,
As one well read in all the points of honor,
And there we are your Schollers.
   Sforza.   True, but such
As farre out-strip the Master; we'le contend
In loue hereafter, in the meane time pray you,
Let me discharge my debt, and as in earnest
Of what's to come, deuide this Cabinet:
In the small body of it there are Iewels,
Will yeeld a hundred thousand Pistolets,
Which honor me to receiue.
   Medina.   You bind vs to you.
   Sforza. And when great *Charles* comands me to his presence,
If you will please to excuse my abrupt departure,
Designes that most concerne me next his mercie,
Calling me home, I shall hereafter meete you,
And gratifie the fauor.
   Hernando.   In this and all things,
We are your Seruants.
   Sforza.   A name I euer owe you.
                          Exeunt MEDINA, HERNANDO, ALPHONSO.
   Pescara. So Sir, this tempest is well ouerblowne,
And all things fall out to our wishes. But
In my opinion, this quicke returne,
Before you haue made a partie in the Court
Among the great ones (for these needy Captains
Haue little power in peace) may beget danger,
At least suspition.
   Sforza.   Where true honor liues,
Doubt hath no being; I desire no pawne
Beyond an Emperors word for my assurance:
Besides, *Pescara*, to thy selfe of all men
I will confesse my weakenesse; though my State
And Crown's restored me, though I am in grace
And that a little stay might be a step

230. emulation,] *38*; ~. *23*   237. in] *23*; an *Gifford*   244. his] *Congress* MS, *McIlwraith*; this *23*   246-7. things, / We] *Coxeter*; things, we *23*

III. i. 261–ii. 17   *The Duke of Milan*   259

To greater honors, I must hence. Alas,
I liue not here, my wife, my wife *Pescara*,
Being absent I am dead. Prethe excuse,
And do not chide for freindship sake my fondnes;
But ride along with me, I'le giue you reasons,   265
And strong ones, to plead for me.
   Pescara.   Vse your owne pleasure,
I'le bere you companie.
   Sforza.   Farewell griefe, I am stor'd with
Two blessings most desir'd in humaine life,
A constant friend, an vnsuspected wife.   [*Exeunt.*]

Actus Tercius. Scæna Secunda.

Enter GRACCHO, OFFICER.

   Officer. What I did, I had warrant for; you haue tasted
My Office gently, and for those soft strokes,
Flea bitings to the Ierks I could haue lent you,
There does belong a feeling.
   Graccho.   Must I pay
For being tormented and dishonor'd?
   Officer.   Fye no,   5
Your honours not empar'd in't: What's the letting out
Of a little corrupt blood and the next way too?
There is no Chirurgion like me to take off
A Courtiers Itch that's rampant at great Ladies,
Or turnes knaue for preferment, or growes proud   10
Of their rich Clokes, and Sutes, though got by brokage,
And so forgets his betters.
   Graccho.   Verie good Sir,
But am I the first man of qualitie,
That e're came vnder your fingers?
   Officer.   Not by a thousand,
And they haue said I haue a luckie hand to,   15
Both men and women of all sorts haue bow'd
Vnder this scepter. I haue had a fellow

264. fondnes;] *Coxeter*; ~, 23   269 SD. *Exeunt.*] *Gifford*; *not in* 23
[II. ii. 4. feeling] *23*; feeing *Cunningham*   11. their] *23*; his *Gifford*   and] *23*;
or *38*

That could indite forsooth, and make fine meeters
To tinckle in the eares of ignorant Madams,
That for defaming of great Men, was sent me   20
Thredbare and lowsie, and in three dayes after
Discharged by another that set him on, I haue seene him
Cap a pe gallant, and his stripes wash'd of
With oyle of Angels.
   Graccho.   'Twas a soueraigne cure.
   Officer. There was a Sectarie to, that would not be   25
Conformable to the Orders of the Church,
Nor yeeld to any argument or reason,
But still rayle at authoritie, brought to me,
When I had worm'd his tongue, and trashed his hanches,
Grew a fine Pulpet man, and was benefic'd.   30
Had he not cause to thanke me?
   Graccho.   There was phisicke
Was to the purpose.
   Officer.   Now for women,
For your more consolation, I could tell you
Twentie fine stories, but I'le end in one,
And 'tis the last that's memorable.
   Graccho.   Prethe doe,   35
For I grow wearie of thee.
   Officer.   There was lately
A fine she waiter in the Court, that doted
Extreamely of a Gentleman, that had
His maine dependance on a Signiors fauor
(I will not name) but could not compasse him   40
On any tearmes. This wanton at dead midnight
Was found at the exercise behind the Arras
With the 'foresaid Signior; he got cleare off,
But she was seis'd on, and to saue his honor,
Indur'd the lash; And though I made her often   45
Curuet and caper, she would neuer tell
Who play'd at push-pin with her.

    18. meeters] *23*; meeter *38*   25. Sectarie] *Massinger MS*; Secretarie *23*
27. Nor] *23 (catchword)*, *38*; Not *23*   or] *23*; of *38*   29. trashed] *editor, after Congress MS* (trashde); trussed *23*; tr⟨ ⟩ *Massinger MS*; trounsed *conj. Greg*; trymmed *conj. McIlwraith*   31. he not] *23*; not he *38*   32. women] *23*; women, Sir, *Gifford*

Graccho. But what follow'd?
Prethe be briefe.
  Officer. Why this Sir, she deliuered,
Had store of Crownes assign'd her by her patron,
Who forc'd the Gentleman to saue her credit, 50
To marie her, and say he was the partie
Found in Lobs pound. So, she that before gladly
Would haue been his whore, raignes o're him as his wife,
Nor dares he grumble at it. Speake but truth then,
Is not my Office luckie?
  Graccho. Goe, ther's for thee, 55
But what will be my fortune?
  Officer. If you thriue not
After that soft correction, come againe.
  Graccho. I thanke you knaue.
  Officer. And then knaue, I will fit you.   *Exit* OFFICER.
  Graccho. Whipt like a rogue? no lighter punishment serue
To ballance with a little mirth? 'Tis well; 60
My credit sunke for euer, I am now
Fit companie, only for Pages and for foot boyes,
That haue perused the Porters Lodge.

          Enter two GENTLEMEN.

  1. *Gentleman.* See *Iulio*,
Yonder the proud slaue is, how he lookes now
After his castigation!
  2. *Gentleman.* As he came 65
From a close fight at Sea vnder the Hatches,
With a she Dunckerke, that was shot before
Betweene winde and water, and he hath sprung a leake too,
Or I'me cousen'd.
  1. *Gentleman.* Lets be merie with him.
  Graccho. How they stare at me! am I turn'd to an Owle? 70
The wonder Gentlemen?
  2. *Gentleman.* I read this morning
Strange stories of the passiue fortitude
Of men in former ages, which I thought

  59. serue] *Congress MS, Mason*; striue *23*   68–9. *rearranged by Gifford*; *23 reads*
Betweene ... weather, / And ... cousen'd. / Lets ... him.   68. water] *Gifford*;
weather *23*

Impossible, and not to be beleeued.
But now I looke on you, my wonder ceases.   75
   Graccho. The reason Sir?
   2. Gentleman.   Why Sir you haue been whip'd,
Whip'd signior *Graccho*. And the whip I take it,
Is to a Gentleman, the greatest tryall
That may be of his patience.
   Graccho.   Sir, I'le call you
To a strickt account for this.
   2. Gentleman.   I'le not deale with you,   80
Vnlesse I haue a Beadle for my second.
And then I'le answer you.
   1. Gentleman. Farewell poore *Graccho*.   *Exeunt* GENTLEMEN.
   Graccho. Better and better still. If euer wrongs
Could teach a wretch to find the way to vengence,
Hell now inspire me.

               Enter FRANCISCO *and* SERVANT.

               How, the Lord Protector!   85
My Iudge, I thank him. Whether thus in priuate?
I will not see him.
   Francisco.   If I am sought for,
Say I am indispos'd, and will not heare,
Or suits, or sutors.
   Servant.   But Sir, if the Princes
Enquire, what shall I answere?
   Francisco.   Say, I am rid   90
Abrode to take the ayre, but by no meanes
Let her know I am in Court.
   Servant.   So I shall tell her.   *Exit* SERVANT.
   Francisco. Within there, Ladies.

               Enter a GENTLEWOMAN.

   Gentlewoman.   My good Lord, your pleasure?
   Francisco. Prethe let me begge thy fauor for accesse
To the Dutches.
   Gentlewoman. In good sooth my Lord I dare not,   95
She's verie priuate.
   Francisco.   Come ther's gold to buy thee

86. priuate?] *38*; ~, *23*

A new gowne, and a rich one.
  Gentlewoman.   I once swore
If e're I lost my maiden-head, it should be
With a great Lord as you are, and I know not how,
I feele a yeelding inclination in me,   100
If you haue appetite.
  Francisco.   Poxe on thy maiden-head,
Where is thy Lady?
  Gentlewoman.   If you venter on her,
She's walking in the Gallerie, perhaps
You will find her lesse tractable.
  Francisco.   Bring me to her.
  Gentlewoman. I feare you'l haue cold entertainment, when   105
You are at your iourneys end, and 'twere discretion
To take a snatch by the way.
  Francisco.   Prethe leaue fooling,
My page waites in the lobbie, giue him sweet meats,
He is trayn'd vp for his Masters ease,
And he will coole thee. *Exeunt* FRANCISCO *and* GENTLEWOMAN.
  Graccho. A braue discouerie beyond my hope,   111
A plot euen offer'd to my hand to worke on,
If I am dull now, may I liue and dye
The scorne of wormes and slaues. Let me consider,
My Lady and her Mother first committed   115
In the fauor of the Dutches, and I whip'd,
That with an Iron pen is writ in brasse
On my tough hart, now growne a harder mettal,
And all his brib'd approches to the Dutches
To be conceal'd, good, good, This to my Lady,   120
Deliuer'd as I'le order it, runs her mad.
But this may proue but courtship; let it be
I care not so it feed her Iealousie.   *Exit.*

Actus Tercius. Scæna Tertia.

Enter MARCELIA, FRANCISCO.

  Marcelia. Beleeue thy teares or oathes? Can it be hop'd,
After a practice so abhor'd and horred,

97. A . . . one.] *Gifford*; A . . . one. *This will tempt me.* 23 (*with 'This . . . me.' in R. H. margin* I] 23; This will tempt me. I *Coxeter*

Repentance e're can find thee?
  Francisco.   Deere Lady,
Great in your fortune, greater in your goodnes,
Make a superlatiue of excellence,   5
In being greatest in your sauing mercie.
I doe confesse, humbly confesse my fault
To be beyond all pittie; my attempt,
So barberously rude, that it would turne
A saint-like patience, into sauage furie: 10
H1^r But you that are all innocence and vertue,
No spleane or anger in you of a woman,
But when a holy zeale to pietie fires you,
May, if you please, impute the fault to loue,
Or call it beastly lust, for 'tis no better;   15
A sinne, a monstrous sinne, yet with it, many
That did proue good men after, haue bin tempted,
And thogh I am croked now, 'tis in your powre
To make me straight againe.
  Marcelia.   Is't possible   [*Aside.*]
This can be cunning?
  Francisco.   But if no submission,   20
Nor prayers can appease you, that you may know,
'Tis not the feare of death that makes me sue thus,
But a loathed detestation of my madnesse,
Which makes me wish to liue to haue your pardon,
I will not waite the sentence of the Duke   25
(Since his returne is doubtfull) but I my selfe
Will doe a fearefull iustice on my selfe,
No witnesse by but you, there being no more
When I offended: yet before I doe it,
For I perceiue in you no signes of mercie,   30
I will disclose a secret, which dying with me,
May proue your ruine.
  Marcelia.   Speake it, it will take from
The burthen of thy conscience.
  Francisco.   Thus then Madam,
The warrant by my Lord sign'd for your death,
Was but conditionall, but you must sweare   35

  III. iii. 3. Deere] *23*; Deerest *Gifford*   12. or] *23*; nor *38*   19 SD. *Aside.*]
Coxeter; *not in 23*

III. iii. 36–66   *The Duke of Milan*   265

By your vnspotted truth, not to reueale it,
Or I end here abruptly.
   Marcelia.   By my hopes
Of ioyes hereafter, on.
   Francisco.   Nor was it hate
That forc'd him to it, but excesse of loue.
And if I ne're returne, so said great *Sforza*,   40
No liuing man deseruing to enioy
My best *Marcelia*, with the first newes
That I am dead, for no man after me
Must e're enioy her, faile not to kill her;
But till certaine proofe   45
Assure thee I am lost (these were his words)
Oberue and honor her as if the soule
Of womans goodnesse only dwelt in hers.
This trust I haue abus'd and basely wrong'd,
And if the excelling pittie of your mind   50
Cannot forgiue it, as I dare not hope it,
Rather then looke on my offended Lord,
I stand resolu'd to punish it.
   Marcelia.   Hold, 'tis forgiuen,
And by me freely pardned. In thy faire life
Hereafter studie to deserue this bountie   55
Which thy true penitence (such I beleeue it)
Against my resolution hath forc'd from me.
But that my Lord, my *Sforza* should esteeme
My life fit only as a page, to waite on
The various course of his vncertaine fortunes,   60
Or cherish in himselfe that sensuall hope
In death to know me as a wife, afflicts me,
Nor does his enuie lesse deserue my anger,
Which though such is my loue, I would not nourish,
Will slack the ardor that I had to see him   65
Returne in safetie.

40. ne're] *Coxeter*; e're 23   44. Must] *Massinger MS* (must); Might 23
faile . . . her] *Massinger marks the phrase for insertion here*; but till certaine proofe 23
(*with 'Faile not to kill her' in R. H. margin*)   44–5. Must . . . her; / But . . . proofe
/ Assure . . . words)] *Gifford*²; Might . . . proofe / Assure . . . words) 23; Might . . . kill
her, / But . . . lost, / (These . . . words) *Coxeter*; Must . . . enioy her / Faile . . . proofe
/ Assure . . . words) *McIlwraith*   47. soule] *Massinger MS*; seale 23   56. Which]
Massinger MS (wᶜh); With 23   63. my] 23; mine 38

Francisco. But if your entertainment
Should giue the least ground to his iealousie,
To raise vp an opinion I am false,
You then distroy your mercie. Therfore Madam
(Though I shall euer looke on you as on 70
My liues preseruer, and the miracle
Of human pitty) would you but vouchsafe,
In companie to doe me those faire graces
And fauors which your innocencie and honor
May safely warrant, it would to the Duke 75
(I being to your best selfe alone known guiltie)
Make me appeare most innocent.
 Marcelia.   Haue your wishes,
And some thing I may doe to try his temper,
At least to make him know a constant wife,
Is not so slau'd to her husbands doting humors, 80
But that she may deserue to liue a widow,
Her fate appointing it.
 Francisco.   It is enough,
Nay all I could desire,—and will make way   [*Aside.*]
To my reuenge, which shall disperse it selfe
On him, on her, and all.   *Shout, and Flourish.*
 Marcelia.   What shout is that? 85

    Enter TIBERIO *and* STEPHANO.

Tiberio. All happines to the Dutches, that may flow
From the Dukes new and wish'd returne.
 Marcelia.   He's welcome.
 Stephano. How coldly she receiues it.
 Tiberio.   Obserue their encounter.
            Flourish.

  Enter SFORZA, PESCARA, ISABELLA, MARIANA,
     GRACCHO, *and the rest.*

Mariana. What you haue told me *Graccho* is beleeu'd,
And I'le find time to stur in't.
 Graccho.   As you see cause, 90
I will not doe ill offices.

---

68. false] *Massinger touches up the* s   79. a] *23; his 38*   83 SD. *Aside.*] *after Coxeter; not in 23*   85 SD. *Shout . . . Flourish.*] *Coxeter; follows* enough, (*l. 82*) *23*

Sforza.   I haue stood
Silent thus long *Marcelia*, expecting
When with more then a greedie hast thou would'st
Haue flowne into my armes, and on my lippes
Haue printed a deepe welcome. My desire   95
To glasse my selfe in these faire eyes, haue borne me
With more then human speede. Nor durst I stay
In any Temple, or to any saint
To pay my vowes and thankes for my returne,
Till I had seene thee.
    Marcelia.   Sir, I am most happie   100
To looke vpon you safe, and would expresse
My loue and duty in a modest fashion,
Such as might sute with the behauior
Of one that knowes her selfe a wife, and how
To temper her desires, not like a wanton   105
Fierd with hot appetite, nor can it wrong me
To loue discreetly.
    Sforza.   How, why, can there be
A meane in your affections to *Sforza*?
Or any act though ne're so loose that may
Inuite or heighten appetite, appeare   110
Immodest or vncomly? Doe not moue me,
My passions to you are in extreames,
And know no bounds, come kisse me.
    Marcelia.   I obey you.
    Sforza. By all the ioyes of loue, she does salute me
As if I were her grand-father. What witch,   115
With cursed spels hath quench'd the amorous heat
That liued vpon these lips? Tell me *Marcellia*,
And truly tell me, is't a fault of mine
That hath begot this coldnesse, or neglect
Of others in my absence?
    Marcelia.   Neither Sir,   120
I stand indebted to your substitute,
Noble and good *Francisco* for his care,
And faire obseruance of me: There was nothing
With which you being present could supply me,

96. glasse] *Massinger MS*; glaze *23*; glase *38*   haue] *23*; hath *38*   107. why,]
Coxeter; ~∧ *23*   109. ne're] *38* (nere); neare *23*

That I dare say I wanted.
 Sforza.   How!
 Marcelia.   The pleasures
That sacred *Hymen* warrants vs excepted,
Of which in troth you are too great a doter,
And there is more of beast in it then man.
Let vs loue temperatly, things violent last not,
And too much dotage rather argues folly
Then true affection.
 Graccho.   Obserue but this,
And how she prays'd my Lords care and obseruance,
And then iudge Madam if my intelligence
Haue any ground of truth.
 Mariana.   No more, I marke it.
 Stephano. How the Duke stands!
 Tiberio.   As he were rooted there,
And had no motion.
 Pescara.   My Lord, from whence
Growes this amazement?
 Sforza.   It is more, deare my friend,
For I am doubtfull whether I haue a being,
But certaine that my lifes a burthen to me.
Take me backe good *Pescara*, show me to *Cæsar*,
In all his rage and furie; I disclaime
His mercie; to liue now, which is his guift,
Is worse then death, and with all studied torments.
Marcellia is vnkind, nay worse, growne cold
In her affection, my excesse of feruor,
Which yet was neuer equal'd, growne distastfull.
But haue thy wishes woman, thou shalt know
That I can be my selfe, and thus shake off
The fetters of fond dotage. From my sight
Without reply, for I am apt to doe
Something I may repent. O, who would place [*Exit* MARCELIA.]
His happinesse in most accursed woman,
In whom obsequiousnesse ingenders pride,

 135. rooted] *Massinger MS, 38*; routed *23*   137. more,] *Coxeter*; ~ˏ *23*
 140. backe] *Massinger MS*; bake *23*; back *38*   141. furie;] *Coxeter*; ~ˏ *23*;
disclaime] *Massinger MS, 38*; discliame *23*   145. excesse] *23*; accesse *38*
 146. yet] *Massinger MS*; it *23*   151 SD. *Exit* MARCELIA.] *Gifford*; *not in 23*

And harshnesse deadly hatred. From this howre
I'le labour to forget there are such creatures;   155
True friends be now my mistrisses. Cleere your browes,
And though my heart-strings cracke for't, I will be
To all, a free example of delight:
We will haue sports of all kinds, and propound
Rewards to such as can produce vs new,   160
Vnsatisfi'd though we surfeit in their store.
And neuer thinke of curs'd *Marcelia* more.   *Exeunt.*

Actus Quartus. Scæna Prima.

Enter FRANCISCO, GRACCHO.

Francisco. AND is it possible thou should'st forget
A wrong of such a nature, and then studie
My safetie and content?
　Graccho.　　　　Sir, but allow me
Only to haue read the elements of Courtship
(Not the abstruce and hidden arts to thriue there)   5
And you may please to grant me so much knowledge,
That iniuries from one in grace, like you,
Are noble fauours. Is it not growne common
In euerie sect, for those that want, to suffer
From such as haue to giue? Your Captaine cast   10
If poore, though not thought daring, but approu'd so,
To raise a coward into name, that's rich,
Suffers disgraces publiquely, but receiues
Rewards for them in priuate.
　Francisco.　　　　　　Well obseru'd.
Put on, we'le be familiar, and discourse   15
A little of this argument. That day,
In which it was first rumour'd, then confirm'd,
Great *Sforza* thought me worthy of his fauor,
I found my selfe to be another thing,
Not what I was before. I passed then   20
For a prittie fellow, and of prittie parts too,
And was perhaps receiu'd so: but once rais'd,

---

154. deadly hatred] *Massinger MS*; deadly   　IV. i. 5. arts] *Coxeter*; acts *23*;
arte *Congress MS*　　11. so,] *Coxeter*; ~ₐ *23*

>   The liberall Courtier made me Master of
>   Those vertues, which I ne're knew in my selfe.
>   If I pretended to a iest, 'twas made one
>   By their interpretation. If I offer'd
>   To reason of Philosophy, though absurdly,
>   They had helps to saue me, and without a blush
>   Would sweare, that I by nature had more knowledge,
>   Then others could acquire by any labor.
>   Nay all I did indeed, which in another
>   Was not remarkeable, in me shew'd rarely.
>   *Graccho.* But then they tasted of your bountie.
>   *Francisco.*   True,
>   They gaue me those good parts I was not borne too,
>   And by my intercession they got that,
>   Which (had I cross'd them) they durst not haue hop'd for.
>   *Graccho.* All this is Oracle. And shall I then,
>   For a foolish whipping leaue to honour him,
>   That holds the wheele of Fortune? No, that sauors
>   Too much of th'antient freedome: Since great men
>   Receiue disgraces, and giue thankes, poore knaues
>   Must haue nor spleene, nor anger. Though I loue
>   My limbes aswell as any man, if you had now
>   A humor to kick me lame into an office,
>   Where I might sit in State, and vndoe others,
>   Stood I not bound to kisse the foot that did it?
>   Though it seeme strange, there haue been such things seene
>   In the memorie of man.
>   *Francisco.*   But to the purpose,
>   And then, that seruice done, make thine owne fortunes.
>   My wife, thou say'st, is iealous I am too
>   Familiar with the Dutches.
>   *Graccho.*   And incens'd
>   For her commitment in her brothers absence,
>   And by her Mothers anger is spur'd on
>   To make discouerie of it. This her purpose
>   Was trusted to my charge, which I declin'd
>   As much as in me lay, but finding her
>   Determinately bent to vndertake it,
>   Though breaking my faith to her may destroy

47. haue] *23*; hath *38*

My credit with your Lordship, I yet thought,
Though at my peril, I stood bound to reueale it.   60
 Francisco. I thanke thy care, and will deserue this secret,
In making thee acquainted with a greater,
And of more moment. Come into my bosome,
And take it from me. Canst thou thinke, dull *Graccho*,
My power, and honours, were confer'd vpon me,   65
And ad to them this forme, to haue my pleasures
Confin'd and limited? I delight in change,
And sweet varietie, that's my heauen on earth,
For which I loue life only. I confesse,
My wife pleas'd me a day, the Dutches, two,   70
(And yet I must not say, I haue enioy'd her)
But now I care for neither. Therefore *Graccho*,
So farre I am from stopping *Mariana*
In making her complaint, that I desire thee
To vrge her to it.
 Graccho.   That may proue your ruine,   75
The Duke alreadie being, as 'tis reported,
Doubtfull she hath play'd false.
 Francisco.   There thou art cosen'd,
His dotage like an ague keeps his course,
And now 'tis strongly on him. But I loose time,
And therefore know, whether thou wilt or no,   80
Thou art to be my instrument, and in spite
Of the old sawe, that sayes, it is not safe
On any termes to trust a man that's wrong'd,
I dare thee to be false.
 Graccho.   This is a language
My Lord, I vnderstand not.
 Francisco.   You thought, sirra,   85
To put a trick on me for the relation
Of what I knew before, and hauing woon
Some weightie secret from me, in reuenge
To play the traytor. Know thou wretched thing,
By my command thou wert whip'd, and euery day   90
I'le haue thee freshly tortur'd, if thou misse
In the lest charge that I impose vpon thee.
Though what I speake, for the most part is true,

   92. thee.] *Coxeter*; ~, 23   93. true,] *Coxeter*; ~. 23

Nay, grant thou had'st a thousand witnesses
To be depos'd they heard it, 'tis in me 95
With one word (such is *Sforza's* confidence
Of my fidelitie not to be shaken)
To make all void, and ruine my accusers.
Therefore looke to't, bring my wife hotly on
T'accuse me to the Duke (I haue an end in't) 100
Or thinke, what 'tis makes man most miserable,
And that shall fall vpon thee. Thou wert a foole
To hope by being acquainted with my courses
To curbe and awe me, or that I should liue
Thy slaue, as thou did'st sawcily diuine. 105
For prying in my councels, still liue mine. *Exit* FRANCISCO.
 Graccho. I am caught on both sides. This 'tis for a punie
In Policies *Protean* Schoole, to try conclusions
With one that hath commenc'd and gon out doctor.
If I discouer, what but now he bragg'd of, 110
I shall not be beleeu'd. If I fall off
From him, his threats and actions go togeither.
And ther's no hope of safetie, till I get
A plummet, that may sound his deepest counsels.
I must obey and serue him. Want of skill 115
Now makes me play the rogue against my will. *Exit* GRACCHO.

[IV. ii] *Actus Quartus. Scæna Secunda.*

Enter MARCELIA, TIBERIO, STEPHANO, *Gentlewoman.*

 Marcelia. Command me from his sight, and with such scorne
As he would rate his slaue?
 Tiberio. 'Twas in his furie.
 Stephano. And he repents it Madame.
 Marcelia. Was I borne
To'obserue his humors, or, because he dotes,
Must I run mad?
 Tiberio. If that your Excellence 5
Would please but to receiue a feeling knowledge
Of what he suffers, and how deepe the least
Vnkindnesse wounds from you, you would excuse
His hastie language.

Stephano. He hath payed the forfeit
Of his offence, I'me sure, with such a sorrow, 10
As, if it had been greater, would deserue
A full remission.
　Marcelia.　Why, perhaps he hath it,
And I stand more afflicted for his absence,
Then he can be for mine! So pray you, tell him.
But till I haue digested some sad thoughts, 15
And reconcil'd passions that are at warre
Within my selfe, I purpose to be priuate.
And haue you care, vnlesse it be *Francisco*,
That no man be admitted.　　　[*Exit Gentlewoman.*]
　Tiberio.　　　How, *Francisco*!
　Stephano. He, that at euerie stage keeps liuerie Mistresses, 20
The stallion of the State!
　Tiberio.　　They are things aboue vs,
And so no way concerne vs.
　Stephano.　　If I were
The Duke (I freely must confesse my weakenesse)
I should weare yellow breeches. Here he comes.

　　　　　　Enter FRANCISCO.

　Tiberio. Nay spare your labour, Lady, we know our exit, 25
And quit the roome.
　Stephano.　　Is this her priuacie?
Though with the hazard of a check, perhaps,
This may goe to the Duke.　[*Exeunt* TIBERIO *and* STEPHANO.]
　Marcelia.　　Your face is full
Of feares and doubts. The reason?
　Francisco.　　　O best Madam,
They are not counterfeit. I your poore conuert, 30
That only wish to liue in sad repentance,
To mourne my desperate attempt of you,
That haue no ends, nor aymes, but that your goodnesse
Might be a witnesse of my penitence,
Which seene would teach you, how to loue your mercie, 35
Am robb'd of that last hope. The Duke, the Duke,
I more then feare, hath found, that I am guiltie.

　　IV. ii. 19 SD. *Exit Gentlewoman.*] *Gifford; not in* 23　　25. exit] 23; Duty *Coxeter*
　　28 SD. *Exeunt* . . . STEPHANO.] *Gifford; not in* 23

Marcelia. By my vnspotted honor, not from me,
Nor haue I with him chang'd one sillable
Since his returne but what you heard.
    Francisco.   Yet, malice
Is Eagle-ey'd, and would see that which is not.
And Iealousie's too apt to build vpon
Vnsure foundations.
    Marcelia.   Iealousie?
    Francisco.   It takes.   [*Aside.*]
    Marcelia. Who dares but only thinke, I can be tainted?
But for him, though almost on certaine proofe,
To giue it hearing, not beleefe, deserues
My hate for euer.
    Francisco.   Whether grounded on
Your noble, yet chast fauors showne vnto me,
Or her imprisonment, for her contempt
To you, by my command, my frantique wife
Hath put it in his head.
    Marcelia.   Haue I then liu'd
So long, now to be doubted? Are my fauors
The theames of her discourse? Or what I doe,
That neuer trode in a suspected path,
Subiect to base construction? Be vndanted,
For now, as of a creature that is mine,
I rise vp your protectresse. All the grace
I hitherto haue done you, was bestowed
With a shut hand. It shall be now more free,
Open, and liberall. But let it not,
Though counterfeited to the life, teach you
To nourish sawcie hopes.
    Francisco.   May I be blasted
When I proue such a monster.
    Marcelia.   I will stand, then,
Betweene you, and all danger. He shall know,
Suspition o're-turnes, what confidence builds,
And he that dares but doubt, when ther's no ground,
Is neither to himselfe, nor others sound.   *Exit* MARCELIA.
    Francisco. So, let it worke; her goodnesse, that deny'd
My seruice branded with the name of Lust,

43 SD. *Aside.*] *Coxeter; not in* 23

Shall now destroy it selfe. And she shall finde, 70
When he's a sutor, that brings Cunning arm'd
With power to be his aduocates, the denyall
Is a disease as killing as the plague,
And chastitie a clew, that leads to death.
Hold but thy nature, Duke, and be but rash, 75
And violent enough, and then at leasure
Repent. I care not.
And let my plots produce this long'd-for birth,
In my reuenge I haue my heauen on earth. *Exit* FRANCISCO.

Actus Quartus. Scæna Tertia.

Enter SFORZA, PESCARA, *three* GENTLEMEN.

Pescara. You promis'd to be merrie.
  1. *Gentleman.*   There are pleasures
And of all kinds to entertaine the time.
  2. *Gentleman.* Your excellence vouchsafing to make choice
Of that, which best affects you.
  Sforza.   Hold your prating.
Learne manners too, you are rude.
  3. *Gentleman.*   I haue my answere, 5
Before I aske the question.
  Pescara.   I must borrow
The priuiledge of a friend, and will, or else
I am, like these, a seruant, or what's worse,
A parasite to the sorrow *Sforza* worships
In spite of reason.
  Sforza.   Pray you vse your freedome, 10
And so farre, if you please, allow me mine,
To heare you only, not to be compel'd
To take your morall potions. I am a man,
And thogh philosophy your mistrisse rage for't,
Now I haue cause to grieue, I must be sad, 15
And I dare shew it.
  Pescara.   Would it were bestow'd
Vpon a worthier subiect.
  Sforza.   Take heed, friend.

      IV. iii. 1. pleasures] *Massinger MS, 23², 38*; pleasure, *23¹*

You rub a sore, whose paine will make me mad,
And I shall then forget my selfe and you.
Lance it no further.
   Pescara.   Haue you stood the shock 20
Of thousand enemies, and out-fac'd the anger
Of a great Emperor, that vowed your ruine,
Though by a desperate, a glorious way,
That had no president? Are you return'd with honor,
Lou'd by your subiects? Does your fortune court you, 25
Or rather say, your courage does command it?
Haue you giu'n proofe to this houre of your life,
Prosperitie (that searches the best temper)
Could neuer puffe you vp, nor aduerse fate
Deiect your valor? Shall, I say, these vertues, 30
So many and so various trials of
Your constant mind, be buried in the frowne
(To please you I will say so) of a faire woman?
Yet I haue seene her equals.
   Sforza.   Good *Pescara*,
This language in another were prophane, 35
In you it is vnmannerly. Her equall?
I tell you as a friend, and tell you plainly
(To all men else, my Sword should make reply)
Her goodnesse does disdaine comparison,
And but her selfe admits no paralell. 40
But you will say she's crosse, 'tis fit she should be
When I am foolish, for she's wise, *Pescara*,
And knows how farre she may dispose her bounties,
Her honour safe: or if she were auerse,
'Twas a preuention of a greater sinne 45
Readie to fall vpon me, for she's not ignorant
But truly vnderstands how much I loue her,
And that her rare parts doe deserue all honour.
Her excellence increasing with her yeeres to,
I might haue falne into Idolatry, 50
And from the admiration of her worth,
Bin taught to think there is no power aboue her,
And yet I doe beleeue, had Angels sexes,

    30. Shall,] *Coxeter* ~, 23   38. reply)] 23¹, 38; ~, 23²   48. honour.]
Gifford; ~, 23

The most would be such women, and assume
No other shape, when they were to appeare 55
In their full glorie.
   Pescara.   Well Sir, I'le not crosse you,
Nor labour to diminish your esteeme
Hereafter of her, since your happinesse
(As you will haue it) has alone dependance
Vpon her fauour, from my Soule, I wish you 60
A faire attonement.
   Sforza.   Time, and my submission
May worke her to it.

               Enter TIBERIO *and* STEPHANO.

                O! you are well return'd,
Say, am I blest? hath she vouchsaf'd to heare you?
Is there hope left that she may be appeas'd?
Let her propound, and gladly I'le subscribe 65
To her conditions.
   Tiberio.   She Sir, yet is froward,
And desires respite, and some priuacie.
   Stephano. She was harsh at first, but ere we parted, seem'd not
Implacable.
   Sforza.   Ther's comfort yet, I'le ply her
Each houre with new Embassadors of more honors, 70
Titles, and eminence. My second selfe
Francisco, shall sollicit her.
   Stephano.   That a wise man,
And what is more, a Prince, that may command,
Should sue thus poorely, and treat with his wife,
As she were a victorious enemie, 75
At whose proud feet, himselfe, his State, and Countrey,
Basely beg'd mercie.
   Sforza.   What is that you mutter?
I'le haue thy thoughts.
   Stephano.   You shall, you are too fond,
And feed a pride that's swolne too bigge alreadie,
And surfeits with obseruance.
   Sforza.   O my patience! 80
My vassall speake thus?
   Stephano.   Let my head answere it

If I offend. She that you thinke a Saint,
I feare may play the Diuel.
    Pescara.   Well said old fellow.   [*Aside.*]
    Stephano. And he that hath so long ingross'd your fauours,
Though to be nam'd with reuerence, Lord *Francisco*,   85
Who as you purpose, shall sollicite for you,
I think's too neere her.
    Pescara.   Hold Sir, this is madnesse.
    Stephano. It may be they conferre of ioyning Lordships,
I'me sure he's priuate with her.
    Sforza.   Let me goe,
I scorne to touch him, he deserues my pittie,   90
And not my anger. Dotard, and to be one
Is thy protection, els thou durst not thinke
That loue to my *Marcelia* hath left roome
In my full heart for any Iealous thought,
(That idle passion dwell with thick-skind Trades-men,   95
The vndeseruing Lord, or the vnable)
Lock vp thy owne wife foole, that must take physicke
From her young Doctor, phisicque vpon her backe
Because thou hast the palsey in that part
That makes her actiue. I could smile to thinke   100
What wretched things they are that dare be iealous;
Were I match'd to another *Messaline*,
While I found merit in my selfe to please her
I should beleeue her chast, and would not seeke
To find out my owne torment, but alas,   105
Inioying one that but to me's a *Dian*,
I'me too secure.
    Tiberio.   This is a confidence
Beyond example.

             Enter GRACCHO, ISABELLA, MARIANA.

    Graccho.   There he is, now speake,
Or be for euer silent.
    Sforza.   If you come
To bring me comfort, say, that you haue made   110

    83 SD. *Aside.*] *Gifford*[2]; *not in* 23   88. ioyning] *Massinger MS*; winning 23
98. phisicque] *Massinger MS* (phisicq̢); *blank left in* 23; lijnge *conj. McIlwraith*
106. Dian] *Massinger MS, 38*; Dion 23   108 SD. Enter ... MARIANA.] *38*; *SD
follows* confidence. (*l. 107*) 23

My peace with my *Marcelia*.
  Isabella.   I had rather
Waite on you to your funerall.
  Sforza.   You are my mother,
Or by her life you were dead else.
  Mariana.   Would you were,
To your dishonor, and since dotage makes you
Wilfully blind, borrow of me my eyes,   115
Or some part of my spirit. Are you all flesh?
A lumpe of patience only? No fire in you?
But doe your pleasure, here your Mother was
Committed by your seruant (for I scorne
To call him husband) and my selfe your sister,   120
If that you dare remember such a name,
Mew'd vp to make the way open and free
For the Adultresse, I am vnwilling
To say a part of *Sforza*.
  Sforza.   Take her head off,
She hath blasphem'd, and by our Law must dye.   125
  Isabella. Blasphem'd, for calling of a whore, a whore?
  Sforza. O hell, what doe I suffer?
  Mariana.   Or is it treason
For me that am a subiect, to endeuour
To saue the honour of the Duke, and that
He should not be a Wittall on record?   130
For by posteritie 'twill be beleeu'd
As certainly as now it can be prou'd,
Francisco the great Minion, that swayes all,
To meet the chast embraces of the Dutches,
Hath leap'd into her bed.
  Sforza.   Some proofe vile creature,   135
Or thou hast spoke thy last.
  Mariana.   The publique fame,
Their hourely priuate meetings, and euen now
When vnder a pretence of griefe or anger,
You are deny'd the ioyes due to a husband,
And made a stranger to her, at all times   140
The dore stands open to him. To a Dutchman

117. lumpe] *Massinger MS*; limbe *23*   131. posteritie] *Massinger MS, 38*;
posterie *23*

This were enough, but to a right Italian,
A hundred thousand witnesses.
 Isabella.   Would you haue vs
To be her bawdes?
 Sforza.   O the mallice
And enuie of base women, that with horror   145
Knowing their owne defects and inward guilt,
Dare lye, and sweare, and damne, for what's most false,
To cast aspersions vpon one vntainted!
Y'are in your natures deuils, and your ends,
Knowing your reputation sunke for euer,   150
And not to be recouer'd, to haue all,
Weare your blacke liuerie. Wretches, you haue rays'd
A Monumentall trophy to her purenesse,
In this your studied purpose to depraue her,
And all the shot made by your foule detraction   155
Falling vpon her sure-arm'd Innocence,
Return's vpon your selues, and if my loue
Could suffer an addition, I'me so farre
From giuing credit to you, this would teach me
More to admire and serue her; you are not worthy   160
To fall as sacrifices to appease her,
And therefore liue till your own enuy burst you.
 Isabella. All is in vaine, he is not to be mou'd.
 Mariana. She has bewitcht him.
 Pescara.   'Tis so past beliefe,
To me it shewes a fable.

    Enter FRANCISCO *and a* SERVANT.

 Francisco.   On thy life   165
Prouide my horses, and without the Port
With care attend me.
 Servant.   I shall my Lord.   *Exit* SERVANT.
 Graccho.   He's come.
What iimmecracke haue we next?
 Francisco.   Great Sir.
 Sforza.   *Francisco,*
Though all the ioyes in woman are fled from me

143-4. Would ... vs / To ... bawdes?] 23; Would you / Haue ... bawdes? *Baldwin*
168. iimmecracke] *Massinger MS; space left before* cracke *in 23*

In thee I doe embrace the full delight 170
That I can hope from man.
   Francisco.   I would impart,
Please you to lend your eare, a waightie secret,
I am in labour to deliuer to you.
   Sforza. All leaue the roome, excuse me good *Pescara.*
Ere long I will waite on you.
   Pescara.   You speake Sir 175
The language I should vse.
   Sforza.   Be within call,
Perhaps we may haue vse of you.
   Tiberio.   We shall Sir.
             [*Exeunt all but* SFORZA *and* FRANCISCO.]
   Sforza. Say on my comfort.
   Francisco.   Comfort? No, your torment,
For so my fate appoints me, I could curse
The houre that gaue me being.
   Sforza.   What new monsters 180
Of miserie stand readie to deuoure me?
Let them at once dispatch me.
   Francisco.   Draw your sword then,
And as you wish your own peace, quickly kil me,
Consider not, but doe it.
   Sforza.   Art thou mad?
   Francisco. Or if to take my life be too much mercy, 185
As death indeed concludes all human sorrowes,
Cut off my nose and eares, pull out an eye,
The other only left to lend me light
To see my owne deformities: Why was I borne
Without some mulct impos'd on me by nature? 190
Would from my youth a lothsome leprosie
Had runne vpon this face, or that my breath
Had been infectious, and so made me shun'd
Of all societies: curs'd be he that taught me
Discource or manners, or lent any grace 195
That makes the owner pleasing in the eye
Of wanton women, since those parts which others
Value as blessings, are to me afflictions,
Such my condition is.

177 SD. *Exeunt . . .* FRANCISCO.] *Coxeter; not in* 23   181. miserie] *23;* miseries *38*

Sforza.   I am on the racke,
Dissolue this doubtfull riddle.
   Francisco.   That I alone
Of all mankind that stand most bound to loue you,
And studie your content should be appointed,
Not by my will, but forc'd by cruell fate
To be your greatest enemie! not to hold you
In this amazement longer, in a word,
Your Dutches loues me.
   Sforza.   Loues thee?
   Francisco.   Is mad for me,
Pursues me hourely.
   Sforza.   Oh!
   Francisco.   And from hence grew
Her late neglect of you.
   Sforza.   O women! women!
   Francisco. I labour'd, to diuert her by perswasion,
Then vrg'd your much loue to her, and the danger,
Deny'd her, and with scorne.
   Sforza.   'Twas like thy selfe.
   Francisco. But when I saw her smile, then heard her say,
Your loue and extreme dotage as a Cloke
Should couer our embraces, and your power
Fright others from suspition, and all fauours
That should preserue her in her innocence,
By lust inuerted to be vs'd as bawdes,
I could not but in dutie (though I know
That the relation kils in you all hope
Of peace hereafter, and in me 'twill shew
Both base and poore to rise vp her accuser)
Freely discouer it.
   Sforza.   Eternall plagues
Pursue and ouertake her, for her sake
To all posteritie may he proue a Cuckold,
And like to me a thing so miserable
As words may not expresse him, that giues trust
To all deceiuing women, or since it is
The will of Heauen to preserue mankind,
That we must know, and couple with these serpents,
No wiseman euer taught by my example

IV. iii. 231–59   *The Duke of Milan*   283

Hereafter vse his wife with more respect
Then he would doe his Horse that do's him seruice,
Base woman being in her creation made
A slaue to man; but like a village nurse
Stand I now cursing, and considering when   235
The tamest foole would doe? Within there, *Stephano*,
Tiberio, and the rest! I will be suddaine,
And she shall know and feele loue in extreames,
Abus'd knowes no degree in hate.

     Enter TIBERIO, STEPHANO, *Guard.*

 Tiberio.   My Lord.
 Sforza. Goe to the Chamber of that wicked woman.   240
 Stephano. What wicked woman, Sir?
 Sforza.   The deuill my wife.
Force a rude entry, and if she refuse
To follow you, drag her hither by the hayre
And know no pittie, any gentle vsage
To her will call on cruelty from me   245
To such as shew it. Stand you staring? Goe,
And put my will in act.
 Stephano.   Ther's no disputing.
 Tiberio. But 'tis a tempest on the suddaine rays'd,
Who durst haue dreamt of? *Exeunt* TIBERIO, STEPHANO, [*Guard.*]
 Sforza.   Nay, since she dares damnation,
I'le be a furie to her.
 Francisco.   Yet great Sir,   250
Exceed not in your furie, she's yet guiltie
Only in her intent.
 Sforza.   Intent *Francisco?*
It does include all fact, and I might sooner
Be won to pardon treason to my Crowne,
Or one that kil'd my Father.
 Francisco.   You are wise,   255
And know what's best to doe, yet if you please
To proue her temper to the height, say only
That I am dead, and then obserue how farre
She'le be transported. I'le remoue a little,

  239. in] 23; of 38 249 SD. STEPHANO, *Guard.*] Baldwin; Steph. 23

284   *The Duke of Milan*   IV. iii. 260–89

But be within your call:—now to the vpshot,   [*Aside.*]
How e're I'le shift for one.   *Exit* FRANCISCO.

Enter TIBERIO, STEPHANO, MARCELIA, *Guard.*

   Marcelia.   Where is this Monster?   261
This walking tree of Iealousie, this dreamer,
This horned beast that would be? O are you here Sir?
Is it by your commandement or allowance,
I am thus basely vs'd? Which of my vertues,   265
My labours, seruices, and cares to please you
(For to a man suspitious and vnthankefull,
Without a blush I may be mine owne trumpet)
Inuites this barbarous course? Dare you looke on me
Without a seale of shame?
   Sforza.   Impudence,   270
How vgly thou appear'st now! Thy intent
To be a whore, leaues thee not blood enough
To make an honest blush; what had the act done?
   Marcelia. Return'd thee the dishonor thou deseruest
Though willingly I had giuen vp my selfe   275
To euerie common letcher.
   Sforza.   Your chiefe minion,
Your chosen fauourite, your woo'd *Francisco,*
Has deerely pay'd for't, for wretch, know he's dead,
And by my hand.
   Marcelia.   The bloodyer villaine thou,
But 'tis not to be wonder'd at, thy loue   280
Do's know no other obiect. Thou hast kil'd then
A man I doe professe I lou'd, a man
For whom a thousand Queenes might well be riuals,
But he (I speake it to thy teeth) that dares be
A Iealous foole, dares be a murtherer,   285
And knowes no end in mischiefe.
   Sforza.   I begin now   *Stabs her.*
In this my Iustice.
   Marcelia.   Oh, I haue fool'd my selfe
Into my graue, and only grieue for that
Which when you know, you haue slaine an Innocent

    260 SD. *Aside.*] *Coxeter; not in* 23   266. cares] *23;* care *38*   270. seale] *23;* soule *McIlwraith*

You needs must suffer.
 Sforza.   An Innocent? Let one
Call in *Francisco*, for he liues (vile creature) *Exit* STEPHANO.
To iustifie thy falshood, and how often
With whorish flatteries thou hast tempted him,
I being only fit to liue a stale,
A bawd and propertie to your wantonnesse.

     Enter STEPHANO.

 Stephano. Signior *Francisco* Sir, but euen now
Tooke horse without the Ports.
 Marcelia.   We are both abus'd,
And both by him vndone, stay death a little
Till I haue cleer'd me to my Lord, and then
I willingly obey thee. O my *Sforza*,
Francisco was not tempted, but the Tempter,
And as he thought to win me shew'd the warrant
That you sign'd for my death.
 Sforza.   Then I beleeue thee,
Beleeue thee innocent too.
 Marcelia.   But being contemn'd,
Vpon his knees with teares he did beseech me
Not to reueale it. I soft-hearted foole
Iudging his penitence true, was won vnto it.
Indeed the vnkindnesse to be sentenc'd by you
Before that I was guiltie in a thought,
Made me put on a seeming anger towards you,
And now behold the issue; as I do,
May heauen forgiue you.   *Dyes.*
 Tiberio.   Her sweet soule has left
Her beauteous prison.
 Stephano.   Looke to the Duke, he stands
As if he wanted motion.
 Tiberio.   Griefe hath stopt
The organ of his speech.
 Stephano.   Take vp this body
And call for his Physitians.
 Sforza.   O my heart-strings.   [*Exeunt.*]

  299. me to] *23*; my self unto *38*   316 SD. *Exeunt.*] *Gifford*; *not in 23*

Actus Quintus. Scæna Prima.

Enter FRANCISCO, EUGENIA.

Francisco. WHY could'st thou thinke *Eugenia* that rewards,
Graces, or fauours though strew'd thick vpon me
Could euer bribe me to forget mine honour?
Or that I tamely would sit downe, before
I had dry'd these eyes still wet with showers of teares   5
By the fire of my reuenge? Looke vp my deerest
For that proud-faire that thiefe-like step'd betweene
Thy promis'd hopes, and rob'd thee of a fortune
Almost in thy possession, hath found
With horrid proofe, his loue she thought her glorie   10
And an assurance of all happinesse,
But hast'ned her sad ruine.
   Eugenia.   Doe not flatter
A griefe that is beneath it, for how euer
The credulous Duke to me proued false and cruel,
It is imposible he could be wrought   15
To looke on her, but with the eyes of dotage,
And so to serue her.
   Francisco.   Such indeed I grant
The streame of his affection was, and ran
A constant course, till I with cunning malice
(And yet I wrong my act, for it was Iustice)   20
Made it turne back-wards, and hate in extreames,
Loue banish'd from his heart, to fill the roome;
In a word, know the faire *Marcelia*'s dead.
   Eugenia.   Dead!
   Francisco. And by *Sforza*'s hand, do's it not moue you?
How coldly you receiue it! I expected   25
The meere relation of so great a blessing
Borne proudly on the wings of sweet reuenge
Would haue cal'd on a sacrifice of thankes,
And ioy not to be bounded or conceal'd!
You entertaine it with a looke, as if   30
You wish'd it were vndone!
   Eugenia.   Indeed I doe,

V. i. 11. an] *Massinger MS; not in* 23

For if my sorrowes could receiue addition,
Her sad fate would encrease, not lessen 'em.
She neuer iniur'd me, but entertain'd
A fortune humbly offer'd to her hand, 35
Which a wise Lady gladly would haue kneel'd for.
Vnlesse you would impute it as a crime,
She was more faire then I, and had discretion
Not to deliuer vp her virgin fort
(Though straight besieg'd with flatteries, vowes, and teares) 40
Vntill the Church had made it safe and lawfull.
And had I been the mistris of her iudgement
And constant temper, skilfull in the knowledge
Of mans malitious falshood, I had neuer
Vpon his hell-deepe oathes to marrie me, 45
Giuen vp my faire name, and my mayden honor
To his foule lust, nor liu'd now being branded
In the forhead for his whore, the scorne and shame
Of all good women.
  Francisco.   Have you then no gall,
Anger, or spleene familiar to your sexe? 50
Or is it possible that you could see
Another to possesse what was your due,
And not growe pale with enuie?
  Eugenia.   Yes of him
That did deceiue me. Ther's no passion that
A maid so iniur'd euer could partake of 55
But I haue deerely suffer'd. These three yeeres
In my desire, and labour of reuenge,
Trusted to you, I haue indur'd the throes
Of teeming women, and will hazard all
Fate can inflict on me but I will reache 60
Thy heart false *Sforza*. You haue trifled with me
And not proceeded with that fiery zeale
I look'd for from a brother of your spirit.
Sorrow forsake me, and all signes of griefe
Farewell for euer; Vengeance arm'd with furie 65
Possesse me wholy now.
  Francisco.   The reason sister
Of this strange metamorphosis?
  Eugenia.   Aske thy feares,

Thy base vnmanly feares, thy poore delayes,
Thy dull forgetfulnesse equall with death.
My wrong else, and the scandall which can neuer
Be wash'd off from our house but in his blood,
Would haue stirr'd vp a coward to a deed
In which, though he had falne, the braue intent
Had crown'd it selfe with a faire monument
Of noble resolution. In this shape
I hope to get accesse, and then with shame
Hearing my sodaine execution, iudge
What honor thou hast lost in being transcended
By a weake woman.
  Francisco. Still mine owne, and dearer,
And yet in this you but poure oyle on fire,
And offer your assistance where it needs not,
And that you may perceiue I lay not fallow,
But had your wrongs stamp'd deeply on my hart
By the iron pen of vengeance, I attempted
By whoring her to cuckold him; that failing
I did begin his tragedie in her death,
To which it seru'd as Prologue, and will make
A memorable storie of your fortunes
In my assur'd reuenge, only best sister
Let vs not loose our selues in the performance,
By your rash vndertaking; we will be
As suddaine as you could wish.
  Eugenia.   Vpon those termes
I yeeld my selfe and cause to be dispos'd of
As you thinke fit.
      Enter SERVANT.
  Francisco. Thy purpose?
  Servant.   Ther's one *Graccho*
That follow'd you it seemes vpon the tract,
Since you left Millaine, that's importunate
To haue accesse, and will not be deni'd,
His hast he saies concernes you.
  Francisco.   Bring him to me, *Exit* SERVANT.
Though he hath lay'd an ambush for my life,
Or apprehension, yet I will preuent him
And worke mine own ends out.

V. i. 101–29 *The Duke of Milan* 289

Enter GRACCHO.

Graccho. Now for my whipping,
And if I now out-strip him not, and catch him,
And by a new and strange way to, hereafter
I'le sweare there are wormes in my braines.
  Francisco. Now my good *Graccho*,
We meet as 'twere by miracle.
  Graccho. Loue, and dutie, 105
And vigilance in me for my Lords safetie,
First taught me to imagine you were here,
And then to follow you. Al's come forth my Lord
That you could wish conceal'd. The Dutchesse wound
In the Dukes rage put home, yet gaue her leaue 110
To acquaint him with your practises, which your flight
Did easily confirme.
  Francisco. This I expected,
But sure you come prouided of good counsaile
To helpe in my extreames.
  Graccho. I would not hurt you.
  Francisco. How? hurt me? Such another word's thy death. 115
Why dar'st thou thinke it can fall in thy will,
T'outliue what I determine?
  Graccho. How he awes me! [*Aside.*]
  Francisco. Be briefe, what brought thee hither?
  Graccho. Care to informe you,
You are a condemn'd man, pursu'd, and sought for,
And your head rated at ten thousand Ducates 120
To him that brings it.
  Francisco. Very good.
  Graccho. All passages
Are intercepted, and choyce troopes of horse
Scoure o're the neighbour plaines, your picture sent
To euerie State confederate with Millaine,
That though I grieue to speake it, in my iudgement 125
So thicke your dangers meet, and run vpon you,
It is impossible you should escape
Their curious search.
  Eugenia. Why let vs then turne Romanes,
And falling by our owne hands, mocke their threats,

117 SD. *Aside.*] Coxeter; *not in* 23   128. let vs then] 23; then let vs 38

And dreadfull preparations.
  Francisco.   'Twould show nobly,
But that the honour of our full reuenge
Were lost in the rash action: No *Eugenia*,
Graccho is wise, my friend to, not my seruant,
And I dare trust him with my latest secret.
We would (and thou must helpe vs to performe it)
First kill the Duke, then fall what can vpon vs,
For iniuries are writ in brasse, kind *Graccho*,
And not to be forgotten.
  Graccho.   He instructs me
What I should doe.
  Francisco. What's that?
  Graccho.   I labour with
A strong desire t'assist you with my seruice,
And now I am deliuer'd of't.
  Francisco.   I tould you.
Speake my oraculous *Graccho*.
  Graccho.   I haue heard Sir
Of men in debt, that layd for by their creditors
(In all such places where it could be thought
They would take shelter) chose for sanctuarie,
Their lodgings vnderneath their creditors noses,
Or neere that prison to which they were design'd
If apprehended, confident that there
They neuer should be sought for.
  Eugenia.   'Tis a strange one!
  Francisco. But what inferre you from it?
  Graccho.   This my Lord,
That since all wayes of your escape are stop'd,
In Millaine only, or what's more, i' the Court
(Whether it is presum'd you dare not come)
Conceal'd in some disguise you may liue safe.
  Francisco. And not to be discouered?
  Graccho.   But by my selfe.
  Francisco. By thee? Alas I know thee honest *Graccho*,
And I will put thy counsell into act,
And suddainly. Yet not to be vngratefull
For all thy louing trauell to preserue me,
What bloody end soe're my starres appoint,

Thou shalt be safe good *Graccho*. Who's within there?
  Graccho. In the deuils name what meanes he?
                    Enter Seruants.
  Francisco.   Take my friend
Into your custodie, and bind him fast,
I would not part with him.
  Graccho.   My good Lord.
  Francisco.   Dispatch,
'Tis for your good to keepe you honest *Graccho*,   165
I would not haue ten thousand Ducates tempt you
(Being of a soft and waxe like disposition)
To play the traytor, nor a foolish itch
To be reueng'd for your late excellent whipping
Giue you the opportunitie to offer   170
My head for satisfaction. Why thou foole,
I can looke through, and through thee, thy intents
Appeare to me as written in thy forhead
In plaine and easie caracters. And but that
I scorne a slaues base blood shold rust that sword   175
That from a Prince expects a scarlet dye,
Thou now wert dead, but liue only to pray
For good successe to crowne my vndertakings,
And then at my returne perhaps I'le free thee
To make me further sport. Away with him,   180
            Exeunt Seruants with GRACCHO.
I will not heare a sillable. We must trust
Our selues *Eugenia*, and though we make vse of
The counsaile of our seruants, that oyle spent,
Like snuffes that doe offend we tread them out.
But now to our last Scene, which we'le so carry,   185
That few shall vnderstand how 'twas begun,
Till all with halfe an eye may see 'tis don.   *Exeunt.*

Actus Quintus. Scæna Secunda.
Enter PESCARA, TIBERIO, STEPHANO.
  Pescara. The like was neuer read of.
  Stephano.   In my iudgement
To all that shall but heare it, 'twill appeare

162. In ... what] 23; What 38   V. ii. 1. read] 23; heard 38

A most impossible fable.
  Tiberio.   For *Francisco*,
My wonder is the lesse because there are
Too many Presidents of vnthankefull men
Rays'd vp to greatnesse, which haue after studied
The ruine of their makers.
  Stephano.   But that melancholy,
Though ending in distraction, should worke
So farre vpon a man as to compell him
To court a thing that has nor sence, nor being,
Is vnto me a miracle.
  Pescara.   'Troth I'le tell you,
And briefly as I can, by what degrees
He fell into this madnesse. When by the care
Of his Physitians he was brought to life,
As he had only pass'd a fearefull dreame,
And had not acted what I grieue to thinke on,
He call'd for faire *Marcelia*, and being told
That she was dead, he broke forth in extreames,
(I would not say blasphem'd) and cri'd that heauen
For all th' offences that mankind could doe,
Would neuer be so cruell as to rob it
Of so much sweetnesse, and of so much goodnesse,
That not alone was sacred in her selfe,
But did preserue all others innocent
That had but conuerse with her: Then it came
Into his fancie that she was accus'd
By his mother and his sister, thrice he curs'd 'em,
And thrice his desperat hand was on his sword
To haue kill'd 'em both, but he restrayn'd, and they
Shunning his furie, spite of all preuention
He would haue turn'd his rage vpon himselfe,
When wisely his Physitians looking on
The Dutches wound, to stay his readie hand,
Cry'd out it was not mortall.
  Tiberio.   'Twas well thought on.
  Pescara. He easily beleeuing what he wish'd,
More then a perpetuitie of pleasure
In any obiect else, flatter'd by hope,
Forgetting his owne greatnesse, he fell prostrate

At the doctors feet, implor'd their ayd, and swore,
Prouided they recouer'd her, he would liue 40
A priuat man, and they should share his dukedom.
They seem'd to promise faire, and euerie houre
Varie their iudgements as they find his fit
To suffer intermission, or extreames.
For his behauiour since—
   Sforza.   As you haue pitty   *Within.*
Support her gently.
   Pescara.   Now be your owne witnesses, 46
I am preuented.

Enter SFORZA, ISABELLA, MARIANA, *the body of* MARCELIA,
        DOCTORS, *Seruants.*

   Sforza.   Carefully I beseech you,
The gentlest touch torments her, and then thinke
What I shall suffer. O you earthly gods,
You second natures, that from your great master 50
(Who ioyn'd the limbes of torne *Hyppolytus*,
And drew vpon himselfe the Thunderers enuie)
Are taught those hidden secrets that restore
To life death-wounded men, You haue a patient
On whom to'expresse the excellence of art, 55
Will bind e'ne heau'n your debtor, though It pleases
To make your hands the organs of a worke
The saints will smile to looke on, and good Angels
Clap their Celestiall wings to giue it plaudits.
How pale and wan she lookes! O pardon me, 60
That I presume dyde o're with bloody guilt,
Which makes me I confesse, far, far vnworthy
To touch this snow-white hand. How cold it is!
This once was *Cupids* fire-brand, and still
'Tis so to me. How slow her pulses beat to! 65
Yet in this temper she is all perfection,
And Mistris of a heat so full of sweetnesse,
The blood of virgins in their pride of youth
Are balles of Snow or Ice compar'd vnto her.
   Mariana. Is not this strange?
   Isabella.   O crosse him not deere daughter, 70

    48. gentlest] *23*; least *38*   49. earthly] *Massinger MS*; earthy *23*

Our conscience tells vs we haue been abus'd,
Wrought to accuse the innocent, and with him
Are guiltie of a fact—!

Enter a SERVANT.

   Mariana.   'Tis now past helpe.
   Pescara. With me? What is he?
   Servant.   He has a strange aspect,
A Iew by birth, and a Physitian
By his profession as he sayes, who hearing
Of the Dukes phrensie, on the forfeit of
His life will vndertake to render him
Perfect in euery part. Prouided that
Your Lordships fauour gaine him free accesse,
And your power with the Duke a safe protection,
Till the great worke be ended.
   Pescara.   Bring me to him,
As I find cause I'le doe.   *Exeunt* PESCARA *and* SERVANT.
   Sforza.   How sound she sleepes!
Heauen keepe her from a lethergie; how long
(But answere me with comfort I beseech you)
Do's your sure iudgement tell you that these lids
That couer richer iewells then themselues
Like enuious night will barre these glorious sunnes
From shining on me?
   1. *Doctor.*   We haue giuen her Sir,
A sleepy potion that will hold her long,
That she may be lesse sensible of the torment,
The searching of her wound will put her to.
   2. *Doctor.* Shee now feeles litle, but if we should wake her,
To heare her speake would fright both vs and you,
And therefore dare not hasten it.
   Sforza.   I am patient,
You see I doe not rage, but waite your pleasure.
What doe you thinke she dreames of now? for sure
Although her bodies organs are bound fast,
Her fancy cannot slumber.
   1. *Doctor.*   That Sir, lookes on
Your sorrow for your late rash act with pitty

   93. wake] *Massinger MS, 38*; make *23*   100. act] *Massinger MS, 38*; art *23*

V. ii. 101–34   *The Duke of Milan*

Of what you suffer for it, and prepares
To meet the free confession of your guilt
With a glad pardon.
   Sforza.   Shee was euer kind
And her displeasure though call'd on, short liu'de
Vpon the least submission. O you powers   105
That can conuey our thoughts to one another
Without the aid of eies, or eares, assist me,
Let her behold me in a pleasing dreame,
Thus on my knees before her (yet that duty
In me is not sufficient) let her see me   110
Compell my mother (from whom I tooke life)
And this my sister, Partner of my being,
To bow thus low vnto her, let her heare vs
In my acknowledgement freely confesse
That we in a degree as high are guilty,   115
As she is innocent; bite your tongues, vile creatures,
And let your inward horror fright your soules
For hauing belide that purenesse, to come neere which
All women that posterity can bring forth
Must be, though striuing to be good, poore Riualls.   120
And for that dog *Francisco* (that seduc'd me
In wounding her to rase a temple built
To Chastitie and sweetnesse) let her know
I'll follow him to hell, but I will find him,
And there liue a fourth fury to torment him.   125
Then for this cursed hand and arme that guided
The wicked steele, I'll haue them ioynt by ioynt,
With burning irons seard of, which I will eate.
I being a vultur fit to tast such carrion,
Lastly—
   1. *Doctor.* You are too lowd, Sir, you disturbe   130
Her sweet repose.
   Sforza.   I am hush'd, yet giue vs leaue
Thus prostrate at her feet, our eies bent downewards,
Vnworthy, and asham'd to looke vpon her,
T' expect her gracious sentence.

    102. the] *Mason*; with 23   103. Sforza.] *Massinger MS* (*SForza.*), *38*; Forza. *23*
107. aid] *Coxeter*; end *23*   111. tooke] *Massinger MS*, *38*; looke *23*   122. rase]
Coxeter; raise *23*   131. Sforza.] *Massinger MS* (*SForza.*), *38*; Forza. *23*

2. Doctor.   Hee's past hope.
1. Doctor. The body to, will putrifie, and then
We can no longer couer the imposture.
    Tiberio. Which in his death will quickly be discouer'd;
I can but weepe his fortune.
    Stephano.   Yet be carefull
You loose no minute to preserue him; time,
May lessen his distraction.

                Enter PESCARA, FRANCISCO, EUGENIA.

    Francisco.   I am no God sir,
To giue a new life to her, yet I'le hazard
My head, I'le worke the sencelesse trunke t'appeare
To him as it had got a second being,
Or that the soule that's fled from't were call'd backe,
To gouerne it againe; I will preserue it
In the first sweetnesse, and by a strange vaper
Which I'le infuse into her mouth, create
A seeming breath; I'le make her vaines run high to
As if they had true motion.
    Pescara.   Doe but this,
Till we vse meanes to win vpon his passions
T'indure to heare shee's dead with some small patience
And make thy owne reward.
    Francisco.   The art I vse
Admits no looker on, I only aske
The fourth part of an hower to perfect that
I boldly vndertake.
    Pescara.   I will procure it.
    2. Doctor. What stranger's this?
    Pescara.   Sooth me in all I say,
There is a maine end in't.
    Francisco.   Beware.
    Eugenia.   I am warn'd.
    Pescara. Looke vp Sir chearefully, comfort in me
Flowes stronglie to you.
    Sforza.   From whence came that sound?
Was it from my *Marcelia*? if it were
I rise and ioy will giue me wings to meet it.

            159. *Sforza.*] *Massinger MS (SForza.), 38*; Forza. 23

Pescara. Nor shall your expectation be deferrd
But a few minuts; your Physitians are
Meere voice, and no performance, I haue found
A man that can do wonders, do not hinder
The Dutches wisht recouery to inquire,
Or what he is, or to giue thankes, but leaue him
To worke this miracle.
   Sforza.   Sure, 'tis my good Angell,
I do obey in all things; be it death
For any to disturbe him, or come neere
Till he be pleas'd to call vs, O be prosperous
And make a Duke thy Bondman.
                    Exeunt all but FRANCISCO *and* EUGENIA.
   Francisco.   Tis my purpose
If that to fall a long wisht sacrifice
To my reuenge can be a benefit.
I'll first make fast the dores, soe.
   Eugenia.   You amaze me.
What followes now?
   Francisco.   A full conclusion
Of all thy wishes. Looke on this, *Eugenia*,
Eu'n such a thing, the proudest faire on earth
(For whose delight the elements are ransack'd
And art with nature studies to preserue her)
Must be when she is summond to appeare
In the Court of death, but I loose time.
   Eugenia.   What meane you?
   Francisco. Disturbe me not, your Ladiship lookes pale
But I, your Docter, haue a ceruse for you.
See my *Eugenia*, how many faces
That are ador'd in Court borrow these helpes,
And passe for excellent, when the better part
Of them are like to this: your mouth smells soure to,
But here is that shall take away the sent,
A precious antidote old Ladies vse
When they would kisse, knowing their gummes are rotten:
These hands to, that disdain'd to take a touch
From any lip, whose owner writ not Lord,

180. studies] *23*; studied *Gifford*   187. excellent] *Congress MS, McIlwraith*;
excellence *23*   189. here] *23*; there *38*   193. owner] *Massinger MS*; honour *23*

Are now but as the coursest earth, but I
Am at the charge, my bill not to be paid to,   195
To giue them seeming beauty. Soe tis done:
How do you like my workmanship?
  Eugenia.   I tremble
And thus to tirannize vpon the dead
Is most inhumane.
  Francisco.   Come we for reuenge,
And can we thinke on pitty? now to the vpshott,   200
And as it proues applaud it. My lord the Duke
Enter with ioy, and see the suddaine change
Your seruants hand hath wrought.

      Enter SFORZA *and the rest.*

  Sforza.   I liue againe
In my full confidence that *Marcelia* may
Pronounce my pardon. Can she speake yet?
  Francisco.   No,   205
You must not looke for all your ioyes at once,
That will aske longer time.
  Pescara.   Tis wondrous strange!
  Sforza. By all the dues of loue I haue had from her,
This hand seemes as it was when first I kist it,
These lips inuite to, I could euer feed   210
Vpon these roses, they still keepe their colour
And natiue sweetnesse, only the nectar's wanting
That like the morning dew in flowry May
Preseru'd them in their beauty.

      Enter GRACCHO.

  Graccho.   Treason, treason.
  Tiberio. Call vp the guard.
  Francisco.   *Graccho*! then we are lost.   215

      [*Enter Guard.*]

  Graccho. I am got off, Sir Iew, a bribe hath done it
For all your serious charge; ther's no disguise can keepe
You from my knowledge,

202. change] *38*; chance *23*   203 SD. SFORZA] *Massinger MS (SForza), 38*; *Forza 23*   *Sforza.*] *Massinger MS (SForza), 38*; *Forza 23*   208. *Sforza.*] *Massinger MS (SForza.), 38*; *Forza. 23*   215 SD. *Enter Guard.*] *Gifford*; *not in 23*   217. disguise can] *23*; disguise / Can *Coxeter*

V. ii. 218-44　　　*The Duke of Milan*　　　299

Sforza.　　　　　　　Speake.
Graccho.　　　　　　　I am out of breath,
But this is—
Francisco. Spare thy labor foole, *Francisco*.
All. Monster of Men.
Francisco.　　　　Giue me all attributes　　　220
Of ill you can imagine, yet I glory
To be the thing I was borne, I am *Francisco*,
Francisco that was rais'd by you, and made
The Minion of the time, the same *Francisco*,
That would haue whor'd this trunke when it had life,　　225
And after breath'd a iealousie vpon thee
As killing as those damps that belch out plagues,
When the foundation of the earth is shaken;
I made thee doe a deed heauen will not pardon
Which was to kill an innocent.
Sforza.　　　　　Call forth the tortures　　　230
For all that flesh can feele.
Francisco.　　　　I dare the worst,
Only to yeeld some reason to the world
Why I pursu'd this course, looke on this face
Made old by thy base falshood, 'tis *Eugenia*.
Sforza. Eugenia.
Francisco.　　Do's it start you Sir? my Sister,　　235
Seduc'd and fool'd by thee; but thou must pay
The forfet of thy falshood. Do's it not worke yet?
What ere becomes of me (which I esteeme not)
Thou art mark'd for the graue, I haue giuen thee poison
In this cup, now obserue me, which thy lust　　　240
Carowsing deeply of, made thee forget
Thy vow'd faith to *Eugenia*.
Pescara.　　　　　O damn'd villaine!
Isabella. How do you Sir?
Sforza.　　　　　Like one,
That learnes to know in death what punishment,

218. *Sforza.*] *Massinger MS (SForza), 38; Forza 23*　　219. thy] 23; your 38
221. ill] *McIlwraith*; all 23　　223-4. *rearranged by Coxeter; 23 reads Francisco . . . you, / And . . . time / The . . . Francisco*　　230. *Sforza.*] *Massinger MS (SForza.), 38; Forza. 23*　　235. *Sforza.*] *Massinger MS (SForza.), 38; Forza. 23*　　240. which] *Massinger MS* (w^(ch)); with 23　　lust] *Massinger MS*; last 23　　243. *Sforza.*] *Massinger MS (SForza.), 38; Forza. 23*

Waites on the breach of faith, O now I feele 245
An *Ætna* in my entrailes! I haue liu'd
A Prince, and my last breath shal be commaund.
I burne, I burne, yet ere life be consum'd
Let me pronounce vpon this wretch all torture
That witty cruelty can inuent.
    Pescara.   Away with him. 250
    Tiberio. In all things we will serue you.
    Francisco.   Farewell sister,
Now I haue kept my word, torments I scorne,
I leaue the world with glory; they are men
And leaue behind them name and memory,
That wrong'd doe right themselues before they die. 255
    Stephano. A desperate wretch.   *Exeunt Guard with* FRANCISCO.
    Sforza.   I come death, I obey thee,
Yet I will not die raging, for alas,
My whole life was a phrensie. Good *Eugenia*
In death forgiue me. As you loue me beare her
To some religious house, there let her spend 260
The remnant of her life, when I am ashes
Perhaps shee'll be appeas'd, and spare a prayer
For my poore soule. Bury me with *Marcelia*
And let out Epitaph be—
    Tiberio.   His speech is stop'd.
    Stephano. Already dead.
    Pescara.   It is in vaine to labour 265
To call him backe, wee'll giue him funerall,
And then determine of the state affaires.
And learne from this example, ther's no trust
In a foundation that is built on lust.   *Exeunt.*

FINIS.

245. breach] *Massinger MS, 38*; breath *23*   256. *Sforza.*] *Massinger MS*
(*SForza.*), *38*; Forza. *23*

THE BONDMAN

INTRODUCTION

(a) *Date*

The Bondman: An Ancient Story can be dated with some precision. Gifford, using information given him by Gilchrist (1805 edn., vol. ii, pp. 2 and 114–15), noted the close relation between the date of licensing and the collapse of a chapel referred to at the end of the play. Herbert's licence is dated 3 December 1623: 'For the Queen of Bohemia's Company; *The Noble Bondman*: Written by Philip Messenger, gent.'[1] At V. iii. 248–52 of the play, we have the following lines:

> Let but a Chappell fall, or a street be fir'd,
> A foolish louer hang himselfe for pure loue,
> Or any such like accident, and before
> They are cold in their graues, some damn'd Dittie's made
> Which makes their ghosts walke.

On Sunday, 26 October 1623, the Jesuit, Father Robert Drury, was preaching in a garret at Hunsdon House, the French Ambassador's house in Blackfriars.[2] The floor gave way and many, including Father Drury, were killed. 'A fine rush of booklets came from various presses', commenting upon this extraordinary sign from a Protestant divinity. No later than October 30, 'W.C.' entered *The fatall Vesper*, and on 15 November Chamberlain wrote to Sir Dudley Carleton, saying that he had sent him 'such bookes and ballets as I can come by touching that fearefull accident in the Blacke-friers.'[3]

---

[1] Adams, *Herbert*, p. 26.
[2] I draw chiefly on John Crow, 'Thomas Goad and *The Dolefull Euen-Song*: An Editorial Experiment', *Transactions of the Cambridge Bibliographical Society*, i (1949–53), 238–259, and Arthur Freeman, 'The fatal vesper and The doleful evensong: Claim-jumping in 1623', *The Library*, 5th Series, xxii (June, 1967), 128–35.
[3] *Letters*, ii. 523.

The firing of a street Gifford and Gilchrist identified as the burning of a house in Broad Street, belonging to Sir William Cockaine, on 12 November. Three neighbouring houses were destroyed, 'to the great danger and damage of many neere inhabitants'.[1] This fire is described in Chamberlain's same letter of 15 November (see Commentary), which also gives us the hitherto unidentified lover: 'Yesterday one Needham a barrester of Grayes Ynne, (whose father I have long knowne in Hartfordshire) hangd himself in Maribone-parke. The cause is not yet come abrode but thought to be some matter of love.'[2]

The 'damn'd Ditties' inspired by the fire and the suicide are not known, but these topical allusions are as firmly fixed as such things can be, and one can say confidently enough that Massinger completed his play within a week or two of its licensing on 3 December 1623.

(b) *Sources*

The sources of *The Bondman* are discussed by the editor in *The Review of English Studies*, xv (1964), 21–6. Massinger seems to have started from the elder Seneca's *controversia* vii. 6;[3] this gave him the outline of the plot and the central issue of Cleora's choice of the slave.

A tyrant allowed slaves to ravish their masters' wives. The leading men of the city fled, among them one who had a son and a daughter. Although all the slaves had violated their mistresses, this man's slave protected the young woman. After the tyrant had been killed, the leading men returned and crucified the slaves. But this particular man freed his slave, and gave his daughter in marriage to him. He is charged by his son with being out of his mind.

To fill out the slaves' revolt, Massinger turned to Diodorus's account of the Servile Wars in Sicily of 135–132 B.C. (XXXIV).[4] Here he would have found the degenerate luxury of the slave-owners, their cruelty, and the ignominy of their treatment at the hands of the rebels; and, most important, the suggestion that the rebellion was

[1] Howes' continuation of Stowe's *Annals* (1631), p. 1035.
[2] *Letters*, ii. 525.
[3] *Controverses et suasoires*, ed. H. Bornecque, Paris, 1932, ii. 100–12, 160–1. The resemblance was noted by G. B. A. Fletcher in a letter to A. K. McIlwraith of 28 Oct. 1932.
[4] Cf. B. T. Spencer's edition of *The Bondman*, Princeton, 1932, pp. 22–7.

Introduction

the natural result of oppression and tyranny. Diodorus also speaks of a kind daughter, who, like Seneca's young woman, is protected by the slaves.

Seneca suggested Archidamus, Cleora, Timagoras, and Pisander (who is both the tyrant and the good slave); Diodorus suggested Cleon, Corisca, and Asotus, and enlarged the idea of Cleora. The summoning of Timoleon from Corinth is an historical incident, belonging to an earlier period of Sicilian history (345–336 B.C.). Plutarch's life of Timoleon was used by Massinger, but probably it was his reading of Diodorus's account of the man that gave him the idea of grafting together incidents from two widely-separated periods. Massinger uses little of the historical record for Timoleon; all that he wanted was an infusion of decisiveness and moral strength to show up the decadence of his Sicilians; the high-minded Timoleon is necessary only as a kind of moral compass-bearing.

To fill out the brief mention in the *controversia* of the departure and return of the leading men of the city, Massinger used a well-known story, found in Justin and Herodotus. In Justin (II. v), the Scythians returned home from a long war to find that their slaves had rebelled and were living with their wives; the Scythians overcame the opposition of the slaves by terrifying them with their whips.

B. T. Spencer followed Gardiner and Boyle in seeing *The Bondman* as a comment on the political scene in England, and, working on the correspondence that Sicily represents England, Carthage represents Spain, Corinth represents Holland and Timoleon represents Maurice of Nassau, interpreted the play as an appeal to King and Parliament to assist the Elector Palatine. If one tries to follow the political allegory out, there are many contradictions, and one may feel dubious about Massinger's urging his monarch on to action in a tragicomedy at the Cockpit.[1] I have said elsewhere that 'a study of Massinger at work on his sources in this play shows a man taking a good deal of trouble to fashion a strong dramatic image of weakness and nobility in society and private conduct. If some critics find that the image reflects particular problems of Massinger's day, it is a commendation of the play's breadth, but not an explanation of the play's function.'[2] In a number of speeches in which political theory is discussed, Massinger seems to have been influenced by Jean Bodin's *Six Bookes of a Commonweale*

[1] Cf. Bentley, iv. 768–9.   [2] *RES*, xv (1964), 26.

(translated by Knolles), 1606: see the notes to I. iii. 90–97 and IV. ii. 51–82.

(c) *Text*

The Bondman was entered in the Stationers' Register on 12 March, 1624:

m^r Harrison Edw. Blackmore   Entred for their Copie vnder the hands of Sr Henry Herbert m^r of the Revell and m^r Cole warden A play called the Bondman by Phi‡l: Messenger   vj^d

(Register D 75: Greg, *Bibliography*, i. 33; Arber, iv. 113.)

Herbert himself noted that the play was allowed to be printed on that day (see Adams, *Herbert*, p. 41, and Bentley, iv. 766). The principal edition of the play was published accordingly, in 1624, by John Harrison and Edward Blackmore, printed by Edward Allde; it will be referred to from now as *24*; the title-page is reproduced on page 311. *24* is in quarto, A–L^4 (44 leaves); see Greg, *Bibliography*, no. 408 (ii. 559–60). The contents are: A1, *blank*; A2^r, *title*; A2^v, '*THE ACTORS NAMES.*'; A3^r, *dedication begins*, '*TO* The Right Honourable, my singular good Lord, P$_{HILIP}$ Earle of *Mountgomery*'; A3^v, *dedication ends, signed* '*Philip Massinger.*'; A4^r, *verse epistle*, 'The *Authors* Friend to the Reader.', *signed* 'W. B'; A4^v, *blank*; B1^r, 'The Bond-man.', *text begins*; L4^v, *text ends*, 'FINJS.'. The text is in roman, 20 lines measuring approximately 80 mm. There are usually 38 lines to the page (39 on D2^v and F4^r; 37 on C1^r).

Two skeletons were used in the printing, one for each inner forme, one for each outer; three of the outer-forme headlines were reset in sheet I. Differences in the style of composition are not marked enough to establish clearly the work of different compositors, but it seems possible that one compositor was responsible for A–E, and a second for F–L.[1]

The extensive press-corrections of *24* have been fully described by A. K. McIlwraith (*The Library*, 5, iv (1950), 238–48; see also K. Povey, ibid., x (1955), 41–8). Sixteen out of the twenty-two

---

[1] In sheets B, C, E, capitalization is twice as heavy as in the later sheets, and there are a number of erroneous capitals (for adjectives and verbs). In the later sheets, lines occasionally begin with lower-case letters; there is only one example in B–E. In F–L, the past of weak verbs (unaccented) is almost always '*d*; there is much variety in the forms in the early sheets. The leading of the Act and Scene headings changes slightly in the later half of the play, and speakers' names are less often abbreviated.

formes are variant, 138 corrections being noted. McIlwraith suggests (p. 244) that Massinger himself kept a close watch on the printer.

The copy used by the printer would appear to have been prepared for publication by Massinger, perhaps from his foul papers, though a transcript or fair-copy cannot be ruled out. Many of Massinger's peculiar spellings are preserved, and these are the more striking in that they appear often as exceptions to the normal usages of the compositors (as with *gard* and *receaue*). Some examples are *stincke, rancke, guifts, ghesse, ghest, of* (off), *to* (too), *course* (coarse), *tearmes, waight, waightie, sease* (seize); see Appendix 2, vol. v. The stage-directions are full, and rather 'literary', describing what is to be, or was, seen on the stage. Slaves enter *'drunke and quarrelling'*; *'Zanthia seemes to sleepe'*; *'Cleora kneeles, then puls off her Gloue, and offers her hand to Pisander'*; *'Makes a lowe curtsie, as she goes off'*; *'Senators shake their whips, and they throw away their weapons, and runne off'*; *'Leads in Cleora'* (*sc.* on to the stage); *'Timandra steps out distractedly'*; *'Plucks off his disguise'*. Some of the directions note properties and business in theatrical fashion (e.g., at III. ii, *'Cleora, Timandra, a Chaire, a shout within'*), but there is nothing outside an author's range; there is, moreover, strong evidence *against* stage-annotation of the manuscript in the marked absence of directions for music and flourishes, and in the vagueness with which groups are designated: *'and the rest'*, *'& other slaues'*, *'and Slaues'*, *'others'*, for example. The absence of 'Enter' before the characters' names at the head of each scene (except the first) and the placing of stops rather than commas between the names show Massinger's frequent practice. Acts and scenes are carefully noted; the final scenes of Acts IV and V are designated 'SCÆNA *Vltima*.'

A curious feature of the stage-directions relates to Cleora's gestures when she is blindfold and vowed to silence in III. ii; when Massinger composed the scene, he seems to have taken trouble to indicate actions in the dialogue. The repetition of these actions as stage directions cannot be needed by either actor or stage-keeper; I imagine the additions are for the reader's sake, but the effect is comic: *'Cleora shakes....* Shake not, best Lady...'. There are seven of these peculiar duplications.

A copy of the 1624 *Bondman* was one of the eight plays bound together about 1633 (now in the Folger Library; see the General Introduction, p. xxxii); there are extensive corrections in Massinger's own hand. An editor must, therefore, be very cautious in his emendations, since every alteration he makes implies that a corruption has been overlooked by the author. The editorial position is further complicated by the fact that Massinger sometimes worked with uncorrected formes (e.g., the inner and outer formes of C) and on occasions let stand readings which are corrected in the corrected formes; every press-correction must be regarded very critically: some of them, indeed, are self-evidently wrong (see, for example, I. iii. 264, 301). Massinger's corrections are referred to in the text notes as *Massinger MS*.

In 1638, in Massinger's lifetime, a second quarto was published (*38*); see Greg, *Bibliography*, no. 408(b) (ii. 560–1). The wording of its title-page follows that of *24*, as far as the author's name; the printer was John Raworth; one version of the title-page reads 'for *Edward Blackmore*', another 'for *Iohn Harrison*'. The two copy-holders of *24* 'divided the edition between them, and in this instance each evidently sold his own share' (Greg, ibid.).

38 improves the punctuation of *24* in many places, and in some places the readings, but it is a reprint of a copy of *24* (with some corrected and some uncorrected formes) without additional authority. Massinger cannot have supervised it; he could not, for example, have allowed the uncorrected *surely* for *Sicily* at I. iii. 83. A feature of *38*'s changes is its curious sense of propriety in language; see, for example, II. ii. 142–3.

On 28 April 1660, Harrison's half-share in *The Bondman* was assigned to William Lee (Greg, *Bibliography*, i. 67–8). The edition which Pepys bought on 25 May 1661 must have been one of the early quartos, since there was no other edition in the seventeenth century. The version of 1719 (see below) is more a rewriting than an edition, but it sometimes corrects the early text, and was consulted by Coxeter. It is referred to in the textual notes as *1719*.

Besides the collected editions, *The Bondman* appeared in *The Modern British Drama*, 1811, i. 203–29, and in *Great English Plays*, ed. H. F. Rubinstein, 1928, pp. 502–60. In 1932 was published '*The Bondman: An Antient Storie*, By Philip Massinger. Edited from the First Quarto with Introduction and Notes by Benjamin Townley Spencer, Ph.D. . . . Princeton. Princeton University Press for the University of Cincinnati.' Spencer's thorough work has greatly eased the preparation of the present edition.

A French translation (*L'Esclave*) appeared in Lafond's collection in 1864 (see Collected Editions, p. lxix).

Introduction

There are copies of *24* in the following libraries and institutions: the Bodleian Library; Boston Public Library; the British Museum (4 copies); Cambridge University Library; Library of Congress; Folger Shakespeare Library (2 copies); Harvard College Library; the Huntington Library; the Pierpont Morgan Library; Princeton University; the Victoria and Albert Museum (2 copies); Yale University Library. The present text has been prepared from the British Museum copy, 11773. d. 3.

(d) *Stage History*

The Bondman was one of the series of plays that Massinger wrote in 1623–5 for Christopher Beeston's company (Lady Elizabeth's or Queen of Bohemia's) at the Cockpit or Phoenix in Drury Lane. Herbert licensed it for acting, as has been seen, on 3 December 1623. The play was presented at court by the company on 27 December: 'Upon St. John's night, the prince only being there, *The Bondman*, by the queene [of Bohemia's] company. Att Whitehail' (Adams, *Herbert*, p. 51). In 1639, the play was still in the Cockpit repertory. It was one of the plays for which the younger Beeston secured official entitlement for the King and Queen's 'young' company, in the list dated 10 August 1639 (Bentley, i. 330–1). The play was very popular in the early years of the Restoration.[1] In March 1660, when Rhodes organized a company at the Cockpit, *The Bondman* was one of the first plays acted, and Thomas Betterton established Pisander as one of his great parts.[2] A year later, on 1 March 1661, Pepys saw Betterton acting in the play at Whitefriars, with Davenant's company, and he went again on 19 March: 'acted most excellently, and though I have seen it often, yet I am every time more and more pleased with Betterton's action' (Bentley, iv. 767). He saw it again, now at Salisbury Court, on 26 March. In 1661 also, perhaps in May, the play appears in the repertory of Killigrew's company (King's) and was played at the Red Bull (Adams, *Herbert*, p. 117). McManaway points out that the play was not included in the divisions of plays between Davenant and Killigrew in 1660 and 1668–9, and suggests that, as both companies were playing it, it was regarded as common property.

On 4 and 25 November 1661 Pepys saw the play given by

[1] My source here is J. G. McManaway, 'Philip Massinger and the Restoration Drama', 1934, reprinted in *Studies*, pp. 3–30.
[2] Downes, *Roscius Anglicanus*, ed. Summers, pp. 17–18.

Davenant's company at his new theatre, the Opera; in spite of Betterton, it was not so well acted. Probably in 1662-3, Dr. Edward Browne saw *The Bondman* at 'Salisbury or Dorset Court'. Nicoll thinks that Jolly's men were acting here at this time; if so, four companies had produced the play in two years (McManaway, pp. 12-14). It was revived again in the 1664 season. Pepys went on July 28; 'It is true, for want of practice, they had many of them forgot their parts a little; but Betterton and my poor Ianthe outdo all the world. There is nothing more taking in the world with me than that play.' This is the last performance he records, but in 1666 he was still reading it: 'and so home, I reading all the way to make end of the "Bondman" (which the oftener I read, the more I like)' (Bentley, iv. 768).

In 1719, an alteration of the play was acted and published: *The Bond-Man: or, Love and Liberty. A Tragi-Comedy. As it is now Acted at the Theatre Royal in Drury-Lane. By His Majesty's Servants. London . . . 1719.* This version of the play was attributed to Betterton (who died in 1710) in *Biographica Dramatica*, but Genest is sceptical (*Some Account of the English Stage*, ii. 644). Spencer thinks that the attribution is right, but it is hard not to agree with Genest that the bookseller's mystification about the author would hardly be necessary were he Betterton ('I shall not say any Thing of the Gentleman's Abilities that took the Trouble to alter it' etc.). In 1740, Mrs. Sarah Dixon (see below) attributed it to 'Mr. Row', who died in 1718. The actors' names are given: Timoleon, Mr. Mills; Pisander, Mr. Walker; Cleora, Mrs. Thurmond. The play is considerably shortened; long narratives and reflective speeches are cut; III. iv is omitted; a song is added; there is a good deal of rephrasing. Although, as M. J. Harley remarks,[1] no attempt has been made to rewrite the whole play in accordance with eighteenth-century ideas, the coarseness is considerably toned down. Genest gives the date of revival as 8 June 1719,[2] and notes (iii. 2) a performance of 29 October with the misleading claim 'acted but twice since the reign of King Charles the 1st, now revived with alterations'. It was also performed for Walker's benefit on 6 June 1720.[3] On p. 161 of *Poems on Several Occasions* by Mrs. Sarah Dixon (Canterbury, 1740) we find this

[1] 'The Eighteenth-century Interest in English Drama before 1640' (unpublished dissertation, University of Birmingham, 1962), p. 221.
[2] ii. 644. Nicoll (*History of English Drama*, 1952, ii. 366) gives Tuesday, 9 June and Friday, 12 June; see also *London Stage*, pt. 2, vol. ii, pp. 542-3, 553, 585.
[3] Genest, iii. 11; see also McManaway, *MLN*, xlix (1939), 118-20.

heading: 'The Play called The Bond-Man being Revis'd and Publish'd by Mr. Row some Years since, the following Prologue and Epilogue were Written in the Country for the Diversion of a Friend.' The undistinguished poems attack modern taste:

> Can it be *Wit*, and Sense, that you are seeking,
> When you spend Hours to hear *Italian* Squeaking?
> . . . . .
> Knowing your blind Side, makes us hope, at least,
> To please *one* Night with an old Play new dress'd;
> Here's nought to make the Ladies look askew;
> And very little which reflects on Beau;
> Some Hints there are, which might the Age improve,
> There's some Morality, and a *World of Love*.

The text of the revival of 1779 at Covent Garden, with alterations by Richard Cumberland, has not survived, but from the newspaper accounts it would seem that the original play was not materially changed. It was played on 13 October, with Wroughton as Pisander and Mrs. Yates as Cleora, and received six or seven performances.[1] There are reviews in *The Town and Country Magazine*, xi (1779), 517–18, and *The Westminster Gazette*, vii (1779), 504. The last-named grumbles at the practice of reviving old plays (see General Introduction, vol. i, p. lv) and goes on, 'The Play was well received, principally on account of some striking political passages in it. The performers in general did justice to their parts.' At any rate, the production was successful enough to inspire a second one some weeks later in Bath, with Mrs. Siddons as Cleora, and Dimond as Pisander.[2] There were five performances in the 1779–80 season, and in the following year (1 March 1781) Mrs. Siddons took the part of Cleora again for the benefit of Mr. and Miss Summers. Spencer notes an American production of 19 June 1795, at the New Theater in Philadelphia, under the title of *The Female Patriot*, the alterations being by Mrs. Rowson, who played Statilia (Timandra).[3]

A curious episode in the play's history is the publication of a broadsheet in 1803, at the time an invasion by Napoleon was feared; it prints I. iii. 213–368. The broadsheet is headed 'COUNTRYMEN',

---

[1] Genest, vi. 140; Nicoll, iii. 250.
[2] Genest, vi. 161.
[3] Spencer, p. 11, acknowledging R. H. Ball's reference to G. O. Seilhamer, *History of the American Theatre*, iii. 176, 181, 184.

and, after a brief account of the situation at the beginning of the play, goes on:

The Scene which follows was written by our great Dramatic Poet, MASSINGER: it is at once ELEGANT, NERVOUS, and SUBLIME; and it would be to call in Question the good Sense, no less than the Spirit and Patriotism of Englishmen, to suppose the forcible Arguments here used, will have less effect upon THEM, than they had on the SYRACUSANS!

The sheet was published by J. Hatchard, 190 Piccadilly.

An Opera called *The Bondman*, by Alfred Bunn, with music by Balfe, played at Drury Lane on 11 December 1846 (Nicoll, iv. 276) has no connexion with Massinger.

The play was broadcast on the Third Programme of the B.B.C. on 29 March 1963, and repeated on 28 June 1964.

THE BOND-MAN:

AN ANTIENT STORIE.

As it hath been often Acted with good allowance, at the Cock-pit in *Drury*-lane: by the most Excellent Princesse, the Lady ELIZABETH her Seruants.

By *Phillip Massinger*.

LONDON,
Printed by *Edw: Allde*, for *Iohn Harison* and *Edward Blackmore*, and are to be sold at the great South dore of Pauls.
1624.

THE ACTORS NAMES.

Timoleon, *the Generall of* Corinth.
Archidamus, *the Pretor of* Siracusa.
Diphilus, *a Senator of* Siracusa.
Cleon, *a fat impotent Lord.*
Pisander, *(disguisde [as* Marullo]) *a Gentleman of* Thebes.
Leosthenes, *a Gentleman of* Siracusa *enamourd of* Cleora.
Asotus, *a foolish Louer, and the sonne of* Cleon.
Timagoras, *the Sonne of* Archidamus.
Cleora, *Daughter of* Archidamus.
Corisca, *a proud wanton Lady, wife to*Cleon.
Olimpia, *a rich Widdow.*
Statilia, [(*disguised as* Timandra)] *Sister to* Pisander, *slaue to* Cleora.
Zanthia, *Slaue to* Corisca.
Poliphron, *(disguisde) friend to* Pisander.
Gracculo. ⎱
Cimbrio. ⎰ Bond-men.
A Iaylor.
[Slaves, Soldiers, Officers, Senators.]

  6. *as* Marullo] *editor; not in 24*
  14. *(disguised . . .* Timandra)] *editor; not in 24*
  20. Slaves . . . Senators] *after Gifford; not in 24*

To
The Right Honourable, my singular good Lord, PHILIP Earle of *Mountgomery*, Knight of the most Noble order of the Garter, &c.

Right Honourable,

How euer I could neuer arriue at the happinesse to be made knowne to your Lordship, yet a desire borne with me, to make tender of all duties, and seruice, to the Noble Family of the *Herberts*, descended to me as an inheritance from my dead Father, *Arthur Massinger*. Many years hee happily spent in the seruice of your Honourable House, and dyed a seruant to it; leauing his, to be euer most glad, and ready, to be at the command of al such, as deriue themselues from his most honour'd Master, your Lordships most noble Father. The consideration of this, encouraged me (hauing no other meanes to present my humblest seruice to your Honour) to shrowde this trifle, vnder the wings of your Noble protection; and I hope out of the clemency of your Heroique disposition, it will finde, though perhaps not a welcome entertainment, yet at the worst a gratious pardon. When it was first Acted, your Lordships liberall suffrage taught others to allow it for currant, it hauing receaued the vndoubted stampe of your Lordships allowance: and if in the perusall, at any vacant houre, when your Honours more serious occasions shall giue you leaue to reade it, it answer in your Lordships iudgement, the report and opinion it had vpon the Stage, I shall esteeme my labours not ill imployde, and while I liue continue,

> *The humblest*
> *of those*
> *that truly honour your Lordship,*
>
> *Philip Massinger.*

9. Herberts] 24²; Harberts 24¹   10. Arthur] 24; Philip 38   23. perusall, at] *Massinger MS*; perusall of 24

The *Authors* Friend to the Reader.

THE PRINTERS *haste calls on*; *I must not driue*
My time past Sixe, *though I begin at* Fiue.
One houre I haue entire; *and 'tis enough.*
Here are no Gipsie Iigges, *no* Drumming stuffe,
Dances, *or other* Trumpery *to delight*,   5
Or take, by common way, the common sight.
The AVTHOR *of this* POEM, *as he dares*
To stand th'austerest Censure; *so he cares*
As little what it is. His owne, Best way
Is to be Iudge, *and* AVTHOR *of his* PLAY.   10
It is his Knowledge, *makes him thus secure*;
Nor do's he write to please, but to endure.
And (Reader) if you haue disburs'd a shilling,
To see this worthy STORY, *and are willing*
To haue a large encrease; *(if rul'd by me)*   15
You may a MARCHANT, *and a* POET *be.*
'Tis granted for your twelue-pence you did sit,
And See, *and* Heare, *and* Vnderstand *not yet.*
The AVTHOR (*in a Christian pitty*) *takes*
Care of your good, and Prints it for your sakes.   20
That such as will but venter Six-pence more,
May Know, *what they but* Saw, *and* Heard *before*:
'Twill not be money lost, if you can read,
(Ther's all the doubt now,) but your gaines exceed
If you can Vnderstand, *and you are made*   25
Free of the freest, and the noblest Trade.
　And in the way of POETRY, *now adayes,*
　Of all that are call'd Workes *the best are* PLAYES.

W. B.

3. *enough.*] editor; ~, 24

The Bond-man

Actus Primi. Scæna Prima.

Enter TIMAGORAS, *and* LEOSTHENES.

Timagoras. WHY should you droope *Leosthenes*, or dispaire
My Sisters fauour? what before you purchased
By Court-ship, and faire language, in these Wars
(For from her soule you know she loues a Souldier)
You may deserue by action.
 Leosthenes.   Good *Timagoras*,   5
When I haue said my friend, thinke all is spoken
That may assure me yours; and pray you beleeue
The dreadfull voice of warre that shakes the City;
The thundring threates of *Carthage*; nor their Army
Raisde to make good those threats, affright not me.   10
If faire *Cleora* were confirmd his prize,
That has the strongest Arme, and sharpest Sword,
I would court *Bellona* in her horrid trim,
As if she were a Mistrisse, and blesse Fortune
That offers my young valour to the proofe,   15
How much I dare doe for your Sisters loue.
But when that I consider how auerse
Your noble Father great *Archidamus*
Is, and hath euer beene to my desires,
Reason may warrant me to doubt and feare,   20
What seeds soeuer I sowe in these warres
Of noble courage, his determinate will
May blast, and giue my haruest to another
That neuer toyld for it.

I. i SD., TIMAGORAS] *Massinger MS (Timagoras)*; *Timagorus 24*   1 and 5. Timagoras] *Massinger MS*; *Timagorus 24*   3. language, in these Wars] *38*; language in these Wars, *24*   8. City;] *Massinger MS*; ~, *24*   13. horrid trim] *1719*; Horrid-trime *24*   20. feare,] *Massinger MS*; ~: *24*   21. these] *38*; this *24*

Timagoras.   Prethee doe not nourish
These iealous thoughts: I am thine, (and pardon me
Though I repeate it) thy *Timagoras*,
That for thy sake, when the bold *Theban* su'd,
Farre fam'd *Pisander*, for my sisters loue,
Sent him disgrac'd, and discontented home.
I wrought my Father then, and I that stopt not
In the careere of my affection to thee,
When that renowned Worthy that brought with him
High birth, wealth, courage, as fee'd Aduocates
To mediate for him, neuer will consent
A foole that only has the shape of man,
Asotus, though he be rich *Cleons* Heire
Shall beare her from thee.

Enter PISANDER.

Leosthenes.   In that trust I liue,
Timagoras. Which neuer shall deceiue you.
Pisander.   Sir the Generall
Timoleon by his Trumpets hath giuen warning
For a remoue.
   Timagoras. 'Tis well, prouide my Horse.
   Pisander. I shall Sir.   *Exit* PISANDER.
   Leosthenes.   This Slaue has a strange aspect.
   Timagoras. Fit for his fortune, 'tis a strong limm'd knaue;
My Father bought him for my Sisters Litter.
O pride of women! Coaches are too common,
They surfet in the happinesse of peace,
And Ladyes thinke they keepe not state enough,
If for their pompe, and ease, they are not borne
In triumph on mens shoulders.
   Leosthenes.   Who commands
The *Carthagenian* Fleet?
   Timagoras.   *Gisco*'s their Admirall,
And tis our happinesse: a rawe young fellow,
One neuer traind in Armes, but rather fashiond

---

   26. it) thy *Timagoras*,] *after Gifford;* it thy *Timagoras*) *24;* it, my *Leosthenes*) *Coxeter*
27. su'd,] *Gifford;* ~∧ *24.*   32. Worthy that brought] *24;* Worthy, brought *Mason;* worthy, that, brought *Gifford*   36. *Asotus*] *38;* *Asotas 24*   37. liue,] *Massinger MS;* loue, *24*

To tilt with Ladyes lips, then cracke a Launce,
Rauish a Feather from a Mistrisse Fanne
And weare it as a Fauour; a steele Helmet
Made horrid with a glorious Plume, will cracke 55
His womans necke.
 Leosthenes.   No more of him, the motiues
That *Corinth* giues vs ayde?
 Timagoras.   The common danger:
For *Sicily* being afire, she is not safe;
It being apparant that ambitious *Carthage*,
That to enlarge her Empire, striues to fasten 60
An vniust gripe on vs (that liue free Lords
Of *Syracusa*) will not end, till *Greece*
Acknowledge her their Soueraigne.
 Leosthenes.   I am satisfied.
What thinke you of our Generall?
 Timagoras.   He is a man *A Trumpet sounds.*
Of strange and reserude parts; But a great Souldier. 65
His Trumpets call vs, I'le forbeare his Character.
To morrow in the Senate house at large,
He will expresse himselfe.
 Leosthenes.   Ile follow you. *Exeunt.*

Actus I. Scæna II.

CLEON, CORISCA, GRACCULO.

 Corisca. Nay good Chucke.
 Cleon.   I haue said it; Stay at home,
I cannot brooke this gadding, you are a faire one,
Beauty inuites temptation, and short heeles
Are soone tripd vp.
 Corisca. Deny me? by my honour
You take no pitty on me. I shall swoune 5
Assoone as you are absent, aske my Man else,
You know he dares not tell a lie.
 Gracculo.   Indeed,
You are no sooner out of sight, but shee

---

57. ayde?] *1719*; ~: *24* I. ii. 2. this] *Massinger MS*; with *24* 4. me?] *Massinger MS*; ~, *24*

Does feele strange qualmes, then sends for her young Doctor,
Who ministers phisicke to her, on her backe,
Her Ladyship lying as she were entranc'd.
(I haue peeped in at the keyhole and obserud them)
And sure his Potions neuer faile to worke,
For she is so pleasant, in the taking them,
She tickles againe.
    Corisca.   And alls to make you merry
When you come home.
    Cleon.   You flatter me, I am old,
And Wisdome cries beware.
    Corisca.   Old, Ducke to me
You are young *Adonis.*
    Gracculo.   Well said *Venus,*
I am sure she *Vulcans* him.
    Corisca.   I will not change thee
For twenty boistrous young things without Beards.
These bristles giue the gentlest Tittillations,
And such a sweet dew flowes on them, it cures
My lippes without Pomatum; heres a round belly,
'Tis a Downe pillow to my backe. I sleepe
So quietly by it; and this tunable nose
(Faith when you heare it not) affords such musicke,
That I curse all night Fidlers.
    Gracculo.   This is grosse,
Not finde she flouts him.
    Corisca.   As I liue I am iealous.
    Cleon. Iealous! of me Wife?
    Corisca.   Yes, and I haue reason,
Knowing how lusty and actiue a man you are.
    Cleon. Hum, hum!
    Gracculo. This is no cunning queane! slight, she will make him
To thinke, that like a Stagge he has cast his hornes,
And is growne young againe.
    Corisca.   You haue forgot
What you did in your sleepe, and when you wakd
Cald for a Cawdle.
    Gracculo.   'Twas in his sleepe,

14. them,] *38*; ~ₐ *24*   18. are] *24*; are a *Coxeter*   34–36. *Verse rearranged by Coxeter*; You ... sleepe, / And when ... Cawdle. / 'Twas *24*

For waking I durst trust my Mother with him.
  Corisca. I long to see the man of warre. *Cleora*
Archidamus Daughter goes, and rich *Olimpia*,
I will not misse the showe.
  Cleon.   There's no contending,   40
For this time I am pleas'd, but I'll no more on't.   *Exeunt.*

Actus I. Scæna III.

ARCHIDAMUS, CLEON, DIPHILUS, OLIMPIA,
CORISCA, CLEORA, ZANTHIA.

  Archidamus. So carelesse we haue beene, my noble Lords,
In the disposing of our owne affaires,
And ignorant in the Art of gouernment,
That now we need a stranger to instruct vs.
Yet we are happy, that our neighbour *Corinth*   5
(Pittying the vniust gripe *Carthage* would lay
On *Siracusa*) hath vouchsafed to lend vs
Her man of men *Timoleon* to defend
Our Country, and our Liberties.
  Diphilus.   Tis a fauour
We are vnworthy of, and we may blush,   10
Necessity compels vs to receiue it.
  Archidamus. O shame! that we that are a populous Nation,
Ingag'd to liberall nature, for all blessings
An Iland can bring forth; we that haue limbs
And able bodies; Shipping, Armes, and Treasure,   15
The sinnewes of the Warre, now we are call'd
To stand vpon our Guard, cannot produce
One fit to be our Generall.
  Cleon.   I am olde and fat,
I could say something else.
  Archidamus.   We must obey
The time, and our occasions; ruinous buildings,   20
Whose bases and foundations are infirme
Must vse supporters; we are circled round
With danger, o're our heads with sayle stretch'd wings,
Destruction houers; and a cloud of mischiefe

38. warre.] *Massinger MS*; ~∧ 24

Ready to breake vpon vs; no hope left vs 25
That may diuert it, but our sleeping vertue
Rowsd vp by braue *Timoleon*.
 Cleon.   When arriues he?
 Diphilus. He is expected euery houre.
 Archidamus.   The braueries
Of *Syracusa*, among whom my sonne
Timagoras, *Leosthenes*, and *Asotus* 30
(Your hopefull heire Lord *Cleon*) two dayes since
Rode forth to meet him, and attend him to
The Citie, euery minute we expect
To be blessed with his presence.
 Cleon.   What shout's this?
 Diphilus. Tis seconded with lowd Musique.
 Archidamus.   Which confirmes 35
His wish'd for entrance. Let vs entertaine him
With all respect, solemnity, and pompe,
A man may merit, that comes to redeeme vs
From slauery, and oppression.
 Cleon.   Ile locke vp
My doores, and gard my gold; these Lads of *Corinth* 40
Haue nimble fingers, and I feare them more
Being within our walls, then those of *Carthage*,
They are farre off.
 Archidamus. And Ladies be it your care
To welcome him, and his followers with all duty:
For rest resolu'd; their hands, and swords, must keepe you 45
In that full height of happinesse you liue:
A dreadfull change else followes. *Exeunt* ARCHIDAMUS, CLEON,
 Olimpia.   We are instructed. DIPHILUS.
 Corisca. Ile kisse him for the honor of my Country,
With any she in *Corinth*.
 Olimpia.   Were he a Courtier,
I haue sweet meats in my Closet should content him, 50
Be his pallat ne're so curious.
 Corisca.   And if neede be
I haue a Couch, and a banquetting house in my Orchard,
Where many a man of honour has not scorn'd
To spend an afternoone.

   I. iii. 50. meats] *Massinger MS*; meat 24

Olimpia.   These men of warre
As I haue heard, know not to court a Lady.
They cannot praise our dressings, kisse our hands,
Vsher vs to our Litters, tell loue Stories;
Commend our feet, and legs, and so scarch vpwards;
A sweet becomming boldnesse: they are rough,
Boystrous and sawcy, and at the first sight
Ruffle, and towse vs, and as they finde their stomacks
Fall roundly to it.
    Corisca.   Troth I like em the better.
I cannot endure to haue a perfum'd Sir
Stand cringing in the hammes; licking his lips,
Like a Spaniell o're a Fermenty pot, and yet
Has not the boldnesse to come on, or offer
What they know we expect.
    Olimpia.   We may commend
A Gentlemans modesty, manners, and fine language,
His singing, dancing, riding of great horses,
The wearing of his cloathes, his faire complexion,
Take presents from him, and extoll his bounty,
Yet, though he obserue, and waste his state vpon vs,
If he be stanch and bid not for the stocke
That we were borne to traffick with; the truth is
We care not for his company.
    Corisca.   Musing, *Cleora*?
    Olimpia. She's studying how to entertaine these Strangers,
And to engrosse them to her selfe.
    Cleora.   No surely,
I will not cheapen any of their Wares,
Till you haue made your Market: you will buy
I know at any rate.
    Corisca.   She has giuen it you.
    Olimpia. No more, they come. The first kisse for this Iewell.

Enter TIMAGORAS, LEOSTHENES, ASOTUS, TIMOLEON *in
blacke, led in by* ARCHIDAMUS, DIPHILUS, CLEON, *followed
by* PISANDER, GRACCULO, CIMBRIO, *and others.*

Archidamus. It is your seate.
Diphilus.   Which with a general suffrage,

58. vpwards;] Gifford; ~. 24   65. Fermenty] *Massinger MS*; Firmenty 24

As to the supreame Magistrate, *Sicilie* tenders,
And prayes *Timoleon* to accept.
    Timoleon.   Such honours
To one ambitious of rule or titles;
Whose heauen on earth, is plac'd in his commaund,
And absolute power on others; would with ioy,
And veynes swolne high with pride, be entertain'd.
They take not me: for I haue euer lou'd
An equall freedome: and proclaym'd all such
As would vsurpe on others liberties,
Rebels to nature, to whose bounteous blessings
All men lay clayme as true legitimate sonnes.
But such as haue made forfeit of themselues
By vicious courses, and their birthright lost;
Tis not iniustice they are mark'd for slaues
To serue the vertuous; for my selfe, I know
Honours and great imployments are great burthens,
And must require an *Atlas* to support them.
He that would gouerne others, first should be
The Master of himselfe, richly indude
With depth of vnderstanding, height of courage,
And those remarkable graces which I dare not
Ascribe vnto my selfe.
    Archidamus.   Sir, empty men
Are Trumpets of their owne deserts: but you
That are not in opinion, but in proofe
Really good, and full of glorious parts,
Leaue the report of what you are to fame,
Which from the ready tongues of all good men
Aloud proclaimes you.
    Diphilus.   Besides you stand bound
Hauing so large a field to exercise
Your actiue vertues offerd you, to impart
Your strengths to such as need it.
    Timoleon.   Tis confessed.
And since you'll haue it so, such as I am,
For you and for the liberty of *Greece*

---

83. Magistrate,] 24²; Magistrates ⁎ 24¹   Sicilie] 24²; surely 24¹; Sicelie Massinger MS

I am most ready to lay downe my life:
But yet consider men of *Syracusa*,
Before that you deliuer vp the power
Which yet is yours to me, to whom tis giuen,
To an impartiall man, with whom nor threats,   120
Nor prayers shall preuaile, for I must steere
An euen course.
   Archidamus. Which is desir'd of all.
   Timoleon. Timophanes my brother, for whose death
I am taynted in the world, and foulely taynted,
In whose remembrance I haue euer worne   125
In peace and warre, this liuory of sorrow,
Can witnesse for me, how much I detest
Tyrannous Vsurpation: with griefe
I must remember it, for when no perswasion
Could winne him to desist from his bad practise,   130
To change the Aristocracie of *Corinth*
Into an absolute Monarchy; I chose rather
To proue a pious and obedient sonne
To my Country my best mother, then to lend
Assistance to *Timophanes*, though my brother,   135
That like a Tyrant stroue to set his foote
Vpon the Cities freedome.
   Timagoras.   'Twas a deed
Deseruing rather Trophees, then reproofe.
   Leosthenes. And will be still remembred to your honor
If you forsake not vs.
   Diphilus.   If you free *Sicilie*   140
From barbarous *Carthage* yoke, it will be said,
In him you slew a Tyrant.
   Archidamus.   But giuing way
To her inuasion, not vouchsafing vs
(That flie to your protection) ayde, and comfort,
Twill be beleeu'd, that for your priuate ends   145
You kild a brother.
   Timoleon.   As I then proceed,
To all posterity may that act be crownd
With a deseru'd applause, or branded with

---

119. giuen,] *Massinger MS*; ~∧ 24   135. brother,] *Massinger MS*; ~∧ 24
145. be] *38*; *not in* 24

          The marke of infamy; Stay yet, ere I take
          This seat of Iustice, or ingage my selfe
          To fight for you abroad, or to reforme
          Your State at home, sweare all vpon my sword,
          And call the gods of *Sicily* to witnesse
The oath you take; that whatsoeuer I shall
Propound for safety of your Common-wealth,
Not circumscrib'd or bound in, shall by you
Be willingly obey'd.
  Archidamus, Diphilus, Cleon. So may we prosper,
As we obey in all things.
  Timagoras, Leosthenes, Asotus. And obserue
All your commands as Oracles.
  Timoleon.   Doe not repent it. *Takes the State.*
  Olimpia. He asked not our consent.
  Corisca.   Hee's a clowne, I warrant him.
  Olimpia. I offred my selfe twice, and yet the Churle
Would not salute me.
  Corisca.   Let him kisse his Drumme,
Ile saue my lips, rest on it.
  Olimpia.   He thinkes women
No part of the republique.
  Corisca.   He shall finde
We are a Common-wealth.
  Cleora.   The lesse your honour.
  Timoleon. First then a word or two, but without bitternesse,
(And yet mistake me not, I am no flatterer)
Concerning your ill gouernment of the State,
In which the greatest, noblest, and most rich,
Stand in the first file guilty.
  Cleon.   Ha! how's this?
  Timoleon. You haue not, as good Patriots should doe, studied
The publike good, but your particuler ends.
Factious among your selues, preferring such
To Offices, and honours, as ne're read
The Elements, of sauing policie,
But deepely skild in all the principles,
That vsher to destruction.

  161. Churle] *Massinger MS*; rle *defective in some copies of 24*   163. rest] *Massinger MS*; I rest *24*

Leosthenes. Sharpe.
Timagoras. The better.
Timoleon. Your Senate house, which vs'd not to admit
A man (how euer populer) to stand
At the Helme of gouernment; whose youth was not
Made glorious by action, whose experience
Crown'd with gray haires, gaue warrant to her counsailes,
Heard, and receiu'd with reuerence, is now fild
With greene heads that determine of the State
Ouer their Cups, or when their sated lusts
Afford them leisure: or suppli'd by those
Who rising from base arts, and sordid thrift
Are eminent for their wealth, not for their wisdome.
Which is the reason, that to hold a place
In Counsell, which was once esteem'd an honour,
And a reward for vertue, hath quite lost
Lustre, and Reputation, and is made
A mercenary purchase.
Timagoras. Hee speakes home.
Leosthenes. And to the purpose.
Timoleon. From whence it proceeds,
That the treasure of the City is ingros'd
By a few priuate men: the publique Coffers
Hollow with want; and they that will not spare
One Talent for the common good, to feed
The pride and brauery of their Wiues, consume
In Plate, in Iewels, and superfluous slaues,
What would maintaine an Armie.
Corisca. Haue at vs.
Olimpia. We thought we were forgot.
Cleora. But it appeares,
You will be treated of.
Timoleon. Yet in this plenty,
And fat of peace, your young men ne're were train'd
In Martiall discipline, and your ships vnrig'd,
Rot in the harbour, no defence preparde,
But thought vnusefull, as if that the gods

181. action] *24³, Massinger MS; Achon 24¹,²*   182. her] *24*; his *Mason* counsailes,] *Massinger MS*; counsels ∧ *24* (els *defective in some copies*)   183. Heard] *24³, Massinger MS*; Hand *24¹,²*   206. no] *24³*; nor *24¹,²*; noe *Massinger MS*

Indulgent to your sloth, had granted you
A perpetuitie of pride and pleasure,
No change fear'd, or expected. Now you finde   210
That *Carthage* looking on your stupid sleepes,
And dull securitie, was inuited to
Inuade your Territories.
    Archidamus.   You haue made vs see, Sir,
To our shame the Countries sicknesse: now from you
As from a carefull, and a wise phisitian   215
We doe expect the cure.
    Timoleon.   Old festred sores
Must be lanc'd to the quicke and cauteriz'd,
Which borne with patience, after i'le apply
Soft Vnguents: For the maintenance of the warre
It is decreed all moneys in the hand   220
Of priuate men, shall instantly be brought
To the publike Treasurie.
    Timagoras.   This bites sore.
    Cleon.   The Cure
Is worse then the disease; Ile neuer yeeld to it.
What could the enemy, though victorious,
Inflict more on vs? all that my youth hath toyld for,   225
Purchas'd with industry, and preseru'd with care,
Forc'd from me in a moment.
    Diphilus.   This rough course
Will neuer be allowd of.
    Timoleon.   O blinde men!
If you refuse the first meanes that is offer'd
To giue you health, no hope's left to recouer   230
Your desp'rate sicknesse. Doe you prize your mucke
Aboue your liberties? and rather choose
To be made Bondmen, then to part with that
To which already you are slaues? or can it
Be probable in your flattering apprehensions,   235
You can capitulate with the Conquerour
And keepe that yours, which they come to possesse,
And while you kneele in vaine, will rauish from you?
But take your owne wayes, brood vpon your gold,

    210. No] *24³*; Nor *24¹, ²*   change fear'd,] *24³*; change, fear'd ᴧ *24¹, ²*
    212. securitie] *24³*; secureship *24¹, ²*

I. iii. 240–73 *The Bondman*

Sacrifice to your Idoll, and preserue 240
The prey intire, and merit the report
Of carefull Stewards, yeeld a iust account
To your proud Masters, who with whips of Iron
Will force you to giue vp what you conceale,
Or teare it from your throates; adorne your walls 245
With Persian Hangings wrought of Gold and Pearle;
Couer the floores on which they are to tread
With costly Median silkes; perfume the roomes
With Cassia, and Amber, where they are
To feast and reuell, while like seruile Groomes 250
You wayte vpon their trenchers; feed their eyes
With massie Plate vntill your Cupbords cracke
With the weight that they sustaine; set forth your Wiues
And Daughters in as many varyed shapes
As there are Nations, to prouoke their lusts, 255
And let them be imbrac'd before your eyes,
The object may content you; and to perfit
Their entertainment, offer vp your Sonnes,
And able men for Slaues; while you, that are
Vnfit for labour, are spurn'd out to starue 260
Vnpittied in some Desart, no friend by,
Whose sorrow may spare one compassionat teare,
In the remembrance of what once you were.
    Leosthenes. The blood turnes.
    Timagoras.   Obserue, how olde *Cleon* shakes,
As if in picture hee had showne him, what 265
He was to suffer.
    Corisca.   I am sicke, the man
Speakes poniards, and diseases.
    Olimpia.   O my Doctor,
I neuer shall recouer.
    Cleora.   If a Virgin,
Whose speech was euer yet vsher'd with feare,
One knowing modestie, and humble silence 270
To be the choysest ornaments of our sexe,
In the presence of so many Reuerend men,
Strucke dumbe with terrour and astonishment,

242. Stewards,] *38*; Steward, *24*; Stewards ∧ *Massinger MS*   249. Amber,] *Massinger MS*; ~: *24*   264. *Cleon*] *24¹*; ~. *24²*

Presume to cloath her thought in vocall sounds,
Let her finde pardon. First, to you, great Sir, 275
A bashfull Mayd's thankes, and her zealous prayers
Wing'd with pure innocence, bearing them to Heauen,
For all prosperitie, that the Gods can giue
To one, whose pietie must exact their care,
Thus lowe I offer.
   Timoleon.   Tis a happie Omen. 280
Rise blest one, and speake boldly: on my vertue
I am thy warrant; from so cleere a Spring
Sweet Riuers euer flow.
   Cleora.   Then thus to you
My noble Father, and these Lords, to whom
I next owe duty, no respect forgotten 285
To you my Brother, and these bolde young men
(Such I would haue them) that are, or should be
The Cities Sword and Target of defence.
To all of you, I speake; and if a blush
Steale on my cheekes, it is showne to reproue 290
Your palenesse; willingly I would not say
Your cowardise, or feare: thinke you all treasure
Hid in the bowels of the Earth, or Shipwrack'd
In *Neptunes* watry Kingdome, can hold weight
When Libertie, and Honour, fill one scale, 295
Triumphant Iustice sitting on the beame?
Or dare you but imagine that your golde is
Too deare a salary for such as hazard
Their blood, and liues in your defence? For me
An ignorant Girle, beare witnesse heauen, so farre 300
I prize a Souldier, that to giue him pay,
With such Deuotion as our *Flamens* Offer
Their Sacrifices at the holy Altar,
I doe lay downe these jewels, will make sale
Of my superfluous Wardrobe to supply 305
The meanest of their wants.
   Timoleon.   Braue masculine spirit!
   Diphilus. We are showne to our shame what we in honour
Should haue taught others.

295. scale,] *24², Massinger MS;* ~? *24¹*   296. beame?] *24², Massinger MS;* ~.
24¹   301. pay,] *24¹, ², 38;* ~∧ *24³*

Archidamus.   Such a faire example
Must needs be followed.
   Timagoras.   Euer my deare Sister,
But now our Families glory.
   Leosthenes.   Were she deform'd
The vertues of her minde would force a Stoicque
To sue to be her seruant.
   Cleon.   I must yeeld,
And though my heart blood part with it, I will
Deliuer in my wealth.
   Asotus.   I would say something,
But the truth is, I know not what.
   Timoleon.   We haue money,
And men must now be thought on.
   Archidamus.   We can presse
Of Labourers in the Countrey (men in-vr'd
To colde and heate) ten thousand.
   Diphilus.   Or if need be,
Inroll our Slaues, lustie, and able Varlets,
And fit for seruice.
   Cleon.   They shall goe for me,
I will not pay and fight too.
   Cleora.   How! your Slaues?
O staine of Honour! once more, Sir, your pardon,
And to their shames, let me deliuer, what
I know in justice you may speake.
   Timoleon.   Most gladly,
I could not wish my thoughts a better organ,
Then your tongue, t'expresse them.
   Cleora.   Are you men?
(For Age may qualifie, though not excuse
The backwardnesse of these) able Young men?
Yet now your Countries libertie's at the stake,
Honour, and glorious tryumph, made the garland
For such as dare deserue them; a rich Feast
Prepar'd by Victory of immortall vyands,
Not for base men, but such as with their Swords
Dare force admittance, and will be her Guests;

---

319. Inroll] *1719*; In roll *24*   our] *Massinger MS*; of *24*
Coxeter; ~. *24*[1, 2]; ~, *24*[3]   334. Guests;]

And can you coldly suffer such rewards
To be propos'd, to Labourers and Slaues?
While you that are borne Noble (to whom these
Valued at their best rate, are next to Horses,
Or other Beasts of carriage) cry ayme,
Like idle lookers on, till their proud worth
Make them become your masters?
    Timoleon.   By my hopes,
There's fire and spirit enough in this to make
Thersites valiant.
    Cleora.   No; farre, farre be it from you,
Let these of meaner qualitie contend,
Who can indure most labour; plough the earth,
And thinke they are rewarded, when their sweat
Brings home a fruitfull Haruest to their Lords;
Let them proue good Artificers, and serue you
For vse and ornament, but not presume
To touch at what is Noble; if you thinke them
Vnworthy to taste of those Cates you feed on,
Or weare such costly garments; will you grant them
The priuiledge and prerogatiue of great mindes,
Which you were borne to? Honour, wonne in warre,
And to be stiled preseruers of their Countrey,
Are Titles fit for free and generous Spirits,
And not for Bond-men: had I beene borne a man
And such ne're dying glories made the prize
To bolde Heroicke Courage; by *Diana*,
I would not to my Brother, nay my Father,
Be brib'd to part with the least peece of honour
I should gaine in this action.
    Timoleon.   Shee's inspir'd,
Or in her speakes the Genius of your Countrey
To fire your blood in her defence. I am rap'd
With the imagination! Noble mayde,
Timoleon is your Souldier, and will sweat
Drops of his best blood, but he will bring home
Triumphant conquest to you. Let me weare
Your colours, Lady, and though youthfull heates
That looke no further then your outward forme,

            344. these] *24*; those *38*

Are long since buryed in me, while I liue,
I am a constant louer of your minde,
That does transcend all presidents.
 Cleora.   'Tis an honour: *Giues her Scarfe.*
And so I doe receiue it.
 Corisca.   Plague vpon it,
She has got the start of vs. I could e'ne burst
With enuy at her fortune.
 Olimpia.   A raw young thing,
We haue too much tongue sometimes, our Husbands say,
And she out-strips vs.
 Leosthenes.   I am for the journey.
 Timagoras. May all Diseases, sloath and lechery bring,
Fall vpon him that stayes at home.
 Archidamus.   Though olde,
I will be there in person.
 Diphilus.   So will I.
Me thinkes I am not what I was; her wordes
Haue made me younger, by a score of yeares,
Then I was when I came hither.
 Cleon.   I am still
Old *Cleon*, fat, and vnweldy, I shall neuer
Make a good Souldier, and therefore desire
To be excusde at home.
 Asotus.   Tis my suite too.
I am a grissell, and these Spider fingers
Will neuer hold a Sword. Let vs alone
To rule the Slaues at home, I can so yerke em,
But in my Conscience, I shall neuer proue
Good Iustice in the warre.
 Timoleon.   Haue your desires:
You would be burthens to vs, no way aydes.
Lead, fairest, to the Temple, first we'le pay
A Sacrifice to the Gods for good successe.
For, all great actions the wish'd course doe run,
That are, with their allowance, well begun. *Exeunt all but the*
 Pisander. Stay *Cymbrio*, and *Gracculo.*   *Slaues.*
 Cimbrio.   The businesse?
 Pisander. Meet me to morrow night, neere to the Groue

374. Plague] *24*; Pox *38*

Neighbouring the East part of the Citie.
Gracculo. Well.
Pisander. And bring the rest of our Condition with you,
I haue something to impart, may breake our fetters,
If you dare second me.
Cimbrio. Wee'l not fayle.
Gracculo. A Cart-rope
Shall not binde me at home.
Pisander. Thinke on't, and prosper. *Exeunt.*

Actus II. Scæna I.

ARCHIDAMUS, TIMAGORAS, LEOSTHENES *with Gorgits*, PISANDER.

Archidamus. So, so, 'tis well, how doe I looke?
Pisander. Most sprightfully.
Archidamus. I shrinke not in the shoulders, though I am olde,
I am tough, steele to the backe, I haue not wasted
My stocke of strength in Feather-beds: heer's an arme too,
There's stuffe in't, and I hope will vse a Sword
As well as any beardlesse Boy of you all.
Timagoras. I am glad to see you, Sir, so well prepar'd,
To indure the trauaile of the warre.
Archidamus. Goe too sirra,
I shall indure, when some of you keepe your Cabins,
For all your flaunting Feathers, nay *Leosthenes*
You are welcome too, all friends, and fellowes now.
Leosthenes. Your seruant Sir.
Archidamus. Pish, leaue these Complements,
They stincke in a Souldiers mouth, I could be merry,
For now my Gowne's off, farewell Grauitie,
And must be bolde to put a question to you,
Without offence, I hope.
Leosthenes. Sir, what you please.
Archidamus. And you will answer truely?
Timagoras. On our words, Sir.
Archidamus. Goe too, then, I presume you will confesse,
That you are two notorious Whore-maisters.
Nay spare your blushing, I haue beene wilde my selfe,
A snatch, or so, for Physicke, does no harme;

II. i. 22-52   *The Bondman*   333

Nay, it is physicke, if vs'd moderately,
But to lye at racke, and manger,
   Leosthenes.   Say we grant this,
For if we should deny it, you'l not beleeue vs,
What will you inferre vpon it?
   Archidamus.   What you'l groane for,   25
I feare, when you come to the test. Old Stories tell vs
There is a Moneth cal'd October, which brings in
Colde weather; there are trenches too, 'tis rumor'd,
In which to stand all night to the knees in water,
In Gallants breeds the tooth-ach; there's a sport too   30
Nam'd lying *Perdieu*, (doe you marke me) tis a game,
Which you must learne to play at: now in these seasons,
And choyse varietie of Exercises,
(Nay I come to you) and fasts, not for Deuotion,
Your rambling hunt-smocke, feeles strange alterations,   35
And in a Frosty morning, lookes as if
He could with ease creepe in a pottle Pot
In stead of his Mistris placket; then he curses
The time he spent in midnight visitations,
And findes what he superfluously parted with,   40
To be reported good, at length, and well breath'd,
But if retriu'd into his backe againe,
Would keepe him warmer then a Scarlet wast-coate,
Or an Armour linde with Furre.

            Enter DIPHILUS, *and* CLEORA.
                      O welcome, welcome,
You haue cut off my discourse, but I will perfit   45
My lecture in the Campe.
   Diphilus.   Come, we are stay'd for,
The General's a fire for a remoue,
And longs to be in action.
   Archidamus.   Tis my wish too.
We must part, nay no teares, my best *Cleora*,
I shall melt too, and that were ominous.   50
Millions of blessings on thee, all that's mine,
I giue vp to thy charge, and sirra, looke

   II. i. 21. snatch] *24*; Smatch *1719*; Smack *Coxeter*   34. fasts,] *Massinger MS*;
~ ᴧ *24*   42. retriu'd] *24²*; retain'd *24¹*   backe] *24²*; lacke *24¹, ²*   44 SD. *At
line 42 in 24*   48. too.] *38*; ~, *24*

You, with that care and reuerence obserue her
Which you would pay to me, a kisse, farewell Girle.
   Diphilus. Peace wayte vpon you, faire one.
                    Exeunt ARCHIDAMUS, DIPHILUS, PISANDER.
   Timagoras.   Twere impertinence   55
To wish you to be carefull of your Honour,
That euer keepe in pay a Guard about you
Of faithfull vertues: Farewell friend, I leaue you
To wipe our kisses off, I know that Louers
Part with more circumstance and ceremony,   60
Which I giue way to.
   Leosthenes.   Tis a noble fauour,   *Exit* TIMAGORAS.
For which, I euer owe you. We are alone,
But how I should begin, or in what language
Speake the vnwilling word, of parting from you,
I am yet to learne.
   Cleora.   And still continue ignorant,   65
For I must be most cruell to my selfe,
If I should teach you.
   Leosthenes.   Yet it must be spoken,
Or you will chide my slacknesse, you haue fir'd me
With the heate of noble action, to deserue you,
And the least sparke of honour, that tooke life   70
From your sweet breath, still fann'd by it, and cherish'd,
Must mount vp in a glorious flame, or I
Am much vnworthy.
   Cleora.   May it not burne heere,
And as a Sea-marke, serue to guide true Louers,
(Toss'd on the Ocean of luxurious wishes)   75
Safe from the rockes of Lust into the harbour
Of pure affection? rising vp an example,
Which after-times shall witnesse, to our glory,
First tooke from vs beginning.
   Leosthenes.   Tis a happinesse,
My duty to my Countrey, and mine Honour   80
Cannot consent too, besides, adde to these,
It was your pleasure, fortifide by perswasion,
And strength of reason, for the generall good,
That I should goe.

    62. you.] *Massinger MS*; ~, 24   71. fann'd] *Massinger MS*; fam'd 24

Cleora. Alas, I then was wittie
To pleade against my selfe, and mine eye fix'd
Vpon the hill of Honour, ne're descended
To looke into the vale of certaine dangers,
Through which, you were to cut your passage to it.
  Leosthenes. Ile stay at home then.
  Cleora. No, that must not be,
For, so to serue my own ends, and to gaine
A petty wreath my selfe, I rob you of
A certaine triumph, which must fall vpon you,
Or Vertue's turn'd a hand-maide to blinde Fortune.
How is my soule deuided! to confirme you,
In the opinion of the world, most worthy
To be belou'd, (with me you are at the heigth,
And can aduance no further) I must send you
To court the Goddesse of sterne Warre, who if
Shee see you with my eies, will ne're returne you,
But grow enamour'd of you.
  Leosthenes. Sweet, take comfort,
And what I offer you, you must vouchsafe me,
Or I am wretched; all the dangers, that
I can incounter in the War, are trifles;
My enemies abroad to be contemn'd;
The dreadfull foes, that haue the power to hurt me,
I leaue at home with you.
  Cleora. With mee?
  Leosthenes. Nay, in you,
On euery part about you, they are arm'd
To fight against me.
  Cleora. Where?
  Leosthenes. Ther's no perfection
That you are Mistris of, but musters vp
A Legion against me, and all sworne
To my destruction.
  Cleora. This is strange!
  Leosthenes. But true, sweet,
Excesse of loue can worke such miracles.
Vpon this Iuory fore-head are intrench'd

87. vale] *Massinger MS*; vayle 24   90. For, so] *Massinger MS*; ~ ₐ ~ 24
91. selfe,] *Massinger MS*; ~; 24   93. Fortune.] *Massinger MS*; ~: 24

Ten thousand riuals, and these Sunnes command
Supplies from all the world, on paine to forfeit
Their comfortable beames; these Rubie lips,
A rich Exchecquer to assure their pay;
This hand, *Sibillas* golden bough to guard them
Through Hell, and horror, to the *Elizian* Springs;
Which who'll not venter for? and should I name
Such as the vertues of your minde inuite,
Their numbers would be infinite.
    Cleora.   Can you thinke,
I may be tempted?
    Leosthenes.   You were neuer prou'd.
For me I haue conuers'd with you no farther,
Then would become a Brother. I ne're tun'd
Loose Notes to your chaste eares; or brought rich Presents
For my Artillery, to batter downe
The fortresse of your honour; nor endeuour'd
To make your blood runne high at solemne Feasts
With Viands, that prouoke (the speeding Philtres);
I work'd no Baudes to tempt you; neuer practis'd
The cunning, and corrupting Arts they studie,
That wander in the wilde Maze of desire;
Honest simplicitie, and Truth were all
The Agents I imployd, and when I came
To see you, it was with that reuerence,
As I beheld the Altars of the gods;
And loue, that came along with me, was taught
To leaue his Arrowes, and his Torch behinde,
Quench'd in my feare to giue offence.
    Cleora.   And 'twas
That modesty that tooke me, and preserues me,
Like a fresh Rose, in mine owne naturall sweetnesse;
Which sulli'd with the touch of impure hands,
Looseth both scent and beauty.
    Leosthenes.   But, *Cleora,*
When I am absent, as I must goe from you,
(Such is the cruelty of my fate) and leaue you

118. guard] *24*; guide *McIlwraith*   128. honour;] *Massinger MS*; ~, *24*
130. prouoke (the speeding Philtres);] *after Coxeter*; prouoke; (the speeding Philtres) ~
24   144. Looseth] *Massinger MS*; Loose *24*   scent] *Massinger MS*; sent *24*

Vnguarded, to the violent assaults
Of loose temptations; when the memory
Of my so many yeares of Loue, and seruice,
Is lost in other obiects; when you are courted
By such as keepe a Catalogue of their Conquests,
Wonne vpon credulous Virgins; when nor Father
Is here to awe you; Brother to aduise you;
Nor your poore seruant by, to keepe such off,
By lust instructed how to vndermine,
And blow your chastity vp; when your weake senses
At once assaulted, shall conspire against you;
And play the traytors to your soule, your vertue;
How can you stand? 'faith though you fall, and I
The iudge, before whom you then stood accus'd,
I should acquit you.
   Cleora.   Will you then confirme,
That loue, and iealousie, though of different natures,
Must of necessity be twins? the younger,
Created onely to defeate the elder,
And spoyle him of his Birth-right? 'tis not well.
But being to part, I will not chide, I will not,
Nor with one sillable, or teare expresse,
How deeply I am wounded with the arrowes
Of your distrust: but when that you shall heare
At your returne, how I haue borne my selfe,
And what an austere penance I take on me,
To satisfie your doubts: when like a *Vestall*
I shew you to your shame, the fire still burning,
Committed to my charge by true affection,
The people ioyning with you in the wonder:
When by the glorious splendor of my suffrings,
The prying eies of iealousie are strucke blinde,
The Monster too that feeds on feares, eu'n staru'd
For want of seeming matter to accuse me,
Expect *Leosthenes*, a sharpe reproofe
From my iust anger.
   Leosthenes.   What will you doe?
   Cleora.   Obey mee,

153. awe] *Massinger MS*; owe *24*   165. Birth-right?] *Coxeter*; ~: *24*
182. me:] *after Coxeter*; ~. *24*

Or from this minute you are a stranger to me:
And doe it without reply. All seeing Sunne,
Thou witnesse of my innocence, thus I close
Mine eies against thy comfortable light, 185
Till the returne of this distrustfull man.
Now binde 'em sure, nay doo't: if vncompeld
I loose this knot, vntill the hands that made it
Be pleas'd to vntie it, may consuming plagues
Fall heauy on me: pray you guide me to your lips, 190
This kisse, when you come backe shall be a Virgin
To bid you welcome: Nay, I haue not done yet:
I will continue dumbe, and you once gone,
No Accent shall come from me: now to my chamber,
My Tombe, if you miscarry: there I'le spend 195
My houres in silent mourning, and thus much
Shall be reported of me to my glory,
And you confesse it, whither I liue or die,
My Chastity triumphs ouer your iealousie.   [*Exeunt.*]

Actus II. Scæna II.

ASOTUS, GRACCULO.

Asotus. You slaue, you Dogge, downe Curre.
Gracculo.   Hold, good young Master,
For pitties sake.
Asotus.   Now am I in my kingdome.
Who saies I am not valiant? I begin
To frowne againe, quake villaine.
Gracculo.   So I doe, Sir,
Your lookes are Agues to me.
Asotus.   Are they so Sir? 5
'Slight, if I had them at this bey, that flout me,
And say I looke like a sheepe, and an Asse, I would make 'em
Feele, that I am a Lyon.
Gracculo.   Doe not rore, Sir,
As you are a valiant beast: but doe you know
Why you vse me thus?

183. reply.] *Coxeter*; ~: 24   192. yet:] *Coxeter*; ~. 24   199 SD. Exeunt.]
1719; not in 24   II. ii. 5. Sir?] *Massinger MS*; ~, 24

Asotus. I'le beat thee a little more,
Then study for a reason, O I haue it,
One brake a iest on me, and then I swore
Because I durst not strike him, when I came home
That I would breake thy head.
   Gracculo. Plague on his mirth,
I am sure I mourne for't.
   Asotus. Remember too, I charge you
To teach my Horse good manners; for this morning,
As I rode to take the ayre, th' untutor'd Iade
Threw me, and kick'd me.
   Gracculo. I thanke him for't.
   Asotus. What's that?
   Gracculo. I say, Sir, I'le teach him to hold his heeles,
If you will rule your fingers.
   Asotus. I'le thinke vpon't.
   Gracculo. I am bruisde to ielly; better be a dogge,
Then slaue to a Foole or Coward.

   Enter CORISCA *and* ZANTHIA.

   Asotus. Heere's my Mother,
Shee is chastising too: How braue we liue!
That haue our slaues to beat, to keepe vs in breath,
When we want exercise.
   Corisca. Carelesse Harlotrie, *Striking her.*
Looke too't, if a Curle fall, or winde, or Sunne,
Take my Complexion off, I will not leaue
One haire vpon thine head.
   Gracculo. Here's a second show
Of the Family of pride.
   Corisca. Fie on these warres,
I am staru'd for want of action, not a gamester left
To keepe a woman play; if this world last
A little longer with vs, Ladyes must studie
Some new found Mistery, to coole one another,
Wee shall burne to Cinders else; I haue heard there haue beene
Such Arts in a long vacation; would they were
Reueal'd to mee: they haue made my Doctor too
Phisitian to the Army, he was vs'de

   14. Plague] *24*; Pox *38*   16. for] *Massinger MS*; yet *24*

To serue the turne at a pinch: but I am now
Quite vnprouided.
  Asotus.   My Mother in law is sure
At her deuotion.
  Corisca.   There are none but our slaues left,   40
Nor are they to be trusted; some great women
(Which I could name) in a dearth of Visitants,
Rather then be idle, haue beene glad to play
At small game, but I am so queasie stomack't,
And from my youth haue beene so vsde to Dainties,   45
I cannot taste such grosse meate; some that are hungrie
Draw on their shoomakers, and take a fall
From such as mend Mats in their Galleries;
Or when a Taylor settles a Petticoate on,
Take measure of his Bodkin: fie vpon't,   50
'Tis base; for my part, I could rather lie with
A Gallants breeches, and conceaue vpon 'em,
Then stoope so low.
  Asotus.   Faire Madam, and my Mother.
  Corisca. Leaue the last out, it smells rancke of the Countrie,
And shewes course breeding, your true Courtier knowes not 55
His Neece, or Sister from another woman,
If she be apt and coming. I could tempt now
This foole, but he will be so long a working.
Then hee's my Husbands Sonne; the fitter to
Supply his wants, I haue the way already.   60
I'le trie, if it will take; when were you with
Your Mistris, faire *Cleora*?
  Asotus.   Two daies sithence,
But shee's so coy forsooth, that ere I can
Speake a pen'd speech I haue bought, and studied for her,
Her woman calls her away.
  Corisca.   Here's a dull thing,   65
But better taught I hope, send of your man.
  Asotus. Sirra, be gone.
  Gracculo.   This is the first good turne,
She euer did me.   *Exit* GRACCULO.
  Corisca.   We'le haue a Scæne of mirth,

57. coming] *Massinger MS* (cõminge); cunning 24   62. *Cleora*?] *Massinger MS*; ~. 24

I must not haue you sham'd for want of practise.
I stand here for *Cleora*, and doe you heare Minion, 70
(That you may tell her, what her woman should do)
Repeat the lesson ouer, that I taught you,
When my young Lord came to visit me; if you misse
In a Syllable or posture!
   Zanthia.   I am perfect.
   Asotus. Would I were so: I feare I shall be out. 75
   Corisca. If you are, I'le helpe you in. Thus I walke musing:
You are to enter, and as you passe by,
Salute my woman; be but bold enough,
You'le speed I warrant you; begin.
   Asotus.   Haue at it.
'Saue thee sweet heart. A kisse.
   Zanthia.   *Venus* forbid, Sir, 80
I should presume to taste your honours lips
Before my Lady.
   Corisca.   This is well on both parts.
   Asotus. How does thy Lady?
   Zanthia.   Happy in your Lordship,
As oft as she thinkes on you.
   Corisca.   Very good,
This Wench will learne in time.
   Asotus.   Does she thinke of me? 85
   Zanthia. O Sir, and speakes the best of you, admires
Your wit, your clothes, discourse; and sweares, but that
You are not forward enough for a Lord, you were
The most compleat, and absolute man: I'le shew
Your Lordship a Secret.
   Asotus.   Not of thine owne?
   Zanthia.   O no, Sir, 90
'Tis of my Lady, but vpon your honour,
You must conceale it.
   Asotus.   By all meanes.
   Zanthia.   Some times
I lie with my Ladie, as the last night I did,
Shee could not say her prayers, for thinking of you,
Nay, she talked of you in her sleepe, and sigh'd out, 95
O sweet *Asotus*, sure thou art so backward,
That I must rauish thee, and in that feruor

She tooke me in her armes, threw me vpon her,
Kis'd me, and hug'd me, and then wak'd, and wept,
Because 'twas but a dreame.
    Corisca.   This will bring him on,
Or hee's a blocke. A good Girle!
    Asotus.   I am mad,
Till I am at it.
    Zanthia.   Be not put off, Sir,
With away, I dare not, fie you are immodest,
My Brother's vp, my Father will heare; shoot home, Sir,
You cannot misse the marke.
    Asotus.   There's for thy counsaile.
This is the fairest interlude; if it proue earnest,
I shall wish I were a Player.
    Corisca.   Now my turne comes.
I am exceeding sicke, pray you send my Page
For young *Asotus*, I cannot liue without him,
Pray him to visit me, yet when hee's present,
I must be strange to him.
    Asotus.   Not so: you are caught.
Loe whom you wish, behold *Asotus* here!
    Corisca. You wait well, Minion, shortly I shall not speake
My thoughts in my priuate Chamber, but they must
Lie open to discouery.
    Asotus.   'Slid shee's angry.
    Zanthia. No, no, Sir, she but seemes so. To her againe.
    Asotus. Lady, I would descend to kisse your hand,
But that 'tis glou'd, and Ciuit makes me sicke;
And to presume to taste your lipps not safe,
Your woman by.
    Corisca.   I hope shee's no obseruer,
Of whom I grace.   ZANTHIA *lookes on a Booke.*
    Asotus.   She's at her booke, O rare!   *Kisses her.*
    Corisca. A kisse for entertainement is sufficient:
Too much of one dish cloyes me.
    Asotus.   I would serue in
The second course, but still I feare your woman.
    Corisca. You are very cautelous.   ZANTHIA *seemes to sleepe.*

---

   99. wept,] *Massinger MS;* ~; 24   119. lipps] 24; lip's *Gifford*   121 SD. Booke. | Kisses her.] *Coxeter;* Booke, | kisses her. 24²; Booke, kisses her. 24¹

Asotus. 'Slight shee's asleepe!
'Tis pitty, these instructions are not printed:
They would sell well to Chamber-maides; 'tis no time now
To play with my good fortune, and your fauour,
Yet to be taken, as they say: a scout
To giue the signall when the enemie comes, *Exit* ZANTHIA.
Were now worth gold: Shee's gone to watch.
A wayter so trayn'd vp were worth a million,
To a wanton Citie Madam.
 Corisca.   You are growne conceited.
 Asotus. You teach me; Lady, now your Cabinet.
 Corisca. You speake, as it were yours.
 Asotus.   When we are there,
Ile show you my best euidence.
 Corisca.   Holde, you forget,
I onely play *Cleora's* part.
 Asotus.   No matter,
Now we haue begun, let's end the act.
 Corisca.   Forbeare, Sir,
Your Fathers wife?
 Asotus.   Why, being his Heyre, I am bound,
Since he can make no satisfaction to you,
To see his debts payd.

Enter ZANTHIA *running*.

 Zanthia.   Madame, my Lord.
 Corisca.   Fall off,
I must trifle with the time too; Hell confound it.
 Asotus. Plague on his toothlesse chaps, he cannot do't
Himselfe, yet hinders such as haue good stomacks.

Enter CLEON.

 Cleon. Where are you, Wife? I faine would goe abroad,
But cannot finde my Slaues, that beare my Litter:
I am tyr'd, your shoulder, Sonne; nay sweet, thy hand too,
A turne or two in the Garden, and then to Supper,
And so to Bed.
 Asotus.   Neuer to rise, I hope, more.   *Exeunt.*

---

142. Hell confound it.] 24; *not in 38*   143. Plague] 24; Pox 38

Actus II. Scæna III.

PISANDER, POLIPHRON, *bringing forth a Table.*

Pisander. 'Twill take, I warrant thee.
Poliphron.   You may doe your pleasure:
But, in my judgement, better to make vse of
The present opportunitie.
Pisander.   No more.

Enter CIMBRIO, GRACCULO, *and Slaues.*

Poliphron.   I am silenc'd.
Pisander. More wine, 'pray thee drinke hard, friend,
And when we are hot, what euer I propound,
Second with vehemency: men of your wordes, all welcome,
Slaues vse no ceremonie, sit downe, heer's a health.
  Poliphron. Let it runne round, fill euery man his Glasse.
  Gracculo. We looke for no wayters; this is Wine.
  Pisander.   The better,
Strong, lusty wine: drinke deepe, this juyce will make vs
As free as our Lords.   *Drinkes.*
  Gracculo.   But if they finde, we taste it,
We are all damn'd to the quarry, during life,
Without hope of redemption.
  Pisander.   Pish, for that
Wee'l talke anon: another rowse, we loose time: *Drinkes.*
When our lowe blood's wound vp a little higher,
Ile offer my designe; nay, we are colde yet,
These Glasses containe nothing; doe me right, *Takes the Bottle.*
As e're you hope for liberty. 'Tis done brauely.
How doe you feele your selues now?
  Cimbrio.   I begin
To haue strange Conundrums in my head.
  Gracculo.   And I,
To loath base water: I would be hang'd in peace now,
For one moneth of such Holy-dayes.
  Pisander.   An age, Boyes,
And yet defie the Whip, if you are men,
Or dare belieue, you haue soules.

II. iii. 11 SD. *Drinkes.*] 24²; *at line 10 in* 24¹

Cimbrio.   We are no Broakers:
Gracculo. Nor Whores, whose markes are out of their mouthes,
    they haue none,   25
They hardly can get salt enough to keep 'em
From stinking aboue ground.
    Pisander.   Our Lords are no Gods!
    Gracculo. They are Diuels to vs, I am sure.
    Pisander.   But subject to
Colde, hunger, and diseases.
    Gracculo.   In abundance.
Your Lord, that feeles no ach in his chine at twentie,   30
Forfeits his priuiledge, how should their Chyrurgions build else,
Or ride on their Foot-cloathes?
    Pisander.   Equall nature fashion'd vs
All in one molde: The Beare serues not the Beare,
Nor the Wolfe, the Wolfe; 'twas ods of strength in tyrants,
That pluck'd the first linke from the Golden chayne   35
With which that thing of things bound in the world.
Why then, since we are taught, by their examples,
To loue our Libertie, if not Command,
Should the strong serue the weake, the faire deform'd ones?
Or such as know the cause of thinges, pay tribute   40
To ignorant fooles? All's but the outward glosse
And politicke forme, that does distinguish vs.
Cymbrio, thou art a strong man; if in place
Of carrying burthens, thou hadst beene trayn'd vp
In Martiall discipline, thou mightst haue prou'd   45
A Generall, fit to lead and fight for *Sicilie*,
As fortunate as *Timoleon*.
    Cimbrio.   A little fighting
Will serue a Generals turne.
    Pisander.   Thou, *Gracculo*,
Hast fluencie of Language, quicke conceite,
And I thinke, couer'd with a Senators robe,   50
Formally set on the Bench, thou wouldst appeare
As braue a Senator.
    Gracculo.   Would I had Lands,
Or money to buy a place; and if I did not

27. Gods!] *editor*; Gods? *24*; Gods—*Gifford*   31. Chyrurgions] *Massinger MS*;
Chyrurgion *24*

Sleepe on the Bench, with the drowsiest of 'em, play with my Chayne,
Looke on my Watch, when my guts chym'd twelue, and weare
A state Beard, with my Barbers helpe, rancke with 'em,
In their most choyce peculiar guifts; degrade me
And put me to drinke Water againe, which (now
I haue tasted Wine) were poyson.
 Pisander.   'Tis spoke nobly,
And like a Gown-man; none of these, I thinke too,
But would proue good Burgers.
 Gracculo.   Hum: the fooles are modest,
I know their insides: Here's an ill-fac'd fellow,
(But that will not be seene in a darke Shop,)
If he did not in a moneth, learne to out-sweare,
In the selling of his Wares, the cunningest Tradesman
In *Syracusa*, I haue no skill; Here's another,
Obserue but what a cousening looke he has,
(Hold vp thy head, man) if for drawing Gallants
Into mortgages for Commodities, cheating Heyres
With your new counterfeit Gold thred, and gumm'd Veluets,
He does not transcend all that went before him,
Call in his patent; passe the rest, they'l all make
Sufficient Becos, and with their brow-antlers
Beare vp the Cap of maintenance.
 Pisander.   Is't not pitty then,
Men of such eminent vertues, should be Slaues?
 Cimbrio. Our fortune.
 Pisander.   Tis your folly, daring men
Commaund, and make their fates. Say, at this instant,
I mark'd you out a way to Libertie;
Possest you of those blessings, our proud Lords
So long haue surfetted in; and what is sweetest,
Arme you with power, by strong hand to reuenge
Your stripes, your vnregarded toyle, the pride,
The insolencie, of such as tread vpon
Your patient suffrings; fill your famish'd mouthes,
With the fat and plentie of the Land; redeeme you
From the darke vale of Seruitude, and seate you
Vpon a hill of happinesse; what would you doe
To purchase this and more?

   73. brow-antlers] *Coxeter*; brow-antlets *24²*; brow ant-lets *24¹*

Gracculo. Doe any thing,
To burne a Church or two, and dance by the light on't
Were but a May-game.
   Poliphron. I haue a Father liuing,
But if the cutting of his throat could worke this,
He should excuse me.
   Cimbrio. 'Slight, I would cut mine owne,
Rather then misse it, so I might but haue
A taste on't, ere I dye.
   Pisander. Be resolute men,
You shall runne no such hazard, nor groane vnder
The burthen of such crying sinnes.
   Cimbrio. The meanes?
   Gracculo. I feele a womans longing.
   Poliphron. Doe not torment vs
With expectation.
   Pisander. Thus then, our proud Masters,
And all the able Freemen of the Citie
Are gone vnto the warres,
   Poliphron. Obserue but that.
   Pisander. Old men, and such as can make no resistance,
Are onely left at home.
   Gracculo. And the proud young foole
My Master: If this take, I'le hamper him.
   Pisander. Their Arsenall, their Treasure's in our power,
If we haue hearts to sease 'em; if our Lords fall
In the present action, the whole countrie's ours;
Say they returne victorious, we haue meanes
To keepe the Towne against them: at the worst
To make our owne conditions: now if you dare
Fall on their Daughters, and their wiues, breake vp
Their Iron Chests, banquet on their rich Beds,
And carue your selues of all delights and pleasures
You haue beene barr'd from, with one voyce cry with me,
Libertie, Libertie.
   All. Libertie, Libertie.
   Pisander. Goe then, and take possession; vse all freedome,
But shed no blood. So, this is well begun,
But not to be commended, til't be done.   *Exeunt omnes.*

116. blood. So, this] *after 1719*; blood: so this 24

Actus III. Scæna I.

PISANDER. TIMANDRA.

Pisander. Why, thinke you, that I plot against my selfe?
Feare nothing, you are safe, these thick-skinn'd slaues,
(I vse as instruments to serue my ends)
Pierce not my deepe designes: nor shall they dare
To lift an arme against you.
    Timandra.   With your will.   5
But turbulent spirits rais'd beyond themselues
With ease, are not so soone layd: they oft proue
Dangerous to him that call'd them vp.
    Pisander.   Tis true,
In what is rashly vndertooke. Long since
I haue considered seriously their natures,   10
Proceeded with mature aduise, and know
I hold their will, and faculties in more awe
Then I can doe my owne. Now for their Licence,
And ryot in the Citie, I can make
A iust defence, and vse: it may appeare too   15
A polliticke preuention of such ills
As might with greater violence, and danger
Hereafter be attempted; though some smart for't,
It matters not: how euer, I am resolu'd;
And sleepe you with security. Holds *Cleora*   20
Constant to her rash vow?
    Timandra.   Beyond beleefe;
To me, that see her hourely, it seemes a fable.
By signes I ghesse at her commands, and serue 'em
With silence, such her pleasure is, made knowne
By holding her faire hand thus; she eates little,   25
Sleepes lesse, as I imagine; once a day
I leade her to this Gallery, where she walkes
Some halfe a dozen turnes, and hauing offred
To her absent Saint a sacrifice of sighes,
She points backe to her prison.
    Pisander.   Guide her hither,   30
And make her vnderstand the slaues reuolt,

III. i. 1. Why, thinke you,] 24^4; ~ ^ ~ ^ $24^{1, 2, 3}$

And with your vtmost eloquence enlarge
Their insolence, and Rapes done in the Citie;
Forget not to, I am their chiefe, and tell her
You strongly thinke my extreame dotage on her,   35
As I am *Marullo*, caus'd this sodaine vprore,
To make way to enioy her.
   Timandra.   Punctually
I will discharge my part.   *Exit* TIMANDRA.

            Enter POLIPHRON.

   Poliphron.   O Sir, I sought you.
You haue mis'd the best sport. Hell, I thinke is broke loose,
There's such varietie of all disorders,   40
As leaping, shouting, drinking, dancing, whoring,
Among the slaues; answer'd with crying, howling,
By the Citizens and their wiues: such a confusion,
(In a word, not to tyre you) as I thinke
The like was neuer reade of.
   Pisander.   I share in   45
The pleasure, though I am absent. This is some
Reuenge for my disgrace.
   Poliphron.   But Sir; I feare,
If your authority restraine them not,
They'le fire the Citie, or kill one another,
They are so apt to outrage; neither know I   50
Whether you wish it, and came therefore to
Acquaint you with so much.
   Pisander.   I will among 'em,
But must not long be absent.
   Poliphron.   At your pleasure.   *[Exeunt.]*

Actus III. Scæna II.

CLEORA, TIMANDRA, *a Chaire, a shout within.*

   Timandra. They are at our gates, my heart! affrights and horrors
Increase each minute: No way left to saue vs;
No flattering hope to comfort vs, or meanes
By miracle to redeeme vs from base lust,

     41. shouting] *38*; shooting *24*   53 SD. *Exeunt.*] *Coxeter; not in 24*

  And lawlesse rapine. Are there Gods, yet suffer 5
  Such innocent sweetnesse to be made the spoile
  Of brutish appetite? Or, since they decree
  To ruine Natures master-peece (of which
  They haue not left one patterne) must they choose,
  To set their tyrannie of, slaues to pollute 10
  The spring of chastitie, and poyson it
  With their most loath'd embraces? and of those
  He that should offer vp his life to guard it?
  Marullo, curs'd *Marullo*, your owne Bond-man
  Purchas'd to serue you, and fed by your fauours. 15
  Nay, start not; it is he, hee the grand Captaine   CLEORA *starts.*
  Of these libidinous beasts, that haue not left
  One cruell act vndone, that Barbarous conquest
  Yet euer practis'd in a captiue Citie.
  He doting on your beauty, and to haue fellowes 20
  In his foule sinne, hath rais'd these mutinous slaues,
  Who haue begun the game by violent Rapes,
  Vpon the Wiues and Daughters of their Lords:
  And he to quench the fire of his base lust, 24
  By force comes to enioy you: doe not wring   CLEORA *wrings her*
  Your innocent hands, 'tis bootlesse; vse the meanes   *hands.*
  That may preserue you. 'Tis no crime to breake
  A vow, when you are forc'd to it; shew your face,
  And with the maiestie of commanding beautie,
  Strike dead his loose affections; if that faile, 30
  Giue libertie to your tongue, and vse entreaties;
  There cannot be a breast of flesh, and bloud,
  Or heart so made of flint, but must receiue
  Impression from your words; or eies so sterne,
  But from the cleere reflection of your teares 35
  Must melt, and beare them company; will you not
  Doe these good offices to your selfe? poore I then,
  Can onely weepe your fortune; here he comes.

    Enter PISANDER *speaking at the doore.*

  Pisander. He that aduances
  A foot beyond this, comes vpon my sword. 40
  You haue had your wayes, disturbe not mine.

    III. ii. 37. selfe?] 24*ᶜ*, *Massinger MS*; ~, 24[1], [2], [3]

Timandra.　　　　　　　　　　Speake gently,
Her feares may kill her else.
　Pisander.　　　　　　Now loue inspire me!
Still shall this Canopie of enuious night
Obscure my Suns of comfort? and those dainties
Of purest white and red, which I take in at　　　　　45
My greedy eyes, deny'd my famish'd senses?
The Organs of your hearing yet are open;
And you infringe no vow, though you vouchsafe
To giue them warrant, to conuey vnto
Your vnderstanding parts, the story of　　　　　　50
A tortur'd and dispairing Louer, whom　　*CLEORA shakes.*
Not Fortune but affection markes your slaue.
Shake not, best Lady; for (beleeu't) you are
As farre from danger as I am from force.
All violence I'le offer, tendes no farther　　　　　55
Then to relate my suffrings, which I dare not
Presume to doe, till by some gratious signe
You shew, you are pleas'd to heare me.
　Timandra.　　　　　　　　If you are,
Hold forth your right hand.　*CLEORA holdes forth her right hand.*
　Pisander.　　　　　　So, 'tis done, and I
With my glad lips seale humbly on your foot,　　60
My soules thankes for the fauour: I forbeare
To tell you who I am, what wealth, what honours
I made exchange of to become your seruant:
And though I knew, worthy *Leosthenes*
(For sure he must be worthy, for whose loue　　　65
You haue endur'd so much) to be my riuall,
When rage, and iealousie counsail'd me to kill him,
(Which then I could haue done with much more ease,
Then now, in feare to grieue you, I dare speake it)
Loue seconded with duty boldly told me,　　　　70
The man I hated, faire *Cleora* fauour'd,
And that was his protection.　　　　*CLEORA bowes.*
　Timandra.　　　　　See, she bowes
Her head in signe of thankfulnesse.
　Pisander.　　　　　　　He remou'd,

---

44. and] 24; are *McIlwraith*　　50. vnderstanding parts,] *Massinger MS*; ~, ~ ∧
24¹, ², ³; ~ ∧ ~ ∧ 24⁴

By th' occasion of the war (my fires increasing
By being clos'd, and stop'd vp) franticke affection 75
Prompted me to doe something in his absence,
That might deliuer you into my power,
Which you see is effected; and euen now,
When my rebellious passions chide my dulnesse,
And tell me how much I abuse my fortunes, 80
Now 'tis in my power to beare you hence,   CLEORA *starts.*
Or take my wishes here, (nay, feare not Madam,
True loue's a seruant, brutish lust a Tyrant)
I dare not touch those viands, that ne're taste well,
But when they are freely offred: only thus much, 85
Be pleas'd I may speake in my owne deare cause,
And thinke it worthy your consideration,
I haue lou'd truly, (cannot say deseru'd,
Since duty must not take the name of merit)
That I so farre prise your content, before 90
All blessings, that my hopes can fashion to mee,
That willingly I entertaine despayre,
And for your sake embrace it. For I know,
This opportunity lost, by no endeauour
The like can be recouer'd. To conclude, 95
Forget not, that I lose my selfe, to saue you.
For what can I expect, but death and torture,
The warre being ended? and, what is a taske
Would trouble *Hercules* to vndertake,
I doe deny you to my selfe, to giue you 100
A pure vnspotted present to my riuall.
I haue said: if it distaste not, best of Virgins,
Reward my temperance with some lawfull fauour,
Though you contemne my person.
            CLEORA *kneeles, then puls off her Gloue, and offers her*
                                           hand to PISANDER.
    Timandra.   See, she kneeles
And seemes to call vpon the gods to pay 105
The debt she owes your vertue. To performe which,
As a sure pledge of friendship, she vouchsafes you
Her faire right hand.
    Pisander.   I am payd for all my suffrings.

87. consideration,] *38*; ~. *24*

Now when you please, passe to your priuate Chamber:
My loue, and dutie, faithfull guards, shall keepe you 110
From all disturbance; and when you are sated *Makes a lowe*
With thinking of *Leosthenes*, as a fee *curtsie, as she goes off.*
Due to my seruice, spare one sigh for me. *Exeunt.*

Actus III. Scæna III.

GRACCULO *leading* ASOTUS *in an Apes habit, with a chaine about his necke.* ZANTHIA, *in* CORISCA'S *Cloathes, she bearing vp her traine.*

Gracculo. Come on, Sir.
Asotus. Oh.
Gracculo. Doe you grumble? you were euer
A brainelesse Asse, but if this hold, I'le teach you
To come aloft, and doe tricks like an Ape.
Your mornings lesson: if you misse—
Asotus. O no, Sir.
Gracculo. What for the Carthaginians? a good beast. 5
                             ASOTUS *makes moppes.*
What for our selfe your Lord? exceeding well. *Dances.*
There's your reward. Not kisse your pawe? So, so, so.
Zanthia. Was euer Lady the first daie of her honour
So waited on by a wrinkled crone? she lookes now
Without her painting, curling, and perfumes 10
Like the last day of Ianuary; and stinkes worse
Then a hot brach in the dogge daies. Further of,
So, stand there like an image; if you stirre,
Till with a quarter of a looke I call you,
You know what followes.
Corisca. O what am I falne to! 15
But 'tis a punishment for my lust and pride,
Iustly return'd vpon me.
Gracculo. How doo'st thou like
Thy Ladiship *Zanthia*?
Zanthia. Very well, and beare it
With as much state as your Lordship.

111 SD. *At line 108 in 24*   III. iii. 3. Ape.] *38*; ~ ^ *24*   5 SD. *At line 4 in 24*

Gracculo. Giue me thy hand;
Let vs like conquering Romans walke in triumph,
Our captiues following. Then mount our Tribunals,
And make the slaues our footstooles.
Zanthia. Fine by Ioue,
Are your hands cleane minion?
Corisca. Yes forsooth.
Zanthia. Fall off then.
So now come on: and hauing made your three duties,
Downe I say, (are you stiffe in the hams?) now kneele,
And tie our shooe. Now kisse it and be happy.
Gracculo. This is state indeed.
Zanthia. It is such as she taught me;
A tickling itch of greatnesse, your proud Ladyes
Expect from their poore Waiters; we haue chang'd parts,
Shee does what she forc'd me to doe in her raigne,
And I must practise it in mine.
Gracculo. 'Tis iustice;
O heere come more.

Enter CIMBRIO, CLEON, POLIPHRON, OLIMPIA.

Cimbrio. Discouer to a Drachma,
Or I will famish thee.
Cleon. O I am pin'de already.
Cimbrio. Hunger shall force thee to cut off the brawnes
From thy armes and thighes, then broile them on the coles
For Carbonadoes.
Poliphron. Spare the olde Iade, he's foundred.
Gracculo. Cutt his throat then,
And hang him out for a scarre-Crowe.
Poliphron. You haue all your wishes
In your reuenge, and I haue mine. You see
I vse no tyrannie: When I was her slaue,
She kept me as a sinner to lie at her backe
In frostie nights, and fed me high with dainties,
Which still she had in her belly againe e're morning,
And in requitall of those curtesies
Hauing made one another free, we are marryed,
And if you wish vs ioy, ioyne with vs in
A Dance at our Wedding.

III. iii. 47-72   *The Bondman*   355

Gracculo.   Agreed, for I haue thought of
A most triumphant one, which shall expresse,
Wee are Lords, and these our slaues.
   Poliphron.   But we shall want
A woman.
   Gracculo. No, here's Iane of Apes shall serue;   50
Carry your body swimming: where's the Musicke?
   Poliphron. I haue plac'd it in yon Window.
   Gracculo.   Begin then sprightly.

    The dance. At the end, enter PISANDER.

   Poliphron. Well done on all sides. I haue prepar'd a Banquet;
Let's drinke, and coole vs.
   Gracculo.   A good motion.
   Cimbrio.   Wait heere,
You haue beene tyr'd with feasting, learne to fast now.   55
   Gracculo. Ile haue an Apple for Iacke, and may be some scrapps
May fall to your share.   *Exeunt* GRACCULO, ZANTHIA,
                        CIMBRIO, POLIPHRON, OLIMPIA.
   Corisca.   Whom can we accuse
But our selues for what we suffer? thou art iust,
Thou all-creating power. And miserie
Instructs me now, (that yesterday acknowledg'd   60
No Deitie beyond my lust and pride)
There is a heauen aboue vs, that lookes downe
With the eyes of Iustice, vpon such as number
Those blessings freely giuen, in the accompt
Of their poore merits: Else it could not be   65
Now miserable I, to please whose pallat
The Elements were ransack'd, yet complain'd
Of Nature, as not liberall enough
In her prouision of rarities
To soothe my taste, and pamper my proud flesh,   70
Now wish in vaine for bread:
   Cleon.   Yes, I doe wishe too,
For what I fed my dogges with.

48-9. *Verse rearranged by Coxeter;* A most ... slaues. *24*   52 SD. *The dance
... PISANDER.*] *after McIlwraith; The dance at the end. | Enter Pisander. 24 (begins
against* Window)   60-1. now, (that ... pride)] *Massinger MS;* now, that ...
pride. *24*   65. be] *24;* ~. *Coxeter*   70. flesh,] *Mason;* ~: *24*   71. Now]
24; Should *Mason*

Corisca. I that forgot
I was made of flesh and blood, and thought the silke
Spunne by the diligent wormes out of their intrals,
Too course to cloathe mee; and the softest Downe 75
Too hard to sleepe on; that disdain'd to looke
On vertue being in ragges; that stop'd my nose
At those that did not vse adulterate arts
To better nature; that from those, that seru'd me,
Expected adoration, am made iustly 80
The scorne of my owne Bond-woman.
  Asotus. I am punish'd,
For seeking to Cuckold mine owne naturall Father.
Had I beene gelded then, or vs'd my selfe
Like a man: I had not beene transform'd, and forc'd
To play an ore-growne Ape.
  Cleon. I know I cannot 85
Last long, that's all my comfort: come, I forgiue both.
It is in vaine to be angry, let vs therefore
Lament together like friends.
  Pisander. What a true mirror
Were this sad spectacle for secure greatnesse!
Heere they that neuer see themselues, but in 90
The Glasse of seruile flattery, might behold
The weake foundation, vpon which they build,
That trust in humane frailtie. Happie are those,
That knowing in their births, they are subiect to
Vncertaine change, are still prepar'd, and arm'd 95
For either fortune: A rare principle,
And with much labour, learn'd in wisdomes schoole!
For as these Bond-men by their actions shew,
That their prosperitie, like too large a Sayle
For their small barke of iudgement, sinkes them with 100
A fore-right gale of libertie, e're they reach
The Port they long to touch at: So these wretches,
Swolne with the false opinion of their worth,
And proud of blessings left them, not acquir'd,
That did beleeue they could with Gyant-armes 105

74. wormes] *Massinger MS*; worme, *24*   92. foundation,] *Massinger MS*; ~ˬ
24   99. too] *Massinger MS*; too too *24*   100. iudgement,] *Massinger MS*;
~; *24*

Fathome the earth, and were aboue their fates,
Those borrow'd helpes that did support them, vanish'd:
Fall of themselues, and by vnmanly suffring,
Betray their proper weaknesse, and make knowne
Their boasted greatnesse was lent, not their owne. 110
  Cleon. O for some meate, they sit long.
  Corisca.   We forgot,
When we drew out intemperate feasts till midnight:
Their hunger was not thought on, nor their watchings;
Nor did we hold our selues seru'd to the height,
But when we did exact, and force their duties 115
Beyond their strength and power.
  Asotus.   We pay for't now,
I now could be content to haue my head
Broke with a ribbe of Beefe, or for a Coffin
Be buried in the dripping Pan.

      Enter POLIPHRON, CIMBRIO, GRACCULO, ZANTHIA,
         OLIMPIA, *drunke and quarrelling.*

  Cimbrio.   Doe not hold me,
Not kisse the Bride?
  Poliphron.   No Sir.
  Cimbrio.   She's common good, 120
And so wee'll vse her.
  Gracculo.   Wee'le haue nothing priuate.
  Olimpia. Hold:
  Zanthia.   Heere's *Marullo.*
  Olimpia.   Hee's your chiefe.
  Cimbrio.   We are equals,
I will know no obedience.
  Gracculo.   Nor superior,
Nay, if you are Lyon-drunke, I will make one,
For lightly euer he that parts the fray, 125
Goes away with the blowes.
  Pisander.   Art thou madde too?
No more, as you respect me.
  Poliphron.   I obey, Sir.
  Pisander. Quarrell among your selues?

---

106. fates,] *Massinger MS*; ~. *24*   107. vanish'd:] *24*; ~, *Coxeter*   122. Olimpia. Hold:] *24*; Pisan. [*coming forward*] Hold! *Gifford¹*   Heere's] *Gifford*; Heere, *24*

Cimbrio. Yes, in our Wine, Sir,
And for our Wenches.
  Gracculo. How could we be Lords else?
  Pisander. Take heed, I haue news will coole this heat, and make you
Remember, what you were.
  Cimbrio. How?
  Pisander. Send off these,
And then I'le tell you. ZANTHIA *beating* CORISCA.
  Olimpia. This is tyrannie,
Now she offends not.
  Zanthia. 'Tis for exercise,
And to helpe digestion, what is she good for else?
To me it was her language.
  Pisander. Staue her of.
And take heed Madam minx, the Wheele may turne.
Goe to your meate, and rest, and from this houre
Remember, he that is a Lord to day,
May be a Slaue to morrow.
  Cleon. Good morallity.
      Exeunt CLEON, ASOTUS, ZANTHIA, OLIMPIA, CORISCA.
  Cimbrio. But what would you impart?
  Pisander. What must inuite you
To stand vpon your guard, and leaue your feasting,
Or but imagine, what it is to be
Most miserable, and rest assur'd you are so.
Our Masters are victorious:
  All. How?
  Pisander. Within
A dayes march of the Citie, flesh'd with spoyle,
And proud of conquest, the Armado sunke,
The Carthaginian Admirall hand to hand,
Slaine by *Leosthenes*.
  Cimbrio. I feele the whippe
Vpon my backe already.
  Gracculo. Euery man
Seeke a conuenient Tree, and hang himselfe.
  Poliphron. Better die once, then liue an age to suffer
New tortures euery houre.

135. Staue her of.] *Massinger MS*; Leaue her off, *24*   139 SD. *Exeunt* ...
CORISCA.] *1719; at line 138 in 24*

Cimbrio.   Say, we submit,
And yeeld vs to their mercy.
   Pisander.   Can you flatter
Your selues with such false hopes? or dare you thinke
That your imperious Lords, that neuer fail'd   155
To punish with seuerity petty slipps,
In your neglect of labour, may be wonne
To pardon those licentious outrages,
Which noble enemies forbeare to practise
Vpon the conquer'd? What haue you omitted,   160
That may call on their iust reuenge with horror,
And studied cruelty? We haue gone too farre
To thinke now of retyring; in our courage,
And daringe, lies our safetie; if you are not
Slaues in your abiect mindes, as in your fortunes,   165
Since to die is the worst, better expose
Our naked breasts to their keene Swords, and sell
Our liues with the most aduantage, then to trust
In a forestal'd remission, or yeeld vp
Our bodies to the furnace of their furie,   170
Thrice heated with reuenge.
   Gracculo.   You led vs on.
   Cimbrio. And 'tis but iustice, you should bring vs off.
   Gracculo. And we expect it.
   Pisander.   Heare then, and obey me,
And I will either saue you, or fall with you;
Man the Walls strongly, and make good the Ports,   175
Boldly deny their entrance, and rippe vp
Your grieuances, and what compel'd you to
This desperate course: if they disdaine to heare
Of composition, we haue in our powers
Their aged Fathers, Children, and their Wiues,   180
Who to preserue themselues, must willingly
Make intercession for vs. 'Tis not time now
To talke, but doe. A glorious end or freedome
Is now propos'd vs; stand resolu'd for either,
And like good fellowes, liue, or die togeather.   *Exeunt.*

164. daringe] *Massinger MS*; during 24

[III. iv]

Actus III. Scæna IIII.

LEOSTHENES, TIMAGORAS.

Timagoras. I am so farre from enuie, I am proud
You haue outstrip'd me in the race of honour.
O 'twas a glorious day, and brauely wonne!
Your bold performance gaue such lustre to
Timoleons wise directions, as the Armie   5
Rests doubtfull, to whom they stand most ingag'de
For their so great successe.
    Leosthenes.   The Gods first honour'd,
The glory be the Generalls; 'tis farre from mee
To be his riuall.
    Timagoras.   You abuse your fortune,
To entertaine her choyce, and gratious fauours,   10
With a contracted browe; Plum'd victorie
Is truly painted with a cheerefull looke,
Equally distant from proud insolence,
And base deiection.
    Leosthenes.   O *Timagoras*,
You onely are acquainted with the cause,   15
That loades my sad heart with a hill of lead;
Whose ponderous waight, neither my new got honour,
Assisted by the generall applause
The souldier crownes it with: nor all warres glories
Can lessen, or remoue; and would you please,   20
With fit consideration to remember,
How much I wrong'd *Cleoras* innocence,
With my rash doubts; and what a grieuous pennance,
Shee did impose vpon her tender sweetnesse,
To plucke away the Vulture iealousie,   25
That fed vpon my Liuer: you cannot blame me,
But call it a fit iustice on my selfe,
Though I resolue to be a stranger to
The thought of mirth, or pleasure.
    Timagoras.   You haue redeem'd
The forfeit of your fault, with such a ransome   30

III. iv. 16. lead;] *38*; ~. *24*   22. wrong'd] *Coxeter*; wrong *24*   29. *Timagoras.*] Massinger MS (*Timago:*) *38*; *Timandra. 24*

Of honourable action, as my Sister
Must of necessitie confesse her suffrings
Weigh'd downe by your faire merits; and when she views you
Like a triumphant Conquerour, carried through
The Streets of *Syracusa*, the glad people
Pressing to meet you, and the Senators
Contending who shall heape most honours on you;
The Oxen crown'd with Girlands led before you
Appointed for the Sacrifice; and the Altars
Smoaking with thankfull Incense to the gods:
The Souldiers chaunting loud hymnes to your praise:
The windowes fill'd with Matrons, and with Virgins,
Throwing vpon your head, as you passe by,
The choycest Flowers; and silently inuoking
The Queene of Loue, with their particular vowes,
To be thought worthy of you; can *Cleora*,
(Though, in the glasse of selfe-loue, shee behold
Her best deserts) but with all ioy acknowledge,
What she indur'd, was but a noble tryall
You made of her affection? and her anger
Rising from your too amorous feares, soone drench'd
In *Lethe*, and forgotten.
   Leosthenes.   If those glories
You so set forth were mine, they might plead for mee:
But I can laye no claime to the least honour,
Which you with foule iniustice rauish from her;
Her beauty, in me wrought a myracle,
Taught me to ayme at things beyond my power,
Which her perfections purchas'd, and gaue to me
From her free bounties; she inspir'd me with
That vallour, which I dare not call mine owne:
And from the faire reflexion of her minde,
My soule receau'd the sparckling beames of courage.
Shee from the magazine of her proper goodnesse,
Stock'd me with vertuous purposes; sent me forth
To trade for honour; and she being the owner
Of the barke of my aduentures, I must yeeld her
A iust accompt of all, as fits a Factor:
And howsoeuer others thinke me happy,

        51. feares] *Massinger MS*; eares 24

And cry aloud, I haue made a prosperous voyage:
One frowne of her dislike at my returne, 70
(Which, as a punishment for my fault, I looke for)
Strikes dead all comfort.
   Timagoras.   Tush, these feares are needlesse,
Shee cannot, must not, shall not be so cruell.
A free confession of a fault winnes pardon;
But being seconded by desert, commands it. 75
The Generall is your owne, and sure; my Father
Repents his harshnesse: for my selfe, I am
Euer your creature; one day shall be happy
In your triumph, and your Mariage.
   Leosthenes.   May it proue so,
With her consent, and pardon.
   Timagoras.   Euer touching 80
On that harsh string? she is your owne, and you
Without disturbance seaze on what's your due.   *Exeunt.*

Actus IIII. Scæna I.

PISANDER, TIMANDRA.

   Pisander. SHE has her health then?
   Timandra.   Yes, Sir, and as often
As I speake of you, lends attentiue eare
To all that I deliuer; nor seemes tyr'de,
Though I dwell long on the relation of
Your suffrings for her, heaping praise on praise, 5
On your vnequal'd temperance, and command,
You hold o're your affections.
   Pisander.   To my wish:
Haue you acquainted her with the defeature
Of the Carthaginians, and with what honours
Leosthenes comes crown'd home with?
   Timandra.   With all care. 10
   Pisander. And how does she receaue it?
   Timandra.   As I ghesse,
With a seeming kinde of ioy, but yet appeares not
Transported, or proud of his happy fortune.

    76. sure;] *24*; ~, *38*   IV. i. 1. then?] *1719*; ~: *24*

But when I tell her of the certaine ruine,
You must encounter with at their arriuall
In *Syracusa*, and that death with torments
Must fall vpon you, which you yet repent not;
Esteeming it a glorious martyrdome,
And a reward of pure, vnspotted loue,
Preseru'd in the white robe of Innocence:
Though she were in your power, and yow spurr'd on
By insolent lust; you rather chose to suffer,
The fruit vntasted, for whose glad possession,
You haue call'd on the furie of your Lord,
Then that she should be grieu'd, or tainted in
Her Reputation—
  Pisander.   Doth it worke compunction?
Pitties she my misfortune?
  Timandra.   Shee express'd
All signes of sorrow, which, her vow obseru'd,
Could witnesse a grieu'd heart. At the first hearing
Shee fell vpon her face, rent her faire haire,
Her hands held vp to heauen, and vented sighes,
In which shee silently seem'd to complaine,
Of heauens iniustice.
  Pisander.   'Tis enough: waite carefully,
And vpon all watch'd occasions, continue
Speech, and discourse of me: 'tis time, must worke her.
  Timandra. I'le not be wanting, but still striue to serue you.
                                    Exit TIMANDRA.
                Enter POLIPHRON.
  Pisander. Now, *Poliphron*, the newes?
  Poliphron.   The conquering Army
Is within ken.
  Pisander. How brooke the slaues the obiect?
  Poliphron. Cheerefully yet; they do refuse no labour,
And seeme to scoffe at danger; 'tis your presence
That must confirme them; with a full consent,
You are chosen to relate the tyranny
Of our proud Masters; and what you subscribe too,

21. yow] *Massinger MS*; still *24*   on] *24*; ~, *Massinger MS*   22. lust;] *24*;
~, *38*   suffer,] *McIlwraith*; ~ˌ *24*   26. Reputation—] *Gifford*; ~. *24*
28. which,] *38*; (which) *24*   37. newes?] *1719*; ~: *24*

They gladly will allow of, or hold out
To the last man.
    Pisander.   I'le instantly among them:
If we prooue constant to our selues, good fortune
Will not, I hope, forsake vs.
    Poliphron.   'Tis our best refuge.   *Exeunt.*

Actus IIII. Scæna II.

TIMOLEON, ARCHIDAMUS, DIPHILUS, LEOSTHENES, TIMAGORAS, *others.*

    Timoleon. Thus farre we are return'd victorious, crown'd
With Wreathes triumphant, (famine, blood, and dearth,
Banisht your peacefull confines,) and bring home
Securitie, and peace. 'Tis therefore fit
That such as boldly stood the shocke of warre,
And with the deere expence of sweat and blood
Haue purchas'd Honour, should with pleasure reape
The haruest of their toyle; and wee stand bound
Out of the first file of the best deseruers,
(Though all must be consider'd to their merits)
To thinke of you *Leosthenes*, that stand,
And worthily, most deere in our esteeme,
For your heroique valour.
    Archidamus.   When I looke on
(The labour of so many men, and ages)
This well-built Citie, not long since design'd
To spoyle and rapine; by the fauour of
The gods, and you their ministers, preseru'd;
I cannot in my height of ioy, but offer
These teares for a glad sacrifice.
    Diphilus.   Sleepe the Citizens?
Or are they ouerwhelm'd with the excesse
Of comfort, that flowes to them?
    Leosthenes.   Wee receaue
A silent entertainment.
    Timagoras.   I long since
Expected, that the virgins, and the Matrons,

        IV. ii. 2. dearth] *24*; death *Gifford*   17. ministers,] *38*; ~ₐ *24*

The old men striuing with their age, the Priests
Carrying the Images of their gods before 'em,   25
Should haue met vs with Procession: Ha! the gates
Are shut against vs!

      Enter aboue, PISANDER, POLIPHRON, CIMBRIO,
           GRACCULO, *and the rest.*

  Archidamus.   And vpon the Walls
Arm'd men seeme to defie vs!
  Diphilus.   I should know
These faces; they are our slaues.
  Timagoras.   The misterie, Rascalls?
Open the ports, and play not with an anger,   30
That will consume you.
  Timoleon.   This is aboue wonder.
  Archidamus. Our Bond-men stand against vs!
  Gracculo.   Some such things
We were in mans remembrance; the slaues are turn'd
Lords of the Towne, or so; nay, be not angry:
Perhaps on good tearmes, giuing security   35
You will be quiet men, we may allow you
Some lodgings in our Garrets, or out-houses;
Your great lookes cannot carry it.
  Cimbrio.   The truth is,
We haue beene bold with your wiues, toy'd with your daughters.
  Leosthenes. O my prophetique soule!
  Gracculo.   Rifled your Chests,   40
Beene busie with your Wardrobes.
  Timagoras.   Can we indure this?
  Leosthenes. O my *Cleora*!
  Gracculo.   A Caudle, for the Gentleman,
Hee'll die a'the pip else.
  Timagoras.   Scorn'd too! are you turn'd stone?
Hold parley with our Bond-men? force our entrance,
Then Villaines, expect—
  Timoleon.   Hold: you weare mens shapes,   45
And if like men you haue reason, shew a cause
That leads you to this desperate course, which must end
In your destruction.

      45. expect—] *1719*; ~. *24*   48. destruction.] *38*; ~? *24*

Gracculo. That, as please the Fates,
But we vouchsafe; speake Captaine.
　　Timagoras. 　　　　　　　　Hell, and Furies!
　　Archidamus. Bay'd by our owne curres?
　　Cimbrio. 　　　　　　　Take heed, you be not wurried.
　　Poliphron. We are sharpe set.
　　Cimbrio. 　　　　　　　And sodaine.
　　Pisander. 　　　　　　　　　　　Briefly thus then,
Since I must speake for all; your tyranny
Drew vs from our obedience. Happy those times,
When Lords were styl'd fathers of Families,
And not imperious Masters; when they numbred
Their seruants almost equall with their Sonnes,
Or one degree beneath them; when their labours
Were cherish'd, and rewarded, and a period
Set to their suffrings; when they did not presse
Their duties, or their wills beyond the power
And strength of their performance; all things order'd
With such decorum, as wise Law-makers,
From each well-gouern'd priuate house deriu'd
The perfect modell of a Common-wealth;
Humanity then lodg'd in the hearts of men,
And thankfull Masters carefully prouided
For Creatures wanting reason. The noble horse,
That in his fiery youth from his wide nostrells
Neigh'd courage to his Rider, and brake through
Groues of opposed Pikes, bearing his Lord
Safe to triumphant victory, old or wounded,
Was set at libertie, and freed from seruice.
The Athenian Mules, that from the Quarrie drew
Marble, hew'd for the Temples of the gods,
The great worke ended, were dismis'd, and fed
At the publique cost; nay, faithfull dogs haue found
Their Sepulchres; but man to man more cruell,
Appoints no end to the suffrings of his slaue;
Since pride stept in and ryot, and o'return'd
This goodly frame of Concord, teaching Masters
To glory in the abuse of such, as are
Brought vnder their command; who grown vnusefull,
Are lesse esteem'd than beasts; this you haue practis'd,

Practis'd on vs with rigor; this hath forc'd vs,
To shake our heauy yokes off; and if redresse   85
Of these iust grieuances be not granted vs,
Wee'le right our selues, and by strong hand defend,
What we are now possess'd of.
    Gracculo.   And not leaue
One house vnfir'd.
    Cimbrio.   Or throat vncut of those
We haue in our power.
    Poliphron.   Nor will we fall alone,   90
You shall buy vs dearely.
    Timagoras.   O, the gods!
Vnheard of insolence!
    Timoleon.   What are your demaunds?
    Pisander. A generall pardon, first, for all offences
Committed in your absence. Libertie,
To all such, as desire to make returne   95
Into their countries; and to those that stay,
A competence of land freely allotted
To each mans proper vse; no Lord acknowledg'd.
Lastly, with your consent, to choose them wiues
Out of your Families.
    Timagoras.   Let the Citie sinke first.   100
    Leosthenes. And ruine sease on all, e're we subscribe
To such conditions.
    Archidamus.   *Carthage*, though victorious,
Could not haue forc'd more from vs.
    Leosthenes.   Scale the Walls,
Capitulate after.
    Timoleon.   He that winnes the toppe first,
Shall weare a murall wreath.   *Exeunt.*
    Pisander.   Each to his place.   105
Or death or victory; charge them home, and feare not. [*Exeunt.*]

    Flourish, and alarmes. Enter TIMOLEON *and Senators.*

    Timoleon. We wrong our selues, and we are iustly punish'd,
To deale with Bond-men, as if we encountred
An equall enemy.
    Archidamus.   They fight like deuills:
            106 SD. *Exeunt.*] *after Gifford; not in* 24

And runne vpon our Swords, as if their breasts
Were proofe beyond their Armour.

Enter LEOSTHENES, *and* TIMAGORAS.

Timagoras. Make a firme stand:
The slaues not satisfied, they haue beat vs off,
Prepare to sally forth.
 Timoleon. They are wilde beasts,
And to be tam'd by pollicie; each man take
A tough whippe in his hand: such as you vs'd
To punish them with, as masters; in your lookes
Carry seuerity, and awe; 'twill fright them
More then your weapons; sauage Lyons flye from
The sight of fire; and these that haue forgot
That duty, you n'ere taught them with your swords,
When vnexpected, they behold those terrors
Aduanc'd aloft, that they were made to shake at,
'Twill force them to remember what they are,
And stoope to due obedience.

Enter CIMBRIO, GRACCULO, *and other slaues.*

Archidamus. Heere they come.
 Cimbrio. Leaue not a man aliue; a wound is but a fleabyting,
To what we suffred being slaues.
 Gracculo. O my heart!
Cimbrio what doe we see? the whippe! our Masters!
 Timagoras. Dare you rebell, slaues?
Senators shake their whips, and they throw away their weapons, and
              runne off.
 Cimbrio. Mercy, mercy; where
Shall we hide vs from their furie?
 Gracculo. Fly, they follow;
O, we shall be tormented!
 Timoleon. Enter with them,
But yet forbeare to kill them; still remember
They are part of your wealth, and being disarm'd,
There is no danger.

111 SD. Enter ... TIMAGORAS.] *Coxeter*; after line 110 in 24   124 SD. Enter
... slaues.] *38*; after line 123 in 24   128. where] *24²*; when *24¹*; where, *Massinger
MS*   130. tormented!] *Gifford*; ~: 24

Archidamus. Let vs first deliuer
Such as they haue in Fetters, and at leasure
Determine of their punishment.
 Leosthenes.   Friend, to you   135
I leaue the disposition of what's mine:
I cannot thinke I am safe without your Sister,
Shee's only worth my thought; and till I see
What she has suffred, I am on the racke,   139
And Furies my tormentors. Pray you leaue mee. *Exeunt.*

Actus IIII. Scæna III.

PISANDER, TIMANDRA.

Pisander. I know, I am pursu'd, nor would I flye,
Although the Ports were open, and a Conuoy
Ready to bring me off: the basenesse of
These villaines, from the pride of all my hopes,
Haue throwne me to the bottomlesse Abisse   5
Of horror, and despayre; had they stood firme,
I could haue bought *Cleoras* free consent,
With the safetie of her Fathers life, and Brothers:
And forc'd *Leosthenes* to quit his claime,
And kneele a Suitor for mee.
 Timandra.   You must not thinke,   10
What might haue beene, but what must now be practic'd,
And suddenly resolue.
 Pisander. All my poore fortunes
Are at the stake, and I must runne the hazard.
Vnseene, conuey me to *Cleora's* Chamber,
For in her sight, if it were possible,   15
I would be apprehended: doe not inquire
The reason why, but helpe me.
 Timandra. Make haste, one knockes, *Exit* PISANDER.
Ioue turne all to the best:

    Enter LEOSTHENES.
      you are welcome Sir.
 Leosthenes. Thou giu'st it in a heauy tone.

140. Furies] *38*; furye's *24* Pray you leaue mee.] *Massinger MS; not in 24*

Timandra.   Alas, Sir,
Wee haue so long fed on the bread of sorrow,
Drinking the bitter water of afflictions,
Made loathsome to, by our continued feares,
Comfort's a stranger to vs.
   Leosthenes.   Feares! your suffrings:
For which I am so ouergone with griefe,
I dare not aske without compassionate teares,
The villaines name, that rob'd thee of thy honour;
For being train'd vp in chastities cold Schoole,
And taught by such a Mistresse as *Cleora*,
'Twere impious in me, to thinke *Timandra*
Fell with her owne consent.
   Timandra.   How meane you, fell, Sir?
I vnderstand you not.
   Leosthenes.   I would, thou didst not,
Or that I could not reade vpon thy face,
In blushing caracters, the story of
Libidinous Rape; confesse it, for you stand not
Accomptable for a sinne, against whose strength
Your o're-match'd innocence could make no resistance;
Vnder which odds, I know *Cleora* fell too,
Heau'ns helpe in vaine inuok'd; the amazed Sunne,
Hiding his face behinde a maske of cloudes,
Not daring, to looke on it; in her suffrings
All sorrowe's comprehended; what *Timandra*,
Or the Citie has indur'd, her losse consider'd,
Deserues not to be nam'd.
   Timandra.   Pray you doe not bring, Sir,
In the chymeraes of your iealous feares,
New monsters to affright vs.
   Leosthenes.   O *Timandra*,
That I had faith enough but to beleeue thee:
I should receaue it with a ioy beyond
Assurance of Elizian shades hereafter,
Or all the blessings in this life, a Mother
Could wish her children crown'd with: but I must not
Credit impossibilities, yet I striue
To finde out that, whose knowledge is a curse,
And ignorance a blessing. Come, discouer

What kinde of looke he had, that forc'd thy Lady,
(Thy rauisher, I will enquire at leasure,)   55
That when hereafter I behold a stranger
But neere him in aspect, I may conclude,
(Though men and Angels should proclaime him honest,)
Hee is a Hell-bred villaine.
 Timandra.   You are vnworthy
To know she is preseru'd, preseru'd vntainted.   60
Sorrow (but ill bestow'd) hath only made
A rape vpon her comforts, in your absence.
Come forth, deare Madam.
      Leads in CLEORA.

 Leosthenes.   Ha!   *Kneeles.*
 Timandra.   Nay, she deserues
The bending of your heart; that to content you,
Has kept a vow, the breach of which a vestall   65
(Though the infringing it had call'd vpon her
A liuing funerall,) must of force haue shrunke at;
No danger could compell her, to dispence with
Her cruell Penance; though hot lust came arm'd
To seaze vpon her, when one looke, or accent   70
Might haue redeem'd her.
 Leosthenes.   Might? O doe not show me
A beame of comfort, and straight take it from me;
The meanes, by which she was freed? Speake, O speake quickly,
Each minute of delay's an age of Torment:
O speake, *Timandra.*
 Timandra.   Free her from her oath,   75
Her selfe can best deliuer it.   *Takes off the Scarfe.*
 Leosthenes.   O blest office!
Neuer did Gally-slaue shake off his chaines,
Or look'd on his redemption from the Oare,
With such true feeling of delight, as now
I finde my selfe possess'd of; now I behold   80
True light indeed; For since these fairest starres,
(Couer'd with cloudes of your determinate will)
Denyde their influence to my optique sense,
The Splendor of the Sunne appear'd to me,
But as some little glimpse of his bright beames   85

  Conuey'd into a Dungeon; to remember
The darke inhabitants there, how much they wanted.
Open these long-shut lips, and strike mine eares
With Musicke more harmonious, then the Spheares
Yeeld in their heauenly motions; And if euer
A true submission, for a crime acknowledg'd,
May finde a gratious hearing, teach your tongue
In the first sweet, articulate sounds, it vtters,
To signe my wish'd-for pardon.
  Cleora.   I forgiue you.
  Leosthenes. How greedily I receiue this! Stay, best Lady,
And let me by degrees ascend the height
Of humane happinesse; All at once deliuer'd,
The torrent of my ioyes will ouerwhelme me;
So, now a little more; And pray excuse me,
If like a wanton Epicure I desire,
The pleasant taste these cates of comfort yeild me,
Should not too soone be swallow'd. Haue you not
(By your vnspotted truth, I doe coniure you
To answer truly) suffer'd in your honour:
(By force, I meane, for in your will I free you)
Since I left *Syracusa*?
  Cleora.   I restore
This kisse, (so help me goodnesse,) which I borrow'd,
When I last saw you.
  Leosthenes.   Miracle of vertue!
One pawse more, I beseech you, I am like
A man, whose vitall spirits consum'd, and wasted
With a long and tedious Feuer, vnto whom
Too much of a strong Cordiall at once taken
Brings death, and not restores him. Yet I cannot
Fixe here: but must enquire the man, to whom
I stand indebted for a benefit,
Which to requite at full, though in this hand
I grasp'd all Scepters the worlds Empires bow to,
Would leaue me a poore Bank'rout; name him, Lady;
If of a meane estate, I'le gladly part with
My vtmost fortunes to him; but if noble,
In thankfull duty studie how to serue him;

  IV. iii. 86. Conuey'd] *38*; Couey'd *24* 117. Empires] *McIlwraith*; Empire *24*

Or if of higher rancke, erect him Altars,
And (as a god) adore him.
  Cleora.   If that goodnesse,
And noble temperance (the Queene of vertues)
Bridling rebellous passions (to whose sway,   125
Such as haue conquer'd Nations haue liu'd slaues)
Did euer wing great mindes to flye to heauen;
He that preseru'd mine honour, may hope boldly
To fill a seat among the gods, and shake of
Our fraile corruption.
  Leosthenes.   Forward.
  Cleora.   Or if euer   130
The powers aboue did masque in humane shapes,
To teach mortality, not by cold precepts
Forgot as soone as told, but by examples,
To imitate their purenesse, and draw neere
To their Cœlestiall Natures; I belieue   135
Hee's more then man.
  Leosthenes.   You doe describe a wonder.
  Cleora. Which will increase, when you shall vnderstand,
He was a louer.
  Leosthenes. Not yours, Lady?
  Cleora.   Yes,
Lou'd me, *Leosthenes*; Nay more, so doted,
(If cleere affections scorning grosse desires   140
May without wrong be stil'd so) that he durst not
With an immodest syllable, or looke,
In feare it might take from me, whom he made
The obiect of his better part, discouer,
I was the Saint, he su'de too.
  Leosthenes.   A rare temper!   145
  Cleora. I cannot speake it to the worth: All praise
I can bestow vpon it, will appeare
Enuious detraction. Not to racke you farther,
Yet make the miracle full; though of all men
He hated you *Leosthenes*, as his riuall: 150
So high yet he priz'd my content, that knowing
You were a man I fauour'd, he disdain'd not
Against himselfe to serue you.

    145. temper] *24²*, *Massinger MS*; tempter *24¹*

Leosthenes. You conceale, still,
The owner of these excellencies.
 Cleora. 'Tis *Marullo*,
My Fathers Bond-man.
 Leosthenes. Ha, ha, ha!
 Cleora. Why doe you laugh?
 Leosthenes. To heare the labouring mountaine of your praise
Deliuer'd of a Mouse.
 Cleora. The man deserues not
This scorne, I can assure you.
 Leosthenes. Doe you call,
What was his dutie, merit?
 Cleora. Yes, and place it,
As high in my esteeme, as all the honours
Descended from your Auncestors, or the glory,
Which you may call your owne, got in this action;
In which I must confesse you haue done nobly,
And I could adde; As I desir'd; but that
I feare, 'twould make you proud.
 Leosthenes. Why Lady, can you
Be wonne to giue allowance, that your slaue
Should dare to loue you?
 Cleora. The Immortall gods
Accept the meanest Altars, that are rais'd
By pure deuotions; and sometimes preferre
An ounce of Frankinsence, hony, or milke,
Before whole *Hecatombes*, or *Sabæan* Gums
Offer'd in ostentation. Are you sicke   *Aside.*
Of your old disease? I'le fit you.
 Leosthenes. You seeme mou'd.
 Cleora. Zealous, I grant, in the defence of vertue.
Why, good *Leosthenes*, though I endur'd
A penance for your sake, aboue example,
I haue not so farre sold my selfe, I take it,
To be at your deuotion, but I may
Cherish desert in others, where I finde it.
How would you tyranize, if you stood possess'd of
That, which is only yours in expectation?
That now prescribe such hard conditions to me?

176. your] *38*; you *24*

Leosthenes. One kisse, and I am silenc'd.
Cleora. I vouchsafe it;
Yet, I must tell you, 'tis a fauour, that
Marullo, when I was his, not mine owne,
Durst not presume to aske; No, when the Citie
Bow'd humbly to licentious Rapes, and lust,
And when I was of men and gods forsaken,
Deliuer'd to his power, he did not presse me
To grace him with one looke or sillable,
Or vrg'd the dispensation of an oath
Made for your satisfaction; The poore wretch
Hauing related only his owne suffrings,
And kiss'd my hand, which I could not denie him,
Defending me from others, neuer since
Solicited my fauours.
   Leosthenes. Pray you, end,
The story does not please me.
   Cleora. Well, take heed
Of doubts, and feares; For know, *Leosthenes*,
A greater iniury cannot be offer'd
To innocent chastity, then vniust suspition.
I loue *Marulloes* faire minde, not his person,
Let that secure you. And I here command you,
If I haue any power in you, to stand
Betweene him and all punishment, and oppose
His temperance to his folly; If you faile—
No more, I will not threaten. *Exit.*
   Leosthenes. What a bridge
Of glasse I walke vpon, ouer a Riuer
Of certaine ruine: mine owne waightie feares
Cracking what should support me: And those helpes,
Which confidence lends to others, are from me
Rauish'd by doubts, and wilfull Iealousie. [*Exit.*]

Actus IIII. Scæna Vltima.

TIMAGORAS, CLEON, ASOTUS, CORISCA, OLIMPIA.

Cleon. But are you sure we are safe?
   Timagoras. You need not feare,

187. lust,] *Gifford*; ~. *24*   211 SD. *Exit.*] *1719; not in 24*

They are all vnder guard, their fangs par'd off:
The wounds their insolence gaue you, to be cur'd,
With the balme of your reuenge.
   Asotus.   And shall I be
The thing I was borne, my Lord?
   Timagoras.   The same wise thing;   5
'Slight, what a beast they haue made thee! *Affricke* neuer
Produc'd the like.
   Asotus.   I thinke so: Nor the land
Where Apes, and Monkies, grow, like Crabs, and Wall-nuts,
On the same tree. Not all the Catalogue
Of Coniurers, or wise women, bound together,   10
Could haue so soone transform'd me, as my Raskall
Did with his whip; Not in outside only,
But in my owne beliefe, I thought my selfe
As perfect a Baboone.
   Timagoras.   An Asse, thou wert euer.
   Asotus. And would haue giuen one legge with all my heart   15
For good securitie to haue beene a man
After three liues, or one and twenty yeares,
Though I had dy'de on Crouches.
   Cleon.   Neuer varlets
So triumph'd o're an old fat man: I was famish'd.
   Timagoras. In deed you are falne away.
   Asotus.   Three yeeres of feeding
On Cullises and ielly, though his Cookes   21
Lard all he eates with marrow, or his Doctors
Powre in his mouth Restoratiues, as he sleepes,
Will not recouer him.
   Timagoras.   But your Ladiship lookes
Sad on the matter, as if you had mis'd   25
Your ten-crowne Amber Possets, good to smoothe
The Cutis, as you call it, and prepare you
Actiue, and high for an afternoones incounter,
With a rough gamester, on your couch; fie on't,
You are growne thriftie, smell like other women;   30
The Colledge of Phisitians haue not sate,
As they were vs'd, in councell how to fill
The cranies in your cheekes, or raise a rampire,

           IV. iv. 12. outside] *24*; my outside *McIlwraith*

IV. iv. 34–55 *The Bondman* 377

With Mummy, Ceruses, or Infants fat,
To keepe off age, and time.
   Corisca.   Pray you, forbeare;   35
I am an alter'd woman.
   Timagoras.   So it seemes;
A part of your honours ruffe stands out of rancke too.
   Corisca. No matter, I haue other thoughts.
   Timagoras.   O strange!
Not ten dayes since it would haue vex'd you more,
Then th' losse of your good name; Pitty, this cure   40
For your proud itch came no sooner! Marry, *Olympia*
Seemes to beare vp still.
   Olimpia.   I complaine not, Sir,
I haue borne my fortune patiently.
   Timagoras.   Thou wer't euer
An excellent bearer; so is all your tribe,
If you may choose your carriage:

       Enter LEOSTHENES, *and* DIPHILUS *with a Guard.*

                          How now, friend,   45
Lookes our *Cleora* louely?
   Loesthenes.   In my thoughts, Sir.
   Timagoras. But why this guard?
   Diphilus.   It is *Timoleons* pleasure;
The slaues haue beene examin'd, and confesse,
Their ryot tooke beginning from your house:
And the first moouer of them to rebellion,   50
Your slaue *Marullo.*   [*Exeunt* DIPHILUS *and Guard.*]
   Leosthenes.   Ha! I more then feare.
   Timagoras. They may search boldly.

                   Enter TIMANDRA.

   Timandra.   You are vnmanner'd Groomes,
To prie into my Ladyes priuate lodgings;
There's no *Marulloe's,* there.

       Enter DIPHILUS [*and Guard*] *with* PISANDER.

   Timagoras.   Now I suspect too;
Where found you him?

   45 SD. Enter ... Guard.] *Gifford; at line 46 in* 24   51 SD. Exeunt ... Guard.]
Gifford; not in 24   54 SD. and Guard] *Gifford; not in* 24

Diphilus. Close hid in your Sisters Chamber.
Timagoras. Is that the villaines sanctuary?
Leosthenes. This confirmes
All she deliuer'd, false.
Timagoras. But that I scorne
To rust my good Sword in thy slauish blood,
Thou now wert dead.
Pisander. Hee's more a slaue, then Fortune,
Or Miserie can make me, that insults
Vpon vnweapon'd Innocence.
Timagoras. Prate, you dogge?
Pisander. Curres snap at Lyons in the toyle, whose lookes
Frighted them being free.
Timagoras. As a wilde beast,
Driue him before you.
Pisander. O Diuine *Cleora*!
Leosthenes. Dar'st thou presume to name her?
Pisander. Yes, and loue her:
And may say, haue deseru'd her.
Timagoras. Stoppe his mouth:
Load him with Irons too. *Exit Guard with* PISANDER.
Cleon. I am deadly sicke,
To looke on him.
Asotus. If he get loose, I know it,
I caper, like an Ape, againe: I feele
The whip already.
Timandra. This goes to my Lady.
Timagoras. Come, cheere you, Sir, wee'll vrge his punishment
To the full satisfaction of your anger.
Leosthenes. Hee is not worth my thoughts; No corner left
In all the spatious roomes of my vex'd heart,
But is fill'd with *Cleora*: And the Rape
Shee has done vpon her honour, with my wrong,
The heauy burthen of my sorrowes song. *Exeunt.*

66. *Timagoras*] *38*; *Timandra 24*

Actus V. Scæna I.

ARCHIDAMUS, CLEORA.

Archidamus. THOU art thine owne disposer. Were his honours
And glories centupled, (as I must confesse,
Leosthenes is most worthy) yet I will not,
How euer I may counsaile, force affection.
   Cleora. It needs not, Sir, I prize him to his worth,   5
Nay, loue him truly, yet would not liue slau'd
To his iealous humours: since by the hopes of heauen,
As I am free from violence, in a thought
I am not guilty.
   Archidamus.   'Tis beleeu'd *Cleora*,
And much the rather, (our great gods be prais'd for't)   10
In that I finde beyond my hopes, no signe
Of ryot in my house, but all things order'd,
As if I had beene present.
   Cleora.   May that moue you
To pitty poore *Marullo*.
   Archidamus.   'Tis my purpose
To doe him all the good I can, *Cleora*;   15
But his offence being against the State,
Must haue a publique triall. In the meane time
Be carefull of your selfe, and stand ingag'd
No farther to *Leosthenes*, then you may
Come off with honour: For, being once his wife,   20
You are no more your owne, nor mine, but must
Resolue to serue, and suffer his commands,
And not dispute 'em; e're it be to late,
Consider it duly. I must to the Senate.   *Exit* ARCHIDAMUS.
   Cleora. I am much distracted; in *Leosthenes*   25
I can finde nothing iustly to accuse,
But his excesse of loue, which I haue studied
To cure with more then common meanes, yet still
It growes vpon him. And if I may call
My suffrings merit, I stand bound to thinke on   30
Marullos dangers; though I saue his life,
His loue is vnrewarded: I confesse,

V. i. SD. CLEORA] *Massinger MS (Cleora)*; Cleor. 24   7. humours:] *38*; ~. *24*

Both haue deseru'd me, yet of force must be
Vniust to one; such is my destiny.

Enter TIMANDRA.

How now? whence flowe these teares?
   Timandra.   I haue met, Madam,
An obiect of such crueltie, as would force
A Sauage to compassion.
   Cleora.   Speake, what is it?
   Timandra. Men pitty beasts of rapine, if o're-match'd,
Though bayted for their pleasure: but these monsters
Vpon a man, that can make no resistance,
Are senselesse in their tyranny. Let it be granted,
Marullo is a slaue, hee's still a man;
A capitall offender, yet in iustice
Not to be tortur'd, till the Iudge pronounce
His punishment.
   Cleora.   Where is he?
   Timandra.   Drag'd to prison
With more then barbarous violence, spurn'd and spit on
By the insulting officers, his hands
Pynion'd behinde his backe: loaden with fetters;
Yet, with a Saint-like patience, he still offers
His face to their rude buffets.
   Cleora.   O my grieu'd soule!
By whose command?
   Timandra.   It seemes, my Lord your brothers;
For hee's a looker on: and it takes from
Honour'd *Leosthenes* to suffer it,
For his respect to you, whose name in vaine
The grieu'd wretch loudly calls on.
   Cleora.   By *Diana*,
'Tis base in both, and to their teeth I'll tell 'em
That I am wrong'd in't.   *As going forth.*
   Timandra.   What will you doe?
   Cleora.   In person
Visit, and comfort him.
   Timandra.   That will bring fewell
To the iealous fires, which burne too hot already
In Lord *Leosthenes*.

Cleora.   Let them consume him;
I am Mistrisse of my selfe. Where crueltie raignes,
There dwels nor loue, nor honour.   *Exit* CLEORA.
   Timandra.   So, it workes.
Though hetherto I haue ranne a desperate course
To serue my brothers purposes, now 'tis fit,
I study mine owne ends.

Enter LEOSTHENES *and* TIMAGORAS.

                   They come. Assist me
In these my vndertakings, loues great Patron,
As my intents are honest.
   Leosthenes.   'Tis my fault.
Distrust of others springs, *Timagoras,*
From diffidence in our selues. But I will striue,
With the assurance of my worth, and merits,
To kill this monster, iealousie.
   Timagoras.   'Tis a ghest
In wisdome neuer to be entertain'd
On triuiall probabilities; but when
Hee does appeare in pregnant proofes, not fashion'd
By idle doubts and feares, to be receiu'd:
They make their owne hornes, that are too secure,
As well as such as giue them grouth, and being
From meere imagination. Though I prize
Cleora's honour equall with mine owne;
And know what large additions of power
This match brings to our family; I preferre
Our friendship, and your peace of minde so farre
Aboue my owne respects, or hers, that if
Shee hold not her true value in the test,
'Tis farre from my ambition for her cure,
That you should wound your selfe.
   Timandra.   This argues for me.
   Timagoras. Why she should be so passionate for a Bond-man,
Falls not in compasse of my vnderstanding,
But for some neerer interest: or hee raise
This mutiny, if he lou'd her (as you say,
Shee does confesse, he did) but to enioy

   68. of] *1719*; from *24*   75. receiu'd:] *Gifford*; ~, *24*

By faire or foule play, what he venter'd for,
To mee's a Riddle.
   Leosthenes.   'Pray you, no more; already
I haue answer'd that obiection in my strong
Assurance of her vertue.
   Timagoras.   'Tis vnfit then,   95
That I should presse it further.
   Timandra.   Now I must
Make in, or all is lost.   TIMANDRA *steps out distractedly.*
   Timagoras.   What would *Timandra*?
   Leosthenes. How wilde she lookes! How is it with thy Lady?
   Timagoras. Collect thy selfe, and speake.
   Timandra.   As you are noble,
Haue pitty, or loue pietie. Oh!
   Leosthenes.   Take breath.   100
   Timagoras. Out with it boldly.
   Timandra.   O, the best of Ladyes,
I feare, is gone for euer.
   Leosthenes.   Who, *Cleora*?
   Timagoras. Deliuer, how. 'Sdeath, be a man, Sir. Speake.
   Timandra. Take it then in as many sighes, as words:
My Lady—
   Timagoras. What of her?
   Timandra.   No sooner heard,   105
Marullo was imprison'd, but she fell
Into a deadly swoune.
   Timagoras.   But shee recouer'd?
Say so, or he will sinke too, hold, Sir, fie,
This is vnmanly.
   Timandra.   Brought againe to life,
But with much labour; she awhile stood silent,   110
Yet in that interim vented sighes, as if
They labour'd from the prison of her flesh,
To giue her grieu'd soule freedome. On the sodaine
Transported on the wings of rage, and sorrow,
Shee flew out of the house, and vnattended   115
Enter'd the common prison.
   Leosthenes.   This confirmes

    97 SD. *At line 96 in 24 editor*; ~, *24*; ~! *1719*   101. *Timandra.*] *1719*; *Timag. 24*   103. Sir.]
107. recouer'd?] *Massinger MS*; ~. *24*

What but before I fear'd.
    Timandra.   There you may finde her,
And if you loue her, as a Sister—
    Timagoras.   Damme her.
    Timandra. Or you respect her safetie, as a louer,
Procure *Marullos* libertie.
    Timagoras.   Impudence
Beyond expression.
    Leosthenes.   Shall I be a Bawd
To her lust, and my dishonour?
    Timandra.   Shee'll runne mad else,
Or doe some violent act vpon her selfe.
My Lord her Father, sensible of her suffrings,
Labours to gaine his freedome.
    Leosthenes.   O, the Diuell!
Has she bewitch'd him too?
    Timagoras.   I'le heare no more.
Come, Sir, wee'll follow her, and if no perswasion
Can make her take againe her naturall forme,
Which by lusts powerfull spell she has cast off,
This Sword shall dis-inchant her.
    Leosthenes.   O my heart-strings!
                    Exeunt LEOSTHENES *and* TIMAGORAS.
    Timandra. I knew, 'twould take. Pardon me, faire *Cleora*,
Though I appeare a traytresse, which thou wilt doe
In pitty of my woes, when I make knowne
My lawfull claime, and onely seeke mine owne.   *Exit.*

Actus V. Scæna II.

CLEORA, IAYLOR, PISANDER.

    Cleora. There's for your priuacy. Stay, vnbinde his hands.
    Iaylor. I dare not, Madam.
    Cleora.   I will buy thy danger.
Take more gold, doe not trouble me with thankes;
I doe suppose it done.   *Exit* IAYLOR.
    Pisander.   My better Angell
Assumes this shape to comfort me, and wisely;
Since from the choyce of all cœlestiall figures,

Hee could not take a visible forme so full
Of glorious sweetnesse. *Kneeles.*
 Cleora.   Rise. I am flesh and blood,
And doe partake thy tortures.
 Pisander.   Can it bee?
That charity should perswade you to discend
So farre from your owne height, as to vouchsafe
To looke vpon my suffrings? How I blesse
My fetters now, and stand ingag'd to Fortune
For my captiuity, no, my freedome rather!
For who dares thinke that place a Prison, which
You sanctifie with your presence? or belieue,
Sorrow has power to vse her sting on him,
That is in your compassion arm'd, and made
Impregnable? though tyranny raise at once
All engines to assault him.
 Cleora.   Indeed vertue,
With which you haue made euident proofes, that you
Are strongly fortified, cannot fall, though shaken
With the shocke of fierce temptations, but still triumphs
In spight of opposition. For my selfe
I may endeauour to confirme your goodnesse,
(A sure retreate which neuer will deceaue you)
And with vnfayned teares expresse my sorrow,
For what I cannot helpe.
 Pisander.   Doe you weepe for mee?
O saue that pretious balme for nobler vses,
I am vnworthy of the smallest drop,
Which in your prodigalitie of pitty
You throw away on me. Tenne of these pearles
Were a large ransome to redeeme a kingdome
From a consuming plague, or stop heauens vengeance
Call'd downe by crying sinnes, though at that instant
In dreadfull flashes falling on the roofes
Of bold blasphemers. I am iustly punish'd
For my intent of violence to such purenesse;
And all the torments flesh is sensible of
A soft and gentle pennance.
 Cleora.   Which is ended
In this your free confession.

Enter LEOSTHENES *and* TIMAGORAS.

Leosthenes. What an obiect
Haue I encounter'd?
   Timagoras. I am blasted too:
Yet heare a little further.
   Pisander. Could I expire now,
These white and innocent hands closing my eyes thus,
'Twere not to die, but in a heauenly dreame
To be transported, without the helpe of *Charon*
To the Elizian shades. You make mee bold:
And but to wish such happinesse, I feare,
May giue offence.
   Cleora. No, for, beleeu't, *Marullo*,
You haue wonne so much vpon me, that I know not
That happinesse in my gift, but you may challenge.
   Leosthenes. Are you yet satisfied?
   Cleora. Nor can you wish,
But what my vowes will second, though it were
Your freedome first, and then in me full power
To make a second tender of my selfe,
And you receiue the present. By this kisse
(From me a virgin bounty) I will practise
All arts for your deliuerance; and that purchas'd,
In what concernes your farther aymes, I speake it,
Doe not despaire, but hope.
   Timagoras. To haue the Hangman,
When he is married to the crosse, in scorne,
To say, gods giue you ioy.
   Leosthenes. But looke on me,
And be not too indulgent to your folly,
And then (but that griefe stops my speech) imagine,
What language I should vse.
   Cleora. Against thy selfe.
Thy malice cannot reach me.
   Timagoras. How?
   Cleora. So, brother;
Though you ioyne in the Dialogue to accuse me,
What I haue done, I'le iustifie; and these fauours,
Which you presume will taint me in my honour,

Though iealousie vse all her eyes to spie out 70
One stayne in my behauiour, or Enuy
As many tongues to wound it, shall appeare
My best perfections. For to the world
I can in my defence alleage such reasons,
As my accusers shall stand dumbe to heare 'em, 75
When in his Fetters this mans worth and vertues
But truly told shall shame your boasted glories,
Which fortune claimes a share in.
  Timagoras.   The base villaine
Shall neuer liue to heare it.
  Cleora.   Murther, helpe,
Through me you shall passe to him.

       Enter ARCHIDAMUS, DIPHILUS, *and Officers.*

  Archidamus.   What's the matter? 80
On whom is your Sword drawne? are you a iudge?
Or else ambitious of the hangmans office
Before it be design'd you? you are bold too,
Vnhand my daughter.
  Leosthenes.   Shee's my valours prize.
  Archidamus. With her consent, not otherwise. You may vrge 85
Your title in the Court; if it proue good,
Possesse her freely: Guard him safely off too.
  Timagoras. You'll heare me, Sir?
  Archidamus.   If you haue ought to say,
Deliuer it in publike; all shall finde
A iust Iudge of *Timoleon.*
  Diphilus.   You must 90
Of force now vse your patience.
              Exeunt omnes præter LEOSTHENES *and* TIMAGORAS.
  Timagoras.   Vengeance rather;
Whirle-windes of rage possesse mee; you are wrong'd
Beyond a Stoicque sufferance, yet you stand,
As you were rooted.
  Leosthenes.   I feele something here,
That boldly tells mee, all the loue and seruice, 95
I pay *Cleora,* is anothers due,

    V. ii. 80 SD. *Enter . . . Officers.*] *1719*; *at line 79 in 24*   93. Beyond] *Massinger MS;* Beyound *24*

And therefore cannot prosper.
 Timagoras.   Melancholy,
Which now you must not yeeld to.
 Leosthenes.   'Tis apparent,
In fact your Sisters innocent, howeuer
Chang'd by her violent will.
 Timagoras.   If you belieue so,   100
Follow the chase still: And in open court
Plead your owne interest; we shall finde the Iudge
Our friend I feare not.
 Leosthenes.   Something I shall say,
But what—
 Timagoras. Collect your selfe, as we walke thither. *Exeunt.*

Actus V. Scæna Vltima.

TIMOLEON, ARCHIDAMUS, CLEORA, *Officers.*

 Timoleon. Tis wondrous strange! nor can it fall within
The reach of my beliefe, a slaue should be
The owner of a temperance, which this age
Can hardly paralell in free-borne Lords,
Or Kings proud of their purple.
 Archidamus.   'Tis most true.   5
And though at first it did appeare a fable,
All circumstances meet to giue it credit;
Which work so on me, that I am compel'd
To be a Sutor, not to be deni'de,
Hee may haue æquall hearing.
 Cleora.   Sir, you grac'd mee   10
With the title of your Mistrisse, but my fortune
Is so farre distant from command, that I
Lay by the power you gaue me, and plead humbly
For the preseruer of my fame and honour.
And pray you, Sir, in charity beleeue,   15
That since I had ability of speach,
My tongue has so much beene enur'd to truth,
I know not, how to lye.

V. iii. SD. CLEORA] *Coxeter*; *Cleon 24*   9. to be] *Massinger MS*; *be 24*

Timoleon.   I'll rather doubt
The Oracles of the gods, then question, what
Your innocence deliuers: and as farre
As iustice with mine honour can giue way,
He shall haue fauour. Bring him in, vnbound: *Exeunt Officers.*
And though *Leosthenes* may challenge from me,
For his late worthy seruice, credit to
All things he can alleage in his owne cause,
Marullo (so I thinke you call his name)
Shall finde, I doe reserue one eare for him,
To let in mercy.

    Enter CLEON, ASOTUS, DIPHILUS, OLIMPIA, CORISCA.

                Sit and take your places;
The right of this faire virgin first determin'd,
Your Bond-men shall be censur'd.
    Cleon.   With all rigour,
We doe expect.
    Corisca.   Temper'd, I say, with mercie.

    Enter at one dore LEOSTHENES, TIMAGORAS; *at the other
        Officers with* PISANDER *and* TIMANDRA.

    Timoleon. Your hand *Leosthenes*: I cannot doubt
You that haue bin victorious in the war,
Should in a combat fought with words come off,
But with assured triumph.
    Leosthenes.   My deserts, Sir,
(If without arrogance I may stile them such)
Arme me from doubt, and feare.
    Timoleon.   'Tis nobly spoken:
Nor be thou daunted (howsoe're thy fortune
Has mark'd thee out a slaue) to speake thy merits;
For vertue though in raggs may challenge more,
Then vice set off with all the trimme of greatnesse.
    Pisander. I had rather fall vnder so iust a iudge,
Then be acquitted by a man corrupt
And partiall in his censure.
    Archidamus.   Note his language,
It relishes of better breeding then
His present state dares promise.

                38. thy] *Massinger MS*; the 24

Timoleon. I obserue it.
Place the faire Lady in the midst, that both
Looking with couetous eies vpon the prize
They are to plead for, may from the faire obiect,
Teach *Hermes* eloquence.
   Leosthenes. Am I fall'n so lowe,
My birth, my honour, and what's dearest to me,
My loue, and witnesse of my loue, my seruice,
So vnder-valewd, that I must contend
With one, where my excesse of glory must
Make his o'rethrow a conquest? shall my fulnesse
Supply defects in such a thing, that neuer
Knew any thing but want and emptinesse?
Giue him a name, and keepe it such, from this
Vnequall competition? if my pride,
Or any bold assurance of my worth,
Has pluck'd this mountaine of disgrace vpon me,
I am iustly punish'd, and submit; but if
I haue beene modest, and esteem'd my selfe
More iniur'd in the tribute of the praise,
Which no desert of mine priz'd by selfe-loue
Euer exacted; may this cause, and minute
For euer be forgotten. I dwell long
Vpon mine anger, and now turne to you
Ingratefull faire one; and since you are such,
'Tis lawfull for me to proclaime my selfe,
And what I haue deseru'd.
   Cleora. Neglect, and scorne
From me for this proud vaunt.
   Leosthenes. You nourish, Lady,
Your owne dishonour in this harsh replie,
And almost proue what some hold of your sex,
You are all made vp of passion. For if reason
Or iudgement could finde entertainment with you,
Or that you would distinguish of the obiects
You looke on in a true glasse, not seduc'd
By the false light of your too violent will,
I should not need to plead for that, which you
With ioy should offer. Is my high birth a blemish?

74. sex,] *1719*; ~. *24*

Or does my wealth, which all the vaine expence
Of women cannot waste, breed loathing in you?
The honours I can call mine owne thought scandals?
Am I deform'd, or for my Fathers sinnes 85
Mulcted by nature? if you interpret these
As crimes, 'tis fit I should yeeld vp my selfe
Most miserably guiltie. But perhaps
(Which yet I would not credit) you haue seene
This gallant, pitch the barre, or beare a burthen 90
Would cracke the shoulders of a weaker bond-man;
Or any other boistrous exercise,
Assuring a strong backe to satisfie
Your loose desires, insatiate as the graue.
   Cleora. You are foule mouth'd.
   Archidamus.   Ill manner'd too.
   Leosthenes.   I speake 95
In the way of supposition, and intreate you
With all the feruor of a constant louer,
That you would free your selfe from these aspersions,
Or any imputation blacke tongu'd Slaunder
Could throwe on your vnspotted virgin-whitenesse; 100
To which there is no easier way, then by
Vouchsafing him your fauour; him, to whom
Next to the Generall, and the gods, his fautors,
The countrie owes her safetie.
   Timagoras.   Are you stupid?
'Slight leape into his armes, and there aske pardon. 105
O, you expect your slaues reply, no doubt
We shall haue a fine oration; I will teach
My Spaniell to howle in sweeter language,
And keepe a better method.
   Archidamus.   You forget
The dignitie of the place.
   Diphilus.   Silence.
   Timoleon.   Speake boldly. 110
   Pisander. 'Tis your authority giues me a tongue,
I should be dumbe else; and I am secure,
I cannot cloathe my thoughts, and iust defence,
In such an abiect phrase, but 'twill appeare

103. his] *Massinger MS* (His); and *24*

Equall, if not aboue my lowe condition. 115
I need no bombast language, stolne from such,
As make Nobilitie from prodigious termes
The hearers vnderstand not; I bring with me
No wealth to boast of, neither can I number
Vncertaine fortunes fauours, with my merits; 120
I dare not force affection, or presume
To censure her discretion, that lookes on mee
As a weake man, and not her fancies Idoll.
How I haue lou'd, and how much I haue suffer'd,
And with what pleasure vndergone the burthen 125
Of my ambitious hopes (in ayming at
The glad possession of a happinesse,
The abstract of all goodnesse in mankinde
Can at no part deserue) with my confession
Of mine owne wants, is all that can plead for me. 130
But if that pure desires, not blended with
Foule thoughts, that like a Riuer keepes his course,
Retaining still the cleerenesse of the spring,
From whence it tooke beginning, may be thought
Worthy acceptance; then I dare rise vp 135
And tell this gay man to his teeth, I neuer
Durst doubt her constancie, that like a rocke
Beats off temptations, as that mocks the fury
Of the proud waues; nor from my iealous feares
Question that goodnesse, to which as an Altar 140
Of all perfection, he that truly lou'd,
Should rather bring a sacrifice of seruice,
Then raze it with the engines of suspition;
Of which when he can wash an *Æthiope* white,
Leosthenes may hope to free himselfe; 145
But till then neuer.
  Timagoras.   Bold presumptuous villaine.
  Pisander. I will go farther, and make good vpon him
In the pride of all his honours, birth, and fortunes,
Hee's more vnworthy, then my selfe.
  Leosthenes.   Thou lyest.
  Timagoras. Confute him with a whippe, and the doubt decided,
Punish him with a halter.
  Pisander.   O the gods! 151

My ribs, though made of Brasse can not containe
My heart swolne big with rage. The lye! Whippe?
Let fury then disperse these clouds, in which   *Plucks off his disguise.*
I long haue mask'd disguis'd; that when they know,
Whom they haue iniur'd, they may faint with horror
Of my reuenge, which, wretched men, expect
As sure as fate to suffer.
 Leosthenes.   Ha! *Pisander!*
 Timagoras. 'Tis the bold Theban!
 Asotus.   There's no hope for me then:
I thought I should haue put in for a share,
And borne *Cleora* from them both; but now
This stranger lookes so terrible, that I dare not
So much as looke on her.
 Pisander.   Now as my selfe,
Thy equall, at thy best, *Leosthenes.*
For you, *Timagoras*; praise heau'n, you were borne
Cleora's brother, 'tis your safest armour.
But I loose time. The base lie cast vpon me,
I thus returne: thou art a periur'd man,
False and perfidious: And hast made a tender
Of loue, and seruice to this Lady; when
Thy soule (if thou hast any) can beare witnesse,
That thou wert not thine owne. For proofe of this,
Looke better on this virgin, and consider,
This Persian shape laid by, and she appearing
In a Greekish dresse, such as when first you saw her,
If she resemble not *Pisanders* sister,
One, call'd *Statilia*?
 Leosthenes. 'Tis the same! my guilt
So chokes my spirits, I cannot denie
My falshood, nor excuse it.
 Pisander.   This is shee
To whom thou wert contracted: this the Lady,
That when thou wert my prisoner fairely taken
In the *Spartan* warre, that beg'd thy libertie,
And with it gaue her selfe to thee vngratefull.
 Timandra. No more, Sir, I intreate you; I perceiue

153. Whippe?] *24*; A Whip! *Coxeter* 157. which, wretched men, expect] *Coxeter* (men!); which wretched men expect, *24*

True sorrow in his lookes, and a consent 185
To make me reparation in mine honour,
And then I am most happy.
   Pisander.   The wrong done her,
Drew mee from *Thebes* with a full intent to kill thee:
But this faire obiect met me in my furie
And quite disarm'd me; being deni'd to haue her 190
By you my Lord *Archidamus*, and not able
To liue farre from her, loue (the Mistresse of
All quaint deuices,) prompted me to treat
With a friend of mine, who as a Pirate sold me
For a slaue to you my Lord, and gaue my Sister 195
As a present to *Cleora*.
   Timoleon.   Strange Meanders!
   Pisander. There how I bare my selfe needs no relation.
But if so farre descending from the height
Of my then flourishing fortunes, to the lowest
Condition of a man, to haue meanes only 200
To feed my eye, with the sight of what I honour'd,
The dangers to I vnderwent; the suffrings;
The cleerenesse of my interest may deserue
A noble recompence in your lawfull fauour;
Now 'tis apparent that *Leosthenes* 205
Can claime no interest in you, you may please
To thinke vpon my seruice.
   Cleora.   Sir, my want
Of power to satisfie so great a debt,
Makes me accuse my fortune; but if that
Out of the bountie of your minde, you thinke, 210
A free surrender of my selfe full payment,
I gladly tender it.
   Archidamus.   With my consent to,
All iniuries forgotten.
   Timagoras.   I will studie
In my future seruice to descerue your fauour
And good opinion.
   Leosthenes.   Thus I gladly fee   *Kissing* STATILIA.
This Aduocate to plead for me.
   Pisander.   You will finde me 216

193. deuices,)] *Massinger MS*; ~, 24   204. fauour;] *Mason*; ~. 24

An easie iudge, when I haue yeelded reasons
Of your Bond-mens falling off from their obedience,
And after, as you please, determine of me.
I found their natures apt to mutinie
From your too cruell vsage; and made triall
How farre they might be wrought on; to instruct you
To looke with more preuention, and care
To what they may hereafter vndertake
Vpon the like occasions. The hurt's little
They haue committed, nor was euer cure
But with some paine effected. I confesse
In hope to force a grant of faire *Cleora*
I vrg'd them to defend the Towne against you;
Nor had the terror of your whips, but that
I was preparing of defence else-where,
So soone got entrance; in this I am guiltie,
Now as you please, your censure.

 Timoleon.   Bring them in,
And though you haue giu'n me power, I doe intreate
Such as haue vndergone their insolence,
It may not be offensiue though I studie
Pitty more then reuenge.

 Corisca.   'Twill best become you.
 Cleon. I must consent.
 Asotus.   For me I'le finde a time
To be reueng'd hereafter.

   GRACCULO, CIMBRIO, POLIPHRON, ZANTHIA, *and
     the rest, with Halters.*

 Gracculo.   Giue me leaue,
I'le speake for all.
 Timoleon.   What canst thou say to hinder
The course of iustice?
 Gracculo.   Nothing. You may see
Wee are prepar'd for hanging, and confesse
We haue deseru'd it. Our most humble suite is
We may not twice be executed.
 Timoleon.   'Twice? how meanest thou?

217. iudge,] *24*; ~. *Gifford*   219. And after] *24*; Then after *1719*; And after you *McIlwraith*   231. of] *24*; for *1719*; our *McIlwraith*

Gracculo. At the Gallowes first, and after in a Ballad   245
Sung to some villanous tune. There are ten-grot-Rimers
About the Towne growne fat on these occasions.
Let but a Chappell fall, or a street be fir'd,
A foolish louer hang himselfe for pure loue,
Or any such like accident, and before   250
They are cold in their graues, some damn'd Dittie's made
Which makes their ghosts walke. Let the State take order
For the redresse of this abuse, recording
'Twas done by my aduice, and for my part
I'le cut as cleane a caper from the Ladder,   255
As euer merry Greeke did.
    Timoleon.   Yet I thinke
You would shew more actiuity to delight
Your Master for a pardon.
    Gracculo.   O, I would dance   *Capers.*
As I were all ayre, and fire.
    Timoleon.   And euer be
Obedient and humble?
    Gracculo.   As his Spaniell,   260
Though he kickt me for exercise, and the like
I promise for all the rest.
    Timoleon.   Rise then, you haue it.
    All slaues. Timoleon, Timoleon!
    Timoleon.   Cease these clamors.
And now the warre being ended to our wishes,
And such as went the pilgrimage of loue,   265
Happy in full fruition of their hopes,
'Tis lawfull, thankes paid to the powers diuine,
To drowne our cares in honest mirth, and Wine.   *Exeunt.*

FINIS.

245. *Gracculo.*] *Massinger MS* (Gra.); *not in 24*   267. lawfull,] *Coxeter;* ~∧ *24*